ADMIRALS OF THE NEW STEEL NAVY

MAKERS OF THE AMERICAN NAVAL TRADITION

Edited by James C. Bradford

Command Under Sail, 1775–1850

Captains of the Old Steam Navy, 1840–1880

Admirals of the New Steel Navy, 1880–1930

Masters of Sea Power, 1930–1990 (in preparation)

ADMIRALS OF THE NEW STEEL NAVY

MAKERS OF THE AMERICAN NAVAL TRADITION
1880–1930

EDITED BY JAMES C. BRADFORD

NAVAL INSTITUTE PRESS
Annapolis, Maryland

Library of Congress Cataloging-in-Publication Data

Admirals of the new steel navy : makers of the American naval tradition, 1880–
1930 / edited by James C. Bradford.
    p.   cm.—(Makers of the American naval tradition)
    Includes bibliographical references.
    ISBN 0-87021-003-3
    1. Admirals—United States—Biography.   2. United States.   Navy—
Biography.   3. Admirals—United States—History.   4. United States—
History, Naval.   5. United States.   Navy—History.   I. Bradford,
James C.   II. Series.
E182.A26   1990
359'.0092'273—dc20
[B]   89-13517
                                                CIP

Printed in the United States of America

3 5 7 9 8 6 4 2

First printing

For John W. and Dorothy B. Huston

CONTENTS

A NAVY SECOND TO NONE

LIST OF ILLUSTRATIONS

PREFACE

A s the American people celebrated their centennial as a nation and sponsored the Philadelphia Exposition to exhibit the products of their advancement to the world, one of their institutions, the U.S. Navy, stood far from the forefront of the world's sea services. At the end of the Civil War, it had been the world's largest navy with the greatest number of vessels and the most officers and enlisted men. It was a technological leader, with its monitors and wood screw-steamers among the best ships of their classes. Yet within a decade the situation had changed.

With the end of the war, the United States turned its interest inward to reconstructing the nation and binding the wounds of civil war, to shifting America from an agricultural to an industrial nation and absorbing the vast numbers of immigrants who worked in the new factories, and to building new cities and expanding westward to settle the plains and mountains of the Great West. The navy had little role to play in any of these activities and was allowed to slip into obsolescence, its ships laid up and its men discharged. Even the navy's pitiful performance in the *Virginius* affair in 1873 failed to shake the nation from its naval lethargy. As European navies undertook the experimentation that resulted in a revolution in warfare at sea, the United States stood by complacently, serenely watching. America seemed to have no need for any but the smallest navy. The United States had no enemies threatening invasion and few overseas interests worth protecting.

It was a grim period for the navy. The reestablishment of the squadron system with ships showing the flag on foreign stations, the shortage of funds that led Admiral David Porter to order captains to record in red in their logs anytime they expended coal to cruise under steam, and long periods between promotions discouraged its officer corps. Naval officers took little solace when reminded that at least they, unlike their predecessors in the Age of Sail, could depend on steady employment and not suffer periodic interludes of unpaid inactivity.

But all was not dark; there were glimmers of hope. Some Americans were beginning to look outward in a search for markets, and a developing steel industry would demand the modernization of the navy. In addition, in 1873, a group of forward-looking officers had formed the U.S. Naval Institute, which would provide a forum for discussion of naval developments. Equally important for the future, though unrelated in the public mind, was the establishment in 1884 of the Naval War College at Newport, Rhode Island. Dedicated to the study of warfare, it as the first institution of its kind in the world.

Within a decade the signs of naval renewal were clear. During the 1880s the first new class of post–Civil War ships, the cruisers *Atlanta, Boston,* and *Chicago,* were designed and built, to be followed shortly by America's first steel battleships, the *Texas* and the *Maine.* During the same decade the Office of Naval Intelligence was established to keep the navy abreast of developments abroad.

If the 1880s were years of rebirth, the 1890s were years of steady growth. The True Blue Saloon incident in Chile was not shrugged off by Americans as the *Virginius* affair had been two decades earlier; instead it shocked the nation into action. Embarrassed that the U.S. Navy did not stand among the world's top ten navies, Congress appropriated funds for a sustained building program. The new ships would be among the best in the world; and one could even argue that by missing the building race of the previous two decades, the navy had suffered no permanent damage—having saved money instead of spending it constructing vessels that rapid technological development would have rendered obsolete before they were launched.

At the end of the decade, the navy fought, and in the eyes of most Americans won, the Spanish–American War; and suddenly the navy was a popular institution. Funds were available to rebuild the Naval Academy, whose buildings had been condemned as unsafe a few years before. With the public captivated by the navy and with Theodore Roosevelt in the White House, everything had changed. The new century brought heady times for the navy. In 1903, Secretary of the

Navy John D. Long wrote a book on *The New American Navy,* in which he extolled the virtues of the service and outlined the role it played in America's destiny. When his superior, Theodore Roosevelt, left office in 1909, the United States, with twenty-seven battleships in service and six more building, had become the world's second or third strongest naval power. Less than a decade later another president, Woodrow Wilson, would call for "a Navy second to none"; and, with World War I in progress, Congress appropriated funds toward that end.

When the United States entered World War I, its leaders were forced for the first time in history to conduct coalition warfare. Divisions quickly developed between naval leaders. William S. Sims, serving in London, placed greatest priority on fulfilling the immediate needs of the Allies in conducting the war. Others, including William S. Benson, feared that Germany might defeat Britain, leaving the United States to fight alone. Equally concerned about the postwar balance of power, Benson and others presented alternative policies designed to enhance the power of the U.S. fleet to act independently.

With the end of the war came a demand by the American people that the nation return to "normalcy." That meant a reduction in taxation and, consequently, the curtailment of naval building. A return to normalcy also implied a retreat from international involvement. The desire for retrenchment in naval expenditures and foreign affairs spawned the Washington Conference of 1921–22, which resulted in a series of treaties aimed at limiting naval armaments while protecting the status quo in China and the Pacific. For the next decade the navy appeared to languish, as it had following the Civil War. The U.S. Navy did not even build to the level allowed by the Five Power Pact of the Washington Conference, but its failure to do so does not mean that no progress was made; there were advances, particularly in the field of aviation.

The 1920s marked the end of an era just as the 1880s had marked the beginning of one. The four decades that straddled the start of the new century witnessed the birth of the modern U.S. Navy. The navy that emerged during this era had more in common with a modern Navy than with the sailing navy and the old steam navy that came before it; but it nonetheless formed a distinct unit—the New Steel Navy. That navy and the individuals who led it are the subject of this book.

Navies, like all other institutions, reflect the societies they serve.

The period between 1880 and 1920 was as much a time of transition for the U.S. Navy as for the United States. The introduction of smokeless powder, compound face-hardened steel armor plate, and high-explosive shells rendered wooden and iron ships obsolete for use against the ships of a modern navy. Thus change was most noticeable in the ships of the U.S. Navy. At the start of the era virtually all were equipped with sails; by the end none were. The first decade was one of constant change in naval technology. The next three decades marked the heyday of the battleship. From the publication of Alfred Thayer Mahan's *The Influence of Sea Power upon History* in 1890 until the Washington Naval Conference of 1921 and 1922, naval strategic thought focused on fleets of battleships, though most of the important battles of the era—Manila Bay and Santiago (1898), Coronel and Falkland Islands (1914), Dogger Bank (1915), and Jutland (1916)—were fought by cruisers. During the era two entirely new ship types, submarines and destroyers, joined the fleet, and shortly after World War I aircraft carriers were developed that would radically alter naval warfare during World War II.

Less apparent, but at least as important, were changes in the sailors who served in these ships. The "iron men" who sailed the "wooden ships" of previous eras were drawn from the lower levels of society and were as likely to be foreign as American citizens. The new steel ships with their sophisticated technology required specialized skills for their operation, and the Progressive Era brought significant reforms to the enlisted force. The U.S. Navy opened recruit depots in sections of the nation away from the coasts, curtailed the practice of enlisting foreigners, and expanded training facilities ashore. Living conditions improved for sailors when the traditional system of issuing food to small groups of men who cooked it themselves was replaced by a general mess staffed by trained cooks. Health and sanitary standards were raised by the establishment of the Nurse Corps in 1908 and the Dental Corps in 1912. A retirement system was introduced in an effort to keep experienced seamen in the service for thirty years.

To examine the officer corps of the New Steel Navy, like studying the ships of the era, is to view a group in transition. John Paul Jones, John Barry, Thomas Truxton, and other leaders of the Continental Navy and the early U.S. Navy received their training in the merchant marine and only entered the navy in time of national peril. The next generation of leaders, men such as Stephen Decatur, John Rodgers, and David Farragut, learned their trade at sea, serving as midshipmen during the Barbary Wars and the War of 1812. The establishment of the Naval Academy in 1845 was a turning point in officer education. Young officers would, for the first time, receive the rudiments of their education and training on shore before serving at sea. The careers that these men entered were tenuous at best, and a second career was virtually a necessity for the officers of the Old Navy. There were far more officers than billets, and junior officers in particular had to expect extended forced furloughs without pay. Such was not the case in the New Navy because shortly after the Civil War the number of officers entering the service was closely controlled, and officers could depend on continuous employment, albeit not necessarily with the navy. French Ensor Chadwick would be detailed to the Lighthouse Service, William S. Benson would be assigned to the Coastal Survey and U.S. Fish Commission, and Henry T. Mayo would serve longer as a junior officer with the Coastal Survey than in the navy proper. By 1900 this practice had changed, however, and in the twentieth century officers are rarely assigned to duties outside the navy.

The educational level of officers was higher during the transitional era than earlier. By the 1870s graduates of the Naval Academy had gained enough seniority to influence policy. Their attitude toward education is most clearly shown by their leadership in establishing the Naval Institute and the Naval War College. The mantle of David Porter in his drive to focus the attention of naval officers on their "real business," preparing for and, if necessary, waging war, was assumed by Stephen B. Luce, who had served under Porter at the Naval Academy. During the early part of the century a "war is the best school of war" attitude had delayed the establishment of the Naval Academy. In the 1880s Luce had to overcome opponents with a similar belief, that "the only place to learn to be an officer is on board a ship," to found the Naval War College, a new type of institution to prepare a new type of officer to lead the New Navy. More recent reformers of the same stripe have included Arleigh Burke and Stansfield Turner.

Seniority and command at sea were virtually the only avenues to promotion in the Old Navy. During the Civil War, Benjamin Isherwood reached flag rank through engineering work. A generation later, Stephen B. Luce, Bradley A. Fiske, and Alfred Thayer Mahan rose through special talents in education, training, and engineering. After World War II, Hyman Rickover received the four stars of a full admiral while serving very little time at sea. Still, George Dewey's rise, which was based more on longevity of service than anything else, was more typical of the officers of the late nineteenth century, and the development of managerial skills so valued by progressives became the surest route to promotion in the New Navy. Gone were the days when a young officer like Stephen Decatur could earn a captaincy by a single act of heroism like burning the *Philadelphia.*

None of this is to argue that the qualities of leadership, coolness under fire, and administrative ability were less valuable in the New Navy than in the Old. The courage demonstrated by John Paul Jones as the *Bonhomme Richard* engaged the *Serapis* and by David Farragut standing in the rigging of the *Hartford* as she entered Mobile Bay foreshadowed that exhibited by George Dewey as he calmly instructed his captain, "You may fire when ready, Gridley," in Manila Bay. The determination William A. Moffett brought to naval aviation was not unlike that which fired Benjamin F. Isherwood in developing new ships and steam engines, and Stephen B. Luce brought the same dedication to his service as the first president of the Naval War College that Franklin Buchanan had shown as first superintendent of the Naval Academy. The element of luck could still make an officer's career, as when a chance meeting with Secretary of the Navy Josephus Daniels led to Henry T. Mayo's transfer to Washington and opened the door to an important command position.

The era of the New Steel Navy was not without its problems. Many officers were as pugnaciously nationalistic as their predecessors. Robley D. Evans's bellicosity at Valparaiso and Henry T. Mayo's quick umbrage at Tampico are more akin to Stephen Decatur's "My country right or wrong" attitude, David Porter's landing at Foxardo, and Andrew Foote's attack on the forts at Canton than to the naval diplomacy of the twentieth century. The modern naval diplomat is more likely to become involved with problems of the nature faced by Mark L. Bristol in Turkey than the ones faced by Robley D. Evans in Chile. Evans's action would bring little but criticism today, whereas Bristol's scrupulous policy of complete neutrality and delivery of humanitarian aid to people in distress could serve as a model for modern officers who find themselves in similar circumstances.

Indeed, the turn of the century marked as great a transition in naval diplomacy as in ships and officers. During the U.S. Navy's first century, naval officers sometimes conducted negotiations with nations that did not maintain regular diplomatic relations with the United States, but more often they found themselves confronting revolutionary forces, pirates, or corsairs. When Robert Shufeldt signed a treaty with Korea in 1883, that was the last time an active duty naval officer would be called upon to fill such a role. Officers who acted as diplomats during the new era were likely to represent the United States at an international conference, as did William T. Sampson at the Prime Meridian Conference of 1884 and Mark L. Bristol at the Lausanne Conference forty years later.

Earlier naval officers had tended to act alone, whereas modern ones often had to work in conjunction with army officers and diplomats, as in the case of Sampson attempting to coordinate operations with General William Shafter at Santiago or Mark L. Bristol working with John V. A. MacMurray in China. Those earlier naval officers often acted alone for no other reason than that consultation with officials at home took weeks if not months, but this situation changed when twentieth-century improvements in communications allowed officials in Washington to direct the actions of officers virtually anywhere in the world. Both civilian and military leaders were more than ready to exercise such control; thus Henry T. Mayo was probably the last naval officer who enjoyed such discretion that he could both follow his orders and nearly involve the nation in a war without consulting his superiors in Washington. As the era of the New Steel Navy drew to a close in the 1920s, Rear Admiral H. S. Knapp explained this difference between the Old Navy and the New in graphic terms: "The ease of modern communications make the most resolute and self-confident man think twice before adopting a course of action that he would adopt without hesitation if so situated that weeks or months would be necessary for consultation with the home government; while the irresolute or self-distrustful man, or one who fears to take responsibility, has under modern conditions a ready reason for doing nothing until he had been told what to do."[1]

The two decades on either side of 1900 saw a greater burst of reformist energy than any other period in the navy's history. Stephen B. Luce worked to bring reform in professional education, Bradley A. Fiske in engineering, William S. Sims in gunnery, and French Ensor Chadwick in administration. Reform was always controversial, however, and the reformers never spoke with a unified voice. Chadwick, who usually supported reform, was strongly opposed to combining line and engineering officers because he believed that such an amalgamation would lead to endless discord within the officer corps and cloud the clear lines of command necessary for the efficient operation of a ship. Officers were keenly aware of the debilitating effects of intraservice dissension. The Sampson–Schley controversy, one of the least positive legacies of the Spanish–American War, was fresh in everyone's mind and embittered relationships within the officer corps for over twenty years. Thus many officers were reluctant to stir controversy, but some reformers were not, and the period witnessed the most overt challenge to civilian control of the navy in the service's history. Some reformers, including William S. Sims and Bradley A. Fiske, believed that a general staff was essential if the navy was to be effectively managed, and they were willing to publicly challenge the secretary of the navy to get one. Other reformers adopted less confrontational tactics. William S. Benson, who is not always considered a reformer, adopted conciliatory tactics and, by working with Secretary of the Navy Daniels, shaped his chief of naval operations position into one that functioned much like a general staff. Benson's promotion over thirty-one more senior officers to become chief of naval operations was in itself controversial, and many officers, including Bradley A. Fiske and William S. Sims, resented it. Technological advances brought other changes, as World War I marked the emergence of submarines and airplanes as effective weapons. The former were adopted into the navy with little trouble, but aircraft posed more serious problems. Mark L. Bristol, William A. Moffett, and others laid the foundation for naval aviation during the 1910s and 1920s, but its full integration into the service would take another decade at least. Victory in World War I and the building of the most powerful navy in the nation's history did not end controversy within its ranks; for even in the afterglow of that victory, William S. Sims clashed with the majority of senior officers regarding the service's wartime record. Thus the decades straddling the start of the twentieth century were marked as much by transition and controversy at their end as at their beginning.

The history of the U.S. Navy can be divided into distinct periods. The story of the Sailing Navy and the men who laid the basis of the Ameican naval tradition has been chronicled in *Command Under Sail*, the first volume in this series. The second volume, *Captains of the Old Steam Navy*, examined the transition from sail to steam, rising professionalism, and the establishment of naval squadrons around the world, which characterized the period from 1820 to 1880. This volume carries the story forward through the transition from the Old Navy to the New. It was a stirring time—"Bully Years," Theodore Roosevelt would call them, a time of embullient nationalism as Americans looked outward beyond the North American continent and confidently accepted Rudyard Kipling's challenge to "take up the white man's burden."

The U.S. Navy was in the forefront of that expansion. Stephen B. Luce, Bradley A. Fiske, and French Ensor Chadwick prepared the navy for the challenge; Alfred Thayer Mahan provided the philosophical underpinning; William T. Sampson, George Dewey, and Winfied Scott Schley won battles that established a new empire; and Henry T. Mayo, William S. Benson, Mark L. Bristol, William S. Sims, and William A. Moffett led the navy into the modern era.

The individuals selected for inclusion in this study are a varied lot. Robley "Fighting Bob" Evans is a transitional figure. He fought at Fort Fisher at the close of the Civil War and led the Great White Fleet on the first leg of its round the world cruise fifty years later. His pugnacity was more typical of the Old Navy than the New, but his attitudes reflected those of the American people in the first flush of an empire as yet untroubled by the moral dilemmas of the Philippine Insurrection or disillusioned by World War I. Mark L. Bristol was a diplomat in the modern sense of the word. A contrast of the styles of Robley D. Evans at Valparaiso and Henry T. Mayo at Tampico with those of William S. Sims in London and Mark L. Bristol in Turkey effectively shows the changing nature of American diplomacy. A comparison of the methods employed by reformers Bradley A. Fiske and William S. Sims with those used by William S. Benson and William A. Moffett to achieve similar changes is equally instructive.

The names of some of the officers in this volume, for example, Alfred Thayer Mahan and William T. Sampson, are familiar, though the exact nature of their contribution is not so clearly understood. What was Bradley A. Fiske's contribution to the reform movement of the early century? In what sense did his work lead to the establishment of the office of chief of naval operations? How did William S. Benson, the first chief of naval operations, mold the office and make it more powerful than many Wilsonians wanted it to be? How do the contributions of William A. Moffett to naval aviation compare with those of Mark L. Bristol? Other officers, Henry T. Mayo and French Ensor Chadwick, for example, are less well known than they deserve to be.

The authors who assess these men are all specialists. Most have previously published works on the events and movements involving their subject. No attempt has been made to impose a common style or a single line of interpretation on them. Some authors summarize ideas presented elsewhere, whereas others offer reappraisals that are less favorable to their subjects than previous studies.

The question of whether leadership is innate or learned is insoluble, and no attempt is made here to answer it.[2] The focus is on the U.S. Navy, a service in transition, and particularly on its officer corps, because as a modern naval leader has written, "Important as ships are, naval history is made by men."[3] This is a truism worth remembering, and one recognized by naval officers from the earliest days of the U.S. Navy. "Without officers what can be expected from a navy?" Thomas Truxton asked Secretary of War James McHenry in 1797. "The ships cannot maneuver themselves. . . . If we are to have a navy, we must make officers to man that navy."[4] Individuals more than ships or administrative agencies link the navy with its past. The U.S. Navy has never had a dominating figure like Horatio Nelson; indeed until World War II no American naval officers were ever presented with an opportunity to command in the Nelsonian tradition of holding the nation's fate in their hands.

As the U.S. Navy entered the modern era it was guided not by one man but by many. They lived in an age of adventure when America exuberantly strode upon the stage of world affairs. The navy, an agency of American power, reflected the nation's pride. The group of men who guided it, shaped its character, and set its course into the twentieth century were a mixed lot. Some appear never to have felt quite at home with the new era; others embraced it with vigor. This is their story. At the same time it is the story of the U.S. Navy on the threshold of greatness.

NOTES

1. H. S. Knapp, "The Naval Officer in Diplomacy," 312.

2. During the. era under examination Alfred Thayer Mahan, *Types of Naval Officers,* and Charles Benedict Davenport, *Naval Officers: Their Heredity and Development,* investigated the problem. Influenced by the new social sciences of the day, the latter classified officers by "temperament," "juvenile promise," and hereditary traits, including "hyperkinetic qualities," "nomadism," and "Thalassophilia" (love of the sea). The subject of leadership continues to intrigue authors. See, for example, John Horsfield, *The Art of Leadership in War: The Royal Navy from the Age of Nelson to the End of World War II,* and Oliver Warner, *Command at Sea: Great Fighting Admirals from Hawke to Nimitz.*

3. James Calvert, *The Naval Profession,* 6.

4. Truxton to McHenry, 3 March 1797, James McHenry Papers, Huntington Library.

ACKNOWLEDGMENTS

This book has been a cooperative enterprise, whose authors have borne with remarkable good humor my requests for clarification, as well as suggestions for changes in wording, and sometimes changes in the emphasis of their essays. To them I first must acknowledge my indebtedness. Dale T. Knobel and Joseph G. Dawson made valuable suggestions for improving both the preface and my own essay. As with previous volumes in this series, my work has been made easier by the assistance of a number of individuals. Being in Malaysia for much of the time, I had to rely on Deborah Guberti Estes and Marjorie B. Kerns at the Naval Institute Press more than I had done when working on previous volumes in the series; and both were unfailingly helpful. Our manuscript editor, Constance M. MacDonald, again applied her sharp eye, and equally sharp pencil, to improve the manuscript in a number of ways. Charles R. Haberlein, head of the photographic section of the Naval Historical Center, and Patty M. Maddocks, director of library and photographic services at the Naval Institute, assisted in the selection of illustrations that bring an added dimension to the essays. Laurie V. Caldwell and Jude K. Swank overcame the difficulties inherent in working with someone far away in preparing the manuscript. My wife, Judy, provided general support. While not contributing directly to this book, John W. and Dorothy B. Huston have for over a decade assisted me in a variety of ways. One could not ask for better friends, and as a token of appreciation I dedicate the book to them.

ADMIRALS OF THE
NEW STEEL NAVY

Silver statue of Bosun Riggin. In October 1891 a liberty party from the
USS *Baltimore* became involved in a brawl in Valparaiso, Chile, in which
two American sailors were killed and seventeen wounded. Silver dimes
contributed by Americans were used to make three statues of one of the
men killed. The sculptor, Alexander J. Doyle, created them "as a gratuitous contribution to the patriotic sentiment" embodied by the victims.
The three statues were presented to President Benjamin Harrison, Secretary of State James G. Blaine, and Secretary of the Navy Benjamin F.
Tracy. Both the public's and the U.S. Navy's reaction to the incident are
indicative of their spirit at the turn of the century. *Courtesy of the Navy
Memorial Museum.*

SHAPERS OF
THE NEW NAVY

STEPHEN B. LUCE: INTELLECTUAL LEADER OF THE NEW NAVY

Rear Admiral Stephen B. Luce was the intellectual leader and the catalyst for professional naval thinking among the generation of officers who became the admirals of America's New Steel Navy. Luce, himself, belonged to an earlier generation, but his contribution to the naval service became the legacy for the new era. As Rear Admiral Bradley Fiske wrote in an obituary in 1917:

> Luce taught the Navy to think, to think about the Navy as a whole.
> . . . More clearly than any other man in American history he saw
> the relations that ought to exist between the central government and
> its military and naval officers. . . . Luce saw strategy as clearly as
> most of us see a material object. To him, more than any other officer
> who ever lived, are naval officers indebted for the understanding they
> have of their profession.[1]

It was with this point in mind that Fiske spoke for his own generation when he dedicated his autobiography to Luce, "who saw the light before others saw it and led the Navies toward it."[2]

Although Luce's impact was large, his contributions were for the most part intangible ones. The preeminent seaman in the navy of his day, he has won respect for his ability and accomplishment in command of ships at sea, yet his achievement was to go beyond that and to use his success and practical knowledge as the basis for a conceptual understanding of the navy as a profession. His greatest achievements were made in peacetime as an administrator, an organizer, a writer, and a teacher. Most important, Luce may be credited with establishing a system of education and training within the U.S. Navy, ranging from the lowest apprentice seaman to the highest level of

3

Stephen B. Luce. Photograph taken during the late 1880s and published in the book *U.S.T.S. Monongahela & the U.S. Naval Training System* (1892). *Courtesy of the Naval Historical Center.*

civil and naval command. His concept of education at the highest level was the basis for the Naval War College as an institution that would foster the continuing development and refinement of tactical and strategic theory, as well as the organizational concepts through which such theories and academic examination could be effectively translated into practice. Despite the intangible quality of his contribution to a rising generation of naval officers, there remain institutions within the U.S. Navy that derive their roles directly from the ideas that Luce championed. Under their present names, they are the Naval Recruit Training Centers, the State University of New York Maritime College at Fort Schuyler, the Naval War College, and the office of the Chief of Naval Operations.

Stephen Bleecker Luce was born in Albany, New York, on 25 March 1827, the third son of Vinal and Charlotte Bleecker Luce.

The original Luce family had come from England and settled in Martha's Vineyard; his mother was from one of the old Dutch families of New York. In 1833 when he was six, his father moved to Washington, D.C., where he obtained an appointment as a clerk in the Treasury Department through family connections with President Martin Van Buren. Family tradition has it that at age fourteen, Stephen went to the White House with his father and personally requested a naval commission from Van Buren. Whatever the circumstances, Van Buren signed his appointment as a midshipman on 19 October 1841.

Assigned first to the receiving ship at New York, Luce spent his first five months in naval life on board the ship of the line *North Carolina,* during the winter of 1841. After his indoctrination, Luce reported to the newly commissioned frigate *Congress* cruising on the Mediterranean and off the east coast of South America. In 1845, Luce was assigned to the ship of the line *Columbus,* then preparing to sail as the flagship of Commodore James Biddle's squadron, which would bring to China the ratification of America's first treaty with that country, and then make the first attempt to establish formal relations between the United States and Japan. On the return leg of the voyage, Luce spent six months in the *Columbus* cruising on the California coast during the Mexican War. After two three-year cruises at sea, Luce, with a number of his contemporary midshipmen, was sent to the newly established Naval Academy, where he became a member of the second class to be sent to the school. The early classes were not expected to follow a finely prescribed curriculum; for the most part, the midshipmen were at Annapolis to review information that they had learned from their seagoing mathematics professors and to prepare for promotion examinations. Luce spent the months between April 1848 and August 1849 studying for his examinations at Annapolis.

In its early years, Annapolis lacked the formal program of education for which it later became known. In 1850, a year after Luce left the Academy, it went through its first reform, during which it was remodeled along the lines of the Military Academy at West Point. The school's need for educational reform and its lack of discipline were readily apparent to Luce, and were the cause of a punishment that hindered his career for years. In March of 1849 the secretary of the navy had authorized midshipmen to participate in the inauguration ceremonies for President Zachary Taylor, but the superintendent of the Academy decided not to take advantage of the opportunity. A number of midshipmen, including Luce, showed their displeasure by

Midshipman Stephen B. Luce. Daguerreotype taken circa 1841 when Luce reported to his first ship, the USS *North Carolina*. Fifty years later Luce wrote a memoir of his experiences during his six months in the *North Carolina* for *Youth's Companion*. *Courtesy of the Newport Historical Society.*

making a demonstration in protest. For his role in this event, Luce lost seventy-two places on the promotion list, moving him from fourth in his class to near the bottom and delaying his promotion to lieutenant for six years.

As a passed midshipman, he then served from 1849 to 1852 in the sloop-of-war *Vandalia* on the Pacific station. Fortunately, part of his personal journal for this period is preserved among his papers. This ledger-size book gives a good picture of the young officer in Honolulu, in San Francisco, and on board ship, and also provides an insight into his reading habits: Milton's *Paradise Lost,* Dickens's *Old Curiosity Shop,* works of Shakespeare, and George Grote's twelve-volume *History of Greece.* In addition, he read the Bible and knew it well. He became familiar with the writings of the French biblical scholar Augustin Calmet, the sailor-poet William Falconer, and such authors as Lord Byron, Theodor Mommsen, and James Fenimore Cooper. While studying these works, Luce provided for his own liberal arts education through broad reading, travel, and experience. As he became proficient in the practical skills of his profession, Luce developed an awareness of the type and quality of men that the naval service required. Understandably, this knowledge grew with the scope of his practical experience.

Following Luce's tour of duty in the *Vandalia* came four years in the Coast Survey. For a brief period in 1853 he assisted Lieutenant James M. Gillis with calculations made from Gillis's observations of Venus and Mars between 1849 and 1852. Luce was then assigned to various survey ships on the Atlantic coast where he continued to gain experience in the scientific aspects of his profession: astronomy, oceanography, cartography, and hydrography. On 7 December 1854, Stephen married a childhood friend, Elisa Henley, daughter of Commodore John C. Henley and a grandniece of Martha Washington. Three children were born of the marriage: John Dandridge Henley Luce (1855–1921), Caroline Luce (1857–1933), and Charlotte Luce (1859–1946).

From 1857 to 1860, Luce served first as a lieutenant in the sloop-of-war *Jamestown* and then on the east coast of Central America. By this point in his career he had gained a wide variety of experience, from which he could draw sound observations about his profession and outline the general direction of his future career. In 1858 the thirty-one-year-old officer wrote in his private journal, "It is my opinion . . . that the navy should be re-organized."[3] These were significant words, for they expressed his early determination to reform the service. In the long journal entry that followed, he discussed the training and education required for officers to lead and organize men. These fields of interest seem unusual when compared to those of other officers at the time, but their selection was very much a product of his own experience.

Orders to the Naval Academy in 1860, as an instructor in sea-manship and gunnery just before the Civil War, provided Luce with his first opportunity to write and to publish. His initial published effort was in the area of practical training: the compilation and re-vision of textbooks for the Naval Academy.

As part of this work, Luce first revised a small gunnery manual that had been written by Lieutenant W. H. Parker in 1859: *Instruction for Naval Light Artillery, Afloat and Ashore*. When Parker re-signed his commission to join the Confederacy, Luce was asked to revise the "rebel" officer's work. Upon completion of that assign-ment, Luce saw the need for a text on seamanship, perceiving the inadequacy of the books on this important subject that were already in print and available in America. In recommending to the comman-dant of midshipmen that a seamanship text be prepared, he noted:

> Compared to the Army with their wealth of professional literature, we may be likened to the nomadic tribes of the East who are content with the vague tradition of the past. Does it seem creditable then, Sir, to this Institution that it should possess no text book on the most important branch taught within its halls?[4]

When his textbook finally was published a year or so later, it was not an original treatise on seamanship but a compilation from a wide variety of sources. Revised over the years, *Seamanship* became the standard American text for the late nineteenth century, appearing in nine different editions. In the area of practical sea training, this book was Luce's major contribution. As each edition appeared, Luce en-sured that the new aspects of shiphandling in steamships were con-sidered, along with guidelines for the newly popular fore-and-aft sailing rig. His attention to these details demonstrated his continuing inter-est in the practical aspects of the art, and his text provided up-to-date information on these matters to the Academy's midshipmen.

At the same time, Luce was an advocate of training under sail as the most appropriate method of teaching practical maritime skills. Not one to be reactionary or anachronistic, Luce strongly believed that practical experience under sail would teach a young man more about the basic nature of ships than experience in any other type of vessel.

Luce's textbooks were all devoted to obtaining a standard routine for all drills, maneuvers, and evolutions at sea; but together they form only a small part of Luce's literary contribution to training.

Within a decade after his first text appeared, Luce had expanded the scope of his work to the broad problems of a training system. This, too, had its origins in Luce's experience in the period 1861–65.

Luce's service during the Civil War was divided between the Naval Academy and the South Atlantic Blockading Squadron. He participated in the early blockade, the operations at Hatteras Inlet, and the Battle of Port Royal, South Carolina. His most fruitful activity during this period, however, had nothing to do with the prosecution of the war. In the summer of 1863, he took his first command, the midshipman practice ship *Macedonia,* to Europe, visiting the naval installations at Portsmouth and Plymouth, England, and Cherbourg, France. The French navy at this time was experiencing a resurgence, and the English were meeting the French challenge, as both nations were developing efficient maritime administrations and excellent training systems. Luce compiled a comprehensive report on European naval training and later used this information as source material in his articles and letters recommending a system that would be appropriate for the United States. Shortly after returning from Europe, Luce was ordered to command the new monitor *Nantucket.*

The poor quality of many of the men in the Union Navy at this time was painfully evident to him. The situation was no better than the one he had perceived in 1858. Wartime service in the navy held few attractions for enlisted men. Blockade duty was arduous and boring, liberty ashore was infrequent, and the grog ration had been stopped in 1862. Even prize money was largely a delusion; only the crews of a few lucky ships received any.

The physical environment and pay were somewhat better for naval officers. A large number of officers was made necessary by the expansion of the navy, and they were easier to recruit than enlisted men. Drawn from both oceangoing ships and river steamers, these new officers performed credibly. The Union Navy would have been unable to perform its demanding task without them, but they did have their limitations.

While in command of the *Nantucket,* Luce resolved to search for remedies to deficiencies he found. During the war he wrote several articles on naval personnel and training for the *Army and Navy Journal,* and after the peace he developed a plan that included an apprentice system for the navy and a parallel program of maritime schoolships for those aspiring to be officers in the merchant marine. Reform of the merchant training system was his first accomplishment, based on the 1862 Morrill Act which established land-grant colleges "to promote the liberal and practical education of the industrial classes in the several pursuits and professions of life." This act was to be the source of the agricultural and mechanical arts colleges and many of the country's state universities. Luce expanded on the original concept and extended it to include the knowledge of nautical sciences among young men in the coastal states.

Luce wrote the draft bill that both extended the Morrill Act to nautical education and authorized the secretary of the navy to lend ships and to detail officers to public maritime schools. This bill was enacted into law on 4 January 1874, and by January of the following year Luce had personally fitted out the sloop-of-war *St. Marys* and drafted plans, rules, and regulations for her to function as the New York State Maritime School. Commander Robert L. Phythian was chosen as the school's first superintendent. Other schools followed in Massachusetts, Pennsylvania, California, Maine, and Texas. To meet the academic needs of these schools, Luce wrote a textbook, *The Young Seaman's Manual.* Taken from *Seamanship,* it provided information needed in the new curriculum he had designed for merchant marine apprentices.

Once this program was effectively organized, Luce transferred his energies to naval training and education. He spent the years from 1877 to 1883 in schoolships, developing a naval apprentice program for training afloat. Eventually transferred ashore with close order drills added, it became the naval training system.

It was during this period that Luce produced a volume of *Naval Songs.* He believed that singing was an effective means of instilling the traditions of the sea and teaching the type of discipline that stresses interdependence.

By the mid-1870s, Luce had established himself well enough in Washington circles to exert some influence with regard to his ideas for reforming the Navy Department. While in command of the *Hartford* at Norfolk, Luce met Congressman W. C. Whitthorne when the Tennessee representative was inspecting the Norfolk Navy Yard in February 1876. Whitthorne, a former Confederate general, served as chairman of the Naval Affairs Committee in the Democratic Party–controlled Forty-fourth (1875–76) Congress, being the first chairman of that committee. Although he came from an inland state that had no navy yard, Whitthorne had become one of the nation's chief spokesmen for naval preparedness. With other legislators, such as Eugene Hale, Benjamin W. Harris, Charles Boutelle, Hilary Herbert, and Henry Cabot Lodge, Whitthorne deserves credit for building the new American navy of the 1880s. Luce's meeting with Whitthorne marked the beginning of a relationship that would be nurtured by fifteen years of correspondence and an exchange of ideas on the state of the navy and needed reforms. In 1878, Luce advocated reforming the Navy Department so that it would more successfully carry out government policy, complement the army, and adequately represent the nation. To achieve these goals, he recommended to Whitthorne the establishment of a "mixed commission" made up of members of Congress and army and naval officers, as well as other prominent citizens. For a time success seemed likely, but ultimately the attempt failed. It was to be thirty years before the Moody Board would consider the basic issues behind this recommendation. Nevertheless, Whitthorne continued to listen to Luce's advice while serving in the House of Representatives and, later, the Senate. In this relationship, Luce had found an outlet in Congress for his views.

It was during this same fertile period in Luce's thought that he came into contact with Colonel Emory Upton, then at the Artillery School at Fort Monroe, Virginia. Through Upton, Luce came to appreciate more fully the practices of the Prussian General Staff, which would become a major factor in Luce's approach to professional education and staff work within the navy. In 1877, Luce had been giving a considerable amount of thought to establishing an advanced school of naval officers. The opportunity came for Luce in 1882 with his assignment as the senior member of a commission to study and to make recommendations on the conditions of navy yards and naval stations. It was during the year that he was engaged in this work that he first came to associate closely with the secretary of the navy, William E. Chandler, and to present to the secretary his ideas on naval education, strategy, and administration.

In the 1880s the United States had just entered a period when rapid technological change would have a continuing and direct effect on the character of its navy. The development of steam and electrical engineering, the screw propeller, the rifled gun, and the study of interior and exterior ballistics, together with the use of iron and then steel, provided a new fabric for sea power that spurred rapid and continued change in ship design, engineering, armor, and weapons.[5] These developments quickly altered the physical character of navies while, at the same time, demanding new types of special expertise. It was the beginning of a period in American naval history, which has continued to this day, in which new equipment would become obsolete almost as soon as it was put to sea. Luce saw that although naval professionals have nothing to gain from restricting technological development, surely their central interest should be in technologies that have a direct usefulness to their profession. For this reason, Luce believed that the most important education naval officers received was that which developed their understanding of the purpose, character, use, and nature of navies.

For Luce, the highest aspect of the naval profession was the study of the art of warfare. This, he believed, was properly divided into several branches, in descending order of importance: statesmanship, strategy, tactics, and logistics. The study of diplomacy, or statesmanship in its relationship to war, was so important to Luce's concept of education that he believed it needed, "to attain any degree of proficiency, such an amount of careful reading as to leave little leisure for extra professional studies."[6]

Luce saw that diplomacy, strategy, tactics, and logistics were fundamental areas that together comprised the highest elements of professional naval thought. In order for naval officers to command effectively, all these areas must be in harmony and reflect even broader aspects of national interests, values, and economics. This, Luce believed, could be done only if a commander had first been given an education at a college dedicated to the broadest perspectives of professional thought.[7]

The Naval War College was Luce's answer to this need. On 8 March 1884, Luce presented to Secretary of the Navy William Chandler a draft of a general order establishing the school. Secretary Chandler appointed Luce to head a board that would elaborate on the subject and make specific recommendations. The board consisted of Luce, his sympathetic friend Commander W. T. Sampson, and Lieutenant Commander Caspar F. Goodrich.

The report of the board, submitted 13 June 1884, concisely argued for establishing an advanced school of naval warfare, and it went on to consider the curriculum and location. Washington, Annapolis, New York, Newport, and Boston were all mentioned, but only the last two locations were critically examined. Newport was favored over Boston because in Rhode Island the college could be located close to a promising fleet base where a school of application could be established. At the same time, it would be distant enough from the daily pressures of policy-making in Washington that it could allow for the proper academic atmosphere and broad reflection. It was also close enough to "the Hub" to ensure that eminent talent from Harvard, Yale, Brown, the Massachusetts Institute of Technology, and other centers could easily visit the college. The Naval War College was established by General Order 325 of 6 October 1884, and the first course was presented from 4 to 30 September 1885.

When Luce first thought about a Naval War College, there were no books or studies about the theoretical character of a navy. One of his main objectives in establishing the college was to have its faculty create the philosophical and theoretical literature that related the basic elements of warfare to the naval profession. The essence of the body of literature could then guide practical application.

To create the fundamental underpinning of professional thought, Luce turned to the study of naval history as a key resource. He believed that from historical knowledge, officers could begin to generalize about the nature of navies and thereby provide the groundwork for professional thought. But, he warned, if this study was to be profitable, one had to be able to identify historical material that could be analyzed and reasoned upon with advantage. Here Luce admonished officers to think broadly and to range freely over the centuries, noting particularly that Thucydides, and other ancient writers, offered much valuable insight even for a technologically advanced culture.[8]

To stimulate a profitable examination of naval history, Luce proposed that it be undertaken by individuals with an intimate knowledge of current practice as well as a wide-ranging theoretical understanding of the art of warfare. Simultaneously, Luce suggested using the conclusions drawn from army history in a comparative way, as a guide to formulating naval theory. The basic ideas in military studies were often directly applicable to the art of naval warfare, Luce believed; but for these concepts to be assimilated properly, someone needed to reformulate and modify them after making a detailed, thorough investigation of a broad variety of naval actions. Luce gave this job to Alfred Thayer Mahan, suggesting that he use Jomini's ideas as a basis in the work of creating naval theory through comparative study.

Luce believed that from a study of detailed cases in naval affairs, new naval generalizations could be established by logical thinking. First, generalizations would be established through inductive reasoning, that is, by proceeding from particulars to generalization; then the process could be reversed, through deductive reasoning, by applying the generalizations as a guide to particulars in the present and in the future.[9]

Luce's central and basic idea about the Naval War College was his belief that a naval officer did something more than just perform a job. He carried out his work as a highly educated, trained specialist operating within a clearly defined area, with established procedures and ethical standards; further, the officer used a highly developed body of theoretical knowledge relating to his field, and had a strong feeling of group identity and shared knowledge with others performing similar work. In short, Luce saw the naval officer as a professional, who, like a doctor, a lawyer, or an educator, should have both advanced education and recognized credentials certifying his achievement in mastering the progressive levels of understanding needed for his chosen career.

The field of education was Luce's focus. In every sense of the word, he was a teacher, and he devoted his entire career to the presentation of his concepts to the naval profession and to the nation. In his thinking he drew a sharp distinction between practical training for specific tasks and the education of the mind for creative functions. Representative of much that was popular among the educational circles of his day, Luce's article "On the Study of Naval Warfare as a Science"[10] best reveals the substance of his educational concepts. With Herbert Spencer, he believed that education was an individual process whereby each person had to discover for himself the nature of the world around him. Largely for this reason, he established the methodology of the Naval War College around individual reading and research. Teachers were not to be sources of information, but rather guides in a cooperative search for knowledge. For Luce and many others, truth was something to be found in basic immutable laws of nature that were fully ascertainable by individuals. At that time the use of comparative study and analogy was popular in the arts, as it was among scientists. The scientists had demonstrated that there were basic laws of the physical universe, and it seemed logical to Luce that similar laws could be found in human nature. These were ideas that Luce brought together and applied in his own self-education, and that he adapted to the Naval War College. They were not unusual ideas at this time, and they were not original with Luce. However, the depth of thought and the successful application of these ideas were unusual in a navy. Therein lies Luce's contribution.

The Naval War College was conceived as only part of Luce's larger scheme for the systematic development of the navy, but in the latter portion of his lifetime, it became the aspect to which he devoted the majority of his attention. Even after its establishment, the development of the War College along the lines that Luce had envisioned was not assured. The history of the Naval War College is the story of not only a battle for survival, but also an effort to retain a conception of curricular study that emphasized the development of naval science and intellectual stimulation rather than the mere training of officers in already preconceived ideas. In both these aspects Luce led the effort and advised those who followed him.

A year after its opening, Rear Admiral Stephen B. Luce turned the presidency of the Naval War College over to Captain Alfred T. Mahan; and Luce took command of the North Atlantic Squadron in 1886. Although markedly successful in this important command, Stephen Luce experienced some disappointment. The War College comprised only the theoretical part of his plan, and it should have been supplemented by a permanent squadron of evolution, a sort of seagoing laboratory where the theoretical work of the college could regularly be tested. Luce tried to make the North Atlantic Squadron perform this function, but his hopes were not completely fulfilled, for at least two reasons: the poor condition of the majority of ships, which made them unsuitable for such work, and the political situation in both Caribbean and Canadian waters, which kept the squadron scattered.

During Luce's command of the North Atlantic Squadron, however, he was able to achieve his objectives on several occasions, and these marked the high points of his command. At these times, the squadron was used as a squadron of evolution, and it was then that ships of the U.S. Navy were first exercised tactically as a fleet. Luce had first attempted this exercise while temporarily serving as commander of the North Atlantic Station in August 1884, when the squadron had made a surprise landing on Gardiner's Island in Long Island Sound. Given only two days of preparation, orders for the landing were issued by Luce while the squadron was at sea. He reported that such an exercise had never previously been attempted in secrecy. Luce's second major exercise took place at Newport on 10 November 1887. In undertaking these exercises, Luce was particularly interested in linking fleet operations with the academic work of the Naval War College. In this endeavor, Luce saw a direct interaction between the work of the college and the fleet exercises. Both exercises were joint operations involving landing operations; and Luce believed that such exercises gave realistic training for actual combat, while at the same time supplementing the comparative study of military and naval subjects that Luce had stressed at the Naval War College. He vainly hoped that these beginnings would develop into an American equivalent of the annual exercises that were then common in Europe.

Closely linked to a broad understanding of statesmanship, policy, strategy, and the broad function of navies in Luce's mind was the need to investigate and to improve one's understanding in those additional elements that comprise the highest aspect of professional thought: tactics and logistics. As strategy is interwoven in the great issues of state that guide it, so an understanding of strategy is essential to and intertwined with logistics and tactics. Luce emphasized that none of the elements can be entirely separated or omitted if officers are to be educated in their profession. The concept of comprehensive control of armed force blends these areas into focus, showing the various elements as gradients of a single concept that forms the essence of the best professional thinking in high command.

Both tactics and logistics are practical matters that involve the direct employment of equipment. Whatever its conception, any military operation is a blend of the two, tactics being the immediate employment of forces to attain strategic objects and logistcs being the provision of the physical resources for tactics to employ. Although practical in nature and dependent upon new technology, both tactics and logistics require a theoretical underpinning that provides a basic understanding upon which action can be taken. Far from being an unnecessary abstraction for practical naval officers, Luce saw that an understanding of theory in these areas sheds light on problems and provides guidelines for responsible executives who must attempt to make optimum decisions in the face of chance, a variety of possible solutions, and limited resources.

Although theory was an important consideration to him and ought to be carefully developed at the Naval War College, Luce believed that the link between theory and practice was a key element that deserved equal attention at the college. "War," he wrote, "is no time for experimentation." [11] He commented: "That 'war is the best school of war,' is one of those dangerous and delusive sayings that contain just enough truth to secure currency: he who waits for war to learn his profession often acquires his knowledge at a frightful cost of human life." [12]

For this reason, Luce promoted naval war gaming and encouraged the experimental use by the fleet of tactics and logistics concepts developed by the Naval War College. Peacetime, he believed, was the proper time to explore and to experiment with new methods and concepts in order to be prepared when war came.

Required to retire on his sixty-second birthday, 25 March 1889, Luce requested that for convenience the date be advanced by a month and a half. On 16 February he ordered his flag struck on board his flagship, the USS *Galena,* at Key West, Florida, and he retired without ceremony to his home at Newport, Rhode Island.

The next twenty-two years were spent in active retirement. During this period, Luce wrote more than sixty articles and maintained a close and active connection with the Naval War College in Newport. In 1892–93, he served as commissioner general of the United States Commission for the Columbian Historical Exposition at Madrid, Spain. In 1901, Luce was ordered to active duty on the retired list at the Naval War College, and he remained in that status until he finally retired on 20 November 1910.

During these years, Luce devoted himself to a number of projects: promotion of the work of the Naval War College; prevention of the amalgamation of the U.S. Coast Guard and the U.S. Navy; improvement of the merchant marine; and, most important in his view, the installation of uniformed direction for the navy in Washington, D.C. This last subject had been of long-standing interest to Luce, who took up the issue again in 1904 at the age of seventy-seven. In 1902

Naval War College. This photograph of the Naval War College viewed from Narragansett Bay, circa 1914, illustrates Luce's dream of basing both a major fleet and the Naval War College in the same location. *Courtesy of the Naval War College.*

and 1903, the annual reports by the chief of the Bureau of Navigation, Rear Admiral Henry C. Taylor, had pointed out that the bureau could not efficiently handle both the administration of naval
personnel and the formulation of war plans. Secretary of the Navy
William H. Moody and President Theodore Roosevelt concurred in
Taylor's opinion, and both urged the Congress to create a naval general staff similar to what had been provided for the army. In April
1904, hearings were held before the House Committee on Naval
Affairs to consider a direct link between the General Board and the
secretary. There was a great deal of opposition to this proposal. The
bureau chiefs feared encroachment on their own departments, and
members of Congress feared a decline in civilian control of the military.

In the midst of this rising controversy, Luce took a radical position. He proposed not merely an adviser, but an entirely new office
that would have the responsibility for fleet operations. In a letter to
Henry Taylor on 25 June 1904, Luce wrote:

> Up to the present time no Secretary has recognized the fact that naval
> operations should be included among his duties. Let this grave over-
> sight be repaired at once by an Executive Order creating under the
> Bureau of Navigation the Office of "Naval Operations." . . . The
> Office should be placed in charge of an officer of rank and one of
> recognized qualifications for its duties. His relations with the Secre-
> tary will be close and confidential. He will be the Secretary's adviser
> on all questions of a military nature. . . . The duties of the office
> will be such as would have gone to the General Staff had one been
> created. Thus will the Secretary obtain, under the law, the substance
> of a General Staff without the empty shadow of the name. There is
> no such thing as spontaneous generation. Plant the seed now and let
> it grow.[13]

The seed grew into the aid for operations and eventually the chief
of naval operations. Its development, however, was slow, and at first
even Taylor had his doubts. He promised to bring the suggestion to
the attention of Secretary Moody before he left office, but Taylor did
have reservations, as he was also trying to establish the General Board
as a naval staff. "If we plant this other seed that you suggest," Taylor
wrote Luce, "I am afraid the two plants would not grow together
well."[14]

Luce pressed forward, and in March 1905 his article "The Department of the Navy" appeared after having been awarded an honorable

mention in the Naval Institute Prize Essay contest. On its publication, he sent a copy of this latest plea for an improved naval organization to Admiral of the Navy George Dewey. "The time for action has come," he wrote Dewey. "I have a plan of action which I would like to lay before the General Board. . . ." [15]

Appearing before the board on 31 March, he outlined in detail his proposal and urged the board to take immediate action in support of an executive order that would activate the plan without waiting for Congress. Legislative sanction, he believed, would follow as a matter of course, as it had for the Naval Academy, the Torpedo Station, the War College, and the naval training services. The matter was considered, but no action was taken.

In November 1906, the annual report of Secretary Charles J. Bonaparte stated that radical reform of the Navy Department was necessary. However, he soon left the navy to become the attorney general. In April 1907, during a visit to Washington, Luce gave the new secretary, Victor Metcalf, copies of his articles on naval administration and several papers on naval efficiency, all with little apparent effect. When Luce returned to Washington three weeks later, he found that the secretary intended to rely on the Congress, which, he felt, would certainly take up the matter at the next session.

Luce was not to be put off. In early October he took advantage of a general order soliciting "suggestions to improve the efficiency of the Navy" to again propose that an office of "Naval Operations" be established that would supervise the military operations of the fleet. Again, no action was taken, as politicians and bureaucrats thwarted the reformers. However, the climate improved in December 1907, as the navy reentered the public spotlight. The Great White Fleet started its well-known cruise around the world, and the hearts of the nation sailed with it.

With the U.S. Navy in the forefront, *McClure's Magazine* published an article in January 1908 entitled "The Needs of the Navy" by Henry Reuterdahl, the Swedish–American artist and American editor for *Jane's Fighting Ships*. Written at the encouragement of Commander William S. Sims, the outspoken inspector of target practice and recently appointed naval aide to President Roosevelt, the article summarized many of Sims's opinions on naval problems, particularly that the navy's bureaus were responsible for design defects in ships under construction and that they had failed to correct such defects as too low freeboard and misplaced armor when the flaws were brought to their attention by officers serving at sea. Repercussions were heard in all quarters. In February, the Senate reacted by ordering an investigation into the problems brought to light by Reuterdahl and Sims.

Luce quickly saw that much of the trouble to which these men pointed could have been avoided if the navy had had more effective central direction. In the spring, Luce took up correspondence with Sims. Here was an opportunity to transmit his views to President Roosevelt through a sympathetic naval aide. The Senate committee was dominated by opponents of reform, and when its investigation began to indicate the need for far-reaching administrative reform, it went into executive session and then abruptly ended its investigation without recommendations. Thus it seemed essential to procure presidential action. While the Senate committee was falling into inaction, Sims and his predecessor as naval aide, Commander Albert L. Key, brought to the president's attention some serious design faults in the battleship *North Dakota,* then under construction. The president ordered the General Board, the War College staff, and a group of junior officers with technical expertise to investigate the matter. This commission met in Newport in July 1908 and gave Luce and Sims the opportunity to talk at length about the basic problem of naval administration. In the midst of the conference, Luce wrote directly to the president and suggested the establishment of a commission to consider and to report upon the reorganization of the Navy Department. Within two days President Roosevelt replied that he would carefully consider Luce's "very interesting suggestion."

In October 1908, Luce published his article "The Fleet" in the widely read *North American Review.* Interest in naval reform continued to grow. It appeared that by December a commission would be appointed to consider the matter. "Hope on hope Ever!" Luce wrote Sims, "We'll get there some time." [16] They did. On 27 January 1909, President Roosevelt appointed a board headed by former Secretary William H. Moody and including former Secretary Paul Morton, Congressman Alston G. Dayton, and retired Rear Admirals Luce, A. T. Mahan, Robley D. Evans, William M. Folger, and William S. Cowles. Through Luce's urging, the board completed its work and submitted its recommendations to the president less than a week before he was to leave office. Roosevelt immediately forwarded the report to the Senate, but no action was taken.

When the administration of President William Howard Taft took office on 4 March 1909, the new secretary of the navy, George von Lengerke Meyer, immediately began to study the matter. Detailed plans were drawn up by a board headed by Rear Admiral William Swift, and in November 1909 Meyer ordered, without congressional authority, the establishment of a system of "aids" who would act as professional assistants to the secretary and serve as an advisory council and general staff. The system was an improvement, although it did not represent the complete reformation that Luce and others had sought. From this beginning it would take more than five years for Congress finally to authorize a reorganization of the Navy Department and to provide for a chief of naval operations "charged with the operations of the fleet, and with the preparation and readiness of plans for its use in war." [17] Other individuals were responsible for bringing this idea to fruition. In early 1912, Luce became quite ill and ceased his work entirely. He died at his home in Newport on 28 July 1917, shortly after his ninetieth birthday.

First and foremost, Stephen B. Luce was a naval officer and seaman, but as such he also was a teacher, writer, organizer, administrator, and leader. During his career, he developed a perception of the navy as a flexible tool for applying force. He believed that if a navy was to fulfill its function successfully, it must be efficiently controlled by leaders who not only were technically proficient, but also understood the political limitations and implications of force. With this basic theme in mind, Luce worked for improvements in education and organization during a time of great technological innovation. He promoted standardized procedures throughout the service, established a basic training program for seamen, and initiated the Naval War College for educating officers who would establish naval policy, develop strategy, and manage the navy's functions. He was greatly influenced by ideas of the scientific study of history in the works of T. H. Buckle and J. K. Laughton and by the military theories of E. B. Hamley, Emory Upton, and Jomini, as well as by the expansionist ideas of Theodore Roosevelt and Henry Cabot Lodge.

Luce appreciated the technological revolution of his age, but he saw such innovation only as an additional reason to improve education and organization in order to use and to control technology properly. He was the acknowledged leader of naval intellectuals and influenced a number of rising officers, among them Bradley Allen Fiske, William Sowden Sims, Henry Taylor, and Alfred Thayer Mahan. Luce was not an original theorist, but a subjective thinker, the leader of a reform faction that was strongly opposed by the technicists within the navy. In his own time, he served as a conduit for the new European military ideas, which became some of the fundamental impulses for the development of American naval education, organization, administration, and strategic theory in the twentieth century.

FURTHER READING

The essay published here is drawn from and summarizes John Hattendorf's earlier work on Luce. More detail can be found in *The Writings of Stephen B. Luce,* edited by Rear Admiral John D. Hayes and John B. Hattendorf; Chapters 1–4 of *Sailors and Scholars: The Centennial History of the U.S. Naval War College,* by John B. Hattendorf, B. Mitchell Simpson III, and John R. Wadleigh; "Luce's Idea of the Naval War College," by John B. Hattendorf; and the entry for "Luce" in Roger J. Spiller, Joseph G. Dawson, and T. Harry Williams, eds., *Dictionary of American Military Biography.*

Luce's midshipman cruise on board the USS *Columbus* is related in Charles Nordhoff, *Man of War Life.* Hattendorf's 1985 annotated edition of *Man of War Life* in the Naval Institute Classics of Naval Literature series includes Luce's article, "A Fo'castle Court Martial." In addition to the studies relating to other naval figures connected with Luce, see Albert Gleaves, *Life and Letters of Stephen B. Luce,* which was written by a naval officer who knew Luce and his family well. Ronald Spector, *Professors of War: The Naval War College and the Development of the Naval Profession,* provides further detail on the early years of the Naval War College. For additional research material, see Evelyn M. Cherpak, comp., *Register of the Papers of Stephen B. Luce,* and *David Foote Sellers and Stephen B. Luce: A Register of Papers,* Stephen B. Luce Papers, Library of Congress.

NOTES

1. B. A. Fiske, "Stephen B. Luce, An Appreciation," 1935–40.

2. B. A. Fiske, *From Midshipman to Rear Admiral.*

3. Private Journal 1858, Stephen B. Luce Papers, Library of Congress (henceforth Luce Papers).

4. Luce to Commandant of Midshipmen, 26 February 1861, Luce Papers.

5. Bernard Brodie, *Seapower in the Machine Age,* 149–67.

6. S. B. Luce, "On the Study of Naval Warfare as a Science," reprinted in Hayes and Hattendorf, eds., *The Writings of Stephen B. Luce,* 65–66.

7. Ibid.; the modern and precise definitions of strategy, tactics, and logistics are from Henry E. Eccles, *Military Concepts and Philosophy,* 69.

8. S. B. Luce, "Tactics and History," in Hayes and Hattendorf, eds., *The Writings of Stephen B. Luce,* 74–75.

9. Luce, "On the Study of Naval Warfare as a Science," ibid., 53.

10. Reprinted in ibid., 45–68.

11. S. B. Luce, "The Naval War College," 685.

12. Luce to H. C. Taylor, 25 June 1904, Luce Papers.

13. Ibid.

14. Taylor to Luce, 29 June 1904, ibid.

15. Luce to Dewey, 24 March 1905, George Dewey Papers, Library of Congress.

16. Luce to Sims, 29 December 1908, William S. Sims Papers, Library of Congress.

17. Act of 3 March 1915.

ALFRED THAYER MAHAN: CHRISTIAN EXPANSIONIST, NAVALIST, AND HISTORIAN

ROBERT SEAGER II

Alfred Thayer Mahan (1840–1914) was the eldest son of Mary Okill and Dennis Hart Mahan (1802–71), professor of civil and military engineering and dean of faculty at the United States Military Academy, and a highly regarded author of military treatises. Alfred was born at West Point on 27 September 1840, spent his first twelve years there, and was filled to the brim as a young boy with the absolute necessity of praying until blue in the face and reading until exhausted. His favorite books as a child and young man were "boarders-away!" naval biographies and other maritime adventure stories. He would become, sequentially, a history buff, amateur historian, world-acclaimed professional historian and, in 1902–3, president of the prestigious American Historical Association. He was raised an Episcopalian of the biblical literalist sort, and by his own later admission succeeded personally in finding and knowing God.

But as a naval officer of heroic proportions Alfred Thayer Mahan was an utter failure.[1] There was nothing swashbuckling about him. He thoroughly disliked the navy in which he served for forty years, and was disliked by almost all who served with him, under him, or over him. His classmates at the Naval Academy "silenced" him during his first class year (1858–59), his shipmates later avoided him in the ward room, and his shoremates generally gave him wide berth. A tall, handsome, brilliant, and enormously vain young man, he was self-assured to the point of arrogance. Indeed, his contentious personality, his humorlessness, and his ill-concealed sense of social and intellectual superiority conspired to condemn him to a life of professional loneliness in the U.S. Navy. With the exception of Samuel

Alfred Thayer Mahan. This sketch of Mahan by Gribayeitoff was published less than a month after he received an honorary Doctor of Laws from Cambridge University in 1894. *Courtesy of the Naval Historical Center.*

A'Court Ashe, a midshipman who briefly befriended him at Annapolis, he had no close personal friends in or out of the service. He was, as his daughter Ellen later observed, "The Cat That Walked by Himself."[2]

Further, he was a naval officer who was deathly afraid of the sea; and he was either a poor shiphandler or was incredibly accident-prone at the conn.[3] He never heard a naval gun fired in anger save during the closing moments of the action at Port Royal, South Carolina, in November 1861, and he spent many of his subsequent waking hours on shore trying to avoid or postpone reassignment to sea duty. His naval career, from tedious blockade duty during most of the Civil War until his assignment to the new Naval War College in 1885, was a dreary succession of antique vessels and underfunded shore installations.

Who, then, was this unusual, personally unpopular, ill-starred shiphandler who was prone to seasickness? He was the man who, between 1890 and 1914, did as much as or more than any other American to introduce his countrymen to new ways of looking at the U.S. Navy's role in American foreign policy decision making, the nation's proper role in world affairs, and the strategic implications and dimensions of national security. He published twenty-one books, eleven of them containing reprintings of many of his 137 articles or serving as the repositories of various preserialized magazine articles. He also penned 107 letters to newspaper editors, mostly to the *New York Times* and mostly contentious. His most important works by far were his seminal *The Influence of Sea Power upon History 1660–1783*, published in 1890, and its sequel, *The Influence of Sea Power upon the French Revolution and Empire, 1793–1812*, published in 1892.[4]

Mahan has been condemned as naval propagandist, imperialist, warmonger, racist, and social Darwinist. He has been praised as patriot, foreign policy realist, brilliant historian, founding father of the Anglo–American "special relationship," and strategic genius. But what has generally been either overlooked or underestimated in evaluations of Mahan is that he was an intensely devout High Church Episcopalian, rooted in New Testament literalism, who combined into a single philosophical, theological, cosmological, and historical system conceptions that presented a Christian view of just war, pusillanimous peace, and Good Samaritan "imperialism." His was a cosmos filled with dialectical conflict, a history in which God continuously intervened, and an earth inhabited by inherently combative men and nation states.

Much of Mahan's adult life was spent as an Episcopal tither, layreader, sometime delegate to annual Episcopal Church general conventions, adviser to and lay-president of the Seamen's Church Institute (Episcopal) of New York, and member of the Episcopal Church Board of Missions; friend, counselor, and contributor to Boone University of Wuchang, China, and to St. Augustine School for Negroes in Raleigh, North Carolina; and frequent contributor to *The Church-*

man magazine, as well as a leading figure in the controversy within the Episcopal Church concerning reform of *The Book of Common Prayer.* Episcopal Christianity in particular and Protestant Christianity in general were always in his heart and mind and were always a prism through which he viewed the secular world. His "spiritual biography," *The Harvest Within: Thoughts on the Life of a Christian* (1909), discloses the depth of this orientation, as does the revealing diary he kept while serving as executive officer in the *Iroquois* in East Asian waters in 1868–69. The most important clue to understanding the mind of Alfred Thayer Mahan lies in his religion.[5]

There was nothing particularly original, however, in Mahan's eclectic cosmology. Nor was his major discovery (in 1884) of the influence of sea power on history original with him, a point he willingly conceded when he came later to realize that men from General Pericles of Athens, Greece, to Representative Washington C. Whitthorne of Columbia, Tennessee, had earlier grasped the idea.[6]

Mahan participated in no stirring battles, chastised no duplicitous tribal chief by leveling his flimsy village, and opened no foreign port to U.S. trade at cannon mouth. On only two occasions (Osaka, Japan, in 1868 and Panama City in 1885) did he participate in putting small bodies of armed seamen on shore to protect American lives and property. Because he was totally unheroic, any analysis of his reputation as one of the most important and influential officers in the history of the U.S. Navy must turn almost entirely on his ideas and teachings: how and from whence those ideas derived, how they applied to the nation and to the world in which Mahan lived, and to what extent, if any, they are still useful to the navy and the nation nearly a century later.

A summary of his ideas, to which the influence of sea power upon history was basic, would include the following:

1. *Conflict, Progress, and Natural Laws in the Universe:* From his uncle, the Reverend Milo Mahan (1819–70), professor of early Christian church history in the General (Episcopal) Seminary in New York City, Mahan derived his belief that motion in the universe and progress in history could be explained in terms of the dialectical clashes of various cosmic forces inherently in opposition to one another. Whereas Milo Mahan was a Pythagorean numerologist and mystic who explained these forces as numbers that stood for conflicting ideas or principles, his nephew, without known assistance from Hegel or Marx, argued that progress in history was the result of "the conflict of two opposites, as in the long struggle between freedom

and slavery, union and disunion in our own land; but the union nevertheless exists. It is not to be found in freedom, not yet in slavery, but in their conflict it is." From his uncle Milo also came the conviction that a universe fashioned and set in motion by an omnipotent, omniscient, and omnipresent Creator was, by definition, suffused with a logic and perfection that could be expressed in the form and fact of natural laws. Mahan therefore believed that there were "laws" of history, war (strategy and tactics), and human behavior. He held, further, that "the first law of states, as of men, is self-preservation," even if such preservation had to be achieved by national expansion.

2. *Inherency of War and Just Wars in Human History:* Mahan viewed war as the earthly manifestation of dialectical conflict in the universe. Given the existence of sovereign states inhabited and governed by aggressive men (ample evidence for which he found in the Bible), and the fact that there was no recorded human history in which war was absent, he concluded that war was both constant and inevitable. Indeed, war was a corrective instrument placed in human hands by the Creator to enable God-fearing and God-loving men to defend that which is good, just, and righteous on earth and oppose forcibly that which is evil, unjust, and wrong. Modern nations in the service of God must be prepared at all times to fight just wars. When such wars were fought to overthrow political tyranny, end human bondage, prevent religious persecution, or remove other obvious moral evils, they were not only righteous and justified in the eyes of God, they contributed mightily to human progress. "Honest collision is evidently a law of progress, however we explain its origin; whether it be in the ordinance of God, or in the imperfection of man."

3. *Pacifism, Arms Limitation, and Rules of War:* Mahan opposed all popular agitation for courts that would arbitrate international disputes, seek to control or outlaw particularly lethal weapons, or otherwise make rules and regulations designed to mitigate the horrors of war. Such activities foolishly denied the historical inevitability of war and compromised the necessity of fighting just wars. He felt, however, that modern wars might be rendered less protracted and less frequent if the profits reaped by nonparticipants were removed. Thus as a U.S. delegate to the First Hague Conference in 1899 and a strident critic of American participation in the Second Hague Conference in 1907, he urged the abandonment of the seventeenth-century international rubric that in wartime "free ships make free goods, except contraband."

4. *Research and Writing of History:* Mahan was convinced that his awareness of the influence of sea power upon history came directly from God. It was clearly one of the laws (or central themes) of history because the creation and proper use of organized sea power in wartime to ensure "command of the sea" had clearly influenced the course of human history, certainly more than had any other single factor. As will be shown below, his belief in the inherency of God-given central themes in the universe, themes that historians could discover through the favor of God and by the use of subordinationist historical methodology, underpinned his attitude toward researching and writing history. Specifically, he believed that "Facts won't lie if you work them right; but if you work them wrong a little disproportion in the emphasis, a slight exaggeration of color, a little more or less limelight on this or that part of the grouping and the result is not truth, even though each individual fact be as unimpeachable as the multiplication table." By working them right, historians could achieve mystical oneness with God by verifying His laws; nor would historians ever err in matters of historical interpretation.

5. *Laws of Naval Strategy and Tactics:* From Antoine-Henri Jomini (1779–1869) by way of Stephen B. Luce (1827–1917), Mahan derived the notion that a nation's "command of the sea" hinged on its recognition and scientific application of the laws of tactical and strategical concentration. These were cosmic laws that operated without reference to technological changes in naval vessels and ordinance. For this reason, fleets or armies, regardless of existing technology, that situated themselves at geographical positions in or near the "strategic center" of a given war—thus affording themselves the greatest amount of offensive mobility or the greatest measure of defensive flexibility— usually won the battles that determined the outcome of the wars that influenced the course of history. And a fleet in battle that could maneuver (concentrate) itself in such a way as to bring, for a decisive moment, a greater part of its firepower and personnel against lesser parts of the firepower and people of its enemy would invariably win the action, the decisive "Big Battle," that would establish "command of the sea" and bring victory. Indeed, as Mahan put it, again in dialectical terms, the very "Art of War consists in concentrating in order to fight and disseminating in order to subsist. . . . The problem is one of embracing opposites."

6. *Battleships as Decisive Naval Weapons:* Finally, Mahan argued that mere commerce raiding during war at sea, *guerre de course,* could never be tactically or strategically decisive. Wars at sea could be

settled conclusively, and "command of the sea" thereby established, only by concentrated fleets of battleships. But such vessels, he had come to believe by 1906, did not necessarily have to be copies of HMS *Dreadnought* and mount batteries composed solely of 10-inch or 12-inch guns. Modern navies, he argued, should maintain the operational flexibility inherent in "balanced" ship sizes and in the employment of "mixed batteries" of greater and lesser caliber guns. But whatever the size of the ships, or caliber of the guns, battlefleets must obey the strategical and tactical laws governing war at sea. The projection of naval power ashore by amphibious or other means seems not to have concerned Mahan.[7]

Mahan's discovery of the influence of sea power on history occurred shortly after Commodore Stephen B. Luce had invited him to join the faculty of the proposed Naval War College, which was scheduled to commence operation in Newport, Rhode Island, on 4 September 1885. Luce told him only that he would be required to give lectures on the "certain general principles" adducing to success or failure in naval warfare.[8] Commander Mahan was no stranger to the scholarly Luce. They had sailed together briefly during the Civil War, and Luce also knew him as the author of *The Gulf and Inland Waters,* a credible volume in the Charles Scribner's Sons series on the navy in the Civil War, which Mahan researched and wrote in five months in 1883 while serving as navigation officer at the New York (Brooklyn) Navy Yard. Why Scribner's picked Mahan for this task is not known, but why Mahan accepted such a pressure-packed assignment is clear: with a wife and three small children to support, he desperately needed the $600 the publisher was offering for the job. Competent as the book was, there was in it no hint of the sea power hypothesis to come. He did, however, make plain his view that the Civil War was in every respect a just war.[9]

The time, place, and circumstance of Mahan's great discovery of his sea power hypothesis are known precisely; it occurred in the library of the English Club in Lima, Peru, in November 1884, while he was reading Theodor Mommsen's *The History of Rome* in preparation for his War College lectures, and while his command, the decrepit *Wachusett,* lay at nearby Callao. Years later, in 1907, he described the exciting moment of his discovery in his autobiography, *From Sail to Steam:*

He who seeks, finds, if he does not lose heart; and to me, continuously seeking, came from within the suggestion that control of the sea was an historic factor which had never been systematically appreciated and expanded. For me . . . the light dawned first on my inner consciousness; I owed it to no other man. . . . I cannot now reconstitute from memory the sequence of my mental processes; but while my problem was still wrestling with my brain there dawned upon me one of those concrete perceptions which turn inward darkness into light—and give substance to shadow. . . . It suddenly struck me, whether by some chance phrase of the author I do not know, how different things might have been could Hannibal have invaded Italy by sea, as the Romans often had Africa, instead of by the long land route.

But much earlier than this, in mid-1894, he had privately assured his wife that he had been "guided to the work which is now so overwhelming praised," and that "the gift and call to write both came from outside." [10]

Whether the Creator had indeed nudged Mahan's mind, or a Gestalt experience of sorts had taken place, cannot be determined. Nonetheless, Mahan's blinding historical insight in November 1884 about sea power in history was destined to change the direction of his boring and lackluster naval career, revolutionize the study of naval history, and make his name a household word in U.S. naval and diplomatic circles and in the parlors of subscribers to such high-toned magazines as *Atlantic Monthly, Harper's Monthly,* and *North American Review*.

In mid-May 1885, Mahan informed Luce that preoccupation with the concerns of the *Wachusett* had rendered his sea power insight "a little vague" since November 1884; but that from "scanty notes" made at the time, his basic approach to his lectures would be, first, to "consider sources of maritime power or weakness—material, personnel, national aptitude, harbors with their positions relative to commercial routes and enemies coasts." He would then "bring forward instances from ancient and modern history, of the effect of navies and the control of the sea upon great or small campaigns," especially Hannibal's defeat in Italy in the Second Punic War. He hoped this approach would lead to the discovery of possible parallels "between the weapons or branches of land forces and those of the sea, if any hints can be drawn as to their use." As for the "subject of naval tactics," a primary theoretical interest of Luce's at this time, "I own I am awfully at sea; but in a study like the above I should hope for light." [11]

Mahan would soon learn that Luce had already discovered the source of that light and would urge Mahan to follow its gleam. Indeed,

Luce was far ahead of Mahan in the conviction that naval officers should study history, especially that of great naval battles, to discover what scientific principles were illustrated in victorious combat, or where disregard for the accepted rules of war had led to defeat. Mahan would also learn that Luce had nothing less in view than to make of the new Naval War College the birthplace of the discovery of the laws and principles comprising the "science of naval warfare." He told the nine men in the first class to report to the college in September 1885 (Mahan was not yet present) that their task was "to raise maritime war to the level of a science." Moreover, "having established our principles by the inductive process, we may then resort to the deductive method of applying those principles to such a changed condition of the art of war as may be imposed by later inventions or by introduction of novel devices." Luce was also certain that although there was yet

> no authoritative treatise on the art of naval warfare under steam . . . we must, perforce, resort to the well-known rules of the military art with a view to their application to the military movements of a fleet, and, from the well-recognized methods of disposing troops for battle, ascertain the principles which govern fleet formations. . . . *It is by this means alone that we can raise naval warfare from the empirical stage to the dignity of a science.*

To make this last point clear he suggested that "the existence of fundamental principles, by which all the operations of war should be conducted, has been placed beyond doubt by the researches of Jomini." Let us, Luce emphasized, as we search for "the science of naval warfare under steam . . . look for that master mind who will lay the foundations of that science, and do for it what Jomini has done for military science." [12]

So it was that through Luce, his commanding officer at the War College, Mahan derived his conception of naval strategy and tactics from Antoine-Henri Jomini, whose numerous works (twenty-seven volumes of military history covering the wars of Frederick the Great, the French Revolution, and Bonaparte) dealt entirely with the strategy and tactics of land armies. In effect, Luce ordered Mahan to study Jomini's land-war tactics and apply their principles to hypothetical fleet combat maneuvers of ironclad vessels under steam. Mahan, of course, obeyed, even though Jomini had observed in his seminal *The Art of War* (1836) that "war in its ensemble is not a science, but an art. Strategy, particularly, may indeed by regulated by fixed laws resembling those of the positive sciences, but this is not true of war viewed as a whole."[13]

Mahan did not reach Newport until October 1885, after the brief twenty-six-day first session of the War College had ended. He was delayed by the fact that the *Wachusett* was unexpectedly ordered to Central American waters in March and April 1885 to protect American lives, property, and transit-treaty rights during revolutionary and international disorders in the area. This enterprise forced Mahan to put a landing party ashore on the Isthmus of Panama in mid-March 1885 to maintain the nation's right of transit, an operation that involved seizing and holding the U.S.-owned railroad and cable station in Panama City. It also involved showing the flag in El Salvador and Guatemala in April, during the chaos there occasioned by the latter's invasion of the former.

The detour of the *Wachusett* to the west coast of Central America was not without its educational advantages. If nothing else, Mahan learned from this experience that the U.S. Navy badly needed a coaling station on that coast, and that U.S. sea power, properly applied, had a critical role to play in sustaining U.S. diplomacy. Further, the experience riveted in his mind an appreciation for the strategic importance of the isthmus, the chaotic political conditions within the weak little nations situated thereupon, and the importance of the transit rights the United States held there. Indeed, the problem of the isthmus would play a major, almost disproportionate, role in Mahan's early studies of sea power and in the curriculum of the infant Naval War College after he became the institution's president in mid-1886.[14]

When Mahan finally conferred with Luce in Newport in October 1885, it was decided between them that Mahan (now captain) would spend the next ten months in New York working up lectures on naval tactics and naval history to be given at the second session of the college, scheduled for a ten-week period commencing 6 September 1886. Three months before that session began, however, Luce (now rear admiral) was detached from the institution and assigned to command the North Atlantic Station, and Mahan became president of the school. Meanwhile, Mahan had gone to work on his lectures in the Astor Library and the New York Lyceum.

It should be kept in mind that during this period of lecture preparation Mahan was attempting to accomplish two quite different research and writing tasks. First, he undertook a review of the tactical maneuvers employed by warring fleets of wooden sailing vessels in line-ahead formation in the seventeenth and eighteenth centuries with a view toward applying them to steel vessels under steam. To the practice of firepower concentration employed in line-ahead formations during the Age of Sail (usually employed without success or decision), he added Jomini's principles of unit or fractional concentration. His problem here was that in 1885–87 there was no tactical combat doctrine for steel and steam vessels; and with the exception of the Austro–Italian battle of Lissa in July 1866, which had been a tactically chaotic melee of iron-clad vessels attempting to sink one another with close-in gunfire or by ramming, there was no body of combat experience to guide him. [15]

Second, he read broadly in the printed accounts of the naval dimensions of the great mercantilist wars for empire in which Britain, France, Holland, and Spain had participated in the period 1660 to

U.S. Naval War College, 1886. The "old" administration building on Coaster's Harbor Island as it appeared when Mahan reported for duty to deliver his lectures on naval tactics and history. Built during the 1820s as an asylum for the poor of Newport, it served as home for the Naval War College from its establishment in 1885 until 1889. *Courtesy of the Naval Historical Center.*

1783, this with the clear intent to document and otherwise demonstrate the truth of the sea power hypothesis he had earlier stumbled upon in Lima in November 1884. In this second task he made no effort to consult primary sources or materials that might conflict with his conviction that the existence or nonexistence of sea power had been (and was) the most powerful factor in determining the course and direction of human history. "Original research was not within my scope, nor was it necessary to the scheme," he later confessed.[16]

The first of these dual historiographical enterprises to see the light was a curious manuscript titled "Fleet Battle Tactics." In its text and in the accompanying hypothetical battle diagrams, Mahan employed, as best he could, elements of Jomini's four main "maxims," or "principles" or "laws," of tactical concentration. As expressed in Jomini's *Study of the Art of War,* they were:

> 1. To throw by strategic movements the mass of an army, successively, upon the decisive points of a theater of war, and also upon the communications of the enemy as much as possible without compromising one's own.
> 2. To maneuver to engage fractions of the hostile army, with the bulk of one's own forces.
> 3. On the battle-field, to throw the mass of the forces upon the decisive point, or upon that portion of the hostile line which it is of the first importance to overthrow.
> 4. To arrange that these masses shall not only be thrown upon the decisive point, but that they shall engage at the proper times and with energy.[17]

These four "maxims," "principles," or "laws" of the "science" or "art" (Jomini's nomenclature varied) of tactical concentration lost something in persuasiveness when Mahan applied them to naval battle tactics in his "Fleet Battle Tactics" essay. As he viewed it, the battleship line, as it commenced action in either line abreast or echelon, would wheel, turn, and perform various precise, complex, and opportunistic geometric evolutions designed to secure, maintain, regain, or increase its concentration of fire ("the essence of scientific warfare," said Mahan) on selected smaller enemy units that would be sent gloriously to the bottom one by one. It was to be a "highly drilled" fleet operation executed by "reasonably perfect ships, reasonably drilled and commanded." In sum, said Mahan, "Perfection is our aim." But in reading "Fleet Battle Tactics" today, one gains the impression that the enemy fleet was expected to sit supinely in the water, watching in awe, as the U.S. battleline, directed by some brilliant naval choreographer, danced nimbly around it and destroyed it piecemeal and totally. Near the end, U.S. torpedo boats and rams, the equivalents of Jominian cavalry, would swiftly stand down on the sinking cripples and put them out of their misery.[18]

Luce did not think highly of his disciple's manuscript on tactics. He told Mahan, after reading the piece, that the main weakness in it was that it did not adequately link recent technological changes in ship design and ordnance with Jomini's principles of land tactics as applied to fleet maneuvers. Luce also informed him that he would be responsible for only two lectures on tactics during the 1886 session and that he had engaged someone else to do the rest. In fine, Mahan's "Fleet Battle Tactics" quickly disappeared from the sight and mind of man, a fate that seems not to have disturbed its author. Moreover, in his future books and articles Mahan never permitted the fact of technological changes in naval vessels and weapons to becloud or set aside his notions of fixed tactical and strategical principles, or laws, of naval warfare that were, he came to believe, inherent in the mathematical orderliness of the universe.[19]

Mahan's study of Jomini's tactical doctrines in 1886 also influenced his conception of naval strategy, some elements of which he discussed in his War College lectures in 1887, and which found their way into his two *Influence* books in 1890 and 1892. Not until 1911, however, did he finally bring his scattered views on strategy together in his *Naval Strategy, Compared and Contrasted with the Principles of Military Operations on Land.* "Naval Strategy," he assured the readers of that opaque volume, is based upon "fundamental truths, which when correctly formulated are rightly called principles; these truths, where ascertained, are themselves unchangeable." He admitted that new light might be shed on the applications of these principles. But the appearance of the submarine, the long-range torpedo, wireless telegraphy, and the airplane by 1911 had not modified or illuminated his "fundamental truths" about naval strategy. These strategical "truths," all with Jominian overtones of tactical concentration, were, as Mahan viewed them, four in number:

1. To understand that the basic goal, and end purpose, of naval strategy is, by fleet action, to "break up the enemy's power on the sea, cutting off his communications with the rest of his possessions, drying up the sources of his wealth and his commerce, and making possible a closure of his ports." This produces "command of the sea."

2. To effect a deployment of battlefleet and support vessels in such manner as to bring a superior force of one's own to bear on an

inferior though significant enemy force in one quarter, while else-where other enemy units are held in check long enough to permit the initial or primary strike force to produce victory; in fine, the "hit and hold" principle.

3. To seek to commence naval war from a central position (or strategic center) so that one's own concentrated naval force may be dispatched offensively along interior lines outward against separated segments of the enemy's force. This positioning increases the likeli-hood of bringing successful hit and hold maneuvers into play. One must never divide his own main battlefleet or dispatch it on eccentric operations.

4. To appreciate and act upon the fact that the main purpose and mission of battlefleets is to bring the enemy's main fleet (or a major segment thereof) to decisive battle, and to destroy it wholly with concentrated fire from guns of one's own capital ships (armored steel battleships). Battlefleets thus must operate offensively, not defen-sively (not as "fleets-in-being"), in bringing the enemy into a deci-sive "Big Battle," victory in which is rewarded with "command of the sea," the fundamental strategic goal of naval warfare.[20]

The dubious relevance of his *Naval Strategy* volume and his "Fleet Battle Tactics" manuscript aside, it was Mahan's second task—to compose lectures that would clearly demonstrate the influence of sea power on history—that he wanted most to accomplish. These lec-tures would become, virtually unchanged, his famous *The Influence of Sea Power upon History, 1660–1783*. In November 1885 he had com-menced reading the printed monographic, biographical, and autobio-graphical literature on the great European imperial wars of the sev-enteenth and eighteenth centuries. By May 1886 he had taken 400 pages of notes and knew exactly what he wanted to prove and how to prove it. It was just a question of arranging his carefully selected facts to fit his thesis and getting it all down on paper. Indeed, on 22 January 1886 he informed Luce that he had chosen the 1660–1783 period to focus upon, had the general schema in mind, and would begin his lectures

with a general consideration of the sea, its uses to mankind and to nations, the effect which the control of it or the reverse has [had] upon their peaceful development and upon their military strength. This will naturally lead to . . . a consideration of the sources of Sea Power, whether commercial or military; depending upon the position of the particular country—the character of its coast, its harbors, the character and pursuits of its people, its possession of military posts in various parts of the world, its colonies, etc.—its resources, in the length and breadth of the word. After such a general statement of the various elements of the problem, illustrated of course by specific examples—the path would be cleared for naval history. . . . I have carefully followed up this period [after 1648] both in respect of naval history and the general struggles of Europe; for it has seemed to me . . . that the attempt to violently separate the naval history from that context will be something like . . . Hamlet with all but the part of Hamlet left out. . . . I expect to begin with Jomini etc. and, having naval conditions constantly before my mind, I should hope to detect analogies—and with an admirable system of one kind of war before me to contribute something to the development of a systematic study of war in another field. . . . I would like this letter, however, to be confidential—in case any of my thunder should turn out *real* thunder.[21]

This statement was, in essence, an outline of his first *Influence of Sea Power* book, which appeared in December 1890.

In analyzing Mahan's seminal volume, one should remember that the first and most influential chapter in the book, "Elements of Sea Power," was written last, that it was tacked onto the hefty manuscript at the very last moment at the request of the publisher to make the whole work "more popular." Mahan agreed to this bastard surgery because he knew history was not "an attractive subject to the public," and because he thought increased sales might encourage the publishers, Little, Brown of Boston, to gamble on a sequel that would carry the story up to 1812, as later they did. In sum, "Elements of Sea Power" was primarily a summary of *European* national motives, opportunities, and aptitudes for the creation and employment of sea power, as Mahan conceived them to have related to the great mercantilist wars for empire fought in the seventeenth and eighteenth centuries. It was a précis of sorts to the rest of the book. The historical illustrations he used in "Elements of Sea Power" to explain national motives, opportunities, and aptitudes for sea power were taken primarily from British and French military and naval experience in 1660–1783. How these examples might be applied to the United States in 1890 was treated briefly, tangentially, and diffidently. "Elements of Sea Power" was not, then, a prescription for or summons to U.S. imperialism, mercantilism, colonialism, or territorial expansion. Mahan sought only to awaken Americans to the need for a navy that could ensure national security in Gulf–Caribbean and eastern Pacific waters, if and when a canal was built across the Isthmus of Panama by a foreign power—a project French interests indeed were attempting at that time. The essay was essentially a call to his countrymen to emerge from twenty-five years of isolation.[22]

The basic thing Mahan sought to demonstrate in the main body of the book was simply this: that among European nations with sea coasts, "in three things—production, with the necessity of exchanging products, shipping, whereby the exchange is carried on, and colonies, which facilitate and enlarge the operations of shipping and tend to protect it by multiplying points of safety—is to be found the key to much of history, as well as of the policy, of nations bordering upon the sea." Mercantilistic imperialism thus boiled down to the relationship of "(1) Production; (2) Shipping; (3) Colonies and Markets—in a word, sea power."[23]

It was "sea power," therefore, that had made eighteenth-century European imperialism and mercantilism really work. Specifically, Mahan described the process whereby strong (usually absolute) monarchs exported the products and people of their kingdoms, in the numerous vessels of their national merchant marines, protected by their large navies, to overseas colonies that were designed to function as closed, monopolized markets. This policy produced favorable trade balances, generating the bullion or raw materials that made the imperial exporting nations and their ruling dynasties even richer and more powerful, as well as better able economically to launch and sustain the mercantilist wars on land and sea (mostly the latter) that served to expand their empires even farther. Britain, thanks to the early emergence of the superb Royal Navy, was Mahan's prime example of the crucial role sea power (merchant and naval) had played in creating the national power, glory, and wealth that was the British Empire of 1890.

Mahan also set forth, in the "Elements of Sea Power" chapter, the six "principal conditions affecting the sea power of nations" and the potentiality of various coastal nations to develop such power, mainly citing illustrative comparisons from British, French, Dutch, and Spanish imperial history of the period 1660–1783. It was only in this comparative context, however, that the United States with its tiny merchant marine and antiquated navy was brought peripherally into the picture. The six conditions Mahan cited were: Geographical Position, Physical Conformation, Extent of Territory, Number of Population, National Character, and Character of Government.

As for Geographical Position, that of the United States was certainly conducive to the development of sea power should the nation choose to undertake such development. Mahan noted, however, that from a strategic and military defense standpoint the relationship between the southern continental United States and the Gulf of Mexico was analogous to England's relationship to its channel, or that of the Mediterranean nations to Suez, especially if a Central American canal were to be constructed. If that occurred, Mahan warned, the Gulf–Caribbean, given a canal outlet, would become "one of the great highways of the world" along which "a great commerce would travel, bringing the interests of the other great nations, the European nations, close along our shores, as they have never been before." This magnetic attraction of world shipping, merchant and naval, to the Gulf–Caribbean would surely involve America in "international complications" eventually calling for "war-ships of the first class, without which ships no country can pretend to control any part of the sea." It would also demand bases in the Gulf–Caribbean sufficient to sustain U.S. naval operations in isthmian waters in the event of political crises in Central America. These bases should be positioned so as to control ingress and egress to and from the Mississippi River. It should be noted that, in this regard, Mahan was thinking almost entirely in terms of coastal strategic defense.[24]

He pointed out that the nation's Physical Conformation included numerous deep harbors with easy access to the sea like those that had been a source of maritime power and wealth in Europe, and that the United States had such assets on three coasts; but the country had no merchant marine, nor was it likely to have one in the foreseeable future. Further, the nation had no colonies because its investment capital found ample opportunity for profit in its economically underdeveloped interior. This would remain the situation for some time to come unless America's isolated "little corner" of the world was pierced by an isthmian canal—in which case the nation would be in for a "rude awakening."[25] In sum, of the three requisites for empire—Production, Merchant Shipping, and Colonies (Closed Markets)—America lacked two. Industrial productive capacity the nation did have.

On the other hand, America's Extent of Territory and Number of Population were sufficient to achieve and sustain sea power capabilities. Also, the National Character of Americans included a necessary amount of commercial aptitude and acquisitiveness; and Americans certainly had the ability to produce sufficient commodities for trade. But modern nations aspiring to sea power must also have a "capacity for planting healthy colonies." By healthy colonies, Mahan did not mean the kind of colonies planted by Spain, Portugal, and France in the sixteenth, seventeenth, and eighteenth centuries. These were simply mercantilistic "cows to be milked," upon which the home government had legislated "a monopoly of its external trade." He meant, instead, colonies like the British planted in North America, possessions that required minimum control from the mother country. They would be colonies settled by people with a "genius for independent action," not colonies rigidly controlled and monopolized by the home government. Therefore, if there were ever in the American future conditions "calling for colonization, it cannot be doubted that Americans will carry to them all their inherited aptitude for self-government and independent growth." He saw no such situation developing, however.

Finally, Mahan admitted that the Character of Government of most of Europe's great sea powers had in the past been absolutist or despotic; but he felt certain that democratic governments could also aspire to sea power even though "Popular governments are not generally favorable to military expenditure."[26]

What concerned Mahan most in all of this was that even with a great U.S. merchant marine, "it may be doubted whether a sufficient navy would follow"; and even if it did follow, whether it would be strong enough and capable enough to meet a potential enemy far at sea, even close to foreign shores, rather than in American waters. Or would it be so weak that it would have to adopt a passive defense strategy and meet the enemy in U.S. coastal waters? The question, then, of the adequacy of the U.S. Navy, Mahan concluded, "is probably now quickening in the Central American Isthmus. Let us hope that it will not come to the birth too late."[27]

In general, Mahan did not in 1890 consider the United States a likely candidate for imperialism, colonialism, or militarism. "I dread outlying colonies," he had told Sam Ashe in 1884, "to maintain which large military establishments are necessary. I see in them the on-coming of a 'strong' central government . . . or perhaps a subversion of really free government." He worried, too, that neither the Republican nor Democratic parties would have the political courage to respond to a foreign challenge at the isthmus, or even have the good sense to assume a sensible defense posture in the Gulf–Caribbean. But Mahan himself did little to change matters. He participated not at all in the political agitation for the New Navy in the 1880s, or in arguments in and out of Congress that linked naval expansion to forced commercial expansion abroad. He favored free trade, he told Ashe in 1884. Indeed, he never advocated artificial U.S. government stimulation of overseas trade with tariffs, subsidies, drawbacks, or gunboats. Nor did he ever link the advent and growth of the New Navy to the advancement of his personal career.[28]

It thus seems reasonably clear that the principal thrust of Mahan's advice to his country on the nation's diplomacy and its defensive strategy at the advent of the so-called imperialist period in American history was not particularly imperialistic. He was an "imperialist," he said, because he was nonisolationist; and an "imperialist" United States, by his definition, was a nation that must abandon isolationism to the extent of aspiring to own, operate, fortify, or otherwise control any future Central American canal. The nation must also have a naval capability in warships, bases, and coaling stations in the Gulf–Caribbean with which to protect that canal and monitor international shipping to, near, and through its eastern approaches. Similarly, in the eastern Pacific the United States must annex Hawaii and establish there a naval presence capable of flanking and otherwise superintending international shipping to and from the future canal's western terminus. The new U.S. Navy, then, need only be large enough to maintain a protective shield in the northern and eastern Pacific for the purpose of defending the thinly populated, underdeveloped West Coast against threat from or attack by an increasingly aggressive Japan. As for the size of the nation's Pacific shield, Mahan was quite specific. In an *Atlantic Monthly* article in 1890, titled "The United States Looking Outward," he wrote:

> It should be an inviolable resolution of our national policy, that no foreign state should henceforth acquire a coaling position within three thousand miles of San Francisco—a distance which includes the Hawaiian and Galapagos islands and the coast of Central America. For fuel is the life of modern naval war; it is the food of the ship; without it the modern monsters of the deep die of inanition. Around it, therefore, cluster some of the most important considerations of naval strategy.[29]

True, Mahan also spoke in the 1890s of the possibility of increased American trade in the Pacific in future years; but he regarded this mainly as a desirable economic by-product of canal acquisition and Hawaiian annexation. It was far less important to him than was the strategic necessity of creating and policing an isthmian-centered, Caribbean–Gulf–Hawaiian–West Coast–Galápagos Islands defense perimeter. Indeed, the strategic importance of an American-controlled canal at the isthmus was almost always in his mind in 1890–

1914. No other strategic subject engaged his attention with such frequency and intensity during these years.[30]

Mahan even suggested in November 1900 that, given the nation's commitment to China in its recently announced Open Door policy, Americans might well consider a "retrenchment of responsibility" and abandon insistence on the Monroe Doctrine in that sector of the Western Hemisphere south of the Amazon valley; or at least extend Open Door (free trade) principles there to all nations, principles of the sort some Americans were then seeking to establish in China.[31]

This is not to say that the highly moralistic Mahan approved the tough methods employed by the Roosevelt administration against Colombia in November 1903 to acquire an acceptable canal right-of-way in Panama. After all, Christians do not steal—or should not. In any event, not until 1912 did he undertake a defense of the legality of U.S. behavior at the isthmus nine years earlier. In this belated exercise he argued that the Roosevelt administration had intervened to restore order in Panama so as to preserve the right-of-transit permitted in Article 35 of the 1846 treaty between the United States and New Granada (predecessor state to Colombia). He specifically separated the dubious morality of the U.S intervention from its legality.

Nor had Mahan been happy when Britain joined with Germany in a naval blockade of the Venezuelan coast, in December 1902, in an attempt to force Venezuela to pay its debts—a blockade in which the Germans had actually bombarded a fort and a town on that coast. He believed that the only good that could come of such arrogant European naval penetration of the Gulf–Caribbean so close to the isthmus was that Congress might be persuaded to authorize "two more battleships." Furthermore, Mahan did not think, as he made clear in February 1903, that the Monroe Doctrine should be used by the United States against Latin Americans to justify compelling them to make good their obligations to their European creditors, because "to do so which has been by some argued a necessary corollary of the Monroe Doctrine, would encroach on the very independence which that political dogma defends." The United States, he asserted, should be "preponderant" in Latin America, not "paramount." The nation would not "find the true complement of the Monroe Doctrine in an undefined control over [Latin] American states, exercised by her and denied to Europe."

Given these temperate views, Roosevelt's crude seizure of Panama in November 1903 was simply too much for Mahan. So too was the president's enunciation of the so-called Roosevelt Corollary to the Monroe Doctrine in December 1904, in which he justified unilateral preventive intervention by the United States in Latin America in order to forestall possible European intervention there. Not until 1908 did Mahan accept the principle underlying the corollary. In thus defending Roosevelt's 1904 policy in the Dominican Republic in 1908, and his 1903 policy in Panama in 1912, Mahan was tardily accepting the fait accompli of both situations. He had not contributed to or participated in the initial decision-making process in either instance, nor was he even consulted.[32]

In addition, it is well to note that Mahan's advocacy of an eastern Pacific defense perimeter, particularly his insistence that Hawaii be annexed, contained a distinct racial dimension that was related to his perception, as early as January 1893, that the Hawaiian Islands were being overrun by immigrant Chinese. He saw this as evidence of the beginnings of a "barbaric invasion" of Western civilization that could be contained only by "a firm hold on the Sandwich Islands by a great civilized, maritime power." An augmentation of U.S. naval power to protect underpopulated California from Oriental inundation (the "Yellow Peril") was clearly indicated, he insisted.

Four years later Mahan viewed increasing Japanese emigration to Hawaii and California in much the same light, and saw the appearance of modern Japanese naval vessels in Hawaiian waters in 1897 as evidence that the Yellow Peril (Japanese manifestation) was about to engulf Hawaii. For the remainder of his life Mahan nursed the conviction, off and on, that there would someday occur a gigantic global military showdown between Orient and Occident, barbarism and civilization, yellow and white, heathen and Christian. That there would be an earlier war of lesser magnitude between the United States and Japan in the Pacific he had no doubt. Some day, in some way, and for some reason, Japan would attack the United States.[33]

Mahan's dogged insistence upon Hawaiian annexation in the early 1890s earned him (so he claimed) exile to sea in 1893, by the anti-annexationist Cleveland administration, as commanding officer of the USS *Chicago*. This banishment, however, led to his triumphal welcome in England where his *Influence* books had been exceptionally well received in British naval, political, and literary circles. His enthusiastic inclusion in such company was a social and professional success that increased his already enormous sense of Anglophilia, cementing forever in his mind a firm belief in the absolute superiority of virtually everything British—their parliamentary system, common law, navy, empire, Anglican Church, manners, and smug confidence in their racial superiority. His subsequent writing clearly reflected these unshakable biases.

But his two-year cruise in the *Chicago* also convinced him that the technology of the steel "naval monsters" of the New Navy had passed him by. The modern vessels truly frightened him. When he returned home in 1896 he retired; forty unhappy years in the U.S. Navy were enough. He had meanwhile decided that he could earn enough in a "second career" as a writer (at five to seven cents a word) to increase a retirement salary of $3,375 to a level necessary to support a wife and two unmarried daughters at home, put a son through boarding school and college, and sustain a gracious life-style of the sort he had observed and admired in England in 1893–94. Beginning in 1897 his literary output thus became increasingly voluminous; it also became increasingly commercial, popular, superficial, and repetitious, focusing far less on history and much more on current events. Daily European and Asian diplomatic crises, conveniently spaced wars (Spanish–American, Boer, Russo–Japanese, Balkan), naval arms races, dangerous peace movements, and various Christian concerns soon became Mahan's principal subjects. "I have committed myself to potboilers," he confessed in June 1896. However, it was these potboilers, mostly magazine articles subsequently collected and reissued in book form, that helped pay for a fine row house in New York City, an elaborate summer place in Quoque, Long Island, and a household staff or four or five servants in both residences. The "Philosopher of Sea Power" lived well from 1897 until his death in 1914.[34]

At the time of Mahan's retirement from the U.S. Navy in November 1896, many Americans had become aware that there was under way in Cuba a bloody revolutionary war of independence against Spain. "Cuba Libre!" was the cry. Seventeen months later, in April 1898, the United States, for purposes of pacification and for reasons essentially humanitarian, intervened militarily in that conflict. This action brought on the 116-day Spanish–American War, which secured the independence of Cuba, and which incidentally (almost accidentally) resulted in U.S. annexation of Spain's colony in the Philippines.

Mahan had virtually nothing to do with the onset of the war. Neither his personal letters nor his publications in late 1897–early 1898 indicate any interest in Cuba save as a strategic pawn in a hypothetical American–German naval war in the Gulf–Caribbean.

He certainly visualized no actual Spanish–American war there.[35] Nor is there credible evidence that Mahan participated importantly in the U.S. Navy's routine contingency planning of naval war with Spain and other nations in the years 1894–98. However, three or four Mahan letters (now lost) written in March 1898 to Assistant Secretary of the Navy Theodore Roosevelt do indicate that he was consulted informally by Roosevelt on blockade strategy and tactics in Cuba in the event of war with Spain, and that he apparently recommended to Roosevelt a tight blockade of Havana, Mantanzas, and the western half of Cuba pending concentration of the U.S. battle-fleet for a decisive action ("Big Battle") against the Spanish home fleet, if and when it arrived in the waters of the Western Hemisphere.[36]

There is no evidence that Mahan ever recommended a naval attack on the Philippines as part of a war with Spain. At no time during the prewar period did he agitate for war with Spain, contemplate or advocate territorial acquisitions as the result of such a war, or even speak out for a free Cuba. He was far too busy writing profitable articles for *Harper's Monthly* that addressed the possibility of future naval war with Germany or Japan and argued the need for creating eastern Pacific and Gulf–Caribbean defense zones in order to maintain U.S. naval preeminence near a possible future canal in Central America. Thus when the USS *Maine* mysteriously exploded in Havana harbor on 15 February 1898, claiming the lives of 260 officers and men, Mahan was not among those splenetic Americans who irrationally blamed it on Spain and called loudly for war. Instead, he advocated a suspension of judgment in the matter and pointed out that the explosion might well have been caused by an accident within the vessel, which, in retrospect, now seems likely. Finally, on 26 March 1898, five weeks after the sinking of the *Maine* and sixteen days before McKinley read his war message to Congress, Mahan and his family departed the United States for a tour of Europe.[37]

Ordered back to Washington on 25 April to serve on the Naval War Board, which was to advise Secretary of the Navy John D. Long on the conduct of the war in ways not made entirely clear, Mahan spent most of the brief war making various strategical and tactical suggestions that dealt principally with operational problems associated with U.S. fleet concentration in Cuban, Caribbean, and Spanish home waters—although by the time he actually reached Washington on 10 May, the fleet was anything but concentrated, and Dewey had already sent Spain's decrepit Asiatic squadron to the bottom of Manila Bay. On 3 July, most of the remainder of Spain's little navy was demolished near Santiago, thus severing the Spanish army in Cuba and the colony itself from the Madrid government. Responding to threats of bombardment of the Spanish coast by the U.S. Navy, Spain wisely asked for a cease-fire. On 12 August the fighting ended. Meanwhile, U.S. infantry units numbering about 11,000 men had reached Manila and occupied the city; Guam and Wake islands, as well as Puerto Rico, had also been seized—all without opposition—and Hawaii had at last been annexed (in July 1898) by treaty with a compliant insular government, earlier (June 1897) negotiated by the equally willing McKinley administration.

Mahan's main contribution to these stirring events was his continued insistence on the annexation of Hawaii. A less obvious contribution was his signing, two weeks after joining the Naval War Board, of a lucrative ("at my price") contract with *McClure's Magazine* that called for a series of five articles on the war. These pieces ran monthly in *McClure's* from December 1898 through April 1899 and were reprinted in book format as *Lessons of the War with Spain* in September 1899, following Mahan's return from participation as an American delegate at the First Hague Conference. The articles remain a valuable primary source on the history of the naval operations of the conflict.[38]

The final report of the Naval War Board, written by Mahan during the third week in August 1898, saluted the nation's acquisition of Hawaii, calling the islands "militarily essential, both to our transit to Asia, and to the defense of our Pacific coast." The report also called for a canal at the isthmus and for eight naval coaling stations—two in the Caribbean, one each in Hawaii, Samoa, Manila, and Guam, and two in the Chushan islands near the mouth of the Yangtze. "Beyond these eight positions," Mahan wrote, "the Board is not prepared to recommend acquisitions." The proposed bases in the central, western, and southwestern Pacific would, however, contribute to the future protection of American commercial interests in and near a China suffering from "the intrusion of European control upon her territory, and the consequent effect upon her trade relations." The report noticeably did not call for annexation of the Philippines.[39]

Mahan accepted the idea of Philippine annexation with the greatest reluctance, observing in the final report of the Naval War Board that from purely a military standpoint all that was needed by the United States in the archipelago was a naval station and coaling facility at the "city and bay of Manila, or Subic Bay, if all Luzon Island be not ceded." A month earlier, on 21 July 1898, he had explained that he had "not yet become wholly adjusted to the new point of view opened to us by Dewey's victory at Manila" even though it had "opened a vista of possibilities which were not by me in the least foreseen," and in spite of the fact that he had long anticipated a massive conflict in the Pacific between East and West. He finally decided that a beneficent God had delivered the Philippines into American hands to be civilized and uplifted. By early August 1898 he was reluctantly following the Republican party line on annexation, having moved gradually from merely acquiring a naval base in Manila, to taking only Luzon, to annexing all of the islands. His arguments, shared by many U.S. senators and other Americans at the time, pointed out that the Filipinos simply could not be returned to the brutal colonial rule of Spain; that they could not be subjected to the domestic political chaos inherent in Emilio Aguinaldo's ill-organized independence movement; and that to withdraw from the islands would "abandon" to other nations "the task of maintaining order in the land in which we have been led to interpose."[40]

This does not mean that Mahan had suddenly become an enthusiastic colonialist in 1898. He had not. The word colony so disturbed him that he referred to the Philippines and Puerto Rico as "dependencies." He hoped that Americans could administer them with the skill, benevolence, and beneficence generally shown by the British in their colonies, but he admitted that the "task is novel to us; we may make blunders."[41] He participated not at all in the public debate on annexation in 1899–1900. He scarcely mentioned the bloody guerrilla war Americans and Fillipinos fought in the jungles of Luzon, Mindanao, and Samar in 1899–1901. Instead, he turned his busy pen to a defense of the British cause in the Boer War in South Africa. He was convinced that the Philippines lay far outside the eastern Pacific defense perimeter he considered the U.S. Navy capable of defending; further, he came to believe by 1911 that the loss of the archipelago by act of war would be no more significant to the United States from a material standpoint than the "loss of a little finger, perhaps a single joint of it. The Philippines to us are less a property than a charge." Moreover, in his 1911 critique of the Naval War College's contingency plan for war with Japan, Mahan roundly attacked the College's recommendation that the U.S. Navy should carry the war to Japanese home waters by way of the Philippines. The distant Philippines were simply indefensible, Mahan argued.[42]

To be sure, Mahan did on occasion in 1899–1900 speak of the Philippines in American hands as a threshold to the markets of Asia as well as a gateway to the Christianization of China; but the fact is that he had little interest in American commercial successes in China. Certainly he had no personal stake in the nation's China trade. He was, however, interested in the thrust of Secretary of State John Hay's first Open Door note on 20 March 1899, which proclaimed U.S. opposition to the increasingly successful efforts of Germany, Russia, France, Britain, and Japan to carve a militarily helpless and administratively hapless China into monopolistic economic spheres of influence. Hay therefore naively asked the powers involved in these assaults on Chinese sovereignty to desist, and to extend to one another and to all nations equality of commercial opportunity in their respective spheres. Of course, they did not.

Mahan played no personal role in the origination or enunciation of what would become known as Hay's Open Door policy. He and Hay were well acquainted, but they were not confidants. Still, Hay's generally ignored plea to the powers in March 1899 certainly comported with Mahan's long-held belief that the United States could peacefully increase markets for its products the world over through free or freer trade mechanisms. Thus when he returned from The Hague Conference in August 1899 he undertook a quick study of recent East Asian history preliminary to writing a series of three lengthy articles for *Harper's Monthly* on the background of the Open Door concept.[43] In June 1900, a month after the last of these pieces appeared, the Boxer Rebellion broke out. And on 3 July 1900, Secretary Hay, fearing that the powers would use the barbarities of the Boxers (which included the slaughter of Christian missionaries) as an excuse to partition China outright, issued his second Open Door note. This asked the powers to respect China's territorial and administrative integrity and "safeguard for the world the principle of equal and impartial trade with all parts of the Chinese Empire."

Mahan was convinced that American industry, thanks to abundant raw materials, superior management techniques, and the manufacture of quality products in great number, could compete effectively in the China market (or any foreign market) against the products of any other industrial nation if free trade (both import and export) were permitted, and if subsidies were not extended to the various foreign traders by their governments. However, he had no idea what the economic potential of the China market might be, and he wisely refrained from any statistical guesswork on the point. But as Paul A.

Varg has demonstrated, there was no market of any consequence for American goods in China in 1900–1912 and even less of a market in the United States for Chinese commodities, facts perceived by resident U.S. capitalists, commercial agents, consuls, and other "Old China Hands" then and later. The volume and value of U.S. exports to China, measured against total U.S. exports abroad in 1900–1912, were infinitesimal. The "China Market" was a myth.[44]

At the same time, Mahan remained wholly opposed to establishing an American colony or economic sphere of influence in China. He did, however, advocate the use of an international naval force to sustain the new Open Door policy. Fearful that imperial Russia, desperate for warm-water ports, was about to burst out of its Manchurian sphere of influence and overrun north China, Mahan proposed in 1900 the creation of a four-power "Teutonic" naval force (Great Britain, United States, Germany, and Japan) that would be deployed on the Yangtze River and in adjacent coastal waters for the purpose of containing "Slav" aggression against China proper and throughout the Eurasian land mass lying between 30° and 40° N.L. and stretching from the Japan Sea and East China Sea westward to the Aegean. He was convinced that Russian control of this "Debated and Debatable Middle Strip" would lead to the czar's domination of all of Eurasia.

Nothing came of this fanciful proposal to internationalize the use of naval force to uphold the territorial integrity of China. Indeed, Mahan dropped the idea during the Russo–Japanese War, which ended soon after Japan's great triumph over Russia at sea in May 1905. This victory was made possible when the Japanese, employing Mahanian doctrine, concentrated their fleet at the outset of the war, scattered Russia's Pacific fleet in the initial Battle of the Yellow Sea, gained control of the strategic center of the conflict, and then with calm tactical precision destroyed the oncoming Baltic fleet, another segment of the strategically divided Russian navy, in the "Big Battle" that was Tsushima.[45]

Tsushima aside, Mahan's primary interest in China's role in Asian affairs in 1899–1901 had to do with bringing the Chinese (then thought to number 400,000,000 souls) to Christ. He was distressed over the wanton slaughter of Christian missionaries by the Boxers, and he saw more of the same behavior occurring in the future unless the world's Christian nations made a massive joint effort to bring "the Asian people within the compass of the family of Christian states; not by fetters and bands imposed from without, but by regeneration promoted from within." The idea of the Open Door, he said, should be viewed as "open not only for commerce, but also for the entrance of European thoughts and its teachers in its various branches, when they seek admission voluntarily, and not as agents of a foreign government." Specifically, he held that Christian teaching and teachers should have the same access to China as did foreign merchants; but he insisted that no Chinese national necessarily need heed the missionaries or their teaching, and that the missionaries, in turn, should not use force to gain their ends. "Commerce has won its way [in China] by violence, actual or feared," he wrote; "thought, both secular and Christian, asks only freedom of speech." As he explained to Theodore Roosevelt in March 1901, a desirable by-product of establishing an international naval squadron on the Yangtze would result if the four sea-power nations involved would "require of China simple, but entire, liberty of entrance for European *thought,* as well as European commerce, China in my judgment will be saved, or rather, & better, will save herself."[46]

In 1902, while waiting for China to save itself from Slavic Russia, assisted by a Christian God and a screen of Western (and Japanese) warships on the Yangtze, Mahan was elected president of the American Historical Association. From this prestigious podium he instructed his fellow historians in the art of writing and presenting history in a manner so simple that it would instruct "the man in the street" about the world in which he lived and would simultaneously serve the God who was omnipresent in history. History, after all, he said, was "the plan of Providence . . . in its fulfillment." In his presidential address to the association, titled "Subordination in Historical Treatment," he equated "subordination" with "tactical concentration," and asked his colleagues to search out and arrange relevant and related facts around a "central idea" (or thesis), the truth of which, as historians, they wished to test.

It was incumbent upon historians, therefore, to search for, discover, and verify by subordinationist methodology ("Facts won't lie if you work them right") those "central ideas" that by act of verification became central themes, or foundation stones, in the fashioning of the "great mosaic" that was God's continuing revelation of Himself to man. One such central theme was Mahan's own concept of the influence of sea power upon history, which he was certain he had verified in his *Influence of Sea Power* books. The task then, of the historian-partners of God was to discover those other central themes of history that permeate the universe, and that upon discovery are further evidence of the very existence of God as well as evidence of His continuing involvement in human history. Some historian, "some favored mind" (Mahan was certain it would not be himself), would someday effect the "final great synthesis" of all the central themes inherent in history and in the universe, an achievement that would in effect bring human beings into mystical, harmonious oneness with God through the "majestic ideal unity" of a fully synthesized history that was nothing less than the "thought of the Divine Architect realized to his Creatures."

Convinced that the universe contained numerous central themes on the verge of being discovered, Mahan later identified two central ideas that appeared worthy of elevation to the status of central themes, saying that he would personally search for them. These ideas were: (1) the influence of continental expansion on U.S. history; and (2) the imminent upsurge of enthusiasm for Jesus Christ, which would soon possess all mankind, surpassing by far past mass enthusiasms for any other figure in human history. Mahan died before testing either of these central ideas, but it seems certain that given the predictability inherent in his subordinationist methodology he would have verified both, thus converting them into central themes ready for incorporation "into the great mosaic which the history of the race is gradually fashioning under the Divine overruling."[47]

It is not surprising that an American naval officer of Mahan's national and international renown as the discoverer of the influence of sea power on history and a devout believer in its concomitant, the inevitability of war, would attract disciples, enemies, and skeptics during his lifetime and after. After all, he was also known as an advocate of U.S. naval preparedness and American expansion (limited principally to the acquisition of coaling stations for the purpose of enhancing national security), and as a spokesman for the conceptual fusion of free trade, free speech, free thought, and free missionary Christianity as a means of uplifting backward peoples in Asia who enjoyed none of these blessings. These controversial views, one and all, intensified the formation and expression of pro-Mahan and anti-Mahan schools of thought, both of which have attracted faculty and students ever since.

Initially, Mahan was attacked by antiimperialists, pacifists, and constitutional strict constructionists as Philippine annexation became the major presidential campaign issue in 1899–1900. He was called a professional killer and worse, and was held solely responsible for

Alfred Thayer Mahan. Photograph taken at the turn of the century. *Courtesy of the Naval Historical Center.*

the unnecessary annexation of Hawaii in 1898. His belief, then and later, that neither the First nor the Second Hague Conference could, should, or would bring perpetual peace to mankind was especially annoying to those pacifists who held that enough peace committees, pamphlets, and speeches, together with the sheer will power of right-thinking people, could somehow usher in a peaceful millennium someday soon. Not so, countered Mahan: "There are no short cuts by which men may be made peaceful. If the world could have been saved by an organization it would have been saved a thousand years ago by the Christian church." Put another way, if the omnipotent God really wanted peace on earth, He had merely to decree it.[48]

On the other hand, disciples of Mahan were decidedly upset, soon after World War I, when the United States took the lead in bringing about a naval arms limitation agreement at the Washington Conference in 1921–22. William O. Stevens, one such true believer, was much distressed with American acceptance of the 5:5:3:1.75:1.75 capital ship tonnage limitation ratio, a decision that threw "overboard [Mahan's] whole philosophy of sea power." The Five Power Treaty, lacking enforcement provisions, was but a "scrap of paper" that left the nation naked in the western Pacific in the face of an aggressive Japan. The "world has scrapped more than battleships," Stevens warned; "it has discarded Mahan's entire philosophy for an experiment in faith."[49]

Such clairvoyance, however, was but a weak zephyr blowing against the pacifist and isolationist gales of the 1920s and 1930s, the general directions of which were distinctly anti-Mahan. In 1935, Tyler Dennett, a distinguished expert on Far Eastern history and affairs, played a strange role in setting this course. Reviewing Mahan's *The Problem of Asia* thirty-five years after its publication, Dennett sharply criticized its author for not correctly predicting in 1900 the situation in China in 1935, especially for not having had the foresight to see that there was no chance in 1899–1900 for successful American free trade in China unless the U.S. government had been willing to subsidize its traders, as had the European governments. This it was not willing to do and had not done. "The last thing desired by a losing competitor is a free field," Dennett explained; "it is as natural for the latter to turn to his government and beg for its interposition as it is for a savage to pray for rain." He also ridiculed Mahan's hope that the adoption of Christianity might speed China's modernization if Hay's Open Door policies were given a chance.[50]

As unreasonable as was Professor Dennett's hindsight assault on Mahan in 1935, Professor Louis M. Hacker had more than matched it the previous year when he charged Mahan with major personal responsibility for the outbreak of World War I. Hacker linked him with the "Merchants-of-Death" interpretation of America's subsequent entry into the conflict, and accused him of participation in a bourgeois conspiracy against the "repressed working masses" in 1885–1900 that sought to protect a degenerate Western capitalism from proletarian revolution by the imperialist device of forcibly dumping its industrial surpluses in overseas markets, colonial and other.[51]

Equally dubious from a historical standpoint was Julius W. Pratt's effort in 1936, in a book titled *Expansionists of 1898,* to link Mahan to a group of conspirators in Washington who designed and executed the so-called Large Policy of 1898. According to Pratt's theory, three capitalist imperialist conspirators—Theodore Roosevelt, John Hay, and Henry Cabot Lodge—conceived, spearheaded, provoked, and otherwise directed a war with Spain over Cuba in 1898 in order to set in motion a chain of events that would eventually result in the annexation of Hawaii and the Philippines, the achievement of a U.S.-dominated canal in Central America, and the acquisition of a number of naval bases and coaling stations in the Caribbean and the Pacific, which would sustain a large navy whose power and presence would stitch the new American empire together. The end purpose of the Large Policy was to effect American penetration of the rich and boundless markets of Asia. There surplus American products would be dumped, in an act that would solve the nation's economic dilemma of overproduction and underconsumption, avoid periodic depression, dampen the revolutionary spirit of the laboring masses, and save American capitalism.

Further, according to Pratt's thesis, Roosevelt, Hay, and Lodge, the three activist capitalist conspirators in Washington, had been influenced by four intellectuals whose books and ideas had provided the conceptual framework in which the Large Policy was launched. Specifically, Pratt linked Mahan's sea power doctrine with the "Social Darwinism" of Professor John Fiske, the Christian missionary Anglo–Saxonism of the Reverend Josiah Strong, and the "Teutonic" racial and political superiority notions of Professor John W. Burgess. From this gang of four—two university professors, a Congregational clergyman, and a retired naval officer—Pratt argued, came a philosophical potpourri of beliefs that identified the United States with ideas of Anglo–Saxon–Christian white racial superiority; and with the notion that most modern nations, including the United States, were guided by Darwinian laws of natural selection that assured the survival only of those nations that were militarily, racially, and religiously most fit. A nation not expanding territorially was by definition declining. A nation not armed and ready for war would soon be gobbled up by one that was, given the jungle environment that was the international state system at the turn of the century. Pratt did not argue that the New York business community had agitated for war against Spain in 1898; instead he noted that Wall Street had actually opposed American military intervention in Cuba in 1897–98, and had only joined the imperialist movement and Large Policy conspiracy when Philippine annexation and the "fabled markets of

China" were revealed to be part of the Roosevelt–Hay–Lodge national agenda.[52]

There is no evidence of any social, professional, or literary connection between Mahan and the other three authors. Nor is there evidence that he had read their books. That his Biblicism scarcely permitted serious consideration of the ideas of Charles Darwin was not an area of analysis Professor Pratt chose to address. It is also doubtful that there ever was a Large Policy; or if there was one, Mahan, who was in Washington during the summer of 1898, was unaware of it. He did not endorse Philippine annexation until late June or early July 1898, and even then he favored only the acquisition of the Manila area or at most the island of Luzon.[53]

That fact aside, there remain many interpretative problems with the history of American expansion at the turn of the century and with Mahan's presumed relationship to it, a connection incorrectly asserted by Professors Hacker and Pratt in the mid-1930s. Nevertheless, the factually feeble Hacker–Pratt thesis was born again in the 1960s and 1970s in the hands of the New Left historians—Cold War critics of the firm U.S. containment policy toward the Soviet Union, and of what they regarded as "American imperialism" in the post–World War II era. Such imperialism, they insisted, had characterized the misguided diplomatic history of the capitalist United States from its founding and was responsible for most of the world's ills from 1776 to the present. In applying this peculiar belief to the events of 1895–1914, these historians gave the Hacker–Pratt version of those events a more pronounced Marxist twist. In so doing, they ironically honored the memory of Mahan by adopting his skewed conviction that "facts won't lie if you work them right," while condemning him as a pliant tool of Wall Street, which he was not. As James A. Field has recently pointed out, the New Left's analysis of American imperialism at the turn of the century has been an exercise in the juggling of fact, half-fact, and no-fact, together with much fancy, to document predetermined Marxist conclusions about the imperialistic evils of Wall Street at the turn of the century and after. This has included a wholly erroneous view of the role played by Mahan in military and foreign policy formulation in Washington in 1898–1900.[54]

The problem is that New Left historians have lacked persuasive evidence that Americans who favored Philippine annexation or the Open Door policy in China were necessarily the "running dogs" of Wall Street; or that they were frightened capitalists who sought the creation of an American empire replete with closed colonial markets that, when properly exploited, would solve the dilemma of U.S. industrial overproduction. For this reason they have developed code names for an American imperialism that boasted very few genuine "imperialists" in either Marxist–Leninist or eighteenth-century mercantilist terms. They often have adopted language in their books and articles that retained such pejorative buzzwords as "empire" and "imperialists" but cloaked them in such phrases as America's "informal empire," "new empire," "empire of the seas," or "commercial empire." Free trade advocates such as Mahan have been referred to as "Free Trade imperialists" or "Open Door imperialists." Obviously, New Left historians have faced semantic problems that demand a very flexible definition of imperialism, and Thomas G. Paterson recently supplied one in his widely used textbook in U.S. diplomatic history:

> Imperialism is the imposition of controlling authority by a stronger entity over a weaker one. If peoples or regions lose the freedom to make their own decisions, they stand in an imperial relationship with whoever is making those decisions. The crucial factor is controlling *power,* and formal means (annexation, for example) or informal means (economic manipulation) can be used to establish it. . . . American economic domination of a country through trade and investment—an informal method of control—is imperialism, even though the United States does not formally annex the territory as a colony.[55]

Under such a definition, almost any American advocate or practitioner of free or freer trade abroad who seeks peacefully to make a profit in a free or open door market is an imperialist, actual or incipient. If such persons fail to make a profit (and many do not), they are merely ill-meaning capitalist bunglers. Mahan would not have understood this definition. To him, empire meant the seizure and exploitation of closed-market colonies of the eighteenth-century mercantilist sort. Further, he had little interest in U.S. acquisition of colonies, however defined, save as bases for the naval defense of the nation in a world in which war was inherent, usual, and frequent.

But whether or not Mahan was an imperialist by any definition, he has certainly not been accepted as a genuine historian by qualified contemporary commentators on his historiographical labors. The first truly detailed evaluation of Mahan as a professional historian came from Julius W. Pratt in 1937. Putting aside his earlier belief that Mahan had participated in the Large Policy conspiracy in 1898, Pratt applied the methodological strictures and standards of a modern graduate-level seminar in history to Mahan's work, and properly gave it a failing grade. He noted that there was nothing original in Mahan's influence of sea power on history concept, that it was narrowly and unacceptably mono-causal, and that it was interpetatively superficial and almost entirely based on secondary sources. He pointed out that Mahan's subordinationist methodology could be used to prove anything and all things on demand, and that his belief in a mystical union with God through the historiographical process was subject neither to verification nor to logic. In sum, historian Mahan was really little more than an earnest propagandist for nationalism, navalism, racism, war, and muscular Christianity, an evaluation that has been the judgment of most professional historians since.[56]

But more important than the relatively esoteric question of Mahan's current status as a historian among historians is the issue of the usefulness of his principles and doctrines to the U.S. Navy in the post–World War II period. To be sure, Mahan's emphasis on the importance of sea power on history was substantially vindicated in that war, but the strategy and tactics used by the U.S. Navy to achieve "command of the sea" had little to do with Mahan's principles of naval warfare. There was no Mahanian concentration of battlefleets on either the Japanese or the American side. Both navies operated with fractional tactical "task forces," often distributed over large areas of ocean. No decisive, war-ending "Big Battle" was fought at sea. It was a war of attrition in which American industry was more than able to replace and augment U.S. losses on, under, and over the sea while Japan's industrial plant lacked that capability. It was a war in which naval air power played a decisive role, as did the U.S. submarine force, in bringing Japan to its knees industrially and economically. Aircraft carriers, submarines, mobile floating decks, amphibious landing craft, radar, variable time fuses, kamikaze tactics— one and all would have mystified Mahan.[57]

Indeed, Mahan's inexplicable disregard of the relationship between naval technology, tactics, and strategy has bewildered his supporters and critics alike—especially his underestimation of the submarine as a decisive *guerre de course* weapon and his overestimation of the battleship as the decisive fleet surface weapon. It was a costly misjudgment, as German U-boats demonstrated in both world wars. Even when the obsolete *U*-9 sank three old British armored cruisers on 22 September 1914, killing 1,460 sailors, Mahan dismissed the event as a freak accident. It did "not greatly impress me from a military standpoint," he wrote; "I have always held that torpedo protection is a matter of scouting—watchfulness, and lapses there will occur. The result will show if I am greatly wrong." He was totally wrong.[58]

During his final years in the public eye and in print, from the convening of the Second Hague Conference in June 1907 until his death in December 1914, Mahan spent much of his literary energy hurling verbal thunderbolts at the peace and arbitration movements, while simultaneously insisting that the U.S. Navy limit the tonnage of its battleships and the caliber of some of the guns mounted thereupon. Much of his literary activity during these years was also devoted to a gratuitous, almost tiresome campaign to warn the British that war with Germany was looming and to explain to them how the Royal Navy might best conduct the naval dimensions of that conflict.[59]

The most significant of the controversial issues he raised in 1907–14, especially in terms of his personal relations with Theodore Roosevelt and his professional reputation within the U.S. Navy, were four in number: (1) his contention that exempting neutral noncontraband private property from destruction at sea during wartime would simply lengthen the duration of conflicts, because of the excessive wartime profits inherent in the hoary U.S. maritime doctrine of "free ships make free goods"; (2) his belief that the tonnage of battleships should not exceed 12,000, as heavier vessels would be "larger than needed, and likely result in too few ships," the greater size of which would not provide a "commensurate gain in offensive power"; (3) his related recommendation that the U.S. Navy's annual tonnage construction allotment from Congress be spread over a "balanced" fleet of battleships, cruisers, and destroyer–torpedo vessels; and (4) his insistence that the all-big-gun (10-inch and 12-inch) batteries being built into the new U.S. battleships should be replaced with more operationally flexible mixed-caliber batteries mounting various combinations of 12-, 10-, 8-, and 6-inch guns. He went to the mat with Roosevelt on all these points, lost all four falls, and was gently nudged out of the president's inner circle for his trouble. By the time war in Europe loomed in 1912, Mahan was widely regarded as an eccentric, quarrelsome "back number" in the U.S. Navy. His main error was that although he was a "battleship navalist," he was not a *Dreadnought* purist.[60]

As controversial as Alfred Thayer Mahan was in his lifetime, his relevance to the contemporary nuclear naval scene is equally arguable. It is not enough to point out that he greatly influenced the way

Americans came to regard their navy at the turn of the century; or that his "analysis of naval history from the beginnings of the age of sail to the early twentieth century" and "where applicable . . . to more recent events" is still being taught to midshipmen at the Naval Academy; or that he importantly influenced the way Assistant Secretary of the Navy, later President, Franklin D. Roosevelt worried about the navy ("My Navy") from 1913 to 1941, particularly with reference to Mahan's strictures against dividing a one-ocean navy between two oceans until the Panama Canal was opened, and only cautiously afterward. "Halve the fleet and it is inferior in both oceans," Mahan warned in his last article on the U.S. Navy in September 1914.[61] Nor is much to be gained from speculation about how Mahan would regard nuclear weapons and power plants, were he suddenly to rise from his grave in Quoque and attend the senior course at the Naval War College.

Nonetheless, the question "Is Mahan still valid?" is valid. One recent writer has suggested that Mahan's "philosophy of seapower, and his outlook on war and peace, have significant application today in the limited war climate," and that perhaps his " 'imperialistic' application of seapower tends to settle international problems on a limited basis rather than by global conflict." This is little more than a trip to the wishing well. Another author maintains that there remains in the U.S. Navy today a dangerous overemphasis on the tactical concentration implicit in Mahan's battleship fixation, save that the aircraft carrier has replaced the battleship as the navy diligently prepares to refight World War II. Still another student of Mahan suggests that his sweeping and sometime contradictory generalizations about the nature of sea power require a "restatement" of his doctrines that will make clear what he was truly driving at, viz.: the integration of American "sea power" (merchant shipping and related maritime industries) with its "sea force" (navy) in such manner as to ensure successful competition for world markets while simultaneously providing for national security.[62]

Although it is doubtful that Mahan visualized such integration for the United States as a realistic maritime goal (he had little expectation that the U.S. merchant marine would ever amount to much), a partial answer to the validity question lies in Thomas Etzold's observation that Mahan's emphasis on the strategic connection between colonies, commerce, and naval bases, together with his disinterest in naval technology and his continuing interest in the tactical concentration of battleships (in much the same manner as ships of the line were deployed in line-ahead formation in the Age of Sail), really says nothing that is useful today. Nor do his teachings about decisive "Big Battles" fought by 1914 battleships or indecisive *guerre de course* fought by 1812 sloops and frigates have much contemporary relevance. Further, Etzold maintains that Mahan's notions about "command of the sea fell as early victim to the advancing technology of the twentieth century," and with that collapse "fell virtually all of the teachings concerning the purpose of naval warfare in a larger conflict environment." But Mahan's tactical and conceptual antiquities aside, Etzold also reminds us that his doctrine of sea power included an appreciation of the fact that the state of a nation's naval technology is importantly determined by both domestic and international political (and budgetary) considerations; and that Mahan's view of sea power consistently and correctly emphasized the point that the key to strategic planning involved, on the part of the planners, a lively and imaginative awareness of geographical imperatives, opportunities, and dangers.[63]

More important, as Philip Crowl has pointed out, Mahan's oscillating reputation as America's premier philosopher of sea power will rise as well as decline, refreshed by the recollection that he asked his nation and his navy some very difficult and pertinent questions, questions still relevant, questions each generation must ask and answer anew: What exactly is the nature of America's "national interest"? How shall the U.S. Navy best be used as an "instrument of national policy"? What is the proper relationship between a nation's sea power and its diplomatic objectives? What are the "moral" dimensions of the employment of military force? How shall the U.S. ships and fleets best be armed, supplied, and deployed? How much navy is enough navy? And, central to all these, can a nation with three extensive and widely separated coastlines afford to neglect possession of sufficient sea power to maintain open sea-lines of commercial and military communication abroad? As Mahan himself put it to the Naval War College class of 1892: "All the world knows, gentlemen, that we are building a new navy. . . . Well, when we get our navy, what are we going to do with it?" That question remains.[64]

And what has the Russian navy learned from Mahan? Enough to claim that the influence of sea power on history was a brilliant insight, so brilliant that it was actually a czarist naval captain named Berezin who first discovered the concept in 1873—or so insisted the late Sergei G. Gorshkov, Admiral of the Fleet of the Soviet Union, commander in chief of the Soviet navy (1956–86), and author of the brilliant *The Sea Power of the State* (1979). But Gorshkov, while paying obeisance to such Mahanian precepts as the importance of overseas naval bases in preparation for global war and the desirability of aggressive tactical approaches to war at sea, so revises Mahan to fit the realities of naval war in the nuclear age, and to the strategic and tactical capabilities of the Soviet navy as it was in the late 1970s, that there is really very little Mahan left in the Mahanian insights he praises. It is clear that Gorshkov parted company with Mahan on the issue of static technology in naval warfare, when he proclaimed the end of the era when a nation's battlefleet could be concentrated for combat, and argued that it must now be dispersed in order to avoid concentrated nuclear missile fire from dispersed frigates and submarines. He correctly pointed out that "command of the sea" strategically availed the U.S. Navy little during the Korean and Vietnam wars, and noted, with ill-concealed pleasure, that the entire American continent had at last become highly vulnerable to nuclear missile attack launched either from distant shore emplacements or from nuclear submarines. Certain it is that Gorshkov, the "Red Mahan," carefully studied the naval history of the two world wars, and was especially impressed by German successes with U-boat *guerre de course,* which almost alone brought Berlin to the edge of victory at sea in both conflicts. Not surprisingly, therefore, the nuclear-powered submarine, armed with nuclear missiles, became Russia's capital ship during Gorshkov's long tenure in office. Indeed, he made it quite plain in his book, and in a number of his professional articles earlier published as *Red Star Rising at Sea* (1974), that Russia had become a world naval power second only to the United States, and intended soon to achieve naval parity with the Americans.

Nor can it be doubted that the Soviet Union today meets Mahan's six "principal conditions affecting the sea power of nations" and aspires to becoming the truly great sea power Gorshkov envisaged. True, Russia has four widely separated seas to defend (Baltic, Black, Northern, and Pacific), which require four self-sustaining fleets and are otherwise encumbered by at least eight major geographical choke points. In addition, the Soviets presently have far too few stable overseas naval bases to assist in the defense of their four sea frontiers. Nonetheless, the recent acquisition of Cam Ranh Bay in Vietnam and Cienfuegos in Cuba has enormously helped the strategic offensive positioning of the Soviet navy.[65]

Is Mahan still valid? Yes. Although there have been many other influences on history besides the existence or nonexistence of sea power, the relationship between the mastery of the sea and the rise, continuation, or fall of various seaboard nation-states since the beginning of recorded history is fairly obvious. And as long as there is no persuasive historical evidence whatever to contradict Mahan's insistence that war is inherent in the universe, in human history, and in the human condition, it is only prudent that the United States remains thoroughly and constantly prepared for war at sea, whatever the future technological dimensions of naval war might be. This may sound partly like advice from the grave at Quogue. It may reflect the influence of the inevitability of war upon Mahan. But as Etzold notes, "Today, the United States is caught in what can only seem a paradox from a Mahanian view: The United States is strong because it *can* use the sea, and weak, or at least vulnerable, because it *must.*" Mahan would relish the dichotomous and dialectical ring of that observation.

FURTHER READING

The most complete and important source for an understanding of Alfred Thayer Mahan is Robert Seager II and Doris D. Maguire, eds., *Letters and Papers of Alfred Thayer Mahan* (1975). Mahan letters known by Seager or Maguire to have surfaced since 1975 have been directed to the attention of the curator of the Mahan Collection at the Naval War College Library in Newport, Rhode Island. For information on the nature, content, and extent of the Mahan Papers at the War College, see John B. Hattendorf, comp., *Register of the Alfred Thayer Mahan Papers* (1987). In addition, Professor Hattendorf and his sister-in-law, Lynn C. Hattendorf, have compiled *A Bibliography of the Works of Alfred Thayer Mahan* (1986). Excellent in every respect, this work supersedes and renders obsolete all other bibliographical treatments of Mahan. Far from excellent is Mahan's autobiography, *From Sail to Steam: Recollections of Naval Life* (1907). It is uniformly self-serving and highly selective from a factual standpoint. Nonetheless, it is an important and unique historical document that must also be consulted.

Four full-length biographies of Mahan have appeared since his death in 1914. The first of these, *The Life of Admiral Mahan* (1920), was written by Charles Carlisle Taylor, sometime British vice consul at New York. Based on interviews with Mahan family members, on conversations with a number of persons who knew Mahan personally, and on a scattering of letters supplied by a few of Mahan's correspondents, Taylor's effort was superficial, episodic, and eulogistic, emphasizing the Anglo–American dimension in Mahan's life and writings.

Taylor's book was followed two decades later by U.S. Navy Captain W. D. Puleston's *Mahan: The Life and Work of Captain Alfred Thayer Mahan, U.S.N.* (1939). The first extended evaluation by a fellow naval officer, it remains a solid, though somewhat dull, encyclopedic and narrowly conceived account of Mahan's professional naval life, which, in Puleston's view, was illuminated throughout by the brilliance and grandeur of Mahan's philosophy of sea power and its influence on history. Although Puleston's sources, both printed and personal, secondary and primary, were far more numerous and more revealing than Taylor's, his hagiographic account was essentially a glowing fitness report on Mahan, into which nothing negative about the man, personal or professional, was permitted to intrude.

The first historiographically professional treatment of Mahan's life and works was William E. Livezey's *Mahan on Sea Power* (1947). Utilizing the perspective of the naval and diplomatic aspects of the two world wars and the historical antecedents of both conflicts, Professor Livezey produced a sophisticated evaluation of Mahan's doctrine of sea power viewed from a modern geopolitical, diplomatic, and technological standpoint, and first questioned the usefulness of the doctrine in a militarily scientific world Mahan never conceived. He also dealt with navies that had moved far beyond Mahan's naive Age-of-Sail technological ken.

Livezey's path-breaking account has recently been supplemented by Robert Seager's *Alfred Thayer Mahan* (1977). Basing his work on much hitherto unused primary source material, Livezey's work, and factual data found only in Taylor, Puleston, and *From Sail to Steam*, as well as a growing body of scholarly monographs and articles about Mahan and the New Navy, Seager attempted to humanize the man, to explain some of the forces and factors that apparently motivated him, and to evaluate his sea power doctrine in conjunction with U.S. imperialism at the turn of the century. Seager emphasized throughout the book Mahan's unorthodox Christian theology, his philosophy of history and of war in history, his Anglophilia in thought, word, and deed, his static conception of naval tactics and technology, his family life and personal financial problems, and his thoroughly controversial, contentious, and unpleasant personality. Of the latter there is no suggestion whatever in Mahan's autobiography.

Although the body of Mahan, Mahan-related, and New Navy materials has expanded enormously since 1945, serious students of the Philosopher of Sea Power should not overlook Richard W. Turk's recent *The Ambiguous Relationship: Theodore Roosevelt and Alfred Thayer Mahan* (1988) or Richard S. West's enduring *Admirals of American Empire: The Combined Story of George Dewey, Alfred Thayer Mahan, Winfield Scott Schley and William Thomas Sampson* (1948). Nor should they overlook such important interpretive essays as James A. Field, "Alfred Thayer Mahan Speaks for Himself"; Philip A.

Crowl, "Alfred Thayer Mahan: The Naval Historian"; and Julius W. Pratt, "Alfred Thayer Mahan."

NOTES

1. This interpretative essay is based substantially, although by no means entirely, on the following works and studies of Mahan by the present author, viz.: Robert Seager II and Doris D. Maguire, eds., *Letters and Papers of Alfred Thayer Mahan* (cited below as *LPATM*); and Robert Seager II, *Alfred Thayer Mahan*, a biography based on *LPATM* (cited below as Seager, *Mahan*). In greater or lesser degree this essay also relies on material found in the author's several articles on Mahan, viz.: "Ten Years Before Mahan: The Unofficial Case for the New Navy, 1880–1890"; "A Biography of a Biographer: Alfred Thayer Mahan," in *Changing Interpretations and New Sources in Naval History*, ed. Robert W. Love, Jr.; "Alfred Thayer Mahan," in *Dictionary of American Military Biography*, ed. Roger J. Spiller; and "Alfred Thayer Mahan," in *Dictionary of Literary Biography: American Historians, 1866–1912*, ed. Clyde N. Wilson. It is also indebted conceptually to recent research by Philip A. Crowl, James A. Field, and Paul A. Varg. For a more traditional interpretation of Mahan see Margaret Tuttle Sprout, "Mahan: Evangelist of Sea Power," in *Makers of Modern Strategy: Military Thought from Machiavelli to Hitler*, ed. Edward Mead Earle.

2. Rudyard Kipling, *The Cat That Walked by Himself*, passim. For Ellen Kuhn Mahan's recollections of her father, see *LPATM*, 3:719–30.

3. For a conflicting view on Mahan's seamanship, see Captain Robert Brent, USN, "Mahan–Mariner or Misfit?" Compare his account of the *Wachusett* collision, which he denies having happened, with Seager, *Mahan*, 140, 261; and *LPATM*, 2:160. It happened.

4. The useful bibliography of Mahan's publications found in William E. Livezey's *Mahan on Sea Power*, 301–19, has been substantially expanded by John B. Hattendorf and Lynn C. Hattendorf, comps., *A Bibliography of the Works of Alfred Thayer Mahan*, which is now the standard bibliographical source on Mahan.

5. Seager, *Mahan*, 575–77. See especially Alfred Thayer Mahan, "The Peace Conference and the Moral Aspect of War"; "War from the Christian Standpoint," in his *Some Neglected Aspects of War*; "The Apparent Decadence of the Church's Influence"; "Twentieth Century Christianity," in his *The Interest of America in Sea Power*, 229–30, 235–36, 243–46; and his 1913 and 1914 articles on "Freedom in the Use of the Prayer Book" and "Prayer Book Revision." See also his "Christian Progress," as well as his various statements, addresses, and lay sermons on Christian and Episcopal Church themes and concerns in *LPATM*, 3:423, 590–91, 597, 598–602, 605, 644–56, 657, 682, 683–84, 693–97, 714–16. His intense religious experience, while on board the *Iroquois*, is printed in full in *LPATM*, 1:145–332.

6. For the derivation of Mahan's notion of the influence of sea power on history, see Lawrence C. Allin, "The Naval Institute, Mahan, and the

Naval Profession"; A. T. Mahan, *From Sail to Steam: Recollections of Naval Life*, 276; J. M. Scammell, "Thucydides and Sea Power"; see, further, Kenneth J. Hagan's perceptive "Alfred Thayer Mahan"; also, Seager, *Mahan*, 199–204, and his "Ten Years before Mahan," passim. Among others who flirted or consorted with the sea power hypothesis were ancient Greeks and Romans: Thucydides, Xenophon, and Tacitus; Englishmen: Francis Bacon, Walter Raleigh, and John Seeley; U.S. Navy officers: Robert W. Shufeldt, Stephen B. Luce, and William Glenn David; and U.S. House members: John F. Miller and William G. McAdoo.

7. For Milo Mahan's theological influence on his nephew, see Seager, *Mahan*, 445–55, 555. Mahan's hostility to disarmament, arbitration, and international courts to end war or mitigate its horrors is expressed in, and the doctrine of "free ships make free goods" is condemned in, his "The Peace Conference and the Moral Aspect of War," 433–37; "The Hague Conference: The Question of Immunity of Belligerent Merchant Shipping"; "Commerce and War," *New York Times*, 17 and 23 November 1898; "The Hague Conference and the Practical Aspect of War"; also in related articles, written in 1907 and 1911, which are reprinted in his *Some Neglected Aspects of War*, and in his *Armaments and Arbitration, or the Place of Force in the International Relations of States*. Mahan's philosophy of history and historiography is discussed in detail in Seager, *Mahan*, 430–58, and briefly below in this essay. The influence of Jomini and Luce on Mahan in the realm of the "laws" of strategy and tactics is skillfully treated in Philip A. Crowl, "Alfred Thayer Mahan: The Naval Historian," 444–77. Mahan's arguments favoring "balanced" fleets and "mixed batteries" are presented in his "Retrospect upon the War between Japan and Russia"; "Reflections, Historic and Others, Suggested by the Battle of the Sea of Japan"; and "The Battleship of All Big Guns." See also Seager, *Mahan*, 519–34, and footnote 59, below.

8. The quotation is Mahan's. Luce's letter of invitation, dated 22 July 1884, has not survived, nor is it clear just what he intended having Mahan cover in the lectures. See *LPATM*, 1:577–78; Seager, *Mahan*, 141–42.

9. Ibid., 134–36.

10. *LPATM*, 1:577–78, 581–82; 2:276, 285; Seager, *Mahan*, 144–47.

11. *LPATM*, 1:606–7.

12. John D. Hayes and John B. Hattendorf, eds., *The Writings of Stephen B. Luce*, 45–68, 71–97, 190–91; see also John B. Hattendorf et al., *Sailors and Scholars: The Centennial History of the U.S. Naval War College*, 11–24. Luce had also discovered that "Religion and war are the two great central facts of history. . . . Religion gave birth to education. War led the way to civilization." Mahan would soon come to accept this idea as well, if indeed he had not already embraced it.

13. Antoine-Henri Jomini, *The Art of War*, 1836, translated [1861] from the French by Captain G. H. Mendell, USA, and Captain W. P. Craighill, USA, 321. This is a later edition of their 1862 English-language

volume. It seems likely that of Jomini's many volumes, Mahan read only this one. See Crowl, "Alfred Thayer Mahan," 444–47.

14. Seager, *Mahan*, 149–58.

15. E. B. Potter and J. Roger Fredland, eds., *The United States and World Sea Power*, 383–87.

16. Mahan, *From Sail to Steam*, 168, 277–78.

17. Jomini, *The Art of War*, 70–71; Crowl, "Alfred Thayer Mahan," 455–56; Seager, *Mahan*, 168–70, 552, 555. The language here is Jomini's as translated by Mendell and Craighill. See Note 13, above.

18. A. T. Mahan, "Fleet Battle Tactics" [1886]. This lengthy, type-written, unpublished study, containing critical marginal comments by Luce, is in the Mahan Collection, Naval War College Library; see also, Seager, *Mahan*, 166–68, 171–73.

19. Mahan, *From Stail to Steam*, 284–85; Seager, *Mahan*, 173.

20. A. T. Mahan, *Naval Strategy, Compared and Contrasted with the Principles of Military Operations on Land*, 1–3, 6–10, 15–18, 31, 49, 53–55, 189, 199, 254, 279, 386, 391–93, 415, 422–23, 428–29. Crowl, "Alfred Thayer Mahan," 457–61, contains an excellent synthesis and critique of Mahan's strategic concepts. Less persuasive is W. D. Puleston's attempt to identify those concepts with the strategic and tactical insights of Karl von Clausewitz in his otherwise useful *Mahan: The Life and Work of Captain Alfred Thayer Mahan, U.S.N.*, 295–98. Jomini's views on land warfare strategy are set forth in his *The Art of War*, 67–69. Most of his observations lend themselves imperfectly to naval warfare. For the difficult gestation of Mahan's volume, *Naval Strategy*, see Seager, *Mahan*, 548–53.

21. *LPATM*, 1:622–24.

22. Seager, *Mahan*, 205–6; Mahan, *From Sail to Steam*, 324–25.

23. A. T. Mahan, *The Influence of Sea Power upon History, 1660–1783*, 14th ed., 28, 53, 71.

24. Ibid., 33–34, 42, 88.

25. Ibid., 39, 42.

26. Ibid., 42–44, 49, 50, 53, 56, 57–58.

27. Ibid., 58, 67, 87–88. Indeed, as early as March 1880 Mahan had told Ashe that the coming of a canal in Panama would require American control of the Isthmus. "To control at the Isthmus we must have a very large Navy—and must begin to build as soon as the first spadeful of earth is turned at Panama." That failing, "we may as well shut up about the Monroe Doctrine at once." *LPATM*, 1:481–82.

28. *LPATM*, 1:572–74; Seager, *Mahan*, 122, 132–34, 140–41; Seager, "Ten Years before Mahan," passim.

29. Reprinted in A. T. Mahan, *The Interest of America in Sea Power Present and Future*, 26. The population density per square mile of the three West Coast states in 1890 was: California, 7.63; Oregon, 3.28; Washington, 5.25. For the entire coast it was 5.83. For Mahan's definition of himself as an "imperialist" (i.e., nonisolationist), see his *From Sail to Steam*, 324.

30. See his articles in the *Atlantic Monthly* (1890, 1893), *The Forum* (1893), and *Harper's Monthly* (1895, 1897), as reprinted in *The Interest of America in Sea Power*, 3–104, 137–214, 271–314. The concept was later reiterated in "The Panama Canal and Sea Power in the Pacific," and in "The Panama Canal and the Distribution of the Fleet." See also James A. Field's excellent "Alfred Thayer Mahan Speaks for Himself," for a persuasive development and evaluation of Mahan's eastern Pacific defense perimeter concept.

31. "The Effect of Asiatic Conditions upon World Policies," *North American Review* (November 1900), in A. T. Mahan, *The Problem of Asia and Its Effects upon International Policies*, 201–2.

32. "Was Panama 'A Chapter of National Dishonor'?"; Mahan, "Panama Unguarded Might Be Seized," *New York Times*, 27 October 1912; Seager, *Mahan*, 498–99. On the Monroe Doctrine and the Roosevelt Corollary thereto, see A. T. Mahan, "The Monroe Doctrine." This article was revised in 1908 in order to change his hostile view of the Roosevelt Corollary and was reprinted in his *Naval Administration and Warfare, Some General Principles with Other Essays*. See also Seager, *Mahan*, 142, 492–94. For the numerous substantial differences of opinion between Mahan and Roosevelt on these and other so-called imperial matters, see Richard W. Turk, *The Ambiguous Relationship: Theodore Roosevelt and Alfred Thayer Mahan*, passim, but esp. 49, 52–54.

33. *LPATM*, 2:92–93, 507; Mahan, *The Interest of America in Sea Power*, 31; Seager, *Mahan*, 248–50, 358, 465, 476–79.

34. *LPATM*, 2:461. For a view of Mahan from the perspective of his literary production, see Seager, "Alfred Thayer Mahan," in *Dictionary of Literary Biography: American Historians, 1866–1912*, ed. Wilson, 47:162–73; also, Seager, *Mahan*, 327–32. Save for his excellent two-volume life of Nelson, which he began while serving in the *Chicago* and finished soon after his retirement in March 1897, Mahan wrote but two more books. His two-volume *Sea Power in Its Relations to the War of 1812*, previously serialized in *Scribner's Magazine*, remains a solid study of naval operations in that conflict. It is Mahan's only book dealing substantially with U.S. history. It is also a fascinating interpretative exercise in how an American Anglophile decides that *both* Britain and the United States had simultaneously fought wholly just wars in 1812–14. See Kenneth L. Moll, "Mahan: American Historian," 132, 137; and Seager, *Mahan*, 506–8, 564–68. His other book, *Naval Strategy* (1911), is discussed elsewhere in this essay.

35. Mahan, *The Interest of America in Sea Power*, 182–84, 291–92, 295, 299, 307–10; *LPATM*, 2:505–6, 532; Seager, *Mahan*, 357–59.

36. Livezey, *Mahan on Sea Power*, 133–37; *LPATM*, 2:37, 734; Seager, *Mahan*, 358–59, 362. The best brief account of various U.S. Navy contingency war plans against Spain is in David F. Trask, *The War with Spain in 1898*, 72–78. See also Turk, *Ambiguous Relationship*, 28–29, 34–35.

37. *LPATM*, 2:532; 3:592–94; Seager, *Mahan*, 357–58, 360–61; H. G. Rickover, *How the Battleship "Maine" Was Destroyed*, 107–30.

38. For Mahan's service on the Naval War Board see Trask, *The War with Spain*, 67–68, 89–90, 119, 203, 280–83, 306, 339, 361, 377; A. T. Mahan, *Lessons of the War with Spain and Other Articles*, 3–204; and A. T. Mahan, "The Work of the Naval War Board of 1898: A Report to the General Board of the Navy," 29 October 1906, in *LPATM*, 3:627–43; see also Seager, *Mahan*, 366–91.

39. *LPATM*, 2:538–39, 581–91; Livezey, *Mahan on Sea Power*, 170–74; Seager, *Mahan*, 391, 395–96.

40. Seager, *Mahan*, 391–95; A. T. Mahan, "The Effect of Asiatic Conditions upon World Policies," reprinted in *The Problem of Asia*, 147–202, esp. 175.

41. A. T. Mahan, "America's Duties to Her New Dependencies," reprinted under the title "The Relations of the United States to Their New Dependencies," in *Lessons of the War with Spain*, 241–53; A. T. Mahan, "Capt. Mahan on Expansion," *New York Times*, 1 December 1898. See also excerpts from a speech he gave on 30 November 1898 printed in *LPATM*, 3:596, under the title "A Distinction between Colonies and Dependencies." The distinction was that "A colony must be a country qualified by its natural conditions, climatic or otherwise, to become incorporated with the mother country." Therefore, he added: "We can't have colonies. The original Roman colony was an outpost of the mother country—an extended Rome in the fullest sense of the word."

42. Seager, *Mahan*, 394. He also later complained that the nation had been "pitchforked" into the Philippines and spoke of the "extreme repugnance" with which the United States had annexed the islands. The clash between the College's contingency war plan against Japan of 1911, and Mahan's critique, or counterplan, can be traced in *LPATM*, 3:380–88, 389–94, 395, 400–402; see also Naval War College, "Notes on Comments of Rear Admiral Mahan," ca. 25 February–1 March 1911, in the Naval War College Library, Newport, R.I.; and Seager, *Mahan*, 483–86.

43. These articles were all titled, "The Problem of Asia." They appeared in *Harper's Monthly* in March, April, and May 1900 and were updated and reprinted in his *The Problem of Asia*, which appeared in December 1900.

44. Ibid., 155, 166, 176–77, 189–90; Paul A. Varg, *The Making of a Myth: The United States and China, 1897–1912*, 36–53; esp. 50–52. In 1900 the value of U.S. exports to China ($7,000,000) was .005 percent of the value ($1,394,000,000) of all U.S. exports that year; it rose to a high ($53,000,000) of 3.5 percent in 1905 ($1,519,000,000) and slipped back to 1.1 percent ($24,000,000) in a total of $2,204,000,000 in 1912. See *The Statistical History of the United States from Colonial Times to the Present*, 550.

45. Mahan, *The Problem of Asia*, 160–66, 176. Livezey, *Mahan on Sea Power*, 191–99, has an excellent analysis of Mahan's idea of the naval containment of Russia at the Yangtze as this related to the Open Door and to a Teuton vs. Slav racial *Götterdämmerung* for the control of Eurasia and

eventually the whole world; see also Seager, *Mahan,* 462–68, Mahan's delight at the way the naval aspects of the Russo–Japanese War played out strategically and tactically can be traced in his articles on the conflict in *Collier's Weekly,* 20 February, 30 April, and 21 May 1904, and 13 May and 17 June 1905; also in *National Review,* May 1906, and U.S. Navy Institute *Proceedings,* June 1906.

46. Mahan, *The Problem of Asia,* 152, 154, 167–69, 174; *LPATM,* 2:707–8. For Mahan's high hope and great concern for Christian missions in China, see his *The Harvest Within,* 75, 83, 85, 106. See also Turk, *Ambigious Relationship,* 44–45, 48.

47. Mahan, "Subordination in Historical Treatment," renamed "Writing of History." For an earlier (October 1897) statement of his subordinational methodology, see his *The Interest of America in Sea Power,* 284–85; also Seager, *Mahan,* 448–51. For Mahan's predictably successful demonstration of the historicity of the resurrection of Jesus by similar methodological devices, see his *The Harvest Within,* 22–24, 30–41, 44–45, 49, 52.

48. Wallace Rice, "Some Current Fallacies of Captain Mahan"; Lucia Ames Mead, "Some Fallacies of Captain Mahan."

49. William Oliver Stevens, "Scrapping Mahan." The Five Powers and their assigned ratios were Britain (5), the United States (5), Japan (3), France (1.75), and Italy (1.75).

50. Tyler Dennett, "Mahan's 'The Problem of Asia.'" In this same article Professor Dennett speculated that Mahan had had the ear of John Hay when the secretary of state was drafting his second Open Door note. See Livezey, *Mahan on Sea Power,* 190–91. There is no evidence to support such speculation.

51. Louis M. Hacker, "The Incendiary Mahan: A Biography," 95:263–68, 311–12; see also Hacker's earlier article, "The Holy War of 1898"; as well as Seager, *Mahan,* 269–70. Captain Ronald B. St. John, USA, has demonstrated that the European (especially, the Anglo–German) prewar naval arms race was already well under way when Mahan's two *Influence* books appeared, in 1890 and 1892. See his "European Naval Expansion and Mahan, 1889–1906."

52. Julius W. Pratt, *Expansionists of 1898: The Acquisition of Hawaii and the Spanish Islands,* 3–28, 217–23, 260–78; Pratt, "The 'Large Policy' of 1898." For two of the very few times Mahan used the phrase "natural selection," see his *The Problem of Asia,* 46, and his *The Harvest Within,* vii. Mahan "was not an evolutionist," wrote Francis Duncan. "Some evolutionists might have granted God an initial role in originating the spark of life, but none would see God intervening in world affairs as late as 1898." Duncan, "Mahan–Historian with a Purpose," 503.

53. Pratt, *Expansionists of 1898,* 231–32. The phrase "large policy," juxtaposed with the phrase "whole policy," appears without clear definition in two letters from Lodge to Roosevelt (who was then in Cuba) dated 24 and 31 May 1898. Both phrases, however, seem to refer to or have to do

with Philippine annexation and/or Puerto Rican annexation, and/or Cuban independence. To add an isthmian canal or the fabled markets of Asia to it at this juncture requires imaginative powers not normally granted serious historians. H. C. Lodge, ed., *Selections from the Correspondence of Theodore Roosevelt and Henry Cabot Lodge,* 1:299, 300, 302. See also Lodge to Roosevelt, 24 June 1898, ibid., 313.

54. James A. Field, Jr., "American Imperialism: The Worst Chapter in Almost Any Book." See also Crowl, "Alfred Thayer Mahan," 466–67. Field comments on the free-wheeling research methodology and socialist interpretative bent found in books and articles on U.S. imperialism by Richard Hofstadter, William Appleman Williams, Walter LaFeber, Thomas J. McCormick, Philip S. Foner, and others. See as well David L. T. Knudson, "A Note on Walter LaFeber, Captain Mahan, and the Use of Historical Sources," and J. A. Thompson, "William Appleman Williams and the American Empire." William Appleman Williams, ed., *From Colony to Empire: Essays in the History of American Foreign Relations,* presents essays by seven of his disciples or co-ideologists seeking to demonstrate in various ways and instances that "free trade" and "open door" approaches to U.S. economic foreign policy are really capitalist–imperialist devices designed to sustain America's sick and evil economic system. For Williams's defense of his Marxist interpretation and peculiar historical methodology see his "Confessions of an Intransigent Revisionist." Particularly imaginative in the management of facts and quotations to prove the existence of a Wall Street conspiracy in 1898 is Foner's "Why the United States Went to War with Spain in 1898." See also Williams, *Empire as a Way of Life,* passim. As for just who influenced whom in the Mahan–Roosevelt relationship (it was probably Roosevelt who most influenced Mahan), see Peter Karsten, "The Nature of 'Influence': Roosevelt, Mahan and the Concept of Sea Power." On the other hand, for a discussion of the degree to which Marxist interpretative models fail to mesh with the facts of American expansion, 1890–1914, see Robert Zevin, "An Interpretation of American Imperialism," 342–49, 355–60.

55. Thomas G. Paterson, *American Foreign Policy: A History to 1914,* 2nd ed., 160.

56. Julius W. Pratt, "Alfred Thayer Mahan," in *The Marcus W. Jernegan Essays in American Historiography,* ed. William T. Hutchinson, 207–226, esp. 209–10, 214–16, 218, 221–25. See also Duncan, "Mahan— Historian with a Purpose," 503. Duncan was among the first historians to recognize the importance of the Christian dimension in Mahan's philosophy and historiography. It was as a Christian, wrote Duncan, that Mahan "saw force to be used not blindly, but as a weapon to overcome evil; as a means for stepping over legal barriers to grapple with problems that cannot be solved by law." In addition, see Richard W. Smith, "Mahan's Historical Method," and Kenneth L. Moll, "Mahan: American Historian," 132, 138– 39. For a view of Mahan as a historian that is highly favorable if not entirely accurate in all particulars, see Jack E. Godfrey, "Mahan: The Man,

His Writings and Philosophy." On Mahan's theologically based historiography and subordinationist methodology, compare and contrast the views of his first three biographers, viz.: (1) Charles C. Taylor, *The Life of Admiral Mahan*, 103, does not discuss the subject; (2) W. D. Puleston, *Mahan*, 237–38, takes a neutral stance on Mahan's methodolgy while avoiding the theological dimensions of his thought; (3) William E. Livezey, *Mahan on Sea Power*, 23–35, substantially concurs with Pratt's analysis in Hutchinson, ed., *Marcus W. Jernegan Essays*.

57. Bernard Brodie, "New Tactics in Naval Warfare."

58. R. A. Bowling, "The Negative Influence of Mahan on Anti-submarine Warfare," 52–59; A. T. Mahan, "The Submarine and Its Enemies," *Collier's Weekly* 39 (6 April 1907): 17–21; Seager, *Mahan*, 535–38, 554; *LPATM*, 3:549; Van der Vat, *The Atlantic Campaign: World War II's Great Struggle at Sea*, 15–16.

59. See, particularly, his "The Hague Conference and the Practical Aspect of War," "Germany's Naval Ambition," "The Battleship of All Big Guns," and the first six articles, initially published in *North American Review* in 1911–12, that are reprinted in his *Armaments and Arbitration*, 1–154.

60. Seager, *Mahan*, 506–10, 521–33; also Turk, *Ambigious Relationship*, 57–61, 71–76, 82–96, 101–8.

61. Frank B. Freidel, *Franklin D. Roosevelt: The Apprenticeship*, 46, 232–35, 238–39, 246–47, 411; William L. Neumann, "Franklin Delano Roosevelt: A Disciple of Admiral Mahan," 712–19; E. B. Potter, ed., *Sea Power: A Naval History*, 2nd ed., vii; A. T. Mahan, "The Panama Canal and the Distribution of the Fleet"; Patrick Abbazia, *Mr. Roosevelt's Navy*, 80, 156, 160–65.

62. Godfrey, "Mahan: The Man, His Writings and Philosophy," 68; Bowling, "The Negative Influence of Mahan on Anti-submarine Warfare," 57; William Reitzel, "Mahan on the Use of the Sea."

63. Thomas H. Etzold, "Is Mahan Still Valid?" 38–43.

64. Crowl, "Alfred Thayer Mahan," 476–77.

65. S. G. Gorshkov, *The Sea Power of the State*, 61, 82–83, 94, 118–19, 123, 178, 217, 223, 246, 258, 262–65, 268–69, 271. S. G. Gorshkov, *Red Star Rising at Sea*, 40, 141; Jurgen Rohwer, "Admiral Gorshkov and the Influence of History upon Sea Power," 150–73; Frank C. Pandolfe, "Soviet Seapower in the Light of Mahan's Principles," 44–46; Bryan Ranft and Geoffrey Till, *The Sea in Soviet Strategy*, 118–22. For a highly critical Chinese analysis of Mahan's doctrines from a Maoist ideological standpoint during the Cultural Revolution, especially as applied to the Open Door period in China, see Francis J. Romance, "A Chinese Commentary on Mahan's Theory of Seapower," 110–12. In this article the Chinese charged that the Soviet Union had embraced the imperialist views of Mahan as an "ideological weapon for its ocean expansion," and they blamed Gorshkov for having "vigorously advocated such fallacies."

ROBLEY D. EVANS:
MASTER OF PUGNACITY

RICHARD W. TURK

R obley Dunglison Evans—"Fighting Bob" to his countrymen—
lost his last battle 3 January 1912, succumbing to a heart attack
in his Washington, D.C., home. Former President Theodore Roosevelt, among others, paid him tribute:

> In Admiral Robley D. Evans not only the navy but the Nation has
> lost a man whose solid services to both navy and Nation were en-
> hanced by that touch of brilliant picturesqueness which has been an
> attribute of so many great naval characters from the days of Benbow
> to the days of Nelson, and from the days of Nelson to those of Far-
> ragut. . . . Probably even the American navy, fertile though it has
> been in gallant fighting men, has never had any man who more thor-
> oughly and joyously welcomed a fight.[1]

As a young ensign, Evans had participated in the storming of Fort
Fisher in 1865, incurring wounds from which he never fully recovered. He commanded the USS *Yorktown* in Chilean waters in 1891–
92, at a time of tension between the United States and Chile. As
captain of the USS *Iowa* he saw service in the Spanish–American War
with the North Atlantic Squadron. He subsequently served with the
Asiatic Squadron (1902–4) and, as commander of the North Atlantic
Fleet, led the vessels on the first leg of their cruise around the world
that commenced in December 1907.

Evans enjoyed a good press throughout his career. Journalist James
Creelman described him as he appeared near the end of his service
with the navy:

> There was something of the human battleship in that grim, brown,
> square-jawed countenance, with its stern gray eyes and fighting chin.

73

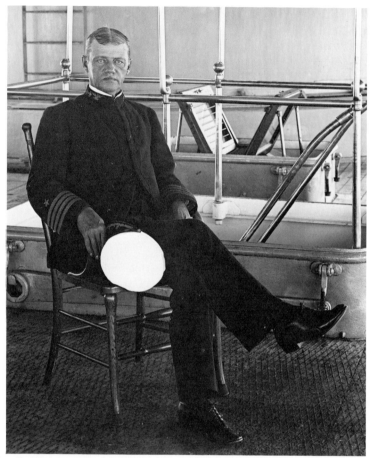

Robley D. Evans. Photograph taken before two of the battleship *Iowa*'s twelve-inch guns in 1898. *Courtesy of the Library of Congress.*

The very slant of the head and the set of the squat, strong figure connected itself with the massive guns thrust out from the ponderous steel turrets behind him, and the steady oak deck beneath him. The crook in the game leg was got forty-one years ago in the terrific assault on Fort Fisher. The powerful shoulder that squared itself occasionally with such a hint of hitting force, was once crushed by a falling steel battlehatch.

And the coarse, almost savage mouth!—how suggestive of a nearly forgotten age of roaring hand-to-hand cutlass fighting and close, fierce ship grapplings, speaking words of command to cold, silent engineers and electricians dealing death to invisible distant foes by the tapping of keys and the moving of switches![2]

A decade earlier, in 1895, the youthful Rudyard Kipling, heretofore no friend of the American navy, had been invited to breakfast with Captain Evans on board the USS *Indiana*. Kipling subsequently toured the vessel, and some weeks later he sent Evans a set of his books. On the title page of *Plain Tales from the Hills,* illustrated by Rufus F. Zogbaum, Kipling wrote the following lines:

> Zogbaum draws with a pencil,
> And I do things with a pen;
> And you sit up in a conning tower,
> Bossing eight hundred men.

> Zogbaum takes care of his business,
> And I take care of mine;
> And you take care of ten thousand tons
> Sky-hooting through the brine.

> Zogbaum can handle his shadows,
> And I can handle my style;
> And you can handle a ten-inch gun
> To carry seven mile.

> 'To him that hath shall be given,'
> And that's why these books are sent
> To the man who has lived more stories
> Than Zogbaum or I could invent.[3]

Evans in truth was a man who "lived more stories" than Kipling could invent. This can easily be confirmed by perusing the first volume of his memoirs, *A Sailor's Log,* published in 1901.[4] In Evans there existed an individual who claimed to detest publicity, but was skilled at the art of self-promotion, an officer of the New Navy who belonged by temperament to the Old, a man by turns progressive and reactionary and perhaps, withal, a charter member of Peter Karsten's "naval aristocracy."

Evans was born 18 August 1846, in Floyd County, Virginia. His father, Doctor Samuel Andrew Jackson Evans, a graduate of the University of Virginia, named his first son Robley Dunglison after one of his medical school instructors. His father died—probably of pneumonia—when Robley was ten, and the family subsequently moved to Fairfax Courthouse. The following year, Robley went to live with his uncle, A. H. Evans, in Washington, D.C. Young Evans spent some of his time on Capitol Hill, where his uncle, a lawyer by profession, served as clerk for the House of Representatives Committee on Claims, and also wrote articles for various papers. The boy also spent "many happy hours" on the waterfront; though he did not know a single naval officer, it occurred to Evans "[I] should like a sea life, and from this time on the idea was never out of my mind."[5] A Utah territorial representative suggested to him that if he could establish residency there, he could obtain an appointment to the Naval Academy at Annapolis. Evans, then thirteen, headed west to Salt Lake City in 1859. The party was attacked twice by Indians, and Evans was wounded in the left ankle. Evans set out on the return trip in midsummer the following year, passed the entrance examination at Annapolis 15 September 1860, and reported five days after that on board the frigate USS *Constitution*, commanded by George Rodgers. To him, and to the commandant of midshipmen, C. R. P. Rodgers, Evans said, ". . . I owe everything in my professional life."[6]

As a Virginian, Evans must have had his loyalties tested by the Civil War, though nowhere does he explicitly say so. His mother, Sally Ann Jackson Evans, apparently wrote a letter of resignation on his behalf (without, however, informing him of it), which was accepted by the Navy Department. The matter eventually was straightened out by C. R. P. Rodgers, but it was years before the mother fully forgave the son for his loyalty to the "old flag."[7] The midshipmen were transferred to Newport, Rhode Island. In the summer of 1863, Evans served variously on board the USS *Marion* (a sloop of war) and the merchant ship *Buckingham*, and as commander of the yacht *America*, searching the offshore waters for the CSS *Florida*. It was just as well they did not find her. Evans graduated from the Naval Academy in October 1863 and reported to the USS *Powhatan*, then outfitting at Philadelphia for the West Indies—an area that Evans was never to remember with any affection. "Our preparations for departure [October 1864] were quickly made, and we said good-bye to the West Indies, yellow fever, rebel sympathizers, heat, filth, and hard service—the whole outfit—without a single pang."[8]

Evans's account of his part in the assault on Fort Fisher in January 1865 certainly must have provided ample food for the retelling in later years. His column assaulted the northeast angle of the fort, where he was singled out by a Confederate sharpshooter, and wounded first in the left leg, then the right knee, and finally the right foot (losing part of one toe). Evans managed to kill his assailant, but spent some hours lying at the foot of the parapet before being rescued. Taken to the Naval Hospital at Norfolk, he overheard doctors say they were going to amputate both of his legs. Evans demurred, threatening to shoot any physician who approached with surgical instruments in tow. Eventually he recovered, but he subsequently had his right knee broken again and reset so that he could walk on it. He was put on the retired list by the Medical Board, but prevailed upon Congress to reinstate him.[9] One is inclined to take his heroic account at face value, but several niggling details seem out of place. At one stage of the assault, Evans claimed he recognized Colonel Lamb, the Confederate commander of Fort Fisher, and took a shot at him.[10] How would he have known Lamb by sight—much less by name—at that time? He also paid tribute to the Union Army, "slowly fighting its way from one gun to another," and to a General Curtis, who was killed, leading his brigade, "shot in the eye."[11] This is extraordinary attention to detail on the part of an individual lying wounded; yet nowhere does he mention the effectiveness of the naval bombardment that enabled the army to advance from one position to another.[12] Finally, why was he still in possession of his service revolver in the hospital at Norfolk, long after his rescue? Perhaps by the time he wrote the account, embellishments that had crept in over years of his telling and retelling the episode had become inseparable from the actual events.

Evans was promoted to lieutenant in July 1866, and to lieutenant commander in March of 1868. His first extended tour of duty was on the Asiatic station, in the USS *Piscataqua*. "Old Gimpy," as he became known in naval circles, was fascinated by the Orient. Like many other officers, he was favorably impressed with the Japanese, but much less so with the Chinese. The young officer drank in the sights and sounds of such ports as Manila, Hong Kong, and Singapore. Alfred Thayer Mahan also served on the Asiatic station at this time, as a lieutenant on board the USS *Iroquois;* but the two officers' accounts of their experiences at similar stages in their careers differ considerably.[13] It is, for example, impossible to imagine Mahan recounting the following story of a snake charmer in Singapore:

> The unfortunate thought came to one of our men that it would be a good idea to get the Mohammedan drunk to see what he would do; so he prepared a dose for him that was very effective. He poured a good stiff drink of brandy into a beer glass, and then filled it with gin instead of water. The charmer took kindly to the drink, and in short time rolled out of his chair on to the floor very drunk, and was soon fast asleep. The bag of snakes had not been thought of up to this time, but it also fell, and the inhabitants quickly spread over the floor. In the meantime five American officers took to the table, and drawing their feet up carefully, remained there until the snake charmer slept off his dose. He snored quietly while the snakes crawled over

and around him, but it was a long time before he finally came to himself, secured his pets, and took them away. We did not repeat that experiment.[14]

When the *Piscataqua* returned home late in 1870, Evans was ordered to duty with the ordnance department at the Washington Navy Yard. During the course of the winter he became engaged to Charlotte Taylor, sister of his Annapolis classmate Henry Clay Taylor. The couple married in July 1871, and Evans's next billet was a two-year hitch as an instructor at the Naval Academy. In his memoirs Evans rather deprecated his own abilities as a teacher, preferring to focus instead on the appointment of the "first colored cadet." He recalled how the black servants at the Academy took the news. His own dining-room steward said to him: "My Lord, Mr. Evans, a nigger done enter the Naval Academy!" The appointee, needless to say, did not last long. "The question of colour was one we were not prepared to tackle," Evans concluded.[15]

In August 1873 he joined the USS *Shenandoah* of the Mediterranean Squadron at Gibraltar. Evans and the *Shenandoah* were caught up in the *Virginius* affair, and the vessel was ordered first to the Caribbean, and subsequently up to Key West to join the naval forces assembled there. "We remained there several weeks, making faces at the Spaniards ninety miles away at Havana, while two modern vessels of war would have done us up in thirty minutes." This episode may have helped Evans to join the ranks of the reformers, as he was convinced the United States "was absolutely without sea power."[16] After the resolution of the affair, the *Shenandoah* was ordered to go out of commission, but Evans managed to obtain a transfer to the USS *Congress* as executive officer. The *Congress,* part of the Mediterranean Squadron, headed for West Africa, looked in on Liberia, and then cruised southward to Cape Palmas, having heard of trouble between American missionaries and the natives thereabouts. "They had threatened to lunch on some of our missionaries," Evans noted, "but had not carried out their threat. A short exercise on shore with a Gatling gun firing at a target . . . convinced them that they really could get on without eating American missionaries."[17]

Back in the Mediterranean, Evans enjoyed a spell of leave with his family (his wife and daughter having accompanied him abroad in 1873, settling in Nice). When Evans rejoined the *Congress,* she, in company with the USS *Franklin,* showed the flag throughout the Mediterranean: Marseilles, Barcelona, Port Mahon, Sicily, the Ionian

Sea, Naples, Malaga, Algiers, Tunis, Malta, and Tripoli. In the last place, an "insult" to the American consul led to the flexing of American military might. The *Congress* was sent "to demand and exact proper reparation" from the pasha. When an officer from the vessel was insulted in turn by the townspeople, a company of marines and a Gatling gun were landed. This misunderstanding was cleared up, but the pasha demurred subsequently when called upon to apologize for the earlier insult. The *Congress* cleared for action, brought her broadside to bear on the town, and, aided by the fortuitous arrival of the USS *Hartford* (which followed suit), received the apology the next day. This was gunboat diplomacy at its best, although Evans's sympathies lay with the pasha, who he thought had shown a willingness to respond to the incident until the American consul, in Evans's view, overreacted by demanding a formal apology.[18] The *Congress* returned to the United States in 1875, represented the navy at the centennial in Philadelphia the following year, and then was decommissioned. Evans, following two months' leave, was ordered to the Navy Department in Washington in the fall of 1876, and while serving there he developed and patented a long-distance signaling lamp. In December 1876 he was ordered to command the training ship USS *Saratoga*. Evans held this billet for four years, and was promoted to commander in July 1878.

Much that happened during the decade of the 1880s had an important bearing on Evans's reputation as a progressive and reformer. He served a two-year stint (1880–82) as equipment officer at the Washington Navy Yard. During this time he was a member of the Naval Advisory Board, in the summer of 1881, and he introduced a resolution recommending that all future naval vessels be constructed of steel.[19] After a brief tour of duty as inspector of the Fifth Lighthouse District, Evans became an inspector of material with the Baltimore & Ohio Railroad, operating from a Pittsburgh office. The B & O was building a large steel bridge over the Susquehanna River at Havre de Grace, Maryland, and the Carnegie firm had the contract. "It was on my suggestion," Evans maintained, "that Mr. Carnegie first seriously considered the question of starting a plate mill for the manufacture of ship plates."[20] Evans subsequently was appointed chief inspector of steel by Secretary of the Navy William C. Whitney, and might well have been considered one of the midwives of the New Steel Navy were it not for the fact that Carnegie, Phipps & Co. proved remarkably reluctant to bid according to the navy's specifications, despite importunings from Secretary Whitney himself.[21] Evans next oversaw the construction of an armored cruiser, the USS *Maine*. In 1889 he applied for a year's leave of absence; he was employed then by a New York firm, owned by Whitney, that manufactured wood fiber at an Appleton, Wisconsin, plant. If, like Mahan, Evans's career had become a "career in stays," this was to change with his appointment to the command of the gunboat USS *Yorktown* in August 1891. With her steel hull and armored deck, the *Yorktown* was one of the navy's newest ships. Evans was pleased with this new command.

In October, Evans and the *Yorktown* were ordered to join the Pacific Squadron at Valparaiso, Chile, an uprising against Chilean President Balmaceda having resulted in victory by the insurgents. The American minister, Patrick Egan, was perceived as hostile to the revolutionary movement and supportive of its opponents. The fact that a number of Balmacedists had taken refuge in the American legation did not improve matters. While the *Yorktown* was en route, the "Baltimore affair" further exacerbated relations. Captain Winfield Scott Schley of the USS *Baltimore* unwisely granted his crew shore leave in Valparaiso, where tempers were running high against the Americans in any case. Although accounts differ as to who provoked whom, fighting erupted between Chileans and the *Baltimore*'s crew, resulting in the death of two of the latter and the wounding of a number of others. The authorities, Schley reported, did not interfere. Egan, accepting Schley's account of the episode, demanded reparation from the Chilean government. His superiors in Washington backed him, although the Chileans, meanwhile, had countered by demanding Egan's recall. The *Yorktown*, after a passage of fifty-one days from New York, arrived in Valparaiso on 3 December 1891.

Evans's sympathies were not hard to discern. He called the attack on the sailors "about the most cowardly and brutal thing I ever heard of." He disapproved of Schley's efforts to demonstrate to the Chilean authorities that the crewmen were "perfectly sober" when the assault occurred:

I did not agree with him in this, for in the first place I doubted the fact, and in the second it was not an issue worth discussing. His men were probably drunk on shore, properly drunk; they went ashore, many of them, for the purpose of getting drunk, which they did on Chilean rum paid for with good United States money. When in this condition they were more entitled to protection than if they had been sober.[22]

Although Evans was not exactly looking for trouble, he was convinced from an early stage that the United States must demand and receive both an apology and reparations from the Chilean government. His diary entries suggest that he kept his temper with some difficulty:

[4 December 1891] It is not my business to make trouble here, and I don't intend to give offense to any one until I have orders from home, and then I shall do it with my guns and not with my tongue.
[7 December 1891] The mob is all for war with the United States, or any one else as far as that goes; but the sensible men know it would be suicide and nothing else. The Baltimore and Yorktown would give their navy a drubbing in two hours, and when the Boston comes we could shell the town into ruins and never be hurt.
[12 December 1891] The President's message . . . is published here to-day. . . . I don't see how Mr. Harrison can help sending a fleet down here to teach these people manners.
[31 December 1891] When the United States is willing to submit the question of the murder of her sailors in uniform to arbitration, I must look for other employment—the navy won't any longer suit me.[23]

Evans was careful to observe proper etiquette in his dealings with foreign warships in Valparaiso roadstead—including Chilean vessels—while at the same time learning all he could about the Chilean warships should matters come to blows. The *Baltimore* had left Valparaiso shortly after Schley's arrival in the port, but Patrick Egan wanted her recalled and on 16 December suggested to Evans that he telegraph Schley at Callao, Peru, to return. Neither Evans nor Schley came under the other's command, and Evans rejected Egan's suggestion, replying that the Navy Department—which was also in cable contact with Callao—would order the *Baltimore* back if necessary. He was apprised on 28 December of a telegram from William R. Grace to the head of the William R. Grace & Company office in Valparaiso. The gist of the message was that Grace was doing everything he could to convince Secretary of State Blaine that war should be avoided. Grace noted that President Harrison favored war, however, and the Navy Department was making preparations for a conflict. Evans decided that the crew of the *Yorktown* would sleep beside loaded guns that night—and every night—until he received better news. On 1 January 1892 he received orders from President Harrison to go to Santiago to confer with Egan, and "ascertain . . . the sentiment of Chile toward the United States." He cabled Washington the de-

sired information on 4 January, noting: "General sentiment of Santiago and Valparaiso brutally hostile to the United States." Throughout this time Evans had been careful not to permit the *Yorktown*'s
crew ashore. Despite his precautions, one of the ship's boats, waiting
for Evans's return from a trip ashore on 7 January, was the target of
rock throwing and taunting by a band of locals on the dock. Evans
headed straight for the *Almirante Cochrane,* whose captain was the
senior Chilean naval officer present, demanded police protection for
American sailors, and said that any repetition of the offense would
lead him to arm his sailors and order them to shoot anyone "who
insulted me or my men or my flag in any way." Evans passed word
of the incident along to the Navy Department. There were no repe-
titions.[24]

The *Yorktown* also provided a haven for some of the refugees in the
American and Spanish legations who were granted safe conduct by
the Chilean government. On 20 January Evans received orders from
the Navy Department to sail for Callao with the refugees. Thus he
had left the danger zone when Blaine's 21 January ultimatum threatening termination of diplomatic relations was delivered to the Chilean authorities. This was followed four days later by a special message from President Harrison to Congress: a virtual invitation to declare
war on Chile. The new Chilean foreign minister meanwhile had sent
the necessary apology, thus nullifying Harrison's message, and in due
course the incident was laid to rest. The extent to which Evans's
reports from Valparaiso heightened perceptions in the United States
that the Chileans would remain intransigent is difficult to determine.
Clearly Evans and the *Yorktown* breathed defiance, daring the Valparaiso mob and the Chilean navy to do their worst. Evans would
not begin a war, but neither would he shy away from one. It also
must be said that Evans, despite disclaimers to the contrary, had
discovered the benefits of a favorable press—and was not averse to
exploiting it in his own interests.[25] "Fighting Bob" Evans he had
become, and "Fighting Bob" he would remain.

Meanwhile, early in 1891, Great Britain and the United States
had reached an agreement that would outlaw pelagic sealing in the
Bering Sea and adjoining waters. Whether it could be extended for
1892 seemed for a time doubtful. Secretary of the Navy Tracy, anticipating an extension, prepared for a combined squadron of revenue
marine vessels and naval ships to enforce the modus vivendi. In March
of that year British agreement was obtained, and Evans was subsequently placed in overall command of the squadron. The govern-

ments of the two countries agreed in the meantime to submit the dispute to an arbitral tribunal in Paris.[26] Evans's squadron consisted of the *Yorktown, Mohican, Adams,* and *Ranger,* and the revenue cutters *Corwin, Rush,* and *Bear.* Not only were the sealers kept out of the Bering Sea by Evans's vessels, but the *Corwin* succeeded in capturing their supply steamer, the *Coquitlan,* severely disrupting their operations.[27] Evans and the *Yorktown* arrived back in San Francisco 8 October 1892. In his annual report, Secretary Tracy noted the Navy Department's "appreciation of the judgment, energy, and skill with which Commander Evans performed the difficult duties assigned to him in the command of the United States naval force in [the] Bering Sea."[28]

Evans's later recounting of the Bering Sea operations relied heavily upon his journals. The entry of 22 September, however, fails to mention the target practice on board the *Yorktown* that took place that day in the harbor of Unalaska. Shooting over open sights in the morning produced indifferent results. When Bradley Fiske's telescopic sight was utilized in the afternoon, the first four shots hit the target, and the fifth was only ten feet away. Evans was not even on board the vessel, and though he mentioned a successful gunnery exercise at sea a few days later (also utilizing the telescopic sight), nowhere are Fiske or his sight, which was to revolutionize naval gunnery, even acknowledged. This is perhaps less surprising when it is noted that Evans earlier had sent an unfavorable report on the sight to the secretary of the navy.[29] In his fitness reports on Fiske, Evans considered the latter's professional ability only "tolerable."[30]

Evans was detached from the *Yorktown* and, after a brief tour of duty with the Lighthouse Board in Washington, was promoted to captain on 27 June 1893 and placed in command of the armored cruiser *New York.* The vessel spent the winter of 1894–95 cruising with the North Atlantic Squadron in the West Indies. In May, Evans was ordered to proceed to European waters, ultimately to participate in ceremonies marking the opening of the Kiel Canal. He was able to spend a few days in England en route, noting in passing: "I came back from London last night (5 June) at midnight, after a most delightful visit. Met many friends there who gave me dinners, luncheons, drives, and made as much fuss over me as if I were named Mahan."[31] Admiral Kirkland, who commanded the European Squadron, transferred his flag to the *New York* on 12 June in Copenhagen, and two days later the vessel headed for Kiel. During the festivities, Evans had occasion to meet and converse with the "picturesque" Kai-

ser Wilhelm II on several occasions, and formed a friendship with
the kaiser's brother, Prince Henry, and the latter's wife, Princess
Irene. Certainly Evans was aware of some of the undercurrents of
European politics, reflected in the behavior of various naval contin-
gents. Whether he felt he and the *New York* were being courted by
the Germans is more problematical; in any event he did not appear
to begrudge the Second Reich a navy commensurate with the size of
its burgeoning commerce.[32]

Evans left the *New York* upon her return home and was ordered to
Philadelphia in October 1895 to fit out and take command of the
USS *Indiana*. He served as her commander until the fall of 1896,
and then was appointed to the Navy Department's Personnel Board
in 1897. Under the guidance of Assistant Secretary of the Navy
Theodore Roosevelt, the board addressed some of the long-standing
differences in rank and pay between members of the line on the one
hand and of the Engineer Corps on the other. That problem had long

The USS *Indiana*. Evans supervised the completion and served as the
first commander of the *Indiana*, the first battleship (BB-1) in the U.S.
Navy. *Courtesy of the Naval Historical Center.*

plagued the navy, and to Evans belongs credit for suggesting a solution. "The scheme of amalgamation [i.e., the creation of a new corps of officers into which the existing engineers would be merged] embodied in that bill was first proposed by me," wrote Evans in his autobiography.[33] The board also provided for the retirement of officers too long in rank, thus improving the flow of promotion from rank to rank and ending the stagnation in some of the lower grades of the service; ensured that existing distinctions between staff officers (i.e., Medical Corps, Pay Corps, chaplains, naval constructors) and line officers would end; improved conditions and pay for both warrant officers and enlisted men; and provided for a reorganization and enlargement of the Marine Corps. Evans's proposal represented something of a volte-face, as it was at variance with the tenor of his remarks in an article that appeared in the *North American Review* in December 1896.[34] Nowhere does Evans explain the reason for his change of mind. Perhaps some of his recent postings to modern battleships helped to convince him of the need for amalgamation. It is also possible that Evans recognized that change was inevitable and, not wishing to find himself in a minority on the committee, sought a workable solution though he remained committed at heart to line officer supremacy.

Evans left Washington in December 1897 on a tour of inspection of lighthouses on the South Atlantic and Gulf coasts. He chanced to be in Key West while the *Maine* was coaling for her one-way trip to Havana. Referring to the subsequent sinking of the vessel, "Fighting Bob" lived up to his sobriquet:

> I felt that if the action of our admiral [Montgomery Sicard] had been different—and it probably would have been had he been younger and not so sick—time at least would have been saved. If he had gone into Havana the morning after the disaster with his whole fleet and said to General Blanco that he had come to find out why these American officers and men, guests of Spain, had been foully murdered, it would, in my opinion, have produced immediate results and saved much time.[35]

With war looming, Sicard was replaced by William T. Sampson as commander of the North Atlantic Squadron, and Evans replaced Sampson as commander of the USS *Iowa*. Upon the outbreak of hostilities, Evans pushed for the bombardment of the Havana defenses by the fleet, although the strategists in Washington had decided that this would be too risky an operation.[36] He subsequently defended the fleet's voyage to and bombardment of San Juan, but whether it was in fact the wisest course to pursue was questionable.[37] Evans was uncharacteristically reluctant to make a judgment in his memoirs about the meandering course pursued by the Flying Squadron under Winfield Scott Schley along the southern coast of Cuba as it searched for Cervera's fleet. Perhaps he felt the Sampson–Schley controversy was generating enough unfavorable publicity for the navy as it was. At the time, his feelings were considerably less restrained, particularly when he learned that Schley intended to return to Key West to coal before having established the whereabouts of Cervera. The following megaphone conversation with his Annapolis classmate, Captain John Philip of the *Texas,* ensued:

> "Say, Jack, what the devil does it mean?"
> "Beats me. What do you think?"
> "Damned if I know, but I know one thing—I'm the most disgusted man afloat."[38]

Cervera was run to ground in Santiago, and Evans and the USS *Iowa* played a significant part in the Battle of Santiago on 3 July.[39]

When the Spanish vessels began to emerge from the harbor at 9:30 a.m., the *Iowa,* the first ship to spot them, hoisted Signal 250, "The enemy is attempting to escape," and opened fire. Within twenty minutes the *María Teresa* and another Spanish ship, the *Oquendo,* were ablaze. The *Iowa* then turned her guns on two destroyers, and joined by fire from the *Texas, Oregon,* and *Indiana* soon put them out of service. American fire was next concentrated on the *Vizcaya,* and within fifteen minutes that vessel too was hammered into submission. With only the *Cristóbal Colón* left in action, Admiral Sampson ordered the *Iowa* and the *Indiana* to break off the chase and return to Santiago to see that the two Spanish ships still in harbor did not leave and attack the American transports anchored at Siboney to the east. En route, Evans swung the *Iowa* toward the beached and burning *Vizcaya* and lowered boats to rescue survivors. The ships in harbor remained there, and at battle's end Spanish admiral Cervera boarded the *Iowa* for the formal surrender. The entire battle had lasted only two hours, but Evans's role in the American victory placed him among the nation's war heros.

Evans left the *Iowa* in October 1898, and would not see another tour of duty at sea until the spring of 1902, when he was appointed to the command of the cruiser division of the Asiatic Fleet. In February of 1901 he had received his promotion to rear admiral, and that fall he was ordered to American Samoa as president of a general court-martial to try the governor of the islands on charges of misconduct. While en route home, he stopped at the Hawaiian Islands, having been commissioned by the president to report upon the overall situation there.[40] The whole question of the defense of the islands he found "most difficult," not least because of the number of Japanese nationals there, "a very ambitious, warlike race, and likely to give trouble in time."[41] The islands, he felt, were in any case too distant to pose a threat to the West Coast even if they fell into enemy hands.

In January 1902 the impending visit of Prince Henry to the United States was announced. The German emperor had requested that Evans serve as his brother's official escort, and this was so ordered. The prince's party arrived in New York City in February, traveled to Washington to make an official call on President Roosevelt, and then returned to the New York City area to witness the launching of the yacht *Meteor,* a vessel the emperor had ordered. Then it was off on an extended tour, to Chattanooga and Lookout Mountain, Chicago, Milwaukee (where both Admiral Evans and the prince agreed that the prettiest women were), Niagara Falls, Boston (where Prince Henry received an honorary degree from Harvard), and back to New York.[42] Evans surmised the visit had been undertaken as a fence-mending operation: to "reestablish . . . cordial relations" that had been strained following the actions of the German squadron at Manila Bay and the perception in the public mind that Germany sought a coaling station in the West Indies. Evans welcomed the thought of an "era of good feeling" between Germany and the United States, should such ensue. "Good-bye to you, Prince Henry, and all your gallant comrades," he wrote. "Good luck and happiness to you all. If you should unhappily be involved in war with some other country, I miss my guess if your enemy doesn't find the German navy a hard nut to crack."[43] It was a tribute from one professional to another.

Evans's request for duty afloat with the Asiatic Fleet not only took him back to a portion of the world that he liked, but one where imperial rivalries and tensions threatened to result in open conflict between the powers. Evans devoted nearly half of his second volume of memoirs (15 of 33 chapters) to the two years spent in Asia. Perhaps by this stage of his career the habit of embellishing a good story had become ingrained. Perhaps, also, he was beginning to fall victim to nostalgia.

Many of the old people of Honolulu and a few naval officers still living and on the retired list will recount to you by the hour the doings of the dear old days before steam and modern guns took all the poetry out of our profession, when the officers flirted, danced, and drank to their hearts' content without fear that the Navy Department would know of their performance.[44]

Whatever the case, one searches in vain for some real substance in Evans's account. What one gets is a disquisition covering an interview with the Dowager Empress of China—"the most remarkable woman in the world"—a belief that if England had only permitted Russia to acquire control of the Bosporus in the 1870s, the "trouble" that came later over Manchuria need not have occurred, and a suspicion that the U.S. Army did not want to defend Subig Bay because Olongapo was too far removed from the pleasures of the Army and Navy Club at Manila![45]

In October 1902 Evans assumed overall command of the Asiatic Fleet, hoisting his flag on board the USS *Kentucky*. Although he did not discuss Russian–American tensions in any detail in his memoirs, it is apparent from his reports then that he entertained serious fears that Russian attempts to consolidate their hold on Manchuria could lead to either renewed antiforeign uprisings in China or perhaps a Russian–American conflict over the Open Door.[46] Evans also went out of his way to minimize the role of Lieutenant William S. Sims in improving gunnery in the fleet at that time, reserving credit instead for members of his own staff.[47] He also became aware of the anti-American feeling on the part of some Filipinos, spending as much time as he did in the Philippines. "Education will in time remedy all this. If it does not, bullets and bayonets, I know, will."[48]

Evans's report to the secretary of the navy covering the first eight months of his command presents a somewhat different picture. His concern for the enlisted men emerges in a variety of ways. Evans advocated the stocking of ships' canteens with beer and wine, maintaining that this would reduce problems encountered during leave ashore. He also suggested incentive pay for gun-pointers, and urged that crews be kept together on board their respective vessels for the duration of a cruise. He desired the stationing of additional shallow-draft gunboats in Chinese waters to protect American interests and American nationals. And he vigorously advocated that "Olongapo, Subig Bay, which, by its location and surroundings, offers by far the most advantageous point in the matter of defense, harbor facilities, and healthful conditions of any place in the islands" be developed as the principal naval station in the Philippines.[49]

The outbreak of the Russo–Japanese War in February 1904 found the Asiatic Squadron at Subig Bay. Evans proposed stationing the cruiser squadron at Chefoo on the Shantung peninsula, and the battleships at Nagasaki, Japan, but was overruled by the Navy Department, with Roosevelt's concurrence. The president wanted to keep American vessels away from the war zone, even at the expense of less-than-perfect protection for American nationals. The gunboat *Helena,* which had been wintering at Newchwang in southern Man-

Theodore Roosevelt and Evans on board the USS *Mayflower.* From left to right are William Emory, Edith (Mrs. Theodore) Roosevelt, Evans, President Roosevelt, and Cornelius Vanderbilt on board the presidential yacht during North Atlantic Fleet maneuvers, probably in 1906. The *Mayflower* was built in Scotland as a steam yacht in 1896, purchased by the U.S. Navy, and converted for use blockading Cuba during the Spanish–American War. Between 1905 and 1929 she served as the presidential yacht for five chief executives. *Courtesy of the U.S. Naval Institute.*

churia, was ordered to leave as soon as possible.[50] In March, Evans was ordered to turn over command of the Asiatic Fleet to Rear Admiral Philip H. Cooper in the following month and to proceed home in the *Kentucky*. This change, however, did not connote dissatisfaction with his actions in the early phases of the conflict; his two-year tour of duty was finished.

That this was indeed the case is evident from the decision later that year to put Evans in command of the North Atlantic Fleet. Roosevelt wrote Henry Cabot Lodge to inform him that Evans, rather than Lodge's brother-in-law, Rear Admiral Charles H. Davis, would receive the posting: ". . . I have been obliged to come to the conclusion, which is also the conclusion of [Paul] Morton, of [William H.] Moody, and of Admiral Converse, that the interest of the Navy requires that Evans should be put in command of the battleship squadron. My judgment and the judgment of these three other men may be all wrong, but it is our best judgment and our clear judgment."[51] Evans hoisted his flag 28 March 1905. Summers were spent in northern waters; winters in the Gulf and Caribbean. Much of the next two years passed uneventfully; an English squadron (Rear Admiral Prince Louis of Battenberg commanding) visited in the fall of 1905; a Cape Cod resident submitted a claim for $39 for the loss of preserves when his shelving collapsed during fleet target practice in Cape Cod Bay; the governor of Jamaica ordered the U.S. Navy out when they engaged in unauthorized rescue efforts following an earthquake there, and was himself removed by the British government for his discourtesy.

All of this activity paled as rumors began to fly in the summer of 1907 that the fleet would go to the Pacific. Evans reported to the president at Oyster Bay, and the projected cruise was thoroughly discussed. Evans's preferred route was via the Straits of Magellan, north to San Francisco, and then westward across the Pacific, rather than eastward via Suez. Roosevelt supported this choice.[52] The command should have served as the capstone to an already distinguished career, but Evans's health was declining. His legs were giving him increasing problems, perhaps because of the old Fort Fisher wounds, gout, or rheumatism—or some combination of the three. That he was a sick man when the fleet left was beyond doubt. Rear Admiral Charles M. Thomas, Evans's second-in-command, noted in his diary:

Mr. [Henry C.] Reuterdahl . . . surprised me much by saying that it was "touch and go" whether or not Evans should take the fleet to the Pacific, and that the subject was brought up at a Cabinet meeting. The opinion of the President and his Cabinet was that Evans is in no condition for the job, but that it would be the better policy to let him go and make the "try," rather than run the risk of a newspaper sensation all over the country by detaching the C. in C. just previous to the sailing of the Fleet.[53]

The cabinet's fears appeared to be justified. Rear Admiral Thomas noted that Evans had taken to his bed two days out from Trinidad, en route to Rio de Janeiro.[54] Evans's chief of staff, Captain Royal Ingersoll, had in effect taken over for him, except for some of the ceremonial duties at various ports of call that devolved upon Thomas. Thomas himself was in a difficult position. Although he admired Evans's grit ("There is not one man in a million who could or would have stood to his post, under such distressing physical disability, as Evans has done. . . ."), he would have been less than human had he not desired the command himself. Hearing subsequently that Evans had decided to step down when the fleet reached San Francisco, he mused:

> I *think* the chances for my being C. in C. next May are fairly good, but if Evans improves so that he can dress himself and drag one leg after the other, I am of the opinion that he will endeavor to hold on until the day of his retirement, Aug. 18 [1908], as he is the greatest Cormorant for *Power* that I have ever known in all my life, and his greatest delight seems to be in "jumping down people's throats." . . . Evans's great ability and general all-around efficiency is universally conceded in the Navy, but he is totally lacking in all those refinements of feeling that go to make up the perfect gentleman.[55]

Evans was true to his word; he requested relief from command in March. In a graceful reply, President Roosevelt paid tribute to his "long and honorable career" and his "mastery" of his profession.[56] Rear Admiral Thomas did indeed command the fleet—for all of one week—9 May to 15 May. He too was not in the best of health. His social duties in the San Francisco area continued; following one such function, Thomas collapsed, and he died on 3 July.[57] Thomas was succeeded by Charles S. Sperry, who commanded the fleet on its voyage across the Pacific in 1908.

Evans retired from active service on 18 August. His remaining years were spent quietly at 324 Indiana Avenue in Washington, D.C. He wrote a series of articles that appeared in *Hampton's Broadway Magazine,* in response to Henry Reuterdahl's criticism of battleship design defects. Evans's defense in turn raised the blood pressure of the insurgents, who were hoping for both administrative reforms, which would break the stranglehold of the bureaus on ship design and construction, and alterations to the vessels themselves, which they believed had serious flaws. "Dewey and Evans ought to be roasted for their statements," commented one.[58] In March 1909, President Roosevelt appointed Evans a member of a board to consider the organization of the Navy Department. Proposed changes pushed by Mahan and the insurgents received his endorsement. Through it all "Fighting Bob" managed to complete and bring out a second volume of his memoirs, although it was not the equal of the first.

Evans, as could have been predicted with some confidence, does appear in Peter Karsten's *Naval Aristocracy*. He married the sister of a fellow officer; his son became an officer in turn, and one of his two daughters married a naval officer. He had a strong sense of national honor, advocated the use of naval force "to correct or uphold" questionable American business practices abroad, and was by turns racist and warmongering. Like many of his generation, he suffered from career anxiety and was assiduous in the pursuit of glory. Karsten quoted Evans's remark at a banquet in San Francisco in May 1908: "If you wish to preserve the peace of the world give us more battleships and fewer statesmen."[59]

Much of Karsten's characterization is based on Evans's memoirs; indeed, Karsten failed to cite many passages that were more damning than those he did use. But the memoirs are only part of the story. Commander Evans discovered that his cruise in the *Yorktown* had made him—thanks to the creative efforts of the American press—a public hero. He subsequently found it useful, given his own proclivities, to live the role created for him as much as circumstances permitted. The memoirs reinforced the portrayal, and were written with his public image very much in mind. All this effort in turn enabled him to rise in his profession no less surely than did Mahan, albeit in a somewhat different fashion.

There existed, alongside the image, a solid professional officer. Let us grant that he may well have been more at home in the Age of Fighting Sail. He cultivated the image of a "Fighting Captain" in an era where the opportunities to win distinction for one's pugnacity were few. By so doing, he served as a bridge between the Old Navy and the New.

FURTHER READING

Despite his prominence, archival material on Evans is relatively sparse. The Evans papers in the Naval Historical Foundation collection consist only of a typescript of the Battle of Santiago as seen from the USS *Iowa*, and some newspaper clippings pertaining to the Spanish–American War. This may explain in part why there has been no study of the rear admiral in the past fifty years. Edwin A. Falk's biography, *Fighting Bob Evans,* was published in 1931, and contains little that cannot be found in Evans's two volumes of memoirs, *A Sailor's Log: Recollections of Forty Years of Naval Life,* published in 1901; and *An Admiral's Log: Being Continued Recollections of Naval Life,* which appeared in 1910. It should be apparent that these sources must be used with some caution. Articles by Evans that appeared from time to time in journals, such as "The Engineer in Naval Warfare" in the *North American Review,* are written with a degree of circumspection, or else, like his memoirs, lean toward the anecdotal.

Works by or about Evans's contemporaries in the service also shed light on certain facets of his career. The papers of his brother-in-law and Annapolis classmate, Henry Clay Taylor, are as sparse as Evans's own. Bradley A. Fiske's memoirs, *From Midshipman to Rear-Admiral*—at any rate those portions dealing with Fiske as a lieutenant on board the *Yorktown*—are useful, as are the Charles M. Thomas papers and the William S. Sims papers. Also illuminating in places are the letters of Theodore Roosevelt and the Grover Cleveland papers (in the last instance, it appears that Evans was a hunting and fishing companion of the former president during the years after the Spanish–American War).

Useful secondary works include Rowena Reed, *Combined Operations in the Civil War,* for the attack on Fort Fisher; Paolo Coletta, *Admiral Bradley A. Fiske and the American Navy;* Frederick B. Pike, *Chile and the United States, 1880–1962: The Emergence of Chile's Social Crisis and the Challenge to United States Diplomacy;* Joyce S. Goldberg, *The Baltimore Affair;* Benjamin F. Cooling, *Gray Steel and Blue Water Navy: The Formative Years of America's Military–Industrial Complex, 1881–1917,* and Cooling's biography *Benjamin Franklin Tracy: Father of the Modern American Fighting Navy;* and Briton C. Busch, *The War Against the Seals: A History of the North American Seal Fishery,* for some aspects of Evans's career in the 1880s and while he was in command of the *Yorktown.* David Trask's *The War With Spain in 1898* is the best one-volume account of that conflict in all its aspects. William R. Braisted's *The United States Navy in the Pacific, 1897–1909,* and Elting E. Morison, *Admiral Sims and the Modern American Navy,* were useful for the period 1902–4, when Evans was with the Asiatic Fleet, as was Richard Challener's *Admirals, Generals, and American Foreign Policy, 1898–1914.* Robert A. Hart's *The Great White Fleet: Its Voyage around the World, 1907–*

1909 is still the standard account of the voyage that should have been the capstone of Evans's career.

NOTES

1. Theodore Roosevelt, "Admiral Evans," *The Outlook* 100 (13 January 1912): 55.
2. Quoted in "The Adventurous Career of 'Fighting Bob' Evans," *Current Literature* 42 (January 1907): 35.
3. Quoted in "Concerning Admiral Evans," *Bookman* 34 (January 1912): 584. Evans maintained that someone noticed Kipling's inscription and gave it publicity; he (Evans) had wanted it to remain private. Robley D. Evans, *A Sailor's Log: Recollections of Forty Years of Naval Life,* 402.
4. Vice President Theodore Roosevelt wrote the author: "I have just been reading your book and I have enjoyed it so much that I cannot resist sending you a line to tell you so. . . . It is not only that I think your book interesting. I feel that in addition it half unconsciously portrays the spirit which makes those of us who have the honor of the country very deeply at heart feel an undying faith in the United States navy." Elting E. Morison and John M. Blum, eds. *Letters of Theodore Roosevelt,* III:99.
5. Evans, *Sailor's Log,* 11.
6. Ibid., 36.
7. Ibid., 47.
8. Ibid., 71.
9. See Evans, *Sailor's Log,* Chapters 8 and 9.
10. Ibid., 89.
11. Ibid., 95.
12. See the account in Rowena Reed, *Combined Operations in the Civil War,* final chapter.
13. Contrast the account in Chapters 10–13 of Evans, *Sailor's Log,* with Mahan's in Robert Seager II and Doris D. Maguire, eds., *The Letters and Papers of Alfred Thayer Mahan,* I:145–332, and Chapter 3 in Robert Seager II, *Alfred Thayer Mahan: The Man and His Letters.*
14. Evans, *Sailor's Log,* 149.
15. Ibid., 156–57.
16. Ibid., 171–72.
17. Ibid., 184–85.
18. Ibid., 203–5.
19. Benjamin F. Cooling, *Gray Steel and Blue Water Navy: The Formative Years of America's Military–Industrial Complex, 1881–1917,* 29; Evans, *Sailor's Log,* 230.
20. Evans, *Sailor's Log,* 234.
21. Cooling, *Gray Steel,* 72–73. Except for the reference to Evans on page 29, Cooling does not mention him at all.
22. Evans, *Sailor's Log,* 258, 259–60.
23. Ibid., 262–63, 265, 279.

24. Ibid., 267–68, 281–82, 287. Evans's report of the rock-throwing episode was released to the press. See the *New York Times*, 13 January 1892, p. 1, col. 1.

25. Evans, *Sailor's Log*, 297–98, 314.

26. See the account in Cooling, *Benjamin Franklin Tracy*, 132–36.

27. The cruise is covered in Chapters 25–28 of Evans, *Sailor's Log*.

28. *Annual Report of the Secretary of the Navy, 1892*, 40.

29. Evans to Tracy, 31 March 1892, R.G. 313: Letters to Navy Department from Commanding Officers of Vessels, Series 17, January 1892–July 1893, National Archives. Cited in Coletta, *Bradley A. Fiske*, 36.

30. Coletta, *Bradley A. Fiske*, 36–37, 39.

31. Evans, *Sailor's Log*, 371.

32. Ibid., 387–88.

33. Ibid., 402. Assistant Secretary of the Navy Theodore Roosevelt, testifying 6 April 1898 before the House Naval Affairs Committee, noted: "As regards the scheme of the bill as it now stands, the first rough outline was presented by Captain Evans, and it was backed up by Chief Engineer Melville." *Navy Reorganization: Hearings Before the Committee on Naval Affairs, House of Representatives, on the Bill* H.R. 7443 *to Combine the Line and Engineer Corps of the Navy*, 55th Congress, 2nd session, House Reports no. 3721, p. 3.

34. Robley D. Evans, "The Engineer in Naval Warfare," *North American Review* 163 (December 1896): 654–60.

35. Evans, *Sailor's Log*, 405–6.

36. David F. Trask, *The War with Spain in 1898*, 90–91; Evans, *Sailor's Log*, 408.

37. Trask, *War with Spain*, 119.

38. Ibid., 124.

39. Evans, *Sailor's Log*, Chapter 39; see also Robley D. Evans, "The 'Iowa' at Santiago," *Century Magazine* 58 (May 1899): 50–62.

40. Robley D. Evans, *An Admiral's Log: Being Continued Recollections of Naval Life*, 9.

41. Evans, *Admiral's Log*, 21–22.

42. Robley D. Evans, "Prince Henry's American Impressions," *McClure's* 19 (May 1902): 27–37; see also Chapters 4–8 of Evans, *Admiral's Log*.

43. Evans, *Admiral's Log*, 77, 79.

44. Ibid., 94.

45. Ibid., 261, 116, 301.

46. William R. Braisted, *The United States Navy in the Pacific, 1897–1909*, 143–45.

47. Elting E. Morison, *Admiral Sims and the Modern American Navy*, 205–53; Evans, *Admiral's Log*, 136–37, 145–52.

48. Evans, *Admiral's Log*, 223.

49. *Annual Report of the Secretary of the Navy, 1903*, 599–620, 651–60.

50. Braisted, *United States Navy*, 155–56, 159–60.

51. Theodore Roosevelt to Henry Cabot Lodge, 16 November 1904; Roosevelt, *Letters,* IV:1032.

52. Theodore Roosevelt to Truman Handy Newberry, 10 August 1907; Roosevelt, *Letters,* V:745; see also Evans, *Admiral's Log,* 394. Roosevelt had heard of a cabal to get rid of both Evans and Davis, and to put Caspar F. Goodrich in command of the fleet. He continued to back Evans. See Theodore Roosevelt to Henry Cabot Lodge, 10 April 1907; Roosevelt, *Letters,* V:645–46.

53. Entry of 20 December 1907, Charles M. Thomas Papers, Naval Historical Foundation Collection, Library of Congress.

54. Entry of 14 January 1908, Thomas Papers.

55. See entries of 20 January and 13 February 1908, Thomas Papers.

56. Theodore Roosevelt to Robley D. Evans, 23 March 1908; Roosevelt, *Letters,* VI:981.

57. Robert A. Hart, *The Great White Fleet: Its Voyage Around the World, 1907–1909,* 168–69.

58. Albert Lemoit Key to William S. Sims, 27 November 1908; Sims Papers, LCMD; quoted in Ronald Spector, *Admiral of the New Empire: The Life and Career of George Dewey,* 177–78.

59. Peter Karsten, *The Naval Aristocracy: The Golden Age of Annapolis and the Emergence of Modern American Navalism,* 125, 130–31, 193, 199, 215–16, 262, 265, 298. The quotation is on page 219.

FRENCH ENSOR CHADWICK: REFORMER, HISTORIAN, AND OUTCAST

MALCOLM MUIR, JR.

Off Santiago on 3 July 1898, Captain French Ensor Chadwick set his eyes on hostile warships for the first and only time in his forty-five-year naval career. This day of triumph for American arms was one of bitter personal disappointment for the thoroughly professional officer. Fate put the fleeing Spaniards out of Chadwick's reach and delivered them instead into the hands of Winfield S. Schley—an officer whom Chadwick despised.

Deprived, then, of the combat success that must cap an officer's record if he is to stand out in the American memory, Chadwick has been largely forgotten. Yet he deserves better. As an outspoken and sometimes abrasive figure in the revitalization of the moribund post–Civil War navy, Chadwick made enemies who kept him from the top commands he deserved. Resigning in 1906 from the organization he had served so ably, Chadwick would turn with great success to the writing of history.

It was history that brought Chadwick to the naval profession in the first place. Born far from the sea in Morgantown, Virginia, 29 February 1844, the boy was a voracious and omnivorous reader, particularly taken with James Fenimore Cooper's *History of the Navy of the United States of America.* Consequently, when his state split over secession in the spring of 1861, Chadwick sought a place at the U.S. Naval Academy. Unionist Congressman William G. Brown rewarded the loyalty of this seventeen-year-old from a slave-holding family with an appointment.

In that fall of 1861, Chadwick reported not to Annapolis but to Newport, Rhode Island, where the Naval Academy had found a safe

French Ensor Chadwick. This photograph of Chadwick appeared in volume 42 of *Harper's Weekly* in 1898. *Courtesy of the Naval Historical Center.*

harbor. With the midshipmen housed in the *Constitution*—"Old Ironsides"—the setting could hardly have been more propitious for a young man brought up on Cooper. Chadwick quickly adjusted to the rigors of a midshipman's life in wartime. Within two years, he participated in actual operations on his summer cruise when the sloop *Marion* hunted for the Confederate raider *Florida*.

Among his classmates at Newport was Winfield S. Schley, the man Chadwick would come to hate more than thirty years later. Among Chadwick's superiors were two lieutenants pivotal in his career: Alfred Thayer Mahan and William T. Sampson. Of the latter, Chadwick formed an early opinion that bordered on awe. Graduating early with his class on 22 November 1864, Chadwick ranked number four. His first assignment took him to the New York Navy Yard to drill recruits, but he soon went to sea in the *Susquehanna* where his hopes for action against either the CSS *Stonewall* or the *Shenandoah* were frustrated by the end of the war.[1]

In the more settled routine of the peacetime navy, Chadwick enjoyed several professional advantages. Except for a prolonged bout with malaria contracted off Panama, he was blessed with robust health. His fortunate marriage in 1878 to Cornelia Jones Miller, a cosmopolitan and active woman, proved a distinct asset. Chadwick's personality was pleasant, even genial, although his honest manner could be direct to the point of brusqueness.[2]

Chadwick mastered his calling in the years following the Civil War with posting to a variety of duties. For instance, he returned to the Naval Academy as instructor in mathematics in 1872; he then served as executive officer on board the *Powhatan,* the old sidewheeler that Matthew C. Perry had taken to Japan in 1853. The Navy Department dispatched Chadwick to Europe in 1879 to study training methods in other fleets. His summary, "Report on the Training Systems for the Navy and Mercantile Marine of England, and on the Naval Training System of France" was published as a Senate document in 1880. Sir Thomas Brassey thought highly of the work and reprinted portions of it in his history of the Royal Navy in 1883. Chadwick was off to a good start as a writer.

His next duty, as assistant inspector of the Third Lighthouse District, also led to publication, in this case of "Aids to Navigation," which included a history of the lighthouse service. With this piece, Chadwick showed his mastery of technical material and his ability to perform research in historical sources. The work, which was published by the Naval Institute, also demonstrated Chadwick's willingness to be outspokenly critical of official inefficiency.

With the U.S. Navy ranking twelfth among the world's fleets and with virtually all the country's warships hopelessly obsolete, there was much for Chadwick to criticize in the early 1880s. Fortunately, the tentative beginnings of a naval renaissance were in the offing, and Chadwick went back to Europe in 1882 to study the latest developments in sea power. In fact, the Navy Department regarded the mission as of such significance that Chadwick was posted the first permanent naval attaché to any overseas port. Chadwick's orders from the secretary of the navy were to report on the organization and methods of Britain's coast guard, lifesaving, and lighthouse services; the care and treatment provided to sick and disabled seamen by the hospital service; inspection and certification of ships and their mates and officers; and the activities of the board of trade and meteorological service that related to maritime affairs. He was to obtain similar information on the lifesaving services of Russia, Norway, Sweden, Denmark, Holland, and Belgium from their embassies in London. These were his formal orders, but the reports he sent home ignore these topics and deal largely with gunpowder, mountings, and turrets; tests of armor plates and new ships; and naval administration and training, thus suggesting that his real mission was to report to the recently established Office of Naval Intelligence on naval advancements and to help the United States acquire examples of modern naval technology.[3]

Chadwick traveled extensively on the Continent—attending, for instance, the German gunboat maneuvers on the River Weser in 1884—but he concentrated his main efforts on the world's naval leader, Great Britain. From the firm Armstrong, he purchased plans for the first American seagoing ship without sails, the *Charleston.* He also bought the drawings for the cruiser *Baltimore* and the small battleship *Texas.* To obtain the most modern pieces of ordnance, Chadwick purchased guns from Cammell and Whitworth. Aware that sea power required more than a strong navy, Chadwick sent home a report on British plans for steamship lines in the Pacific. When established, these links would increase British influence in the area at the expense of the United States; and Chadwick asked if the American government could respond by subsidizing American steamship companies in the same region.[4]

Chadwick's work proved so valuable that his stay in London was extended several times, and ultimately he remained at the Court of St. James until 1889, that is, for seven years. His service was called "conspicuously efficient," and Secretary of the Navy Benjamin Tracy in the 1889 annual report singled out Chadwick for special commendation. As the first naval attaché, he remained longer at that post than any later officer, and his record established the British attachéship as the Office of Naval Intelligence's "most important, profitable and desirable overseas assignment."[5]

Chadwick returned to the United States to put the new gunboat *Yorktown* (PG-1) into commission. "She is a beautiful little ship," he wrote to a friend in London, "quite the equal of any of her sort aboard."[6] He pushed his crew to get her ready for a voyage to Europe as part of the Squadron of Evolution with the cruisers *Atlanta, Boston,* and *Chicago,* the first ships of the New Steel Navy. Tracy wanted to test some of the principles being worked out at the Naval War College, an institution as new as the steel ships themselves. As the squadron neared Portugal, it ran into a bad storm that the three cruisers weathered nicely. The much smaller *Yorktown* had rougher going. Gale winds broke the gunboat's tiller and forced Chadwick to lay to. Threatened with broaching, Chadwick improvised a sea anchor, rode out the storm, and proved that he had not lost his seamanship in his years on the beach.

Chadwick's tour in the *Yorktown* lasted from 1889 to 1891. During that time, he exerted very substantial influence on the upper reaches of the navy—far beyond what would be expected of an officer with the rank of commander. One of his objectives was nothing less than a fundamental overhauling of the structure of the Navy Department. As early as 1886, as an attaché from London, he had written very strong letters to William C. Whitney, President Cleveland's secretary of the navy, attacking the bureau system. Briefly, Chadwick argued that the heads of the bureaus were too independent for the good of the service. With no authority short of the secretary of the navy himself to coordinate their activities, the bureau chiefs often were more interested in their own departments than in the navy as a whole. Jealous of their prerogatives, the bureau chiefs frequently maintained their positions by appeals to Congress.

A year later, while Chadwick was home on leave, Whitney asked his advice concerning the formation of a board to assess ship designs submitted to the government. Chadwick replied that such a board should consist of representatives from various branches of the navy and one or two civilians. He also suggested names of officers to serve on this board and outlined his ideas concerning the most important qualities to be sought in the design of new ships: speed, seaworthiness, range, offensive and defensive power, and healthy, comfortable quarters for the officers and men.[7]

When Benjamin Harrison moved into the White House in 1889, Secretary Tracy sounded out Chadwick on departmental reorganization. Chadwick, readying the *Yorktown* for sea, wrote the new secretary in the strongest possible terms:

> I believe no such example of defective organization exists in any civilized country as that which has existed for many years in ours of the

Navy, nor has there in this generation at least been anything approaching it in badness outside of Turkey, Spain or Russia. We have . . . established a system the like of which exists nowhere else, and . . . which had the result (and necessarily) of reducing the service to a painful exhibition of worthless vessels and decaying navy yards.[8]

Tracy acted swiftly, and in less than a month made sweeping changes, the most significant being the consolidation of the five building bureaus into the Board on Construction. Chadwick was pleased with the changes but felt that they did not go far enough.

By 1890, Chadwick's reputation was such that Alfred Thayer Mahan, president of the Naval War College, recommended to Tracy that Chadwick succeed him to that post. When Chadwick failed to show much interest, Mahan proposed that his own tenure at Newport be extended—perhaps just what Chadwick wanted.[9] Certainly Chadwick had a high opinion of Mahan's work and a continuing interest in strategic matters. For instance, in an 1892 letter to Tracy, Chadwick mused on the importance to the United States of the first true American battleships, which had just been laid down, and he forecast with prescience that these new ships would, in a decade, help make the United States the dominant naval power in both the Caribbean and the Pacific.[10]

Chadwick played an active part in one of the most significant of the Tracy reforms. In 1891, the commander sat on the Pythian Board, which altered the navy's method of officer promotion. Chadwick very much favored selection by merit rather than mere length of service, helped write the board's report to that effect, and in usual outspoken fashion personally encouraged Tracy to push the change through.

By this time, Chadwick was counted as one of the leading Young Turks, along with such contemporaries as Bradley A. Fiske, William S. Sims, and Stephen B. Luce. And when Chadwick received a number of top posts in quick succession, he got his chance to put his ideas into practice. In the summer of 1891, he went to the New York Navy Yard to oversee the construction of warships at that facility. Perhaps his most important effort there was to carry on Tracy's fight against the spoils system ashore by fostering the merit system. For instance, he assigned yard superintending positions to the most capable individuals, regardless of politics. He also set up impartial boards to pick the best mechanics by an open selection process. In the first half of 1892, he implemented these same changes at the Washington Navy Yard.

In August 1892, Chadwick moved over to head the Office of Naval Intelligence, a body demoralized by the mismanagement of its previous chief, Captain Charles H. Davis. Hampered by a shortage of qualified personnel and by a serious cutback in funding due to the depression that began in 1893, Chadwick nevertheless made some significant advances. He stressed closer ties with the Naval War College and provided that body with studies on the value of the Hawaiian Islands for the United States and on the type of navy the United States would need if war came with Germany. One expert on the Office of Naval Intelligence observed that Chadwick in his short tour "has been a force in upbuilding the Service which has not been fully appreciated."[11] But Chadwick's biographer nonetheless concludes: "Despite his best efforts, Chadwick could not revive the ONI. But . . . given more time, Chadwick might have smoothed out the problems besetting . . . his office. . . ."[12]

After less than a year, Chadwick moved again. In June 1893, he benefited from the changes wrought by the Pythian Board to jump over one hundred senior officers into the chairmanship of the Bureau of Equipment, where he would stay for four years. His office had a multitude of responsibilities in an age of rapid technological change, so Chadwick had the chance to prove again his capacity for hard work and his grasp of detail. For example, his bureau helped standardize the electrical lighting systems just coming into naval service; his Naval Observatory established a new standard for accuracy in setting time; and his staff experimented unsuccessfully with setting up a homing pigeon system. One of Chadwick's largest responsibilities was to oversee the provision of new battleships such as the *Iowa* and the *Oregon* with electrical plants. His belief that officers should live like gentlemen led him to purchase Royal Copenhagen china, Dorflinza glassware, and Gorham silver for their use on board ship. His concerns extended to living conditions for the crew and led him to recommend the use of aluminum water tanks and the study of electric ventilation systems. With his continuing concern for the professional development of his fellow officers, Chadwick also devoted much energy to building up the new ships' libraries. His catholicity of interests and taste for governmental efficiency are evident in his provision of every wardroom with a copy of Woodrow Wilson's *Congressional Government*. Later, in corresponding with that political scientist, Chadwick would damn congressional irresponsibility and ineptitude, especially as exemplified by such independent powers as "Czar" Reed and "Uncle Joe" Cannon.[13]

This exchange of letters simply reflected Chadwick's continuing interest, writ large, in reducing intraorganizational wrangling. In 1894, he returned to his attack on the bureau system with an article in the Naval Institute *Proceedings,* calling for a reduction in the number of bureaus and a restructuring of the entire Navy Department. His most radical suggestion was for the creation of a general staff to oversee naval operations and to formulate war plans. Although he received some support from Mahan, his arguments bore no immediate fruit. In the long run, however, his ideas anticipated the General Board created in 1900 and the Office of the Chief of Naval Operations set up in 1915.[14]

Chadwick's tour with the Bureau of Equipment came to an end in November 1897 when he went back to sea wearing the new rank of captain and commanding the modern cruiser *New York.* A plum assignment, this powerful warship, as big as some of the Navy's early battleships, flew the flag of Rear Admiral Montgomery Sicard, commander of the North Atlantic Squadron.

Late in January 1898, President William McKinley ordered the armored ship *Maine* detached from the formation and sent to Havana. Chadwick's cruiser was at sea on exercises when word arrived of the *Maine*'s destruction. On 19 February, Sicard appointed Chadwick to the board of inquiry headed by Chadwick's old friend William Sampson. A logical choice as recent chief of the Bureau of Equipment, Chadwick was an expert in such matters as electricity and coal, both key elements in the investigators' considerations.

When the board began its hearings, Chadwick thought it probable that the *Maine* explosion was accidental; but his reading of the evidence convinced him otherwise. Having reached this conclusion, Chadwick fervently hoped for war. On 24 March, he wrote Assistant Secretary of the Navy Theodore Roosevelt, with whom he had corresponded for some years:

> I hope to heaven we shall not listen to any Wall Street compromise. Why should the dirty Jews who have supported this thing go off smiling with full pockets. Honor and economy are both on the side of immediate action. It will be nothing for us to take Cuba.[15]

Chadwick's anti-Semitism, all too common in that day, was mirrored by the man's racism. He believed strongly that the United States should take up the white man's burden from the degenerate, half-Moorish Spaniards.

With war close at hand, Secretary of the Navy John D. Long replaced the ailing Sicard with Sampson, who made Chadwick his chief of staff. Because Chadwick remained commanding officer of the *New York,* he now performed two jobs. Rear Admiral Bowman McCalla later concluded, "No one . . . could have filled the difficult double duties of such a position better than he."[16]

Chadwick took an active part in planning strategy with Sampson. He supported Sampson's proposal on 23 April to strike at the Spanish forts protecting Havana, a plan rather on the model of Farragut's celebrated actions in the Civil War, but the Navy Department rejected such a scheme for fear of Spanish mines and the lack of any troops on hand to exploit a successful operation.[17]

With the outbreak of war imminent, Sampson and Chadwick prepared instead to blockade Havana. On the day Congress declared war, 25 April, the *New York* with the battleships *Iowa* and *Indiana*

The USS *Maine* Court of Inquiry, 1898. Court members (left to right) Chadwick, Chairman William T. Sampson, and William R. Potter examine Ensign Wilfred V. Powelson on board the U.S. Lighthouse Service tender *Mangrove*. Another court member, Adolph Marix, appears in the white coat. The proceedings were concluded in March 1898, and this photograph was published in the 12 April 1898 issue of *Uncle Sam's Navy. Courtesy of the Naval Historical Center.*

supported by lighter ships, was cruising east of the city when Spanish batteries at Matanzas opened fire. Chadwick pressed Sampson to retaliate. Once Sampson granted permission, Chadwick rushed down the ladder from the bridge and shouted to the officer in charge of the portside 8-inch gun: "Aim for 4000 yards, at that bank of earth on the point."[18] The subsequent salvos, which caused no damage, were the first American shots of the war.

For the next five days, Sampson's ships cruised along the north coast of Cuba looking for trouble, but their only excitement came at Cabanas where some dismounted Spanish cavalrymen fired their rifles at the American squadron and were driven away by 4-inch gunfire from the *New York*. The vessels then headed to Key West for coal and news. Here welcome telegrams informed Sampson of George Dewey's victory at Manila and of Spanish Rear Admiral Pascual Cervera's departure from the Cape Verde Islands. Although Cervera's cruiser–destroyer force was quite inferior to Sampson's squadron, the enemy ships might well make mischief by striking at American ports. To allay nervous Americans, the Navy Department formed a separate entity, the Flying Squadron, under Winfield S. Schley, Chadwick's classmate at the Naval Academy in 1864, and ordered it to remain on the North American coast.

Chadwick thought a Spanish descent on U.S. ports possible but unlikely. He considered it far more probable that Cervera would make for Cuba. To interdict such a move, Chadwick began pressing for an expedition to capture Puerto Rico. Sampson agreed that San Juan was a likely base for Cervera; consequently his squadron arrived off that port on 12 May, although no troops were available to effect a landing. In the ensuing exchange of fire between Sampson's ships and the fortifications, the *New York* suffered a Spanish hit that killed one man, wounded two, and did some minor damage to the cruiser while the Spanish defenses suffered no observable damage.

Two days later, Cervera appeared at Curaçao and then turned north toward Cuba. Both Sampson and Chadwick now thought the Spanish commander would seek refuge in the southeastern Cuban port of Santiago, but Secretary Long instructed the American forces to concentrate themselves off Havana and Cienfuegos on the western side of the island. Sampson's ships were to seal off the former port, while Schley's Flying Squadron, now under Sampson's orders, would watch Cienfuegos. When intelligence arrived that the Spaniards had indeed put into Santiago, Sampson directed Schley to blockade them there.

To the surprise of Chadwick and Sampson, Schley's movement to Santiago seemed dilatory in the extreme; once off the harbor, Schley proposed to abandon his position to return to Key West for coal. Chadwick became increasingly incensed at Schley's behavior, especially when Sampson's squadron reached Santiago on 1 June. At a glance, Chadwick regarded Schley's dispositions about ten miles off the port as both timid and defective. Sampson immediately instituted a closer and tighter blockade.

His fleet patrolled without important incident for the next three weeks. To break the monotony, the American ships shelled with little effect Spanish batteries east of Morro Castle. The *New York* during the 6 June bombardment closed to within 2,000 yards of the enemy guns and once again suffered some minor damage for her pains. On 18 June, Chadwick took the *New York* to the newly acquired base of Guantanamo Bay and then looked over the coast at Daiquiri with an eye to its suitability as a landing site.

Two days later, thirty-seven transports arrived, carrying the American expeditionary force under Brigadier General William R. Shafter. Chadwick acted as Sampson's liaison to the army commander. In their initial conference, Chadwick understood Shafter to say that his army's objective was to capture the forts guarding Santiago harbor so that the navy could attack Cervera. Later, Shafter would flatly deny any such intention. The seeds had been sown for a bitter interservice dispute.[19]

Initially, though, the landings proceeded as smoothly as could be expected. To make up for the army's lack of landing craft, Chadwick supplied the boats and crewmen to get the troops ashore. But with his feet dry, Shafter advanced toward the city of Santiago rather than toward the forts protecting the entrance to the harbor. Meeting greater Spanish resistance than expected, Shafter called upon the navy at first for fire support; and when that failed to cow the Spaniards, he asked Sampson to force the harbor entrance. Sampson declined. By this time, he and Chadwick were utterly disillusioned with Shafter's management.[20]

In this frame of mind, the two officers prepared to go ashore on Sunday, 3 July to confer with Shafter. The *New York* thus had left her blockading station and was about seven miles east of the harbor entrance when Chadwick, dressing in his cabin, heard distant gunfire. Dashing to the bridge wearing leggings and spurs, Chadwick saw the Spanish ships coming out. If they headed eastward, the *New*

York would be in the thick of the fight. Instead, they fled to the west. Chadwick and Sampson were startled to see Schley's flagship, the *Brooklyn,* first turn away from the enemy before taking up the pursuit.

Because of her position, the *New York* missed most of the action. As the cruiser hurried past the harbor entrance, Spanish batteries fired on her for fifteen minutes. Chadwick wanted to reply, but Sampson preferred to save ammunition for the enemy ships. Thus, the only shots fired by the *New York* were 4-inch rounds directed with deadly effect at the damaged torpedo boat *Furor.* After passing the grounded cruiser *Oquendo,* Chadwick briefly had the cruiser *Vizcaya* in his sights but held fire when the *Iowa* fouled his range. Before the *New York* could catch up, the last Spanish survivor, the *Cristóbal*

The USS *New York*. Chadwick commanded the armored cruiser *New York,* Admiral Sampson's flagship, at the Battle of Santiago. *Courtesy of the National Archives.*

Colón, was mortally damaged by Schley's *Brooklyn* and the *Oregon.* Partially aground and with her seacocks open, the *Colón* was going down in waters with a deeply shelving bottom. Chadwick hurried on board the sinking ship and thought he saw a chance to save her by pushing her ashore. In a feat of consummate seamanship, Chadwick placed the *New York*'s bow against the *Colón*'s quarter and with the help of lines nudged her onto the beach, thereby obviating the possibility of the *Colón*'s breaking in half. Had the *New York* not been handled with finesse, one observer noted, she too would have gone aground.[21]

Despite the totality of the naval victory, the Spanish troops around Santiago refused to surrender. Consequently, on 6 July, Sampson sent Chadwick to confer with Shafter on a joint strategy. The two agreed to tighten the grip on the forts and the city, which the navy would bombard after giving the Spanish time to evacuate noncombatants. These operations went forward, and the Spanish capitulated to Shafter on 16 July, whereupon the army commander refused to permit Chadwick, as the navy's representative, to sign the surrender agreement. Shafter excused his behavior on the grounds that Sampson had not mentioned the army in his report of the 3 July naval battle. Then, as the Spanish flag came down from Morro Castle, Shafter and Sampson both rushed boarding parties to seize the few Spanish ships lying in the harbor. This donnybrook was resolved only after appeals by both departments to President McKinley and then to the Supreme Court! The latter eventually ruled in favor of the navy, but the episode left a bitter taste in Chadwick's mouth and underlined in his mind the need for greater coordination in the future between the two services.

Chadwick was even more rankled over the extravagant attention paid by the press and the public to Schley. Many papers had hardly mentioned Sampson in their dispatches of the 3 July naval battle. Chadwick quickly entered the swelling controversy in defense of the man he would later call "one of the greatest characters in our navy and one of the finest in our country." Privately, Chadwick wrote to McKinley protesting Schley's promotion to rear admiral. As the debate continued into 1899, Chadwick allowed a war correspondent access to some of his official wartime dispatches, a step that earned Chadwick a letter of reprimand from Secretary Long.

Even more damaging, Chadwick gave an interview the next spring to a *Brooklyn Eagle* reporter in which he generally flayed Schley, objected to his promotion, and suggested that he ask for a court of inquiry. Chadwick later maintained that his remarks were intended to be "entirely private," but it is hard to believe that he was so naive. Such comments from a top officer on such a hot topic naturally made the front pages, and not just of the *Brooklyn Eagle*. Secretary Long reacted strongly, writing Chadwick that the president, who had recently praised Schley, was personally embarrassed. Long then handed Chadwick a letter of severe reprimand for "inexcusable indiscretion." Chadwick was lucky to escape a court-martial, and his career was badly damaged, as many fellow officers would never forgive him for exposing intraservice conflict to the public.[22]

Bittersweet, then, must have been the honors that came Chadwick's way in the midst of the controversy. His home state of West Virginia celebrated Chadwick Day on 10 October 1899. He and Sampson arrived in Morgantown by special train to be greeted with a parade and a reception in which the governor presented Chadwick with a commemorative sword. Ultimately, the Navy Department did reward Chadwick's Spanish–American War efforts by advancing him five numbers in rank.[23]

Also, just before the final storm broke over the *Brooklyn Eagle* interview, Long recognized Chadwick's professional merit by naming him to head the Naval War College and then made him a charter member of the General Board. At Newport, Chadwick stressed the study of history; among works that he encouraged the students to read were those of Jomini, Colomb, and Mahan. Chadwick's guest-speaker list reflects his wide-ranging interests: the historians Frederick Jackson Turner and John Bassett Moore, naval officers Stephen B. Luce and Bowman McCalla, and former Confederate general Fitzhugh Lee.

Strategic and tactical questions received their fair share of attention in the curriculum Chadwick devised for the war college. From gaming exercises, Chadwick became convinced that all the navy's battleships should be concentrated in the Atlantic, a finding that he conveyed to President Theodore Roosevelt. Under Chadwick, the college also looked for the first time at amphibious warfare.

Chadwick was careful to coordinate the work of the Naval War College with the new General Board. Although it was not yet as powerful as he would have liked, the board represented the sort of step forward that Chadwick had been advocating for decades. It immediately began to prove its usefulness by mulling over a variety of significant issues such as the formation of a naval reserve and the

establishment of a Marine Corps battalion for expeditionary service—
the Fleet Marine Force in embryo. On other matters, Chadwick proposed to the General Board that the United States take steps to acquire the Danish West Indies, and that the U.S. Navy set up a
training center on the Great Lakes. In 1903, Chadwick favored, along
with such innovators as William S. Sims, Homer Poundstone, and
Bradley Fiske, the construction of an all-big-gun battleship—this
three years before HMS *Dreadnought* was commissioned.[24]

Busy and as interested in technology as ever, Chadwick also sat on
a special board to establish battleship characteristics, and in 1901 on
the radio board that interviewed Guglielmo Marconi. Experienced
with the problems of carrier pigeons as the chief of the Bureau of
Equipment, Chadwick was quick to embrace the radio.

Chadwick looked to the future as he helped to form the New
Navy, but he could not escape the past. The Sampson–Schley controversy simply would not die. In 1901, Chadwick and a number of
other officers gave information to Edgar S. Maclay, a historian writing on the Spanish–American War. Maclay's conclusions about Schley's
conduct were so caustic that Schley demanded a court of inquiry, a
move Chadwick may have hoped Schley would take a year earlier
when he stated his views to a reporter from the *Eagle*. Lasting for
almost seven weeks, the court called Chadwick to the stand twice.
As expected, his testimony was hostile to Schley on a number of
points, and the court eventually found Schley negligent on several
counts. George Dewey, the chairman of the court and a long-time
friend of Schley, disagreed with the majority; in fact, Dewey blamed
Sampson's supporters for the continued controversy, which he (and
President Roosevelt) felt was bad for the navy.

That Dewey's star was in the ascendant boded ill for Chadwick,
who was removed from the General Board on 26 January 1904. The
stated reason, that Dewey preferred a small board, was shown to be
a mere subterfuge by the appointment shortly thereafter of two lower-
ranking officers to the board.

In November 1903, his term at the Naval War College over,
Chadwick requested assignment first to the Asiatic and then to the
Caribbean Station, but both commands, and another, went to officers
who were his junior. The less important South Atlantic command
proved to be the best Chadwick could obtain. Writing to a friend in
March 1904, he confided that, "I have accepted the South Atlantic
because in the present unrest anything at sea is better than nothing;

Chadwick on board the USS *Brooklyn* in Tangier. Chadwick is shown with one of the seven Moorish chiefs invited on board his flagship when he commanded the South Atlantic Squadron during the Perdicaris Affair. The photograph was taken by a correspondent for *Collier's* magazine and was published in the July 1904 issue. *Courtesy of the U.S. Naval Institute.*

otherwise retirement would have been better than the humiliation to which I have been subjected."[25]

A month later Chadwick assumed command of the South Atlantic Squadron, composed of Schley's old flagship, the *Brooklyn,* plus the aged *Atlanta* and two gunboats. His first cruise took him into the Mediterranean, where in June 1904 he became involved in the tangled Perdicaris affair in Morocco. Tension over the kidnapping of an American citizen, Ion Perdicaris, by the rebel chieftain Ahmed ben Mohammed Raisuli led to fears for the safety of the U.S. consulate in Tangier. Chadwick sent marines ashore, the first American troops on that ground in almost a century. The arrival of the European Squadron made its commander, Theodore Jewell, the senior American officer on the scene. The arrival of British and French forces brought the crisis to an end, but their actions appear to have kindled in Chadwick a distrust of those European nations.

Chadwick returned home in early 1905. When his older ships were sent into reserve, freeing their personnel for the large number of new ships coming into service, Chadwick's command began melting away. Hoping to turn this development to his advantage, Chadwick sought transfer to the more important command of either the Caribbean or the Asiatic Squadron. On 6 October 1905, Chadwick became a rear admiral, but the promotion took him nowhere. In fact, he found himself passed over a second time as squadron commands were given to three officers his junior. Next he asked for a place back on the General Board, only to be told that Admiral Dewey had reduced the size of that body. Instead, Chadwick was offered League Island Navy Yard. Rather than accept it, Chadwick chose retirement, which became official on 28 February 1906, one day before his sixtieth birthday.

At an age when most men would relax in their front porch swings, Chadwick embarked in a second profession: writing. More correctly, he now entered full-time the waters he had tentatively tested earlier. Back in 1892, Putnam's had published a pamphlet by Chadwick entitled "Temperament, Disease, and Health." Right after the Spanish–American War, he had written articles that had appeared in *Scribner's* and the *Century Magazine* on the naval side of that conflict. Those articles had received enough favorable attention that the Harper publishing company had asked Chadwick in 1903 to compose a book-length study on the background to the Civil War for its prestigious "American Nation" series. That project had been put on a back burner when Chadwick returned to sea duty in 1904. Still, he did manage to assess the Russo–Japanese naval balance in 1904 for *Collier's,* and in 1905 he continued his perennial crusade for naval reorganization with the article "The Great Need of the United States Navy" in *Munsey's Magazine.*

Once retired, Chadwick turned with his usual energy to the writing of history. So deeply did he immerse himself that he paid little attention for almost a decade to contemporary matters, although he lodged a strong protest in 1914 against the naming of a new destroyer the USS *Schley.* Chadwick joined the American Historical Association, strongly supported the Naval History Society, which was founded in 1909, and came to be on close personal terms with such leaders in the field as James Ford Rhodes and Albert Bushnell Hart.

Chadwick's output was prodigious. Within ten years, he had written four books, edited another, published nine articles, and contributed lengthy chapters to two more volumes. His first major undertaking was to complete for Harper the volume *Causes of the Civil
War, 1859–1861.* Chadwick's work in the original sources was typically thorough. Albert Hart considered the first draft too long in
places, questioned Chadwick's emphasis on Fort Sumter and his
omission of other topics, but thought so much of the final product
that he tried unsuccessfully to get Chadwick an honorary degree from
Harvard.[26]

Chadwick looked next to the Spanish–American War. Calling his
study a "monument to Sampson," Chadwick delved into newspaper
accounts, the *Congressional Record,* English and Spanish books, the
reports of the secretary of the navy, ships' logs, and other archival
sources. Determined to produce a balanced and authoritative account, Chadwick spent eight months immersed in the Spanish government records at Madrid. In 1909, Scribner's published the first
volume of the trilogy: *The Relations of the United States and Spain:
Diplomacy.* Although some of the language sounds dated today, with
its talk of a "century of racial strife" and the "Moro-Iberian characteristics of the modern Spaniard," the work stands up quite well in
its treatment of the Monroe Doctrine and the first Cuban revolt.

But Chadwick's best work appeared in 1911, with publication of
the second and third volumes of the set, *The Relations of the United
States and Spain: The Spanish–American War.* In straightforward style,
Chadwick recounted the military course of the struggle; and although he steered clear this time of the Sampson–Schley shoals, he
did not hesitate to come to some pointed conclusions. He particularly castigated the army for its unpreparedness and the entire military establishment for its pathetically inadequate provisions for interservice cooperation.

When the volumes were released, they received much favorable
notice. Typically, the *New York Times* called them "The worthiest of
the contributions to the history of our latest war." Roosevelt recommended that Chadwick send copies to the crowned heads of Spain,
Great Britain, and Germany, all of whom knew Chadwick personally. In fact, Chadwick's history has withstood the test of time. Graham Cosmas, writing in 1971, called it "the most thorough and
judicious military account of the conflict." David Trask, in 1981,
praised Chadwick's work as "the only important general history of

the conflict," and added that more recent treatments "do not add measurably to Chadwick's findings." In perhaps the highest praise of all, the three volumes were reprinted, unchanged, in 1968.[27]

With the outbreak of World War I, Chadwick began collaboration with George H. Allen of the University of Pennsylvania on the *History of World War I*, published by George Barrie's in 1916. Naturally, Chadwick concentrated on the naval side of the conflict, and given his strongly heretical views on the war, his treatment was surprisingly evenhanded. At the same time and at the age of seventy, Chadwick edited the papers of Admiral Graves and other documents pertaining to the naval side of the Yorktown campaign for the Naval Records Society.

Actually, Chadwick's selection to assist in the Allen study of World War I is surprising, as, his abilities as a historian aside, his views on the war had isolated him from virtually all of his colleagues in the naval profession. In fact, Chadwick had become one of the few prominent American defenders of Germany. How he arrived at this point is something of a puzzle: he was of English descent; his service in London as attaché had been pleasant; and he had enjoyed, at least for a time, many English friends. In 1901, as president of the Naval War College, he had warned the officers there about German expansionist designs on Brazil.[28]

He claimed in 1915 that it was the Moroccan crisis that had opened his eyes to "La perfide Albion." Be that as it may, in the fall of 1914, he wrote Secretary of the Navy Josephus Daniels blaming the war on Great Britain, especially on King Edward VII, that "mischief maker" who had arranged the Anglo–French alliance. Chadwick urged strongly that arms sales to Great Britain be banned, and in April 1915 he wrote to his old correspondent Woodrow Wilson to press the same case.[29]

As the war ground on, Chadwick increasingly saw cosmic forces— in his words, "deeply occult forces"—at work. Germany must survive, he argued, or Europe would be divided between Russia and Great Britain, the Slavic threat would move to the North Sea, and the British would turn on the United States, treating it as badly as they had Germany. Behind it all, he sensed the Jew:

> We should cry a halt to that besmirched Jew, Isaacs, and his fellows, British, French, American. We are racking our country asunder at their command. . . . Our country has never been so thoroughly in the hands of the plutocracy as now.[30]

This sort of nonsense caused him to break with most of his old friends.

Chadwick saw in the Moroccan crisis the start of World War I. An angry exchange of letters, in which Chadwick questioned Roosevelt's North African policy and Roosevelt cast aspersions on Chadwick's patriotism and loyalty as a citizen and naval officer, brought to an end two decades of correspondence.

In the end, his views on the war probably contributed to Chadwick's physical collapse. Shortly after the United States declared war on Germany, he suffered a severe paralytic stroke. Henceforth an invalid, he was nursed by his ever faithful wife, Cornelia, until he expired of pneumonia on 27 January 1919. Chadwick was buried with full military honors back home in Morgantown, West Virginia.

It was a sad ending to a life of accomplishment. If Chadwick's maverick views cut him off, at the last, from the realm of policymakers, that same outspokeness had done his navy and his country a great deal of good over the years. His accomplishments as America's first naval attaché, his substantial grasp of a number of disparate fields, his intolerance of inefficiency, and his sheer capacity for hard work made him one of the truly significant, if underrated, figures in the rebirth of the U.S. Navy. That his most lasting memorial, his history of the Spanish–American War, is a first rate piece of scholarship is all the greater tribute to this multifaceted man.

FURTHER READING

Chadwick has attracted only one biographer: Paolo E. Coletta, whose *French Ensor Chadwick: Scholarly Warrior* is a balanced assessment of Chadwick as an officer and as a man. Coletta does, however, gloss over Chadwick's anti-Semitism, racism, and virulent male chauvinism (Chadwick in 1915 wrote an article excoriating women teachers who, he complained, feminized male youths). Coletta's annotated bibliography and extensive essay on sources are especially valuable.

Among those works that give passing mention to Chadwick, Jeffrey M. Dorwart's *Conflict of Duty: The U.S. Navy's Intelligence Dilemma, 1919–1945* offers an appreciation of Chadwick's importance to the Office of Naval Intelligence. Walter Millis, in *The Martial Spirit,* and Hyman G. Rickover, in *How the Battleship "Maine" Was Destroyed,* both give some attention to Chadwick's role on the Sampson board of inquiry. Ivan Musicant's *U.S. Armored Cruisers: A Design and Operational History* offers glimpses of Chadwick's war service on board the *New York*. Robert Seager II, in *Alfred Thayer Mahan: The Man and His Letters,* examines fleetingly the relationship between Chadwick and Mahan, especially in the early 1890s. Although

Ronald Spector's *Admiral of the New Empire: The Life and Career of George Dewey* is disappointing on the Sampson–Schley affair and its aftermath, Spector does offer some valuable information on Chadwick's fear of German expansion in 1901. In the popular *Admirals of American Empire,* Richard S. West, Jr. pays substantial attention in passing to Chadwick.

Of those officers close to Chadwick, Robley D. Evans, in his two volumes *A Sailor's Log* and *An Admiral's Log,* and Caspar Goodrich, in *Rope Yarns from the Old Navy,* are both valuable. Winfield S. Schley's *Forty-Five Years under the Flag* is predictably hostile. Unfortunately, William T. Sampson died before he could write his memoirs, although W. A. M. Goode's *With Sampson through the War* partially compensates for this gap.

Very few of Chadwick's private papers survive. Aside from slim folders at the University of West Virginia and at Princeton, all relating to his publishing activities, no single collection of Chadwick papers exists. Some of Chadwick's official correspondence is scattered in various record groups in the National Archives, and a handful of early letters reside in the ZB and ZV files at the Historical Research Branch of the Navy Historical Center, Washington, D.C. Compensating for these problems to a substantial degree and readily accessible to the researcher is the lengthy and excellent volume entitled *French Ensor Chadwick: Selected Letters and Papers* edited by Doris M. Maguire. Elsewhere, some of Chadwick's correspondence relating to the Naval War College can be found in the *Letters and Papers of Alfred Thayer Mahan,* edited by Robert Seager II and Doris M. Maguire. Other Chadwick letters appear in the *Papers of John Davis Long,* edited by Gardner W. Allen.

For a complete listing of Chadwick's publications, see Coletta's biography of Chadwick. For assessments of Chadwick's abilities as a historian, consult Graham Cosmas, *An Army for Empire;* Walter R. Herrick, Jr., *The American Naval Revolution;* and David F. Trask, *The War with Spain in 1898.*

NOTES

1. Paolo E. Coletta, *French Ensor Chadwick: Scholarly Warrior,* 11–15.
2. Richard S. West, Jr., *Admirals of American Empire,* 247. Chadwick and his wife had no children.
3. Jeffrey M. Dorwart, *Conflict of Duty: The U.S. Navy's Intelligence Dilemma, 1919–1945,* 138.
4. Chadwick to William C. Whitney, 7 October 1887, in Doris D. Maguire, ed., *French Ensor Chadwick: Selected Letters and Papers,* 158–59.
5. Dorwart, *Conflict of Duty,* 138; Albert Gleaves, *The Life of an American Sailor: Rear Admiral William Hemsley Emory, USN,* 123; Coletta, *Chadwick,* 31–38. Chadwick's wife, Cornelia, was the niece of U.S. Ambassador Lowell. Chadwick and Lowell became friends, and that relationship must have facilitated Chadwick's contacts with British officials and industrialists.

6. Chadwick to Henry White, 7 May 1889, in Maguire, *Chadwick, Letters and Papers,* 156–57.

7. Chadwick to William C. Whitney, 28 September and 9 October 1886, and Whitney to Chadwick, 2 April 1887, in ibid., 124–27, 139–41, 144–48.

8. Chadwick to Benjamin F. Tracy, 31 May 1889, in ibid., 172–75.

9. Coletta, *Chadwick,* 54. Coletta believes that Chadwick's reticence was probably deliberate in order to keep Mahan at Newport. Robert Seager II, *Alfred Thayer Mahan: The Man and His Letters,* 223, 241.

10. Chadwick to Tracy, 21 May 1892, in Maguire, *Chadwick, Letters and Papers,* 172–75.

11. Dorwart, *Conflict of Duty,* 6.

12. Coletta, *Chadwick,* 60.

13. In fact, Chadwick privately published in 1901 an essay entitled "An Unresolved Problem in Our Governmental System," in which he condemned the "vicious" committee system. See Coletta, *Chadwick,* 136–37.

14. French E. Chadwick, "Naval Department Organization," U.S. Naval Institute *Proceedings* 20, no. 3 (1894): 493–526.

15. Chadwick to Theodore Roosevelt, 24 March 1898, in Maguire, *Chadwick, Letters and Papers,* 187.

16. Quoted in Paolo E. Coletta, *Bowman Hendry McCalla: A Fighting Sailor,* 79. Chadwick had an equally positive view of McCalla and had written letters in his behalf when McCalla was court-martialed for striking a seamen on board the *Enterprise,* and tried to obtain his appointment to Boards of Survey concerning several ships during the time McCalla languished at Mare Island after his court-martial.

17. David F. Trask, *The War with Spain in 1898,* 90.

18. Ivan Musicant, *U.S. Armored Cruisers: A Design and Operational History,* 31.

19. Trask, *The War with Spain in 1898,* 203–5.

20. Coletta, *Chadwick,* 88.

21. W. A. M. Goode, *With Sampson through the War,* 209–10; French E. Chadwick, *The Relations of the United States and Spain: The Spanish–American War,* 2:157.

22. *New York Times,* 27 April 1900, 1:5; 1 May 1900, 11:3, 2 May 1900, 1:1, 3 May 1900, 2:2; Coletta, *Chadwick,* 104–7; Robert Seager II and Doris D. Maguire, eds., *Letters and Papers of Alfred Thayer Mahan,* 673.

23. ZB File, Historical Research Branch, Naval Historical Center, Washington, D.C.

24. Coletta, *Chadwick,* 115–21.

25. Chadwick to Alston G. Dayton, 5 March 1904, in Maguire, *Chadwick, Letters and Papers,* 323–25.

26. For a complete listing of Chadwick's publications, see Coletta, *Chadwick,* 225–27.

27. *New York Times,* 24 September 1911, 16:565; Graham A. Cosmas, *An Army for Empire,* 1; Trask, *The War with Spain in 1898,* ix.

28. Ronald Spector, *Admiral of the New Empire: The Life and Career of George Dewey*, 132.

29. Chadwick to Joseph Daniels, 24 September 1914, Maguire, *Chadwick, Letters and Papers*, 539–41.

30. Chadwick to Daniels, 31 August 1915, Chadwick to Daniels, 5 October 1915, Maguire, *Chadwick, Letters and Papers*, 603–7, 610–11.

BRADLEY ALLEN FISKE:
INVENTOR AND REFORMER
IN UNIFORM

BENJAMIN FRANKLIN COOLING

A clue to one of the Steel Navy's most gifted officers appears on the title page of his autobiography.[1] Bradley Allen Fiske's self-styled list of accomplishments suggests that he was the greatest naval inventor of his day, an author of facile pen and eclectic tastes, and a well-respected senior leader in the Steel Navy. Not appearing in any order under his name, Fiske's list includes:

> Former Aide for Operations of the Fleet,
> President of the U.S. Naval Institute,
> Gold Medalist of the U.S. Naval Institute,
> the Franklin Institute of Pennsylvania,
> and the Aero Club of America.
> Author of "Electricity in Theory and Practice,"
> "War Time in Manila,"
> "The Navy as A Fighting Machine," etc.
> Inventor of the Gun Director System,
> the Naval Telescope Sight, the Stadimeter,
> the Turret Range Finder, the Horizonmeter,
> the Torpedoplane, etc. etc. etc.

One quickly perceives that Fiske was no ordinary sailor. Holder of nearly sixty patents for his inventions, he also authored six books and over sixty articles during his lifetime. In addition, he ably served the U.S. Navy as junior officer, senior commander, reformist administrator, and philosopher of both sea and air power in the best tradition of Luce and Mahan. He has been accorded credit as progenitor of the office of the Chief of Naval Operations, the Naval Consulting

Bradley Allen Fiske. Photograph taken in October 1912 while Fiske commanded a division of the Atlantic Fleet. *Courtesy of the Naval Historical Center.*

Board, the Naval Research Laboratory, and even the Council of National Defense and National Security Council. As such, he merits recognition among the makers of American naval tradition. Most of these accomplishments came despite internal naval opposition. Fiske was a maverick, a "Young Turk" in the Progressive Era navy. Carrying more spirit than weight in his diminutive 130-pound body, Fiske was always a loyal member of the Annapolis "band of brothers." Yet, at times, he allowed his blue-and-gold professionalism to place him at variance with accepted precepts of civil–military relations in a democracy. Above all, however, Fiske's moral integrity and strength of character stood as a model for combating institutional powers of reactionism and negativism.[2]

Fiske's early years were unpretentious. Born to an Episcopal clergyman's family in upstate New York, in 1854, he quickly entered the orderly world of established church and loving relatives. He displayed youthful inventive genius on questions of desalination and two-part cuff buttons. When his family moved to parishes in the Midwest, the visits of an uncle then attending the Naval Academy (and later to die while fighting under Farragut at New Orleans during the Civil War) led Fiske to matriculate at the school in 1870. He proceeded through four years of solid technical education, graduating with a reputation for intelligence, spirit, dancing, and attraction to Annapolis belles. He befriended Washington Irving Chambers and Albert Michelson, both destined to contribute meaningfully to scientific and professional knowledge. Above all, Midshipman Fiske professed a "profound reverence for the navy" and the desire to be a good officer.[3]

The Annapolis class of 1874 joined a navy in the throes of postwar budgetary retrenchment and rapid obsolescence. The United States had turned inward, binding up wounds of civil war and seeking to finish development of the country. Stirrings of the search for overseas markets could be sensed, although neither government nor the business community yet proved ready to pursue them. Such a "continentalist" focus obviated the need for a sizable fleet. The navy's cruising squadrons returned to showing the flag on foreign stations, but the great wartime fleet of ironclads and steam sloops disintegrated in reserve or were scrapped. Naval leaders basked in the rich afterglow of a victory over an inferior, if rebellious, Southern Confederacy. But, generally, citizens might ask with some validity, "Who is going to fight with us?" Potential European enemies remained unsure of future directions for sea power and busied themselves with experimentation. Together, the world's navies stood on the threshold of revolution, a revolution born of invention and technology—a revolution that Bradley Fiske would join.[4]

Newly married by 1882, Fiske chafed at the tedium of a naval career. He saw little chance of anything beyond "a tiresome alternation of monotonous cruises at sea and profitless tours ashore." He spent much of his time tinkering with inventions—a device for measuring a ship's speed, a sounding machine or fathometer, a boat-detaching contraption, and a breech-loading, rapid-fire musket (quickly judged by naval authorities as no better than that already in service). The U.S. Navy did adopt Fiske's signal lantern, but when he turned to marketing his mechanical pencils and a typewriter, he was quickly faced with threats of patent infringement. Undaunted, Fiske continued to use ship and shore assignments for his creative talents. But, on at least three occasions, he thought seriously of leaving the navy.[5]

The catalyst for keeping Fiske in the service proved to be electricity. Spurred on by Park Benjamin, an old Annapolis classmate and now scientific consultant in New York, Fiske took leave to study the subject. Thomas Alva Edison had invented the electric light, and Alexander Graham Bell the telephone, and Fiske saw great potential for electricity in the navy. He determined to blend the twin facets of line duty and science to mold his career. Line duties would have to come first (which Fiske occasionally forgot), but here was a way for him to apply his restless, inventive mind to improve the sea service. Lacking formal naval laboratory facilities, Fiske would improvise, using ships and shore billets as testing grounds for his schemes, while relying on support from the private sector for the materials to make his inventions.[6]

Fiske's interest in electricity coincided with the American naval renaissance of the 1880s and 1890s. As the United States began to look outward for new markets, isolationism gave way to imperialism, stimulated by a complex blend of culture, idealism, and economics. Whether or not commerce followed the flag or vice versa, expansionism promised international conflict—hence the need for a modernized navy. Congress authorized money for the rebuilding program, and American industry and inventors provided the tools. All of this required steel ships, larger ordnance, and an industrial base, as well as organizational and administrative means to bring it about. Officers and men with foresight, determination, and creative energy soon appeared, Fiske among them. Yet, they would be frustrated by the traditionalism and entrenched bureaucratic attitudes that are predictable in an old-line institution. The thirty-year "transition" to the mature Steel Navy would be fraught with roadblocks, but also with opportunities, as Bradley Fiske would discover as he helped the Steel Navy along the road to completion.[7]

Fiske was assigned to supervising some of the first ordnance work for the "ABCD" cruisers—the first steel warships of the reborn fleet. But, he also found time to write authoritatively on the application of electricity to operating the new warships. Publication of his ideas would be vital, both for sharing information with brother officers and for establishing his credentials in the scientific community. His textbook *Electricity in Theory and Practice* (1887) would enjoy ten printings and a twenty-two-year sales run. At the same time, Fiske moved apace with his inventions. Inter- as well as intraship communication via telephone, apparatus designed to work both the ordnance and ammunition hoists via electricity, and even devices for easing shipyard operations with labor-saving electricity came from his fertile brain. He forged ties with commercial organizations such as the Western Electric and General Electric companies, which provided space, money, and support for his inventive work.[8]

As new warships joined the fleet, everyone discovered "kinks" that needed correcting to make them seaworthy and operational. For one thing, Fiske discovered that open-sight gunnery no longer obtained in this age of greater range for guns and greater speed for vessels. Fiske soon applied his talents to gunnery problems. He affixed a telescope to the sight bar of a gun in 1886, training and elevating the piece using electric motors. This contrivance showed great promise for continuous battery fire. By 1896, he had added other devices such as an electrical range finder (for which the Franklin Institute awarded Fiske its Elliott Cresson Gold Medal in 1893), and the basic scheme for a gunnery plotting room below decks. Though Fiske met continual rebuffs for his ideas in the U.S. Navy, foreign naval ministries found many of those ideas most attractive.[9]

Fiske began to expand his range of interest into areas appropriately termed the "nerves of a warship." These included vital functions such as steering and communication, as Fiske developed an engine-order telegraph, a helm indicator, an engine speed and direction indicator, and an electric steering mechanism. Despite some often very tepid responses from his fellow officers, Fiske could note that by the winter of 1896 a number of American warships were serving as floating test sites for his inventions. His range finders could be found on board the cruisers *Baltimore, San Francisco, Columbia, New York,* and *Cincinnati,* as well as the battleships *Maine, Texas, Indiana, Massachusetts,* and *Oregon.* His range indicators similarly were employed in the *San Francisco, Cincinnati, Maine, Texas,* and *Indiana,* and were on order for the *Massachusetts* and the *Oregon.* Stadimeters (which proved basically as reliable for range finding as Fiske's more sophisticated equipment) found use in the *New York, Cincinnati, Maine, Texas, Indiana, Columbia,* and other cruisers *Raleigh, Montgomery,* and *Minneapolis.* Helm-indicators had been issued to the *New York, Indiana,* and *Massachusetts;* and the *New York* also had a speed and direction indicator and the steering telegraph (as did the *Indiana* and the *Massachusetts*)—all of Fiske's invention. Sensitive to criticism, Fiske noted specifically that this equipment was radically new, and not a mere copy of or improvement on someone else's invention.[10]

Fiske's sensitivity was well founded. "I was frequently told by officers that an officer who really understood his profession could not have seriously considered such a ridiculous idea [as the naval telescope sight]," he noted in his memoirs. Commander Robley D. Evans, Fiske's commanding officer on board the *Yorktown* in 1891, thought so little of the device that he dismissed Fiske's contribution out of hand. Commodore Frank Ramsay, chief of the Bureau of Navigation in the 1890s and "czar" over personnel matters, had openly declared that all naval officers were the same except in rank, and he deplored Fiske's defiance of precedent. Perhaps it was Fiske's personality, his inventive genius, or his appearance of being more brilliant than others in an institution that stood for rank, order, and playing it safe. Still, this was a new age, a New Navy, wherein precocious but loyal bantams like Fiske could contribute as much as the gold-braided senior captains of holystoned deck or Washington bureau.[11]

Later generations might take technology for granted, as they did electricity; but it was not so in Fiske's day. Technology remained mysterious, and Fiske's era was captivated by this mystery. The mystery went beyond gun deck and steam room. Fiske himself caught the spirit when he recorded his "almost awe-struck feeling" in 1911 at being able to transmit a wireless order to a subordinate battleship squadron that was over the horizon and beyond visual signaling. A half-hour later, he wrote, that ship "with white foam at her bow, dashing forward to rejoin us" thrilled him, even though he knew fully well how it was all accomplished. Fiske clearly understood what this portended for the future, and how different it was from the past. But, how could he unravel the mystery for his brother officers so that they could learn to master the technology so vital to the navy's success? From the earliest, Fiske determined to change men's attitudes to help them prepare for the mission of war.[12]

Of course, the conservatism of men like Ramsay may have aided Fiske. Ramsay had once said that one officer could as easily resolve a mechanical design problem as any other, so officers should continuously rotate between ship and shore assignments. This posture forced Fiske to test his apparatus under actual conditions at sea. Furthermore, despite Ramsay and Evans, Fiske found some persons who were amenable to his ideas. Superiors such as Bowman McCalla and John G. Walter as chiefs of navigation, and Montgomery Sicard, William Folger, and William Sampson in similar billets at the ordnance bureau, as well as Fiske's shipboard commanders such as Francis Bunce of the *Atlanta,* Winfield Scott Schley of the *Baltimore,* and J. C. Watson of the *San Francisco,* all proved supportive. Such reformist or insurgent colleagues as Austin Knight, William Sims, and

Albert Gleaves also traded ideas and banter in the course of stimulating Fiske's work. Beyond the mere world of invention, however, Fiske's mind was shaped by the naval intellectuals of the period—Henry C. Taylor, Stephen B. Luce, and Alfred Thayer Mahan; and he was indebted to still others, such as Captain Royal B. Bradford (to Fiske, the true father of electricity in the navy), for their ideas and advice. When Fiske opined in his memoirs that *"nobody was the father of the new navy* [his emphasis]," he was making an important observation. The creation of a powerful yet delicate instrument such as a navy required hard work and teamwork. It also took abrasive friction to set it in motion, with a man of Fiske's temperament and perseverance sharpening the new tools of technology on the rock of traditionalism.[13]

Fiske had the opportunity to test one of his devices in battle before the end of the century. Of course, all of his instruments on board American men-of-war were tested during the short war with Spain; but Fiske personally worked his own stadimeter, a device for measuring ranges by a two-mirror system, during the battle of Manila Bay. He had gone out to the Far East in 1897 as lieutenant and navigation officer in the rather innocuous gunboat *Petrel*. The cruise in the Orient proved basically uneventful, and Fiske found time to experiment with his sounding machine and dabble at radio wave experiments. He met naval officers of the rising imperial Germany and judged them nautically superior to his comrades in the American service. He enjoyed relaxing interludes with his wife, Josephine Harper, and their daughter, Caroline, who perpetuated the naval tradition of following loved ones around the globe for chance meetings at places like Hong Kong in the days before overseas bases. Then, with the destruction of the USS *Maine* at Havana, Cuba, on 15 February 1898, Fiske and the small Asiatic Squadron had their first real encounter with combat.[14]

Commodore George Dewey took his squadron into Manila Bay on 1 May 1898 and destroyed the anchored Spanish fleet in a brief but glorious battle. Fiske had rigged up a platform high on the *Petrel*'s mast, where he took ranges with his stadimeter during the conflict, transmitting these ranges to the ship's commander below, and thence to the gun captains. Thus, Fiske has been cited as the first person to direct naval gunfire from aloft during a battle. The result was less effective fire than Fiske would have liked. Searching for an explanation for the generally dismal performance of the flotilla as a whole, Fiske concluded that it resulted from working their pieces. Fiske himself came away from the battle of Manila Bay with the *Petrel* commander's accolades for "eminent and conspicuous conduct," and Dewey included his name on a short list of officers who had excelled in their work. Dewey, henceforth, became one of Fiske's idols.[15]

The "Young Turks," or reformists such as Fiske, rose through attrition and sequential promotion to positions of power during the fifteen years after the war with Spain. For much of the time, Fiske continued to alternate sea and shore duty, serving during the Philippine Insurrection in lesser billets on board the *Yorktown* and the monitor *Monadnock,* and from 1903 to 1906 as executive officer of the aging battleship *Massachusetts* in the Atlantic fleet, before ever receiving his first command—the fast, protected cruiser *Minneapolis*—at age fifty-two! He cheered on and helped a jingoistic nation in wresting control of the newly acquired Philippines from the insurgency of Emilio Aguinaldo, and he marveled that Filipinos did not yearn for statehood as citizens back home did. Very soon, Bradley Fiske openly embraced the naval and imperial philosophies of Mahan and the navalists. Allied with congressional imperialists such as Senator Henry Cabot Lodge and Congressman Richmond P. Hobson, the navalists viewed the United States as an industrial and commercial giant among nations and demanded a big navy, big warships, and naval power "second to none." Such policies were appropriately reflected in Republican politics and control of Washington after the Spanish–American War.[16]

Fiske's creative energies never flagged during this period. Possibly periodic tours such as his assignment as inspector of ordnance at the E. W. Bliss Company in Brooklyn permitted him the time he needed for creative thought. Yet, despite progressively more responsible and demanding assignments after 1906, including command of the armored cruiser *Tennessee* in 1908–10, Fiske continued to invent and add significantly to useful naval devices. He patented improvements to automotive torpedoes and a whistle to alert shipboard crew members to the closing of watertight doors during an emergency, and he upgraded many of his earlier target and range-finding inventions. He rejoiced at reports from friends about their success with his range finders elsewhere in the Great White Fleet. By 1912, this restless inventor turned to yet another new field—aeronautics, patenting a torpedo-carrying airplane and proclaiming to all who would listen that he had not just discovered a new weapon, but a whole new method of warfare. By 1917, Fiske confidently predicted that a study comparable to Mahan's would someday emerge dealing with the impact of air power on history. But, it was also true that, through the years, many of his early inventions had grown obsolete. Other officers, such as William Sims, used their more entrepreneurial assets to force modernization and systemization of such matters as gunnery drills upon a recalcitrant naval bureaucracy. In retrospect, it seems that Fiske fit the image of the true scientist. Content to tinker with and create ever newer mechanisms, he often left their institutional implementation to other people.[17]

By 1911, Fiske's career had assumed new directions, befitting a man of recognized brilliance and energy but tasking in terms of responsibility for the formulation of policy and the higher art of naval warfare. Promoted to rear admiral on 3 August of that year, Fiske was also elected president of the Naval Institute. He had served on the principally advisory General Board, and would serve also on the Joint Army–Navy Board and as president of the Naval War College. Certainly a worthy successor to Taylor, Luce, and Mahan at the school, he had developed interests by this stage that lay more in overall naval improvement than in merely upgrading the curriculum. During all of this, Fiske found time to jointly patent an automatic gun-pointing device with fellow inventor Elmer Sperry, and to earn distinction as the first admiral to fly in an airplane. He also argued persuasively for greater recognition of inventors in the U.S. Navy.[18]

The apex of Fiske's career would result from his widening of interests and vistas as a senior naval leader. From 1913 until 1915 he served as aid for operations in the administration of Secretary of the Navy Josephus Daniels. Here lay all of the seminal career opportunities available to one of Fiske's years and experience; here was a chance to apply his intense passion for progressive reform as a means of bringing the sea service up to strength and proficiency for its mission; but here, too, lay the greatest challenge in Fiske's career. His nemesis, in this instance, would come less from the rigid constraints of institutionalism (which he had battled his whole career) than from a personality conflict with the top civilian in the department and his distinct differences with the political agenda of the new Democratic administration of Woodrow Wilson. Secretary Daniels personified the peace-focused New Freedom philosophy of the Wilson administration. A North Carolina newspaper editor with an aversion to aristocratic military and naval leaders and industrialists (it was said), Daniels feared the loss of civilian control in the Navy Department. Even his predecessor, George Von Lengerke Meyer, had told Daniels at their first official meeting to keep the control and

power in the department "here," tapping the large desk in the secretary's office. Therefore, when Daniels concentrated on social reforms such as abolition of liquor consumption on board ship and
greater education for the rated enlisted force, he particularly tried to
avoid decisions that would accrue power to the admirals and the
naval line. He especially opposed the reformers' demand for a counterpart of the U.S. Army's new general staff, and establishment of a
powerful chief of naval operations who would control both civil and
military functions in the U.S. Navy. In short, Daniels and Fiske
quickly embarked on a collision course.[19]

Part of Fiske's problem was that although he liked Daniels personally, he doubted Daniels's ability to manage the navy. In fact, he
doubted any civilian's ability to manage the navy. He held to the
rather grandiose notion that a secretary should be "a Hercules of
intellect, a man capable of mentally grasping a difficult problem in
the way a trained wrestler physically grasps an antagonist." Fiske's
idols were navy men, strong of mind and character—Taylor, Luce,
Mahan, and Dewey. Taylor had convinced Fiske of the need for
"foresight" in deciding a course of action. He had made a "futurist"
of Fiske. Moreover, Taylor weaned officers from too close attention
just to "the materials of warfare such as guns, etc.," said Fiske in
his memoirs. He showed them that material objects were merely the
tools of strategists, "just as a workman uses a hammer." Luce and
Mahan similarly broadened Fiske's thought patterns, and all his teachers
received their pupil's gratitude for their knowledge, farsighted goals
for the navy, and tact.[20] In Fiske's estimation, Josephus Daniels lacked
all these qualities.

The principal points of contention between Fiske and Daniels contrasted the secretary's focus on the economic, moral, and social aspects of naval improvement and Fiske's focus on the military side.
From about 1903, when Fiske had heard Luce leccture on the lack
of any comprehensive naval policy, the inventor had been obsessed
with resolving that problem. By 1905, he had begun to shift his
writing from technical subjects to topics that would guide the rest
of his professional life—organization, policy, and preparedness. His
tour with the relatively new General Board (established in 1900)
convinced him of the impotence of that largely advisory body. Its
war planning seemed nothing more than the collection of discon-
nected data, and it lacked the power to control the independent bureaus, which Fiske and such other reformers as William Sims held
accountable for poorly designed warships and the neglect of funda-

Josephus Daniels. While serving as aid for operations, the highest position in the uniformed navy, Fiske had an abrasive relationship with the man he served, Secretary of the Navy Daniels. *Courtesy of the Library of Congress.*

mentals such as gunnery training. Fiske likewise found Republican Secretary Meyer's stopgap measure of an aid system inadequate. In theory, four aids—for operations, material, inspections, and personnel—would coordinate the bureaus engaged in those areas of activity; but Congress failed to legally sanction the arrangement, and the aids became merely additional advisers to the secretary with no real power. The ideal solution to Fiske and the reformers was the model of the German military staff. However, they undoubtedly miscalculated the deep-seated American aversion to such trappings of European militarism, and particularly the Wilson administration's distrust of that system.[21]

Fiske's duties as aid for operations were clearly delineated in Meyer's final report as secretary. The incumbent in this billet would give "his entire attention and study to the operations of the fleet." Working in conjunction with the War College and the General Board on war plans and strategic matters under normal circumstances, the aid also would be "prepared to advise promptly as to the movements of ships and to submit such orders as are necessary to carry into effect campaign plans recommended by the General Board and approved by the Secretary" in any emergency. Meyer believed that the navy was "on a war basis, the council of his [four] aids serving as a strategy board." This would have been impossible under the arrangement that existed prior to the aid system, as the chief of the Bureau of Navigation had so many normal duties attending his position that he could not devote sufficient time or thought to strategic and operational issues. Whether or not Daniels clearly understood the role of his aids or how to employ them to best advantage remains unclear. What becomes readily apparent is that Fiske's energetic pursuit of his advisory duties ran counter to what Daniels wanted from his admirals—thus becoming a potential source of conflict.[22]

Fiske's estrangement from Daniels and the Wilson adminstration mounted between 1913 and 1915. He got nowhere with schemes for reorganization via a general staff, or expanding personnel strengths, or improving fleet preparedness, despite apparently clandestine support from Assistant Secretary of the Navy Franklin D. Roosevelt. Convinced now that Germany was the nation's greatest potential enemy, he testified before Congress about German naval maneuver plans under unified command (something scarcely envisioned in the American service); but the Wilson administration remained unconcerned. Nor could Fiske convince Daniels to increase expenditures for such things as naval aviation. Diplomatic crises with Japan (concerning Japanese workers in California) and Mexico (involving American interest in that country's political stability) hardly daunted Wilsonian determination to conduct diplomatic affairs peaceably and not pour money into armaments. Fiske became increasingly frustrated and shrill in his criticism of civilian neglect of preparedness. His own ardor, personality, and saber-rattling understandably irritated administration officials as the admiral became known as "Granny Fiske," and Daniels even took to pocketing Fiske's anxious memoranda and decision requests, losing them between office and home in an attempt to defuse the bantam blue-suiter. Both sides had a point. The Wilsonians believed that providing professional advice about military options was the proper role for generals and admirals in a democracy. They respected such advice; but they did not want any military man dictating national policy, no matter how right the advice might be. Wilson told Daniels about Joint Board suggestions for fleet movements in the Far East at the time of the Japanese crisis, adding that "we are considering this matter with another light, on the diplomatic side, and must determine the policy." When the Joint Board persisted in its belligerent stance and someone leaked its recommendations to the press, Wilson's patience snapped. He told his secretaries of war and navy to disband the board until he authorized their return to session. Daniels blamed the brink-of-war situation squarely on Fiske and the army's political general, Leonard Wood.[23]

The conflict between navalists and the Wilsonians had become increasingly public by 1914. Release of a General Board report of 1913 calling for a forty-eight-battleship fleet by 1920 escalated the squabble. Admirals George Dewey (venerable hero of Manila Bay) and Charles E. Vreeland of the General Board testified before Congress as to naval weakness, thus joining Fiske in the call for reform. However, the Wilson administration counterattacked, reducing its annual call for new ship authorization, and a simmering feud sapped energies at both ends of Pennsylvania Avenue. Washington, in fact, remained calm even as war clouds appeared ominously over Europe by late summer 1914. Fiske, for one, continued his crusade for fleet concentration and training, arguing that the Wilson administration was wrong in keeping major naval units inertly stationed in Mexican waters rather than returning them to home ports for refitting and preparation for possible American involvement in disintegrating world affairs. Navy General Board meetings became heated as he clashed with such administration favorites as Victor Blue, chief of navigation, and Albert Winterhalter, aid for material. Scarcely concealing his disdain for Wilsonian pacifism, Bradley Fiske, for all his commendable professional zeal, displayed appalling ignorance of political finesse in the capital. By autumn, as the war in Europe showed no sign of a quick conclusion, he embarked upon a two-front campaign to win acceptance for his programs. Ultimately, he succeeded only in bringing his own career to an end.[24]

On 9 November 1914, Fiske penned "the most important" paper he ever wrote. Directed to Daniels, its subject was the U.S. Navy's unpreparedness for major war. Fiske denied any desire to see America embroiled in the European struggle that had erupted in August. But, he warned that the navy had to be ready if called upon to act because "during the next five years we must expect a great number of causes of disagreement between this country and other countries." He proceeded methodically to catalog the navy's weaknesses. Citing his own study of past wars, consultations with fellow professionals, and his perception of the current situation, Fiske concluded that insufficient numbers of officers and men, faulty departmental organization precluding proper preparation for war (the need-for-a-general-staff issue), and insufficient fleet training due to the ill-advised positioning of the fleet in Mexican waters lay at the root of the problem. Daniels read the memorandum and remained unmoved. Fiske's wording may have put him off; perhaps the secretary was simply beyond listening to Fiske's familiar complaints. Daniels returned the document to the admiral, and Fiske filed the paper for future reference.[25]

Daniels's refusal to take Fiske's professional advice seriously (some said the Wilson administration refused to take the question of American involvement in the European war seriously) caused the naval officer to try other approaches. He proposed openly to Daniels that any naval maneuvers in 1915 should be weighted so that the defending American fleet would be overwhelmingly beaten by an imaginary German fleet—in order to awaken the public to the need for preparedness. Daniels naturally vetoed that scheme. Fiske then turned to his allies on Capitol Hill, such as Alabama congressman and Spanish war naval hero Richmond P. Hobson and his Massachusetts colleague Augustus P. Gardner. The three men enjoyed similar views about a strong navy and abhorred Wilsonian pacifism. None thought Daniels knew how to manage the navy, either. Hobson, like Fiske, had publicized the state of America's defenses, and he willingly responded to Fiske's suggestion that the naval officer brief the legislators about naval problems. At the time, only those officers specifically sent by the War or Navy Departments to testify on the Hill, or invited by Congress, could appear before that body, so Fiske's move bordered upon insubordination. Daniels and the Wilson administration remained unresponsive as Congress and the public became aroused over what they heard of naval unpreparedness. So Fiske escalated the issue yet another notch. Meeting clandestinely with Hobson at his Washington residence, Fiske and several other officers masterminded a bill designed to give the navy a chief of operations with fifteen assistants who would form a sort of general staff. They couched their intentions in careful wording, describing their proposal as a body responsible for naval preparedness and the general direction of the navy, under the secretary of the navy. In fact, under the proposed system, the General Board, the Naval War College, even the bureau chiefs would lose power. Paul Y. Hammond accurately described it as a structure that provided not for "a Chief of Staff, but a powerful command general," ironically the very thing the U.S. Army on its side had obviated in the Rootian reforms, which established a chief of staff in place of a commanding general. The naval reformers seemed to want confrontation by establishing a powerful counterpoise to the naval secretary in this battle over preparedness and construction of the world's ranking navy.[26]

At this point an avowedly irate Secretary Daniels effectively quashed Fiske, Hobson, and the reformers' demand for a general staff. By threatening resignation, Daniels defanged the Hobson bill. The position of chief of naval operations was set up, but it lacked the organizational assistance of fifteen subordinates, and the key clause in the legislation read that incumbents would "be charged with the operations of the fleet, and with the preparation and readiness of plans for its use in war." The sweeping change envisioned by Fiske and his colleagues had to await the onset of another crisis and war in 1941–42. Yet, perhaps as maritime historian Robert G. Albion felicitously phrased it, Fiske and the zealots missed an essential point. Nothing so pivotal had happened since the 1842 reorganization, and even in reduced fashion, the onset of the position of chief of naval operations provided opportunities for professional coordination and operational direction simply lacking under the old scheme.[27]

The events culminating with rejection of the Hobson bill in Congress essentially completed Fiske's alienation from the Wilsonians. Fiske continued to badger the secretary on preparedness issues, but increasingly lost influence as a new corps of Daniels's uniformed confidantes rose to power. Only the Republican opposition in Congress used Fiske's ideas, and then mostly as political ammunition against the administration. Daniels effectively muzzled Fiske by bluntly informing the admiral: "You cannot write or talk any more; you can't even say that two and two make four." The final blow came when the secretary banished Fiske to the Naval War College so that this quarrelsome subordinate would have no access whatsoever to politicians or press in official Washington. Fiske's own billet as aid to the secretary would become redundant with inception of the position of chief of naval operations. As parent of this new slot, Fiske might have justifiably expected appointment to it. His feud with Daniels killed that possibility. Fiske resigned the aid position in early 1915, and watched from the sidelines as the Wilson administration swung increasingly toward preparedness, forced to do so both by events in Europe and by outside pressure from Congress and the public. Congress itself responded with the Navy Act of 1915, an act that incorporated many of the reforms long advocated by Fiske and the reformers. A Council on National Defense, expanded naval construction (156 ships in three years), more money for naval aviation, a naval experiments laboratory, increased enlisted strength, a naval reserve, and even staff help for the CNO were numbered among its provisions. Little wonder that Fiske's friends credited the admiral's efforts in winning this singular victory.[28]

Fiske's final year on active service, before his mandatory retirement due to age on 13 June 1916, proved both unpleasant and demeaning to an officer termed the Navy's Emory Upton because, like that army officer, he demanded a rational national military policy and organization. Considered the U.S. Navy's most brilliant senior officer, Fiske was denied service on the General Board or the new Naval Consulting Board on inventions, where he might have continued useful, if by now muted, service to the navy. Assistant Secretary of the Navy Franklin D. Roosevelt approved Fiske's continuing work with seaplanes, but internal naval opposition during the subsequent American participation in World War I thwarted even that useful service. In retirement, Fiske soon became the darling of the Republican opposition, and when he published his memoirs in 1919, the book could be viewed to some degree as both a forum for further naval reformist ideas and a way to settle old scores with a rather vindictive Secretary Daniels. Still, Fiske concluded that in his two years with Daniels he had accomplished some of his goals, including establishment of an aeronautical division, institution of war problems for fleet exercises, increased congressional awareness of the needs of the navy, and creation of the office of the chief of naval operations. Fiske added a somewhat inexplicable comment about his example "proving that the country trusts army and navy officers more than it trusts any one else." In any event, Bradley Fiske might take small comfort that his stormy petrel ways had helped prepare the U.S. Navy for the test of World War I.[29]

Insurgents such as Fiske and Sims eventually found vindication in the preparedness hearings and legislation of 1915–16, as well as postwar investigations of the wartime record of the Navy Department. Unfortunately, the unsavory cast of such investigations, the blatantly partisan exploitation of the admirals by Republican ideologues, and the return of peace lessened their impact. The reformers hoped that Republican Presidents Warren G. Harding and Calvin Coolidge might restore the navalism of the Roosevelt–Taft years, but they were disappoitned. The United States willingly turned isolationist, placing its faith in demobilization and disarmament via naval treaties. Fiske turned increasingly to his causes and experiments following his wife's death in 1919. He continued a ceaseless carping about Wilson and Daniels long after people ceased to heed his words. As a retired sage of the sea service, Fiske still had many perceptive things to say. He suggested, for example, that the country would experience difficulties in defending its Far East possessions in the wake of the drastic naval limitation treaties. He argued forcefully that war with Japan was inevitable.[30]

Finishing his term as president of the Naval Institute in 1923 (the longest on record), Fiske became involved with the National Security League. He fought the navy unsuccessfully for recognition as inventor of the torpedo plane. At least the prestigious Aero Club of America recognized his contribution and awarded him its coveted Gold Medal for that invention. Fiske also found time to produce a magnetic torpedo-ignition system. Returning to optical mechanisms, he finished what would be the forerunner of the microfiche reader. However, his greatest concern remained national weakness in a hostile world. As late as 1936, amid congressional investigations of military–industrial fraud and the resurgence of Germany, Fiske warned *New York Times* readers that America would remain unprepared because politicians would not listen to their military advisers.[31]

When Bradley Fiske died on 6 April 1942, the country was again at war. The navy had suffered a resounding defeat at Pearl Harbor, and the fall of the Philippines seemed imminent. The Roosevelt administration and the navy rushed to consolidate command and control of the overall planning and coordination responsibilities, with direct command over the operating forces and definite authority over offices and bureaus of the department under the chief of naval operations—final consummation of Fiske's reform. Whether or not Fiske ever learned of this milestone remains unclear. He was certainly aware that his dire prediction about war with Japan had come true, and he probably attributed it to unpreparedness. More obvious was the fact that the man who was president in 1941–42 had seen Fiske's earlier battles with Daniels and the Wilsonians firsthand and understood the need for organizational change in the midst of crisis. Roosevelt and Secretary of the Navy Frank Knox provided a more receptive civilian climate for change than the Wilsonians had. Still, in the twilight of his life, Fiske probably looked less to those earlier fights, and instead peered into the future, focusing on changes in warfare. His final great work, published posthumously, emphasized "Air Power." Although Fiske did not live to see the vindication of this crusade either, such pupils of his as Bill Halsey and Chester Nimitz had learned from their teacher much as Fiske had learned from Taylor, Luce, and Mahan. It would take a combination of sea and air power to give America and its democratic allies the ultimate victory in World War II.[32]

Fiske's biographer, Paola Coletta, has studied the admiral more than anyone else has, perhaps, and he has concluded that three themes emerge from Fiske's memoirs, and thus his life. The first part of Fiske's life witnessed the transition of the navy from wood and sail to steel and steam. Fiske's own inventions played a vital role in the transition. Fiske's later life became enmeshed in the conflicts of senior officer with senior officials and national policies. The unifying thread remains Fiske as individualistic inventor and reformer and his battles with inertia, traditionalism, and naval bureaucracy. Yet, any evaluation of Fiske as Steel Navy admiral must move beyond mere memoir and biography (although both should be read concurrently with this essay).[33]

Fiske was undoubtedly a gifted and versatile naval officer. Basically, his service differed little from that of most of his peers in the New Steel Navy. His memoirs, in fact, portray in sharp and often witty fashion how an officer functioned, thought, and responded to his career in that service. Yet, upon this prosaic professional base, Fiske built an impressive record also as inventor, author, lecturer, and thinker. Anyone whose productivity in writing alone stood second only to that of the great Mahan (and may even had exceeded his talents in variety of topics) merits high praise. Bradley Fiske contributed significant writings on electrical engineering, the history of inventions, military history, naval organization, operations, and personal reminiscences of war and peace. He wrote perceptively and suggestively about defense policy issues. Moreover, few ever exceeded Fiske among naval officers in the prodigious outpouring of inventions—inventions with practical utility to operatives in the New Steel Navy. If Fiske has not found a niche among great scientists, it may be because his contribution lay in the naval field. Yet, without such a person, the New Steel Navy would have remained cyclopsian in nature.

True, Fiske functioned best in a laboratory context. He was a pathfinder in such matters as gunnery, electronics, and mechanics, but he left to such others as Sims, or the Briton Sir Percy Scott, fame as entrepreneurs. Moreover, by working with private suppliers such as General Electric, Western Electric, the American Rangefinder Company, and the Bliss Company, Fiske expanded the defense industrial base in its natal years. Using the fleet as his workshop, and friendships with such men as Park Benjamin, Frank J. Sprague, and Elmer A. Sperry, Fiske established a rudimentary research and development framework for his field. He, like others in armor and ordnance, forged the bond of teamwork between the public and private sectors that made possible the modern American Steel Navy.

Fiske's role as senior naval reformer remains more controversial. That he was vigorous, opinionated, and contentious was undeniable. That he was also dedicated to duty—duty adequately defined at the time by Meyer's aid system—also seems unquestionable. Whether or not he might have ridden out the storm with Daniels and truly presided over development of the World War I navy remains speculative. He always claimed, throughout his career, to have been thwarted by "the law of higher powers." Despite the gift of high intelligence, his scientific brilliance, and a commendable career record, Fiske dismally misread the climate of those higher powers during the Wilson years. Perhaps the halcyon days of Republican navalism simply proved too heady for men of Fiske's dedication. Accordingly, he suffered two years of indifference and finally ostracism from Daniels. An unswerving belief in his crusade clouded Fiske's appreciation of the art of persuasion in Washington's political climate. He acted much like that other preparedness thorn in the Wilsonians' side, Major General Leonard Wood, sometime army chief of staff. In fact, Wilsonians openly compared Fiske and Wood to one another. Both military professionals believed in Samuel Huntington's "neo-Hamiltonian" principles of national might and power, and clearly felt that they alone among Americans should be listened to on matters of military issues such as personnel, organization, and war planning. Both Fiske and Wood miscalculated the strong streak of Jeffersonian liberalism in such leaders as Woodrow Wilson, Josephus Daniels, and Secretary of War Newton D. Baker. In the end, both officers became shrill critics, causing Wilson's uncharitable characterization of Fiske as "a perfect old granny whose ideas are perfectly negligible."[34]

The Fiske–Daniels confrontation over preparedness and control of the U.S. Navy can be seen in the classic context of American civil–military relations. On the one hand rests the constitutional provision for civilian control of the military. On the other side stands the issue of the moral and professional ethics of an officer faced with questionable policies of that civil authority. Fiske and the reformers sought national military preparedness, but they used that theme to mask such naval organizational reforms as the general staff. They sought vertical control of the navy by uniformed professionals. They viewed civilians—especially those, such as Josephus Daniels, whom they thought incompetent—as a roadblock. Daniels naturally viewed their actions as a direct challenge to time-honored civilian control, and was even aligned with naval bureau chiefs, who themselves feared loss of power to the new omnipotent chief of naval operations and his general staff. In the end, Daniels and civilian control won out, as the new position of CNO remained subordinate and not equal to the secretary; lacked a staff organization; and was limited to control of the military, not the civil side, of the naval institution. It remained for successive chiefs of operations, starting with Admiral William S. Benson, to patiently and judiciously build that office into a meaningful tool of authority by cooperating with the policies of civilian secretaries. But, in 1915, all of this posed a dilemma for an officer such as Fiske.[35]

Like most other reformers, Fiske would not settle for less than total success with his agenda. Yet, he faced the professional choice between stepping down as aid or continuing the fight for his goals within the context of an administration whose policies were a complete anathema to him. Such is the quandary faced by many military professionals at some time in their careers. One year prior to his mandatory retirement, Bradley Fiske relinquished the pivotal advisory position of aid for operations. He could no longer advise a statutory superior who openly rejected that advice. Daniels had not fired him, but had merely maneuvered the controversial Fiske into the move.

Fiske's long preparedness fight and enactment of a general staff demanded courage. His resignation as aid took courage. He stood for the higher good of the U.S. Navy, as he saw it, not petty personal gain or blind loyalty to superiors. His credo came straight from Annapolis—responsibility, fortitude, virtue, and honor. He defied authority to work on his inventions and to inform a nation on national military conditions. He particularly identified his mission as a

naval officer with advising his civilian superiors about combat preparations, war planning, and organizing for mission accomplishment.
Bluntly put, he laid his career on the line to awaken both superiors
and the public alike to the perils of an unprepared U.S. Navy. As
he told a Naval Academy alumni dinner audience in 1915, should
naval officers fail to speak out against the civilian secretary on issues
like the naval staff or preparedness for fear of their careers, then such
officers were "unworthy of the uniform we wear," and failed their
country as effectively in peacetime as if they had deserted its flag in
war. One must always wonder, however, would Fiske ultimately have
been more effective had he stayed the course, remained as aid, and
simply waited for events in Europe in 1916–17 to bear out his theories? Here again is the quintessential dilemma for the military professional. Can more be accomplished on the inside than on the outside of an organization in a delicate policy situation?

     In the end, like most admirals of the Steel Navy, Fiske preferred
the more amiable climate of Rooseveltian navalism, jingoism, and
service with the Great White Fleet. A man of impeccable principles
and demeanor, Fiske could not accommodate the political winds of
the Democrats. Fiske's greatest fault was what maritime historian
Robert Albion has styled "his chronic allergy to civilian influence."
Hardly a naval secretary appears favorably in Fiske's writings. These
stringent blue-and-gold attitudes conflicted with the political neces-
sities of civil–military relations in America. Did this result from a
deep-seated animosity to blind authority? Did Fiske perceive some
linkage between his beloved technology and the dawning of an era
when civilian management of the armed services would eclipse the
role of uniformed professional? He recorded in 1921 that the technological revolution (in which he himself figured so prominently)
had made naval officers mere "tiny parts" that seemed to be dimin-
ishing as the "Modern Military Machine" grew larger and more complex. With his realization that the day of the manager as opposed to
the hero had dawned, Fiske's inventions, his reformist goals, and his
rebellion against civilian authority may have reflected a desire to ease
his band of brothers through a stormy time of transition, while fighting
a rearguard action against what he saw as the pernicious effect of the
civilianization of war management.[36]

     Bradley Fiske ultimately appears as a blend of inventor and re-
former. His experience in one sector shaped his approach to the other.
Buffeted as an inventor by uniformed bureaucrats, he moved to counter
those effects as a senior leader only to discover other countervailing

forces at work in Washington in the form of unreceptive civilians. Both facets of the man prove important to an understanding of the maturing of the Steel Navy. Possibly few of his contemporaries truly appreciated his duality; certainly many historians today neglect even his contributions to the technology of warfare.[37] Without range finders, telescopic gun sights, stadimeters, or the internal electrical systems on board ship, the keys to naval success were limited. In the Steel Navy, the future belonged to technologists; the day of heroic sea captains and block-and-tackle seamen had passed. Beyond that, in the realm of organization and policy, the future belonged to systems managers with foresight, enterprise, and mechanical aptitude, and, above all, to leaders who understood the art of the possible. Fiske would have preferred that these professionals be in the navy, not civilians. In fact, they proved to be both. The future that faced Fiske when he rose to policy level rank belonged to persons of versatility, creativity, and a will to improve the navy. If Fiske stumbled at this level, he still provided a good model. He was a versatile officer, a creative genius, and an insurgent with a desire to test the system. In time, the navy was a better place because of Bradley Fiske.

FURTHER READING

Basic to any study of Fiske and the Steel Navy are his memoirs, *From Midshipman to Rear Admiral,* and Paolo E. Coletta's definitive biography, *Admiral Bradley A. Fiske and the American Navy.* Lacking a well-defined body of original papers, Fiske's published writings (a comprehensive listing appears in Coletta) will also prove invaluable. Particularly important are representative articles such as "The Naval Battle of the Future," "Range Finders," "American Naval Policy," "The Civil and Military Authority," "The Naval Profession," "The Paramount Duty of the Army and Navy," "Naval Preparedness," "Torpedo Plane and Bomber," "How We Shall Lose the Next War, and When," and "Air Power, 1914–1943," the last published posthumously. Most assuredly, Coletta has attempted comprehensiveness with additional articles on Fiske, including, "The Perils of Invention: Bradley A. Fiske and the Torpedo Plane," "The 'Nerves' of the New Navy," and "Bradley A. Fiske, Naval Inventor." Francis Duncan's short but incisive "Commentary," which accompanies the third of these essays in Richard A. Von Doenhoff, *Versatile Guardian; Research in Naval History,* suggests the customary restraints on autobiography. Coletta, however, has obviously done the most detailed and widespread work on Fiske, probing both original documents and published works. His footnotes and bibliography are virtually encyclopedic. See also his essay on Daniels in *American Secretaries of the Navy,* edited by Coletta, Jack Bauer, and Robert Albion.

The milieu of the Steel Navy should be followed in such older works as Harold Sprout and Margaret Sprout, *The Rise of American Naval Power, 1776–1918,* and *Toward a New Order of Sea Power: American Naval Policy and the World Scene, 1918–1922;* or John D. Long, *The New American Navy.* Recent interpretations include Walter J. Herrick, *The American Naval Revolution;* Peter Karsten, *The Naval Aristocracy: The Golden Age of Annapolis and the Emergence of Modern American Navalism;* John D. Alden, *The American Steel Navy;* and George T. Davis, *A Navy Second to None: The Development of Modern American Naval Power.* Robert William Love, Jr., *The Chiefs of Naval Operations,* contains some salient comments regarding Fiske and that office. All of these works have useful bibliographies. Supplemental reading can be done among a plethora of biographies and memoirs, and in other works, such as Fiske's own *Wartime in Manila,* to capture the ambience of the era.

For technical dimensions of Fiske's period, see Monte A. Calvert, *The Mechanical Engineer in America 1830–1910: Professional Cultures in Conflict;* L. S. Howarth, *History of Communications–Electronics in the United States Navy;* and perhaps the most comprehensive study of its type, Peter Padfield, *Guns at Sea.* Samuel P. Huntington, *The Soldier and the State: The Theory and Politics of Civil–Military Relations,* and Paul Y. Hammond, *Organizing for Defense: The American Military Establishment in the Twentieth Century,* are especially helpful for understanding the organizational web of Fiske, Daniels, and the navy. A new study of the U.S. Navy, which must be read for its perspective, is Edward L. Beach, *The United States Navy: Two Hundred Years.* The work of Elting E. Morison will always prove stimulating, especially his chapter "Gunfire at Sea: A Case Study of Innovation" in *Men, Machines, and Modern Times.* As yet, we lack any comprehensive view of all facets of the naval–industrial and business complex of the Steel Navy era, one that would include not merely heavy armaments production, but the types of material that concerned Fiske, Sims, Michelsen, and others. This remains the most understudied facet of the naval progress of the era.

NOTES

1. Bradley A. Fiske, *From Midshipman to Rear Admiral,* title page.

2. See the definitive biography by Paolo Coletta, *Admiral Bradley A. Fiske and the American Navy,* for all aspects of Fiske's life and career.

3. Fiske, *From Midshipman to Rear Admiral,* 19. For perceptive comments on the role of Annapolis, see Peter Karsten, *The Naval Aristocracy: The Golden Age of Annapolis and the Emergence of Modern American Navalism,* esp. Chapter 2.

4. Appropriate contrasts between "Old" and "New" Navies after the Civil War can be followed in Walter Herrick, Jr., *The American Naval*

Revolution, esp. Chapter 1; Frank M. Bennett, *The Steam Navy of the United States,* esp. Chapters 28–38; and John D. Alden, *The American Steel Navy,* prologue.

5. Fiske, *From Midshipman to Rear Admiral,* esp. Chapter 5.

6. Fiske's life and thoughts at this time are explained well in ibid., Chapter 6; and Coletta, *Fiske,* Chapter 3. For Fiske's concept of his career, see also Coletta, "Bradley Allen Fiske" in *Dictionary of American Military Biography,* ed. Roger J. Spiller, I:324.

7. Appropriate coverage in text and illustration of the fullest dimensions of the "New" Navy can be followed in Alden, *The American Steel Navy,* although the frustrations of the young insurgents and progressives may best be seen in memoirs such as Fiske's own writings.

8. On Fiske's work with electricity see his *Electricity in Theory and Practice; or the Elements of Electrical Engineering,* "The Electric Railway," "The Civilian Electrician in Modern War," and "Electricity in Naval Life."

9. Paolo E. Coletta, "Bradley A. Fiske: Naval Inventor," in Richard A. Von Doenhoff, ed., *Versatile Guardian; Research in Naval History,* 90–92; Fiske, "The Invention and Development of the Naval Telescope Sight," U.S. Naval Institute *Proceedings* (June 1909): 405–7.

10. Fiske, *From Midshipman to Rear Admiral,* 208–13, esp. 211; also Paolo Coletta, "The 'Nerves' of the New Navy," 122–26.

11. Fiske, *From Midshipman to Rear Admiral,* 129, 161–63, 171; Karsten, *Naval Aristocracy,* esp. part II.

12. Fiske, *From Midshipman to Rear Admiral,* 494.

13. In addition to Karsten, *Naval Aristocracy,* Fiske's supporters are clearly noted in his memoirs, *From Midshipman to Rear Admiral,* 68, 81, 84, 98, 107–9, 120–21, 128–29, 170–71, 177–80, 186–87, 191–97, 198, 201, 221–22.

14. Fiske, *From Midshipman to Rear Admiral,* Chapters 15–16; also, his reminiscence *Wartime in Manila,* as well as the last three chapters in Herrick, *Naval Revolution,* for general background on the Spanish–American war.

15. In addition to Fiske's own writings, Coletta, *Fiske,* Chapter 6, covers his actions in the Far East. See also, U.S. Navy, *Naval Operations of the War with Spain: Appendix to the Report of the Chief of the Bureau of Navigation,* II:80–82.

16. See Fiske, "The Naval Profession" and "Naval Power"; Karsten, *Naval Aristocracy,* Chapter 7; George T. Davis, *A Navy Second to None,* Chapter 9.

17. Fiske, "Air Power," U.S. Naval Institute *Proceedings;* on Sims and Fiske, see Elting E. Morison, *Men, Machines, and Modern Times,* Chapter 2, and *Admiral Sims and the Modern American Navy,* esp. Chapters 8–9; and Karsten, *Naval Aristocracy,* 232–33, 266–67.

18. Fiske, *From Midshipman to Rear Admiral,* Chapters 28–33.

19. Coletta, *Fiske,* Chapter 10; Fiske, *From Midshipman to Rear Admiral,* Chapter 34; Arthur S. Link, *Woodrow Wilson and the Progressive Era,* 1910–

1917, 28–29; and E. David Cronon, ed., *The Cabinet Diaries of Josephus Daniels, 1913–1921,* preface.

20. Fiske, *From Midshipman to Rear Admiral,* 65, 220–21, 370–78, 535; on Fiske, Luce, and Dewey, see Fiske's articles "Admiral Dewey: An Appreciation" and "Stephen B. Luce: An Appreciation."

21. Representative Fiske writings in this period included: "American Naval Policy," "The Civil and Military Authority," "The Naval Profession," "Courage and Prudence," "A Fair Basis for Competition in Battle Practice," "Naval Power," "The Diplomatic Responsibility of the United States Navy," and "The Paramount Duty of the Army and Navy." On the aids system, see Coletta, *Fiske,* 102–3.

22. Secretary of the Navy, *1912 Annual Report,* 6.

23. See in addition to Coletta, *Fiske,* Chapters 10–12; Link, *Wilson,* Chapters 4–5, esp. 86; Cronon, *Daniels Diaries,* 52–68, esp. 66; Carroll Kilpatrick, ed., *Roosevelt and Daniels: A Friendship in Politics,* 211–12; and Joseph L. Morrison, *Josephus Daniels: The Small-d Democrat,* 54–55.

24. This phase is particularly well covered by Coletta, *Fiske,* Chapter 13.

25. Fiske published in toto the famous memorandum of 9 November 1914, which he considered his most important piece of writing; see *From Midshipman to Rear Admiral,* 555–60.

26. Robert G. Albion, *Makers of Naval Policy 1798–1947,* 172–73; Josephus Daniels, *The Wilson Era: Years of Peace, 1910–1917,* 241–43; Fiske, *From Midshipman to Rear Admiral,* Chapters 35–36; and Paul Y. Hammond, *Organizing for Defense: The American Military in the Twentieth Century,* 71–77. For a firsthand view of the Fiske–Daniels feud over the CNO question, see U.S. Cong., 66th, 2d Sess., Senate, *Naval Investigation: Hearings before the Subcommittee of the Committee on Naval Affairs,* esp. I:695, II:2972–80.

27. Fiske, *From Midshipman to Rear Admiral,* Chapter 37; Coletta, *Fiske,* Chapters 14–15, 17, esp. 166; Albion, *Makers of Naval Policy 1798–1947,* 218–19.

28. Coletta, *Fiske,* 179–80.

29. Fiske, *From Midshipman to Rear Admiral,* 587–88; Coletta, *Fiske,* 282.

30. Coletta, *Fiske,* Chapter 18; representative Fiske writings in this period include: "The Warfare of the Future," "The Defense of the Philippines," "Possibilities for Disarmament," "How We Shall Lose the Next War, and When," "Pacifists and Militarists," "Delusions of Pacifists," and "War and Peace."

31. Fiske, letter to editor, *New York Times,* 17 September 1936, 16; on Fiske's torpedo plane, see Paolo Coletta, "The Perils of Invention: Bradley A. Fiske and the Torpedo Plane," 111–27.

32. Fiske, "Air Power, 1914–1943," U.S. Naval Institute *Proceedings* (May 1942): 686–94; Edward L. Beach, *The United States Navy: Two Hundred Years,* 470–71.

33. Probably the best appraisal of Fiske appears in Coletta, *Fiske,* Chapter 19.

34. Arthur S. Link, ed., *The Papers of Woodrow Wilson,* 45:387; also Cronon, *Daniels Diaries,* 166, 201; Daniels, *The Wilson Era,* 292; and for War Department organizational change, see James E. Hewes, Jr., *From Root to McNamara,* 3–21; on neo-Hamiltonianism, see Chapter 10 of Samuel P. Huntington, *The Soldier and the State;* also useful are Charles Oscar Paullin, *Paullin's History of Naval Administration, 1775–1911,* 437–40, and Paul Y. Hammond, *Organizing for Defense,* Chapter 3.

35. See representative Fiske writings at the height of his fight with Daniels, including: *The Navy as a Fighting Machine,* "Naval Principles," "Naval Preparedness," "Naval Defense," and "The Next Five Years of the Navy: What We Shall Shall Get for the Billion Dollars We Shall Spend." On Benson and Fiske, see Mary Klachko with David Trask, *Admiral William Shepherd Benson: First Chief of Naval Operations,* esp. Chapter 3.

36. On Fiske's aversion to civilians see Albion, *Makers of Naval Policy,* 205; Fiske, *From Midshipman to Rear Admiral,* 202, 413–15, 535–36; Karsten, *Naval Aristocracy,* 328–29, 392–93.

37. Lack of appreciation of Fiske and Sims seems apparent in the writing of historians of technology; see for example, Thomas A. Palmer, "Military Technology," in *Technology and Western Civilization,* ed. Melvin Kranzberg and Carroll W. Pursell, Jr., vol. 1, *The Emergence of Modern Industrial Society from Earliest Times to 1900,* 489–502; and Edward L. Katzenbach, Jr., "The Mechanization of War, 1900–1919," in *Technology and Western Civilization,* ed. Kranzberg and Pursell, vol. 2., *Technology in the Twentieth Century,* 548–61. A similar neglect of Fiske even appears in Kenneth J. Hagan, ed., *In Peace and War: Interpretations of American Naval History, 1775–1984.*

Heroes of the Spanish–American War. Colored lithograph published in 1898 by F. H. Cline & Holpuch Co. *Courtesy of the Library of Congress.*

BUILDERS OF
THE NEW EMPIRE

WILLIAM T. SAMPSON:
PROGRESSIVE
TECHNOLOGIST AS
NAVAL COMMANDER

JOSEPH G. DAWSON III

Who is not proud to say 'I served under Sampson'[?]" wrote Richard Wainwright, who had commanded the yacht *Glouces-ter* in Sampson's North Atlantic Fleet during the Spanish War. Wainwright concluded that Sampson's "works will live while sea power remains an American necessity." Another young officer, impressed by Sampson's example, called him "the most brilliant officer of his time."[1]

These accolades honored the memory of a man whose role in the battle of Santiago brought his name to public prominence. Command off Cuba capped a forty-year career during which Sampson logged enough time at sea to advance in the service. Although he was most famous as a wartime commander, many of Sampson's assignments required technical and scientific expertise, and it was as a technologist that Sampson made his greatest contributions to the U.S. Navy in the late nineteenth century. It is unfortunate that the battle that made Sampson famous also led to an acrimonious controversy with Winfield S. Schley over command responsibility, which overshadowed all of Sampson's technological services, embittered his final years, and continues to haunt his reputation.

The son of Scotch–Irish parents, William Thomas Sampson excelled in his studies at town schools in Palmyra, New York, where he was born in 1840. With a family of seven children, his parents had no savings to finance a college education. But Sampson favorably impressed William Southwick, a man of means in Palmyra, who contacted Congressman Edwin B. Morgan about appointing Sampson

William T. Sampson. Engraving from a photograph taken just prior to the Spanish–American War. A similar portrait was included as a vignette with a colored lithograph of the USS *New York* published as a supplement to the *Boston Sunday Herald,* 29 May 1898. *Courtesy of the Naval Historical Center.*

to one of the national service academies. In September 1857, Sampson reported as a cadet at the U.S. Naval Academy.[2]

Arriving at Annapolis in an ill-fitting store-bought suit, Sampson nevertheless made an impression on Second Classman Alfred Thayer Mahan, a cadet officer in the gun crew in which Sampson first served. Mahan recalled the youngster having an "unusually fine complexion, delicate regular features, and brown eyes remarkable both in shape and color," with a physique giving "an impression of slightness amounting to fragility." Studying diligently, Sampson mastered the sciences (especially physics) and engineering. In 1861, he ranked first of twenty-seven cadets in his class, a standing he had maintained for three years, the last year while holding the position of cadet adjutant—commanding officer of the cadet battalion. Although saddened by departures from Annapolis of Southern naval cadets in early 1861, Sampson took a firm stance against secession.[3]

The cannon shots at Fort Sumter in April 1861 forced the U.S. Navy to expand and transformed Sampson and other cadets of his class from students to officers. In the first year of the Civil War, Sampson hopscotched through several assignments. As midshipman, he served briefly at the Washington Navy Yard under Commander John A. B. Dahlgren, the noted gun designer and ordnance expert, and then in the frigate *Pocahontas* patrolling the Potomac River. In the rank of acting master, he transferred to the frigate *Potomac*. Also assigned to the *Potomac* was Master Winfield S. Schley, USNA Class of 1860; the two young officers served together for a year, cruising the Gulf of Mexico. On 16 July 1862, Sampson was promoted to lieutenant and posted as an instructor to the Naval Academy, which had temporarily moved from the slave state of Maryland to the safety of Newport, Rhode Island.[4]

After two years at Newport, including supervising cadets on a cruise to Europe in the frigate *Macedonian,* Sampson drew his first real combat assignment, as executive officer of the monitor *Patapsco,* which was assigned to Rear Admiral John Dahlgren's South Atlantic Blockading Squadron off Charleston, South Carolina. On the night of 15 January 1865, the ship was ordered to remove Confederate obstructions from the harbor, near Fort Sumter. While doing so, the *Patapsco* struck a submarine torpedo (mine), and went under in fifteen seconds, taking with her sixty-two members of the crew. When the mine exploded, Sampson was standing on the turret roof. With an unhurried motion, according to survivors, the lieutenant stepped off the turret as the water rushed over his shoes. The captain of the *Patapsco* concluded "that the cool intrepidity displayed by Lieutenant Sampson . . . deserves the highest praise."[5]

Following the Civil War, Sampson served for two years in the steam frigate *Colorado,* flagship on the European Station. Lieutenant Commander George Dewey, one of his fellow officers in the *Colorado,* remembered Sampson as having "a most brilliant mind and the qualities of a practical and efficient officer." Sampson was promoted to the rank of lieutenant commander 25 July 1866.[6]

The following year Sampson returned to the United States and received his second posting to the Naval Academy, this time with

the academic rank of instructor in the Department of Natural Philosophy. Two years later he was promoted to head of the department,
which later changed its named to "Physics and Chemistry."[7]

Ordered to sea in June 1871, Sampson served as executive officer
in the screw sloop *Congress* on the European Station. While in the
Congress, and subsequently on detached duty in command of the gunboat *Alert* (March–August 1875), Sampson undoubtedly noticed the
improved quality of modern ships and guns in European navies. In
contrast, the U.S. Navy lagged behind in new ship construction and
appeared increasingly antiquated.[8]

In mid-1874 Sampson once more became head of the Department
of Physics and Chemistry at Annapolis, laying the foundation for his
future administrative assignments in the navy. In his departmental
report of 1877, Sampson revealed his approach toward scientific education for naval officers. In Sampson's view, "Every branch of a
naval officer's profession furnishes many illustrations of the applications of science, and an officer will better comprehend the application when he understands the scientific principles upon which they
are based." Anticipating future technological demands, he concluded
that the modern officer "should be prepared by scientific training to
adapt himself to the great and rapid changes that are liable at any
moment to arise in his profession." Sampson personally conducted a
number of experiments, and, beyond his own efforts, he prompted
the experiments of others.[9] His greatest success as a mentor came
with Albert A. Michelson, a brilliant ensign recently graduated from
the Academy.

In 1877, Sampson assigned Michelson to teach physics to cadets,
and to replicate an experiment of the French physicist Jean Foucault
using a rotating mirror to measure the velocity of light. Michelson
conducted a series of tests in order to measure the speed of light
from different points and under various circumstances. At Sampson's
urging, beginning in April 1878 Michelson combined his efforts with
those of astronomer Simon Newcomb, director of the Nautical Almanac Office in Washington, D.C. Their experiments resulted in
1879 in Michelson's accurate measurement of the velocity of light.
Meanwhile, in the summer of 1878, Sampson himself participated in
a special scientific expedition to Wyoming to observe a solar eclipse.
The expedition's work allowed scientists to make adjustments in ta-
bles in the *Nautical Almanac*.[10]

After an interlude at sea commanding the screw gunboat *Swatara*
on the Asiatic Station (December 1879–81),[11] Sampson was posted
as assistant superintendent of the Naval Observatory at Washington,

D.C. He provided continuity, as the observatory had four superintendents during his tour in office (1882–84). Sampson's duties included taking readings of stars for navigational purposes and sending expeditions to various points within the United States and overseas to take additional star sightings, permitting revisions in navigational charts. During this shore assignment, Sampson married for the second time. In 1863 he had married Margaret S. Aldrich of Palmyra, by whom he had four daughters, but the first Mrs. Sampson had died in 1878. In 1882, Sampson married Elizabeth S. Burling of Rochester, and they would have two sons.[12]

While at the observatory, Sampson supported a plan to improve the professional education of American naval officers. In May 1884, he agreed to serve on a three-officer board convened to offer advice to the secretary of the navy concerning postgraduate education. The three officers—Rear Admiral Stephen B. Luce (chairman), Sampson, and Caspar Goodrich—strongly recommended that the federal government establish a naval postgraduate college, where officers would "bring to the investigation of the various problems of modern naval warfare the scientific methods adopted in other professions." The board concluded that knowing "electricity in its application to torpedoes, chemistry in application to explosives, metallurgy in relation to ordnance and steam as a motive power, are only means to the end of which a navy may be said to exist—*success in war.*" Secretary William E. Chandler approved the board's recommendation (which had been proposed previously by others, only to be rejected). When the fledgling Naval War College subsequently opened in September 1885, the U.S. Navy took a major step toward modernity.[13] In the meantime, the government called upon Sampson for his scientific expertise, designating him one of the U.S. delegates to the International Prime Meridian and Time Conference. The conference delegates voted overwhelmingly to make Greenwich the prime meridian, which was Sampson's choice.[14]

Leaving the Naval Observatory in October 1884, Sampson became inspector of ordnance at the Torpedo Station, Newport, Rhode Island. He assembled an excellent staff and applied his scientific knowledge to improving explosives, undersea mines, and detonators. In a detailed report accompanied by photographs, Sampson discussed a variety of test results for explosive charges in submarine mines and experiments with cubical torpedoes, among other devices.[15]

Sampson did not limit his study to machinery but reflected on the entire problem of improving America's coastal defense. His expertise in the field led to his appointment to the Endicott Board in May

1885. Headed by Secretary of War William C. Endicott, the board was ordered to study and make recommendations regarding America's coastal fortifications. Composed of two naval officers, Sampson and his good friend Caspar Goodrich, four army officers, and two civilians, the board met for several months before issuing a lengthy report in January 1886, including an appendix by Sampson entitled "Floating Batteries." Revising his paper for the Naval Institute *Proceedings,* Sampson concluded that coastal defense must be a joint army–navy responsibility; otherwise U.S. naval forces would have to be greatly increased. Sampson went into detail on the several types of vessels (gunboats, torpedo boats, and other ships) that would be needed to comprehensively defend the Atlantic, Gulf, and Pacific coasts. Dozens of forts would be needed to defend America's shoreline, and the Endicott Board recommended that the federal government appropriate money for long-term contracts to American steel companies, giving them the incentive to manufacture the heavy artillery pieces needed to arm the forts. Thus the nation could provide for its own defense needs rather than buying manufactured items abroad. Sampson would address this same subject again when he later became the navy's inspector of ordnance. [16]

Departing the Torpedo Station in the summer of 1886, Sampson assumed another administrative position—superintendent of the Naval Academy. In his fourth tour at his alma mater, Sampson intended to improve cadet retention while modernizing the Academy. To achieve these goals, Sampson proposed changes in cadet studies, training, and grading, planned to add to or remodel the institution's physical plant, and hoped to eliminate all forms of hazing.

Within thirty days of becoming superintendent, Sampson proposed a number of changes in the academic and training regimen to Secretary of the Navy William C. Whitney. As it stood, the curriculum called for four years of study at Annapolis and two years training at sea before a cadet returned to the Academy for final examinations. To save money and time in training young officers, Sampson urged deleting the two years of training at sea and recommended that cadets stand final examinations at the end of their fourth year at Annapolis and then receive their commissions. Under Sampson's design, cadets not passing their final examinations would be honorably discharged from the navy and could begin civilian careers without having to spend two years at sea. In part a cost-cutting measure, his plan also would reduce the number of formal examinations administered to cadets and naval officers during their careers. Sampson contended that "no other professional corps and no other body of men in the world except the *literati* of China is required to pass so many examinations." Sampson made another change in regard to cadet studies, one that became his most long-lasting reform. He instituted what came to be called the "aptitude for the service grade," a mark that took on increasing importance and was carried on throughout the twentieth century. Separated from academic scores, the "aptitude for the service grade" evaluated a cadet's leadership qualities and indicated the likelihood that he would make a good naval officer. Cadets earned this significant grade depending upon how they deported themselves on training cruises and performed other professional duties. Though the Naval Academy Board of Visitors endorsed most of Sampson's proposed changes, the two years of post-Annapolis seatime were not dropped until 1912.[17]

Sampson directed his efforts toward another reform, but here met with only partial success. Hazing had been a long-standing practice among cadets at the Academy. The pranks, begun while the Academy was at Newport, had grown increasingly more dangerous as older cadets forced fourth classmen through various physical exercises and torments, such as eating soap and standing on their heads, and delighted in suspending the plebes out of upper-story barracks windows. In 1874, Congress made hazing a court-martial offense, but despite action by Sampson's predecessor, Francis M. Ramsay, the practice continued. Sampson believed that little infractions led to greater misdeeds, and decided "to bring to trial every form of hazing no matter how trifling." Accordingly, courts-martial heard the cases of two cadets accused of hazing in 1886, convicting and dismissing both of them. The superintendent saw to it that charges were brought against five other cadets in 1887, though none was dismissed. The major hazing incident during Sampson's superintendency involved thirteen cadets in 1888. Nine of them were convicted, and Sampson ordered them dismissed from the Academy. However, President Grover Cleveland reinstated all but one of the cadets after they served a brief punishment tour. Despite this reversal of Sampson's order, other cadets took the lesson, and hazing incidents declined.[18]

Sampson took other actions to modernize the Academy. In the strongest terms, he argued that a modern stream cruiser must replace the antiquated practice ship *Constellation,* the venerable veteran that dated from 1791 (a new ship was provided in 1894). Moreover, Sampson urged that the Academy also deserved its own modern examples of guns and cannon, rather than some leftovers on loan from the Ordnance Bureau. The cadets should have modern engines for classes and laboratories. Other items on Sampson's list of proposed improvements included enlarging the library building, increasing the number of books, and efficiently organizing the card file system; switching from gas to electric lighting in Academy buildings; and purchasing several acres of land near the Academy for use as drill and athletic fields. The navy instituted most of these changes by the mid-1890s. Using language that presaged the "progressive" reforms of the early twentieth century, Sampson established two new departments—the Department of Discipline to improve the behavior, character, and morale of cadets, and the Department of Physiology and Hygiene to improve cadet morals by stressing the ill-effects of alcoholic beverages "and other stimulants." By the end of Sampson's tenure as superintendent, his changes and improvements in discipline and academics had improved cadet retention, reducing dismissals of cadets from 22 percent of the battalion in 1887 to 14 percent in 1889.[19]

After several years ashore, Sampson returned to sea duty, assigned to the new protected cruiser *San Francisco*. In July 1890, he moved to California to oversee the final steps in completing the ship and to supervise speed tests and sea trials. Sampson sailed in the *San Francisco* to Chile in March 1891, but after commanding the ship for little more than a year he received orders in June 1892 for yet another administrative assignment—inspector of ordnance at the Washington Navy Yard.[20]

Sampson served as inspector of ordnance from mid-September 1892 to January 1893, preparing to become chief of the Bureau of Ordnance (a position he held from early 1893 to May 1897). As inspector of ordnance, Sampson surveyed work under way and observed the final construction of a modern naval gun factory, which was able to cast 13-inch guns. His duties offered a kaleidoscope of technological responsibility: supervising the manufacture of gun mounts for capital ships, accepting or rejecting powder furnished under contract by such firms as E. I. Du Pont de Nemours & Co., approving shell casings produced by Winchester and other concerns, and testing a variety of mechanical systems. As a part of his work, Sampson evaluated Ensign Joseph Strauss's designs for double-decked turrets (8-inch guns above and 13-inch below) for the new battleships *Kentucky* and *Kearsarge*. Although it presented difficulties, especially in regard to moving ammunition by hoists passing through the turrets, which created dangers from flash and explosion, Sampson approved Strauss's design.[21]

While at Ordnance, Sampson sustained an interest in improving American industry's capability to produce high-technology items such as nickel–steel armor. Sampson believed that such industrial capability was "an important aid to the national defense."[22] In the fall of 1893, Sampson led an investigation on behalf of the Navy Department into the Carnegie Steel Company's failure to provide the quality of armor plate specified in its contract. Subsequently, other cases of questionable manufacturing practices or lack of quality control came to light in the armor scandals, which also involved Linden Steel Works and Standard Steel Casting Company. In the Carnegie case, Sampson recommended a fine equaling 15 percent of the price of armor delivered during 1892–93, but President Cleveland reduced the fine to 10 percent. Sampson wanted to force Carnegie Steel and other companies to deliver the high-quality armor they were capable of producing, specifically, "Harveyized" steel, using an expensive hardening process developed by an American, Augustus Harvey. "Harveyized" steel had passed extraordinary naval tests in 1890, and Sampson believed that though it was more costly it was worth the price. He would not accept second-rate steel for use in America's new ships.[23]

Besides obtaining high-grade steel, other technological problems challenged Sampson during his tenure as Ordnance chief, such as developing turret-turning systems for the navy's new battleships and cruisers. Overall, Sampson concluded that the "good control [of] electricity is preferable to any other method of turning turrets." Although he received assistance from experts such as Bradley A. Fiske, an experienced inventor and naval officer, Sampson found that interbureau rivalries prevented him from resolving the turret system question to his satisfaction.[24]

Another problem plaguing Sampson during his years at Ordnance concerned the quality of powder. In his reports as chief of Ordnance, Sampson remarked on the poor quality of powder delivered from major suppliers, such as Du Pont. In 1895, he wrote that the "difficulty of obtaining a satisfactory brown powder for the larger calibers, as well as the many inconveniences attendant upon the use of brown powder, emphasize the importance of developing a smokeless powder for all calibers." During 1896 Sampson and his inspectors at Ordnance accepted 699,847 pounds of brown powder as being of satisfactory quality while rejecting 835,700 pounds of powder as substandard.[25]

By mid-1896, rumors began to circulate that war was likely between the United States and Spain over the rebellion in Cuba. Although a *New York Times* headline announced that war was "Not Believed to be Probable," in December Secretary of the Navy Herbert called a special board (with Sampson as a member) to consider naval plans in the event of war with Spain. This board developed one of several plans considered by the Navy Department prior to the outbreak of war. In May of 1897, Sampson left the Ordnance Bureau to take command of the 11,000-ton battleship *Iowa,* the U.S. Navy's most modern ship.[26]

By 1897, Sampson (age fifty-seven) had been in the navy for forty years, and, although it was not obvious at the time, his health was declining. It is impossible now to determine exactly what may have afflicted him, but it could have been Alzheimer's disease.[27] In the coming months, it appears that the disease made increasing inroads on Sampson's health, while permitting him days in which he seemed fit. Occasionally, a naval secretary would require an officer to undergo a medical examination, the results of which could force his retirement. At that time, however, the American military services required no regular medical checkups for senior officers; thus Sampson hid his declining health from superiors and subordinates. That Sampson and his army counterpart in the Santiago Campaign, Major General William R. Shafter (who at age sixty-three was six feet tall, weighed 300 pounds, and suffered from gout),[28] held combat command overseas in time of war is another confirmation that reforms were needed in the American military services.

In early 1898, U.S. relations with Spain worsened, prompting President William McKinley to send the battleship *Maine* to Havana, as a symbol of American interest in Cuba. On 16 February an explosion ripped apart the *Maine,* killing 260 officers and sailors; wild speculation about the explosion made war between Spain and the United States likely, but President McKinley demanded information about the causes of the *Maine*'s destruction. Sampson was appointed president of a court of inquiry, and over the next month, assisted by the other court members including Captain French E. Chadwick, he inspected the ship's wreckage and heard testimony from survivors and witnesses. Sampson issued a report on 21 March 1898 concluding that the *Maine* had been sunk by an explosion caused by an unknown external source. Even with all his ordnance and technological experience, Sampson remained convinced that the *Maine* was "destroyed by [an] external agency," although subsequent investigations indicated that an internal explosion, probably due to spontaneous combustion of coal near ammunition stores, had blown up the ship.[29]

Three days after the *Maine* court concluded its work, Sampson replaced Montgomery Sicard as commander of the U.S. North Atlantic Squadron, the navy's most prestigious post. On 21 April, Sampson was appointed acting rear admiral, boosted over more than a dozen senior officers, including the flamboyant Winfield Schley, who was given command of the independent Flying Squadron to protect the East Coast from Spanish raiders.[30] Naturally, some officers grumbled about Sampson's promotion, but peacetime seniority lists did not dictate combat assignments. Adding to the ill-feelings over Sampson's promotion was the fact that in 1895 Sampson and his friend French Chadwick had surprised the establishment, voting to allow low-ranking officers full participation in the Line Officers Association, heretofore dominated by top-ranking senior officers. Furthermore, Sampson lacked the warm personality or professional flair that might have smoothed relations with his high-ranking fellows. A writer for *McClure's* noted that the admiral was "not an affable man," and Mahan, no glad-hander himself, called Sampson "statuesque and unemotional."[31]

Refusing to bicker with his detractors, Sampson bent to his duties. He knew that Admiral Pascual Cervera and a six-ship squadron were approaching the Caribbean, and considered the defeat of this enemy fleet his first goal. However, in early May, General Nelson A. Miles proposed that the army make a landing that summer or fall near Havana, Cuba. In view of Miles's proposal, Sampson drew up a plan to reduce the Spanish forts at Havana as a prelude to an army landing. Secretary Long and Alfred Thayer Mahan advised caution, emphasizing that Sampson must not jeopardize his capital ships by exposing them to coastal artillery. The naval balance in the Atlantic seemed so close that the loss of one or two ships could tip it in favor of the Spanish.[32]

While the army hastily gathered an expeditionary force at Tampa, Sampson intended to intercept Admiral Cervera's squadron by stationing ships off the most likely resupply points, including San Juan, Puerto Rico, and Cienfuegos (on Cuba's south coast), Havana, and Santiago. Sampson's squadron steamed to Havana, and, after establishing a blockade, went on to Puerto Rico where he hoped to find

Cervera. Learning that Cervera was not in San Juan, Sampson ordered his ships to bombard the city's forts. The squadron neither inflicted nor sustained much damage, but the action gave crews and officers needed gunnery practice. Leaving San Juan, Sampson's squadron went to Cap Haitien, Haiti, where he received messages from the U.S. consul in Curaçao and Secretary Long. The consul related that Cervera's ships had briefly stopped at Curaçao and then left on the evening of 15 May, "destination unknown." Secretary Long ordered Sampson back to Key West for recoaling, because he, like Sampson, was still concerned that Cervera would slip by undetected and threaten the coast of the United States. Accordingly, Long directed Schley to move the Flying Squadron to Key West, where he arrived on 18 May, in preparation for steaming to the Gulf or the Caribbean. Meanwhile, the Spanish evaded the American dispatch boats stationed to watch for them, and sailed from Curaçao to Santiago.[33]

Schley departed Key West for Cienfuegos on 19 May, but that evening the Navy Department informed Sampson that Cervera had already reached Santiago. On the twentieth of May, the department reiterated this information and urged Sampson to order Schley on to Santiago. Sampson seemed doubtful about these reports, and his doubts crept into his message, sent by dispatch boat, to Schley, informing him of Cervera's location and directing him to leave Cienfuegos lightly guarded and proceed to Santiago. The dispatch boat met Schley at Cienfuegos on the twenty-second, just after his arrival.[34]

By 23 May, Sampson concluded that Cervera was in Santiago. Again, at Long's urging, he sent a message to Schley, but he again allowed doubts or qualifications to creep into the orders, which reached Schley on 24 May: "Spanish squadron *probably* at Santiago de Cuba— 4 ships and 3 torpedo boat destroyers. *If* you are satisfied that they are not at Cienfuegos, proceed with all dispatch, *but cautiously* to Santiago de Cuba, and *if* the enemy is there blockade him in port [emphasis added]."[35]

Upon reaching Cienfuegos, Schley was derelict in his responsibilities, neither making prompt contact with Cuban insurgents nor putting a reconnaissance party ashore to confirm or deny that Cervera was in port. Instead, Schley drifted off Cienfuegos and only through the efforts of Commander Bowman McCalla did he learn that Cervera was not in Cienfuegos; then, on 24 May, still hindered by mechanical difficulties with his collier and by heavy seas that hampered two of his auxiliaries, Schley proceeded slowly toward Santiago.[36]

Meanwhile, in Washington, President McKinley convened a meeting of his military advisors. Informed that mounting a major expeditionary force in mid-1898 would seriously strain U.S resources, and convinced that the Spanish fleet was at Santiago, the president ordered that it, not Havana, should become the target of American operations. On 27 May, Sampson received orders first to verify the location of the Spanish fleet and then to leave Schley to blockade the port while he proceeded to Tampa to escort army transports to the area.

On 26 May, the day of the strategy meeting, Schley began a series of actions that mystified his squadron officers, angered Long, and alarmed Sampson. Shortly after arriving near Santiago, and without sending a reconnaissance party ashore, Schley decided, in what might be interpreted as going against orders, to return to Key West, claiming that heavy seas prevented the recoaling of his ships. The Flying Squadron began retracing its old route westward toward Cienfuegos. Following one day's slow steaming Schley ordered his ships to pause, and began recoaling when they found calmer seas; subsequently, they seemed to drift for several hours. Schley then signaled a change of course back to Santiago. Robley Evans, captain of the *Iowa,* recalled, "As there had been no conference of commanding officers, we were all completely bewildered as to what his peculiar maneuvering might mean." Echoing Evans's views, Seaton Schroeder an officer in the *Massachusetts,* recalled his "astonishment" at Schley's order to leave Santiago in the first place, and his mystification at being ordered to "lay to" for several hours during the night of 27–28 May. Once Secretary Long learned of Schley's bewildering behavior, he had grounds to remove him from command. No doubt Schley's removal would have caused a controversy, but replacing him for cause then would not have led to any greater controversy than erupted later between Schley and Sampson. Long simply responded to Schley's perplexing actions with clear orders: confirm Cervera's presence in Santiago. Otherwise, Long told Schley, "You must surmount difficulties regarding coaling by your own ingenuity and perseverance."[37]

Sampson, too, sent a stream of messages to Schley; indicative is one dated 27 May: "You will please proceed with all possible dispatch to Santiago to blockade that port. If, on arrival there, you receive *positive* [original emphasis] information of the Spanish ships having left you will follow them in pursuit." Although this note did not reach Schley for several days, it was obvious that Sampson wanted action and that Schley was losing Sampson's confidence. Therefore, on 28 May, Sampson decided to take the North Atlantic Squadron to Santiago. Because of divided counsel among the senior Spanish officials, who maintained contact with Spain by undersea cable, Admiral Cervera accommodated the Americans by remaining docilely in Santiago.[38]

Towing two monitors, and naturally slowed in the process, Sampson's squadron made its way to Santiago, arriving on 1 June. For some unknown reason, Sampson waited until 11 June to order a reconnaissance to confirm the location and disposition of Cervera's squadron in Santiago, but in the meantime he was quick to reorganize the blockade. Displeased with Schley's blockading arrangement, Sampson set about instituting a close blockade of his own design, "gradually shortening the radius of the [blockade's] arc of patrol from six to four miles during the day and to three at night." Always one to stress technology, on 8 June the admiral incorporated powerful searchlights into his tactical plan, ordering that ships alternately train their searchlights on the mouth of Santiago harbor at night. Sampson aimed to reduce confusion and increase his chances of victory by setting out careful prebattle dispositions for the ships of his squadron—redesignated the North Atlantic Fleet on 21 June. Incorporating Schley's Flying Squadron, Sampson's new command clamped a lid on Santiago channel; each ship maintained a specific spot on the blockading arc, bows pointing toward the channel entrance, one battleship prepared to close in if the Spaniards came out. Most officers later agreed with John W. Philip, captain of the *Texas*, that it was "the blockade that made the battle [of Santiago] possible." Within a week of arriving off Santiago, the fleet settled down to a routine: alert patrolling; vigilant searchlight duty; waiting for provisions and mail from Key West, Florida; recoaling at the recently captured base at Guantanamo, Cuba. There were some distractions: reports of another Spanish squadron bearing down on American waters proved erroneous; sinking a collier near the harbor entrance failed to block the channel; Cuban insurgent General Calixto Garcia visited Sampson in his flagship; the Navy Department considered reassigning some of Sampson's ships to a proposed "Eastern Squadron" that would attack the Spanish coast, but the matter was dropped.[39]

Along with these distractions, Sampson dealt with a demand that always challenged the patience of top naval officers: cooperating with a senior U.S. Army officer in command of an expeditionary force. In the Spanish War, unlike more mature (but still difficult) unified command arrangements of wars in the twentieth century, no single officer was placed in charge of the Santiago campaign. Sampson had to share command responsibilities with Major General William Shafter, an irascible officer whose experience focused on leading small units against Indians on the Trans-Mississippi frontier. Shafter believed that the navy must force its way through the channel (despite mines and other hazards), bombard Spanish fortifications, and defeat Cervera's squadron, which otherwise might fire on Shafter's soldiers as they drew near the city. Sampson, on the other hand, was under orders from Secretary Long not to risk his capital ships unnecessarily, especially against a mined channel covered by guns on shore. Sampson wanted the army (perhaps in cooperation with the Cubans) to neutralize the Spanish emplacements along the channel; then the navy could clear the mines. Sampson and Long agreed with Alfred Mahan: "If we lost ten thousand men, the country could replace them; if we lost a battleship, it could not be replaced." Of great concern to the navy's leaders was a potential catastrophe in which the loss of three or four American capital ships would be a terrible blow to national morale and might appear to put the opposing naval forces on a more equal footing, notwithstanding the evident American superiority in gunnery, ships' conditions, and sheer numbers. Shafter, Secretary of War Russell Alger, and U.S. Army officers saw their service braving the risks of battle and unhealthy jungle camps while the U.S. Navy stood safely offshore. The army's leaders had no sympathy with the navy's apparently cavalier attitude toward soldiers' lives, as indicated by Sampson's message to Secretary Long on 6 June: "If 10,000 men were here city and fleet would be ours within forty-eight hours." [40]

In fairness to both Sampson and Shafter, there were no recent models of army–navy cooperation; experiences of combined operations in the Civil War seemed long in the past. Furthermore, neither formal instructions nor past experience indicated how staff officers from the two services should consider common problems, reach compromises, and draft operations orders directing forces to take enemy objectives around Santiago. The lack of interservice coordination indicated further need of reform in the American military services.

On 20 June, Sampson, assisted by Chadwick, met with Shafter and Cuban officers about eighteen miles west of Santiago at Aserraderos, where they shared their misimpressions and departed, each believing the other would support his overall plans to defeat the Spanish. They did agree that the navy would protect and assist Shafter's troops coming ashore, first at Daiquiri and later at Siboney (22–24 June).[41]

Meanwhile, the Spanish minister of marine authorized the governor general of Cuba, Ramon Blanco y Erenas, to assume command over all imperial forces in Cuba, including Cervera's squadron. The admiral's ships were in deplorable condition, with fouled bottoms that significantly reduced their speed. The armored cruiser *Cristóbal Colón* was missing its two 10-inch heavy guns, and the *Vizcaya* and *Almirante Oquendo* had inoperable guns in their batteries. Facing an American fleet of superior numbers and in excellent operating condition, Cervera believed it would be a mistake to challenge the enemy at sea. At this point officials in Washington goaded Shafter into action—the fighting of 1 July on San Juan Heights. Misinterpreting the attack as coming from strength and indicating additional assaults, Governor General Blanco ordered Cervera's six-ship squadron to sortie. Reluctantly Cervera prepared to comply with the orders.[42]

On the same day, 2 July, Shafter, convinced that his troops had survived a "terrible fight" at San Juan Hill, renewed his demand that Sampson enter the harbor and attack the Spanish squadron. Sampson again refused to attempt to force the harbor entrance until the army captured the forts and the mines were removed. Having kept most of his fleet continuously on duty, Sampson gave permission for the battleship *Massachusetts,* the cruisers *New Orleans* and *Newark,* and the auxiliary *Suwannee* to coal at Guantanamo on 3 July. The battleships *Indiana, Oregon, Iowa,* and *Texas,* the armored cruiser *Brooklyn* (under Schley), and several auxiliaries remained on station. Sampson also picked 3 July, a Sunday, to hold another personal meeting with Shafter. The general was too ill with gout to come to Sampson, so on the morning of the third Sampson had already donned leggings and spurs in preparation for the ride to the army camp. As he stood on the bridge of the cruiser *New York,* Sampson appeared anxious. Associated Press correspondent W. A. M. Goode, sailing with Sampson, recalled the admiral saying, "If I leave, I'm sure something will happen." Goode noted that Sampson "was not in very good health, and was well-nigh worn out with the tremendous strain of the past month. . . . The physical and mental strain . . . had confined him once or twice to his bed."[43]

At approximately 8:55 a.m. the *New York* swung out of line, steaming away to the meeting with General Shafter. Although Sampson had not officially relinquished command, he was off station, making

Schley senior officer on the scene. The next half hour was a typical Sunday morning on blockade: officers in dress uniform inspected lines of sailors; nothing appeared extraordinary. At 9:25 the *New York* was almost out of signal distance. Spotters suddenly shouted down to decks and bridges below that they sighted smoke in the channel. Then came the call: "They're coming out!" In the *Texas,* Captain Philip looked at his watch; it read 9:36 a.m. Electric gongs sounded general quarters as Philip looked toward the harbor mouth. Brightly decorated, "the Spanish ships came out as gaily as brides to the alter." Signal flags snapped up in the *Iowa:* "Enemy is attempting to escape." The response was the same throughout the American fleet: sailors dashed to their guns; officers went to battle stations. Sampson's long-standing orders to "close in towards [the] harbor entrance" automatically went into effect. A disaster almost befell the Americans at the outset, when, because of misspoken or misunderstood orders by officers on the bridge of the *Brooklyn,* Schley's ship nearly collided with the *Texas.* The two ships sorted themselves out with no damage and took up pursuit of Cervera, whose squadron had turned west toward the Gulf of Mexico. Meanwhile, at the moment the Spanish ships debouched from the channel, Sampson was heart-struck. He ordered the *New York*'s helmsman to "turn back immediately." The admiral's next thought was: "Oh, that we had wings!" The *New York* vainly raced to reach the battle before it was over.[44]

In three and one-half hours Cervera led his squadron to destruction. Despite being understrength (with ships away coaling), Sampson's fleet (minus the admiral) overwhelmed its enemy. All six Spanish vessels were sunk or forced to beach themselves. No American ship received serious damage. The Spanish lost 474 men killed and wounded; 1,750 officers and sailors were taken prisoner, including Cervera himself. The Americans lost one killed and one wounded.[45] The Atlantic Fleet's lopsided victory at Santiago, coupled with Commodore George Dewey's remarkable victory over a Spanish squadron at Manila on 1 May, forced Spain to sue for peace. These naval victories lifted the United States from the rank of fifth- or sixth-rate power to a new military force that had to be recognized by the major nations. Sampson's technologically perfect blockade and his preparations for battle thus had contributed significantly to America's new status.[46]

On 3 July, however, these results were not assured, and Sampson desperately wanted to join in the battle himself. Instead, even as the *New York*'s engines propelled the ship toward the fighting, the ad-

Battle of Santiago. Dr. Alfonso Saenz, a Spanish Navy surgeon, painted this view of the battle in 1899 at Spain's Ferrol navy base. It was subsequently purchased by George J. Seabury of New York and hung in the Army Navy Club. *Courtesy of the Naval Historical Center.*

miral became a witness after the fact. One by one, the *New York* passed the Spanish ships as they lay dead in the water or beached; in one instance, Chadwick ordered guns fired at the crippled Spanish destroyer *Furor,* which had already been severely damaged by salvos from other American ships. Such was the *New York*'s (and Sampson's) limited participation in combat. No American officer, including Schley, had any semblance of direct control over the U.S. ships during the fighting itself. Therefore, Santiago was "a captain's fight."[47] Unable to restrict the battle to a small area by closing in on the channel mouth, the Americans broke from Sampson's blockade arc. The Spanish, despite foul bottoms, faulty ammunition, and inoperable guns, managed to string out the pursuing Americans along seventy-five miles of the Cuban coast in a pursuit-and-fire exercise.

Neither Sampson's excellent management of the blockade nor his use of searchlights was at issue on 3 July; it was a question of who deserved credit for the naval victory. It is worth noting that back in April, "Fighting Bob" Evans, captain of the *Iowa,* had considered himself in command of Sampson's squadron when the admiral left station to pursue an unidentified ship. In that case, Sampson was absent for several hours. If Evans had happened upon Cervera's squadron then, few would have awarded Sampson credit or blame for a battle's outcome; at that time, Evans would have been the senior officer pres-

Sampson's cabin on board the USS *New York.* This photograph was published as the frontispiece to W. A. M. Goode's *With Sampson through the War* (1899). *Courtesy of the Naval Historical Center.*

ent.[48] Undoubtedly, the circumstances on 3 July were more complicated. In the *New York,* Sampson was physically present to witness
scenes of destruction. If Sampson had been ashore at Shafter's headquarters, the victory at Santiago would have belonged to Schley.

The controversy between Sampson and Schley started as soon as
the *New York* approached the *Brooklyn,* at about 1:45 p.m. on 3 July.
Schley ordered a signal sent to Sampson: "We have gained a great
victory. Details will be communicated." It was brief, but not insult-
ing, and Schley had used "we" to begin the message. Five minutes
passed. The return signal from the *New York* read: "Report your
casualties." Schley may not have known that Sampson had demanded
the same report from each American ship as he approached them,
but it seemed to Schley (and his friend, journalist George Graham)
that the message was unnecessarily curt; was this not a time of victory and jubilation? Schley reported as ordered, and then tried again
to produce a friendly exchange: "This is a great day for our country."
Chadwick, on the bridge with Sampson, merely acknowledged re-
ceipt, declining to send a histrionic reply. A short while later, Chadwick left the *New York* to inspect the Spanish ship *Cristóbal Colón,*
which had been beached by her captain. In Chadwick's absence a
staff officer prepared a brief dispatch (five sentences) for Sampson to
send to Secretary Long. It began: "The fleet under my command
offers the nation as a Fourth of July present the whole of Cervera's
fleet." Journalists quickly noted two things about Sampson's dispatch: first, the admiral made no mention of Schley, and, second,
the dispatch seemed to copy the wording of a telegram from General
William T. Sherman to President Abraham Lincoln after Sherman's
army captured Savannah, Georgia, in 1864. Sampson's rather boast-
ful message, and his failure to mention Schley, combined with newspaper coverage of Schley's peculiar maneuvers between Cienfuegos
and Santiago, his "loop" to escape colliding with the *Texas,* and his
efforts to gain commander's laurels for the Santiago victory, fueled
the Sampson–Schley controversy in the weeks, months, and years to
come.[49]

As contention within the U.S. Navy marred Sampson's victory,
the U.S. Army still struggled in the trenches outside Santiago. Shafter continued to demand that Sampson act against the Spanish forts.
Sampson rejected the demand. The admiral and the general exchanged notes saying they could not travel. Shafter was ill because
of the heat; it is not clear whether the admiral just wanted the general to meet him on board ship or if Sampson was genuinely ill,

Sampson on board the USS *New York*. A comparison of this photograph, taken in the winter of 1898–99, with the preceding portrait reflects the rapid deterioration of Sampson's health in a period of less than a year. *Courtesy of the Naval Historical Center.*

perhaps a recurrence of his chronic malady. Shafter complained to Army Adjutant General Henry C. Corbin that "if Sampson will force an entrance with all his fleet to the upper bay, we [the Army] can take the city within a few hours." Corbin notified Shafter: "The President directs that you confer with Admiral Sampson *at once for cooperation in taking Santiago* [emphasis added]." In reply, Shafter protested that with the Spanish fleet destroyed and no naval threat imminent, Sampson should act "at any cost." If the navy did not attack first, Shafter concluded that "the country should be prepared for heavy losses among our troops." Responding again on behalf of McKinley, Corbin demanded that Shafter and Sampson confer "and determine a course of cooperation best calculated to secure desirable results, with least sacrifice." Secretary Long urged Sampson to coordinate plans with the army, but it was obvious that the Navy Department did not want to jeopardize any capital ships.[50]

The stalemate between the U.S. Army and the U.S. Navy in Cuba continued for several days. Because of Sampson's persisting illness (after the war he specified that he "was suffering from a headache"), Chadwick stepped in to handle negotiations between the interservice rivals. After two days of dealing with Chadwick, Shafter telegraphed the War Department: "No assault will be made of advance from our present lines until the Navy comes into the bay."[51] On 10 July, in order to spur negotiations between Shafter and the Spanish, Sampson agreed to order his ships to bombard enemy positions. The shelling caused little damage but made a good display.[52]

On 11 July, Commanding General of the Army Nelson A. Miles arrived in Cuba, and initially he supported Sampson's idea that the army attack the Spanish forts. Within a few days, however, Miles joined Shafter in a united army front against the navy. Furthermore, another divisive interservice issue had arisen. Sampson wanted a naval officer present at negotiations with the Spanish and he was especially concerned about "the surrender of shipping and the harbor," but Shafter declined to allow a naval officer to join the negotiations.[53]

On 14 July, Spanish and American representatives reached agreement on the surrender of Santiago. When Sampson learned of the capitulation ceremonies late on the afternoon of 16 July, he ordered Captain Chadwick to represent the navy, but he arrived too late to participate. Eventually Sampson was allowed to sign the articles of capitulation. Not surprisingly, officers of the two services argued for several days over which of them would man captured Spanish vessels. As if these disputations were not enough, Miles and Sampson sent several telegrams arguing over how the navy should assist the army in the coming campaign against the Spanish in Puerto Rico.[54]

Simultaneous with the interservice squabbles, the Sampson–Schley controversy was boiling in earnest, fueled by Alfred T. Mahan, who established the basic pro-Sampson argument:

> The latter [Schley] is a gallant man and a good officer; but Sampson has borne the burden and the responsibility of the long watch before Santiago, and was unquestionably responsible for the disposition of the ships. *The shame would have been his had Cervera escaped from bad dispositions* [emphasis added].

Soon salvos arced back and forth in the newspapers, defending or criticizing either Sampson or Schley. On 7 August, the *New York Sun* printed a letter from Mahan emphasizing that Sampson deserved the accolades of victory, and that criticism of Sampson was "designed to deprive an eminent officer of the just reward of his toils." The bitterness intensified when Sampson was promoted eight places on the permanent naval list, but Schley was advanced only six places; these promotions put Sampson one up on Schley. As a twentieth-century historian concluded: "Put another way, the man who missed the Battle of Santiago was promoted above the man who was in the thick of it."[55]

By the end of 1898, only six months after Santiago, the Sampson–Schley controversy was in full cry, and Sampson's health began to fail noticeably. On 29 December, Secretary Long (who was pro-Sampson) accompanied the admiral on a visit to President McKinley. Long's description of Sampson shows how far his health had deteriorated: "Really I see nothing more pathetic than the Admiral. He is worn to skin and bone. His eyes are large and almost appealing. I fancy he half falters as he walks."[56]

For most of 1899, Sampson remained in command of the North Atlantic Station, but evidently his health would not permit him to continue at sea. In September he left his ships and loyal captains, and in October he took charge of the Boston Navy Yard, a sedentary sinecure that was not physically demanding. During the year, newspaper and magazine articles perpetuated the Sampson–Schley controversy. In December, Secretary Long issued an order to naval officers not to engage in public discussion of the affair. In the last three months of 1899, Sampson made several public appearances, including receptions or banquets in his honor at Palmyra and Rochester, New York, and at Boston.[57]

During 1900, Sampson remained in uniform though he had an opportunity to leave the U.S. Navy when the trustees of the Massachusetts Institute of Technology offered him its presidency. He elected to stay in the navy where, perhaps, he had been promised active duty until mandatory retirement in 1902. He attended to official matters and, when possible, participated in the affairs of the U.S. Naval Institute, serving as president of the Institute from 1897 to 1902.

If Sampson hoped for active duty, he was disappointed. Illness plagued his last years, and Alfred Thayer Mahan later recalled that "after the Spanish War, [Sampson's] prolonged frail health and incipient decay had wasted the vigorous frame I had once known, and set on him the mark of death's approach." Furthermore, Mahan noted that in Sampson's "conversation, ordinarily, there was nothing more noticeable than a certain impassivity of manner that was readily mistaken for indifference or lack of response. This at times gave offence, particularly in his later years, when bodily weakness imparted lassitude to his speech."[58]

In early September 1901, Sampson was stricken again and went into seclusion at Lake Sunapee, a retreat near Manchester, New Hampshire. By this time Rear Admiral Schley had finally asked for an official court of inquiry to settle the numerous questions of the Sampson–Schley controversy. His request was forced by publication of the third volume of Edgar S. Maclay's *History of the United States Navy*, which condemned Schley's actions and decisions during the entire Santiago Campaign. The court consisted of Admiral George Dewey (president) and Rear Admirals Francis M. Ramsay and Arthur E. K. Benham. Sampson's doctor, Henry G. Beyer, made it clear to Secretary Long that the admiral was too ill to testify, being gripped by "a mental depression, the most constant symptom of which is a certain form of aphasia characterized by his mixing up words." Sampson's absence made a complete investigation impossible. The court issued its findings in December after hearing dozens of witnesses, including Schley himself. The court found two to one (Dewey dissenting) that Schley's command in the Santiago campaign before 1 June 1898 "was characterized by vacillation, dilatoriness and lack of enterprise." Furthermore, the court judged that "the turn of the *Brooklyn* to the eastward was made to avoid getting her into dangerous proximity to the Spanish vessel," raising the question of cowardice on Schley's part. Yet both Ramsey and Benham complimented Schley for having "encouraged in his own person his subordinate officers and men to fight courageously." Dewey, however, dissented from the negative conclusions of the majority, and found that Schley's conduct had been effective and competent. But, most important, Dewey went beyond the findings of the court's other members and concluded that: "Commander Schley was the senior officer of our squadron off Santiago when the Spanish attempted to escape. . . . He was in absolute command and is entitled to the credit due to such a commanding officer for the glorious victory which resulted in the total destruction of the Spanish ships." The report of the court and Dewey's dissent led Schley to appeal the verdict to President Theodore Roosevelt.[59]

Sampson's last six months were spent in bed under the close care of his wife, who frequently called physicians to their house. In February 1902, a visitor revealed that the admiral was "unable to recognize even the members of his family, who surround his bedside. He does not know he has been retired [from the Navy]." Late that month, President Roosevelt, in an attempt to put the Sampson–Schley controversy to rest, announced his support for Sampson and endorsed the verdict of the majority of the court of inquiry. Although Long supported Sampson, the publication of Long's own account of his years as naval secretary, as well as other articles and essays, kept the controversy alive for years to come.[60]

Sampson died in Washington D.C., on 6 May 1902 from a cerebral hemorrhage. He was buried in Arlington National Cemetery.[61]

Sampson's main legacies to the U.S. Navy consist of the improvements he instituted at the Naval Academy and his emphasis on technology. Certainly he was not the lone naval officer of the 1880s and 1890s to stress technology; Bradley Fiske and several others demonstrate that the navy, more than the army, has always needed an officer corps with scientific and technical expertise. But Santiago also indicated that Sampson, whose life until then seemed largely devoted to scientific work and administration, was a technologist who also could organize and lead a battle fleet effectively in wartime. Surely that would have been the verdict if Sampson had been present throughout the battle at Santiago. He knew other admirals, including John A. Dahlgren and Samuel F. Du Pont, whose reputations had foundered on blockade duty. Had the *New York* taken a more direct part in the victory over Cervera's squadron, Sampson, like Dewey and Roosevelt, would have been a hero of the hour.

Instead, Sampson became involved with Schley in a ceaseless controversy over who deserved credit for Santiago. Although only one year younger than Sampson, Schley lived until 1911, defending himself and his conduct to the end, and publishing a popular autobiography. Sampson would have agreed with an aphorism attributed to Lord Nelson: "The great thing in all military service is health." The collapse of his health left Sampson with no other choice than to have his friends make his claim as victor of Santiago. One of those friends, Robley Evans, supported his admiral stoutly, concluding that "Sampson at Santiago had completed the work so brilliantly begun by Dewey at Manila."[62] Unfortunately for Sampson, his other legacy to his navy was the bitter controversy that divided its officer corps into "Sampsonites" or "Schleyites" for the rest of their lives.

FURTHER READING

Unlike George Dewey, whose reputation improved even after his death in 1917, William T. Sampson and his accomplishments dropped from public view following his death in 1902. Richard S. West, Jr. revived attention to Sampson's multifaceted career and the Sampson–Schley controversy in *Admirals of American Empire,* the best secondary account of Sampson's life.

While conducting his research, West interviewed one of Sampson's sons, Commander Ralph E. Sampson, USN, retired. In the interview Commander Sampson revealed to West that his mother had burned most of the admiral's personal papers and correspondence (note by West, William T. Sampson Collection, in Special Collections Division, Nimitz Library, U.S. Naval Academy, Annapolis). Therefore, a close study of official records of one kind or another is central to a reevaluation of Sampson's naval career. Crucial are the various documents and reports in the *Annual Reports of the Secretary of the Navy* during the 1870s, 1880s, and 1890s. Beneficial are the Records of the U.S. Naval Academy, Letters Sent by the Superintendent of the U.S. Naval Academy (Main Series), 1865–1907, in the National Archives, which contain many letters, mostly about routine matters, during the years when Sampson was superintendent of the Academy.

A variety of letters and reports concerning Sampson's squadron and fleet operations are in the Area Files of the Naval Records Collection, Area 8, in the National Archives. Some of these documents are also available in *Annual Report of the Secretary of the Navy for 1898* and U.S. Department of War, *Correspondence Relating to the War with Spain* (2 vols.). Records of Naval Operating Forces in the National Archives contain copies of many important documents regarding Sampson's squadron and fleet operations, including Circular Letters Issued by Rear Admiral William T. Sampson, March–August 1898; Reports of Naval Engagements from Commanding Officers of Vessels; Information Copies of Letters Received from Commanding Officers of Vessels, March–August 1898; and the Journal of Rear Admiral William T. Sampson, March–August 1898. By far the most important of these is the "Journal," actually a compendium of reports, messages, letters, memoranda, and orders, including the printed "Squadron Bulletins" for the summer of 1898. Some of these documents also are found in *Annual Report of the Secretary of the Navy for 1898* and *Correspondence Relating to the War with Spain.*

Of the many secondary treatments of the Spanish War, David Trask's *The War with Spain in 1898* is the complete description and analysis. Still useful is French E. Chadwick's two-volume *The Relations of the United States and Spain: The Spanish–American War.* Particularly helpful in highlighting the army–navy disagreements is Louis J. Gulliver's article "Sampson and Shafter at Santiago."

Several contemporary magazine articles or books help give the pace and flavor of the blockade and battle of Santiago. Among the best is W. A. M. Goode's *With Sampson through the War.* Various officers and officials wrote memoirs or recollections that give glimpses or descriptions of Sampson. Most significant is Alfred T. Mahan's 1902 essay "Sampson's Naval Career," originally published in *McClure's Magazine* and included in Mahan's book, *Retrospect and Prospect*. Mahan's essay provides important descriptions of Sampson's declining health after Santiago, as do several accounts in the *New York Times*.

NOTES

1. Richard Wainwright, "William Thomas Sampson," 456; Caspar F. Goodrich, *Rope Yarns from the Old Navy*, 23.

2. William T. Sampson File, Palmyra King's Daughters Free Library, Palmyra, New York; *New York Times*, 7 May 1902; Richard S. West, *Admirals of American Empire*, 24–25; Cyrus Baldwin [Principal of Palmyra Union School] to Secretary of the Navy Isaac Toucey, 4 June 1857, William T. Sampson Personal File, Naval Historical Center, Operational Archives Branch, Washington, D.C. Sampson's father's menial occupation (he was a day laborer) and low social standing certainly contrasted with the background of most other "Annapolites." According to Peter Karsten, fewer than 7 percent of cadets' families came from the working class. Karsten, *The Naval Aristocracy*, 12.

3. Alfred T. Mahan, *Retrospect and Prospect*, 292; Edward W. Callahan, *List of Officers of the Navy*, 626–27; West, *Admirals of Empire*, 25–26; Carroll S. Alden and Ralph Earle, *Makers of Naval Tradition*, 273; Charles E. Clark, *My Fifty Years in the Navy*, 24–25; Park Benjamin, *The United States Naval Academy*, 228.

4. West, *Admirals of Empire*, 54–55; *New York Times*, 20 February 1899; Goodrich, *Rope Yarns*, 23.

5. West, *Admirals of Empire*, 56–60; a glowing account of the *Patapsco* incident appeared in *McClure's Magazine* 11 (June 1898): 181; *Official Records of the Union and Confederate Navies*, Series I, 16:176–78; Mahan, *Retrospect and Prospect*, 302.

6. *New York Times*, 20 February 1899; George Dewey, *Autobiography*, 139.

7. James R. Soley, *Historical Sketch of the U.S. Naval Academy*, 195; *New York Times*, 20 February 1899.

8. West, *Admirals of Empire*, 116–17; "William Thomas Sampson, Record of Service," in Sampson File, Biographical Files, Naval Historical Center.

9. *Army and Navy Journal* 12 (19 December 1874): 298, "Board of Visitors Report," in *Annual Report of the Secretary of the Navy, 1878–79*, 46; *Ann. Rept. Sec. Navy, 1877–78*, 62–63; Alden and Earle, *Naval Tradition*, 274–76.

10. Dorothy M. Livingston, *Master of Light: Albert A. Michelson*, 46, 54–58, 62; *Army and Navy Journal* 15 (28 July 1878): 739.

11. Robert E. Johnson, *Far China Station*, 189, 191.

12. Gustavus A. Weber, *The Naval Observatory*, 34–39; West, *Admirals of Empire*, 55, 119–22, 127, 129.

13. Ronald Spector, *Professors of War*, 23–24; John Hattendorf et al., *Sailors and Scholars: The U.S. Naval War College*, 17–21; "Letter from the Secretary of the Navy Report [on] an Advanced Course of Instruction of Naval Officers . . . ," *Senate Exec. Doc. No. 68* (48th Cong., 2nd Sess., Serial 2263), 3–4.

14. *Army and Navy Journal* 22 (11 October 1884): 201.

15. *Ann. Rept. Sec. Navy, 1885–86*, 242–45, 249; Alden and Earle, *Naval Tradition*, 275–76.

16. "Floating Batteries," in *House Exec. Doc. No. 49* (49th Cong., 1st Sess., Serial 2395), 305–13; Sampson, "Outline of a Scheme for the Naval Defense of the Coast," 169–232. See also Robert Browning, *Two If by Sea; Development of American Coastal Defense Policy*, 158–64.

17. Whitney's Report, in *Ann. Rept. of Sec. Navy, 1886–87*, 17; Sampson's Report, ibid., 80–81 [quotation]; Richard S. West, "The Superintendents of the Naval Academy," 804–5; W. D. Puleston, *Annapolis: Gangway to the Quarterdeck*, 114; Benjamin, *Naval Academy*, 331–32, 334; "Board of Visitors Report," in *Ann. Rept. Sec. Navy, 1887–88*, 72–73; *New York Times*, 17 November 1887; Alden and Earle, *Naval Tradition*, 227; Sweetman, *The U.S. Naval Academy*, 125.

18. *New York Times*, 26 September 1886; 24 and 25 August, 17 November 1887 [quotation]; 25 July, 18 August, and 4 September 1888; *Ann. Rept. Sec. Navy, 1887–88* (Serial 2539), xlii, 77, 79; Sampson's Report, in *Ann. Rept. Sec. Navy, 1888–89* (Serial 2639), 26; Sweetman, *U.S. Naval Academy*, 124. See the letters from Sampson to parents of the thirteen cadets regarding prospective courts-martial for their sons, all dated 13 July 1888, Record Group (hereafter R.G.) 405: Records of the U.S. Naval Academy, National Archives (hereafter NA), Washington, D.C.

19. Benjamin, *Naval Academy*, 338, 413; *Ann. Rept. Sec. Navy, 1887–88* (Serial 2539), xlii, 80–81; *Ann. Rept. Sec. Navy, 1888–89*, 25–26, 32; *Ann. Rept. Sec. Navy, 1889–90*, 427; *Ann. Rept. Sec. Navy, 1891*, 167; *New York Times*, 17 November 1887; Order from Sampson Establishing Dept. of Discipline, 25 January 1890, in U.S. Naval Institute *Proceedings* 16 (1890): 173–74. Concerning the need for modern guns and engines, see Sampson to Secretary of the Navy, 6 April 1889, in R.G. 405. Sampson ended up being dissatisfied with the plans for the design of the practice ship; see Sampson to Montgomery Sicard, 30 May 1889, ibid. See also West, *Admirals of Empire*, 126–27; Peter Karsten, *The Naval Aristocracy*, 327.

20. West, *Admirals of Empire*, 175–77; Robert Johnson, *Thence Around Cape Horn*, 145; *Army and Navy Journal* 29 (14 and 21 May 1892): 660, 684.

21. "William Thomas Sampson, Record of Service," Naval Historical Center; *New York Times*, 7 May 1902; West, *Admirals of Empire*, 178–80.

22. "Sampson's Report on Ordnance," in *Ann. Rept. Sec. Navy, 1894–95*, 242, 246 [quotation]. See also Sampson to Hilary Herbert, 1 February 1895, in *Sen. Exec. Doc. No. 56* (53rd Cong., 3rd Sess., Serial 3275), 1–3.

23. "Sampson's Report on Ordnance," in *Ann. Rept. Sec. Navy, 1893–94*, 233–34; William T. Sampson, "Face Hardened Armor," 818–21; Benjamin F. Cooling, *Gray Steel and Blue Water Navy*, 116–18; West, *Admirals of Empire*, 181.

24. "Sampson's Report on Ordnance," in *Ann. Rept. Sec. Navy, 1894–95*, 239–40; Bradley Fiske, *From Midshipman to Rear Admiral*, 198–203; Francis Duncan, "Commentary" [on P. E. Coletta's "Bradley A. Fiske: Naval Inventor"], in *Versatile Guardian: Research in Naval History*, ed. Richard A. Von Doenhoff, 121–23; West, *Admirals of Empire*, 184.

25. "Sampson's Report on Ordnance," in *Ann. Rept. Sec. Navy, 1894–95*, 235; ibid., *1895*, 201; ibid., *1896*, 276.

26. *New York Times*, 7 June 1896; Spector, *Professors of War*, 92–93; David Trask, *War with Spain*, 76–77; *Ann. Rept Sec. Navy, 1897*, 274.

27. Edward L. Beach, *The United States Navy*, 365–66.

28. William H. Leckie, "William Rufus Shafter," in Roger J. Spiller et al., eds., *Dictionary of American Military Biography*, III:979.

29. William T. Sampson, "The Atlantic Fleet in the Spanish War," 913; Hyman G. Rickover, *How the Battleship "Maine" Was Destroyed*, 48–50, 57, 60, 65–66, 67–70, 91; West, *Admirals of Empire*, 191–93.

30. Trask, *War with Spain*, 121; John D. Long to Sampson, 21 April 1898, in "Journal of William T. Sampson," Box 8A, R.G. 313: Records of the Naval Operating Forces, NA (hereafter R.G. 313).

31. Peter Karsten, *Naval Aristocracy*, 357; L. A. Coolidge, "Stories of the Fighting Leaders," 181; Mahan, *Retrospect and Prospect*, 293.

32. French Ensor Chadwick, "The Navy in the War," 529; Robert Seager, *Alfred Thayer Mahan*, 362; Albert Barker, *Everyday Life in the Navy*, 275; French Ensor Chadwick, *Relations of the United States and Spain: The Spanish–American War*, II:70–76, 322; Trask, *War with Spain*, 90–91, 108, 172–74, 180.

33. Edwin A. Falk, *Fighting Bob Evans*, 272; Sampson, "Atlantic Fleet," 894; Trask, *War with Spain*, 116–20.

34. Trask, *War with Spain*, 121; George E. Graham, *Schley and Santiago*, 81–83, 99–102.

35. Sampson to Schley, 21 May 1898, in *Ann. Rept. Sec. Navy, 1898*, II:466.

36. Graham, *Schley and Santiago*, 116–17. See also Trask, *War with Spain*, 122–23; Paolo E. Coletta, *Bowman Hendry McCalla*, 85; Goode, *With Sampson through the War*, 125; Margaret Long, ed., *Journal of John D. Long*, 257; John Long, *The New American Navy*, I:276.

37. Winfield S. Schley, *Forty-five Years under the Flag*, 278–81; Robley Evans, *Sailor's Log*, 429; Seaton Schroeder, *A Half Century of Naval Service*,

178 BUILDERS OF THE NEW EMPIRE

216–17; Long, *Journal of Long,* 226–27; Trask, *War with Spain,* 124–25; Long to Schley [through cable office, Mole St. Nicolas, Haiti], 27 May 1898, in *Ann. Rept. Sec. Navy, 1898,* II:397.

38. Sampson to Schley, 27 May 1898, *Ann. Rept. Sec. Navy, 1898,* II:475; Trask, *War with Spain,* 125–27, 131.

39. Evans, *Sailor's Log,* 417; Sampson, "Atlantic Fleet," 889, 897, 900–901; John Philip, "The 'Texas' at Santiago," 88; Henry C. Taylor, "The 'Indiana' at Santiago," 67; Sampson's plans to "close and engage" are in his "Order of Battle," 2 June 1898, "Journal of William T. Sampson," Box 8A, R.G. 313, NA. Sampson's orders on using searchlights (8 and 11 June 1898) are in *Ann. Rept. Sec. Navy, 1898,* II:513; see also Chadwick, *Spanish–American War,* I:348–49, 357, 362–63; Trask, *War with Spain,* 139, 209, 273–75.

40. Louis J. Gulliver, "Sampson and Shafter at Santiago," 799–800; Trask, *War with Spain,* 207; Paolo E. Coletta, *French Ensor Chadwick,* 87; Mahan, *Lessons of War with Spain,* 251; Graham Cosmas, *An Army for Empire,* 206; Sampson to Long, 6 June 1898, in *Ann. Rept. Sec. Navy, 1898,* II (Serial 3754), 485.

41. "Sqd. Bulletin No. 8," 20 June 1898, in "Journal of William T. Sampson," Box 8A, R.G. 313, NA; Chadwick, *Spanish–American War,* 32–39; Sampson, "Atlantic Fleet," 904–5.

42. Trask, *War with Spain,* 202, 214; Gulliver, "Sampson and Shafter at Santiago," 800.

43. Chadwick, "The 'New York' at Santiago," 114; Goode, *With Sampson through the War,* 194; Goode, "The Destruction of Cervera's Fleet," 425; Shafter to Sampson, 2 July 1898, and reply, in *Ann. Rept. Sec. Navy, 1898,* II (Serial 3754), 504; Trask, *War with Spain,* 252–53, 262.

44. Charles B. Davis, ed., *Adventures and Letters of Richard Harding Davis,* 230; George Graham, "The Destruction of Cervera's Fleet," 405; Philip, " 'Texas' at Santiago," 88, 90; Francis Cook, "The 'Brooklyn' at Santiago," 96; Sampson, "Atlantic Fleet," 906–7. The various captains gave various times of sighting the Spanish, each time differing by a few minutes. See the messages from each ship, dated 3 July 1898, in "Information Copies of Letters Received from Commanding Officers of Vessels," Box 8A, R.G. 313, NA.

45. Trask, *War with Spain,* 265.

46. Ibid., 141; Chadwick, *Spanish–American War,* II:129–31.

47. Goode, *With Sampson through the War,* 199–207. For another view, see Stephen B. Luce, "The Spanish–American War," 616–21.

48. Falk, *Fighting Bob Evans,* 256.

49. West, *Admirals of Empire,* 265; Chadwick, *Spanish–American War,* II:154; Coletta, *Chadwick,* 90–91; Sampson to Long, 3 July 1898, *Ann. Rept. Sec. Navy, 1898,* II:505. The original proposed "Fourth of July present" message was evidently longer, but Sampson trimmed it down. See Sampson to Long, 3 July 1898, "Journal of William T. Sampson," Box 8A, R.G. 313, NA. A copy of Sampson's full report to Long, 16 July

1898, is in R.G. 45: Area File of the Naval Records Collection, Area 8, NA. See also Trask, *War with Spain*, 266.

50. *Correspondence Relating to the War with Spain*, I:87–89, esp. Shafter to Corbin, 5 July 1898 (two messages), Corbin to Shafter, 5 July 1898 (two messages). See also Trask, *War with Spain*, 292, and Chadwick, *Spanish–American War*, II:203.

51. Sampson later gave some comments on his indisposition in the *New York Times*, 17 October 1899; Coletta, *Chadwick*, 94–95; Shafter to Adjutant General, 9 July 1898, *Correspondence Relating to the War*, I:115.

52. Trask, *War with Spain*, 302; detailed reports of the shelling are in "Journal of William T. Sampson," Box 8A, R.G. 313, NA.

53. Ibid., 304–5; Virginia W. Johnson, *The Unregimented General: A Biography of Nelson A. Miles*, 330; Sampson to Shafter, and reply, both dated 13 July 1898, in *Ann. Rept. Sec. Navy, 1898*, II:624.

54. Trask, *War with Spain*, 316, 320, 350–52; Gulliver, "Sampson and Shafter at Santiago," 802–4. Chadwick, *Spanish–American War*, II:249–52; *Correspondence Relating to the War*, I:297–98.

55. Mahan to J. S. Barnes, 9 July 1898, in Seager and Maguire, *Letters of Mahan*, II:562; see also Mahan to Edith Roosevelt, 17 July 1898, and Mahan to Henry Cabot Lodge, 27 and 29 July 1898, ibid., 563, 569, 571, 573–77; *New York Times*, 2 August 1898; Seager, *Mahan*, 401–2 [quotation on 402].

56. *New York Times*, 25 October and 24 December 1898; *Ann. Rept. Sec. Navy, 1898*, II:592–94; John D. Long, *America of Yesterday*, 209.

57. "William Thomas Sampson, Record of Service," in Sampson File, Naval Historical Center; *New York Times*, 16 and 24 February, 16 October, and 13 and 15 November 1899; *Army and Navy Journal* 37 (18 November 1899): 273, (2 December 1899): 322, (23 December 1899): 399; Long, *New American Navy*, II:44–45; West, *Admirals of Empire*, 299.

58. Mahan, *Retrospect and Prospect*, 292, 301 (originally published in *McClure's* in July 1902). See also reports on Sampson in *New York Times*, 17 February and 11 October 1900, and Wainwright, "William Thomas Sampson," 455.

59. *New York Times*, 29 August, and 1, 3, and 24 September 1901; Spector, *Admiral of New Empire*, 117–19; Henry G. Beyer to Long, August 1901, in G. W. Allen, ed., *Papers of John Davis Long*, 56; *Record of Proceedings of a Court of Inquiry into the Case of Rear Admiral Winfield Scott Schley, USN*, II:1829–30.

60. *New York Times*, 2, 17 [quotation], and 21 December 1901, and 10 February 1902 [quotation]; Long, *America of Yesterday*, 233; Long, *New American Navy*, II:46–48; West, *Admirals of Empire*, 302; Luce, "Spanish–American War," 626–27.

61. *New York Times*, 7 and 10 May 1902.

62. Schley, *Forty-five Years under the Flag*; Robert D. Heinl, *Dictionary of Military and Naval Quotations*, 144; Evans, *Sailor's Log*, 449.

WINFIELD SCOTT SCHLEY: THE CONFIDENT COMMANDER

HAROLD D. LANGLEY

The future admiral was born at Richfields, Frederick County, Maryland on 9 October 1839, the son of John Thomas and Georgianna Virginia McClure Schley. His ancestry was German and Huguenot on his father's side and Scotch–Irish on his mother's. A few days after the birth, General Winfield Scott, a hero of the War of 1812 and an old friend of Schley's father, visited the Frederick area. John Schley decided to name his infant son in honor of the general. Scott was flattered and subsequently served as sponsor of the child at the baptism.[1]

Schley grew up in a rural area, within sight of sections of the Appalachian Mountains, surrounded by rich bottomland that produced abundant yields of grain. The family followed an early-to-bed, early-to-rise routine common to farmers. The young Schley hunted, fished, and hiked, unaware that he was building a strong body for his future professional life. His education took place in the local school.

This idyllic life came to an end when his mother died in 1848. Believing that the country was unhealthy, John Schley sold his farm and moved his family to the city of Frederick. In this urban environment Schley grew to manhood. Schley enjoyed himself as a student at the Frederick Academy and later at St. John's College in Annapolis, but he never lost his love for the scenes of his boyhood life.

During his primary school years he heard much about the Mexican War exploits of his namesake and sponsor, General Winfield Scott. The general had earlier suggested to Schley's father that the boy consider a military career, promising that if he did so, he would use

Winfield Scott Schley. This photograph was printed in Schley's *Forty-five Years under the Flag* in 1904. *Courtesy of D. Appleton-Century Company, Inc., New York.*

his influence to obtain the youth an appointment to West Point. When Winfield Schley was of the proper age, however, Scott was embroiled in a dispute with Secretary of War Jefferson Davis, and so was without influence at a crucial point in Schley's life. But new opportunities opened up for the boy.

When he was about seventeen years of age, Schley discovered the writings of Captain Frederick Marryat on life in the Royal Navy.

From reading "Midshipman Easy" and other Marryat stories, Schley developed an unquenchable desire for a life at sea. In the fall of 1854, William Henry Hoffman was elected to Congress partly because of the efforts of Schley's relatives in his district. Once in Congress, Hoffman showed his appreciation by nominating Schley for an appointment as an acting midshipman in the U.S. Navy, and in September 1856 the nineteen-year-old was admitted to the U.S. Naval Academy.[2]

Life at the Naval Academy consisted of a sequence of courses in mathematics, the sciences, navigation, naval architecture, steam, gunnery, and other technical specialties, as well as some work in history, international law, and languages. Midshipmen had the choice of learning French or Spanish. Schley chose Spanish, although he later lamented that his course load did not allow him to devote more time to it. He learned the rudiments of grammar and vocabulary, and he took advantage of opportunities to speak the language during midshipmen cruises to European ports. His work with Spanish continued after graduation, and in the course of his early career he became quite fluent in it.

This interest in Spanish was an exception to Schley's general approach to academic life. At Annapolis he became the leader of a group known as "The Pelicans," an association of young men who rebelled against the serious tone of life at the Academy and who found relief in practical jokes and other forms of fun. Schley was an athletic, self-confident youth and a natural leader. He was also graceful, well mannered, a good dancer, and a marvelous raconteur. Both women and men admired him. His vanity over the small size of his feet led his classmates to give him the nickname "Peggy." It was inevitable that some of his less confident and socially accomplished classmates resented him.

As a boy growing up in both the country and the city, Schley showed an interest in people and what they did, and his naturally open, outgoing, and friendly manner drew others to him. These characteristics were very much in evidence at the Naval Academy. While learning the various aspects of seamanship in the ship *Preble* during a practice cruise in September 1857, her young sailors maneuvered into the edge of a violent hurricane. Midshipmen had to take their turns at the wheel, in boats, and aloft reefing and furling sails. They had to work in wet clothing, and to try to rest in crowded, poorly lit, and badly ventilated quarters, renewing their strength and energy with hardtack, "salt junk," pork and beans, rancid butter, wormy cheese, and the poorest-quality beverages. In addition, a midshipman was allowed only one gallon of water each day for washing, cooking, and drinking. Schley's brief exposure to these conditions made him sympathetic to the daily lives of enlisted men and their endless work routines. This understanding, in turn, helped Schley to forge bonds of loyalty, comradeship, and mutual respect with the men who came under his command.[3]

Schley graduated from the Naval Academy in June 1860, ranked eighteenth in a class of twenty-five. With his warrant as a midshipman came orders to join the steam frigate *Niagara,* then fitting out in New York for a cruise to the Far East under the command of Captain William W. McKean. McKean's orders were to take back to Japan the members of that nation's first diplomatic mission to the United States. The embassy consisted of three princes and several attendants, secretaries, and interpreters. It was an unusual environment for a new officer.

En route to Japan, the ship stopped at Batavia in the Dutch East Indies where a member of the embassy party purchased a monkey, which soon became a pest. It threw food on the deck, creating stains and garbage that had to be cleaned up by the sailors. Whenever a sailor attempted to punish it, the monkey would climb into the rigging and hang by its tail, well out of the reach of the sailors. Something needed to be done, but the fact that the monkey belonged to a member of the diplomatic group limited the options open to the crew. Someone suggested that the tail of the monkey be greased. Although Schley did not take credit for the idea, his reputation for pranks at the Academy tends to point the finger of suspicion in his direction—but whatever the case, the monkey's tail was so lubricated. The next time the animal made a mess, a sailor chased after it, and the monkey predictably headed for the high rigging—where the grease on its tail caused it to lose its balance, fall overboard, and drown. The death of the monkey was duly reported to the captain and to the Japanese owner, and as the officer on watch when all this happened, Schley was called upon for an explanation. The captain suspected Schley had caused the death of the monkey, but neither the captain nor the Japanese owner knew about the greasing, and the inventive Schley was able to convince both that the monkey had committed suicide. The monkey story—told, retold, and elaborated upon in the U.S. Navy—helped to earn Schley a reputation as a witty and resourceful officer. As for the enlisted men on the ship— they loved Schley.[4]

After delivering the diplomatic party to Japan, the *Niagara* visited China, Aden, and Cape Town before heading for Boston. Whey they left the United States, Schley and other officers of the *Niagara* knew that Abraham Lincoln had been nominated for president, but they had had no news of the election or of the South's response to it. As they approached the coast of the United States, the crew were surprised to see few American vessels at sea. It was only after they took on a pilot that they heard the news of the secession of the Southern states, the attack on Fort Sumter, and President Lincoln's proclamation of a blockade. It was a time of great anxiety and personal stress. Unsure about who was loyal and who was not, the Navy Department demanded that everyone under its jurisdiction take a loyalty oath. Anyone who would not do so was dismissed. Although he was out of touch with his family and did not know their views about the crisis, Schley had no hesitation about taking the oath. Later he would learn from his father that the family had expected him to be true to the Union. Having declared himself, Schley anticipated active duty; and he did not have long to wait.[5]

The *Niagara* sailed for New York where she took on coal, stores, and ammunition; and from there the ship headed south. On 12 May 1861, she took up her blockading station off Charleston, South Carolina. Her duty was to stop vessels bound for that city and to inform them of the imposition of the blockade. Sometimes a vessel disregarded the warning and attempted to make the port. Usually a shot across the bow was sufficient to make captains reconsider such a move, but there was one notable exception in those early days of the war.

The ship *General Parkhill* ignored three warning shots and was soon captured. No weapons or ammunition were found on board, but two Palmetto flags indicated a sympathy for the secessionist cause. It was decided to send the ship as a prize of war to Philadelphia under the command of Midshipman Schley—a risky assignment for a young officer. Manpower shortages made it necessary to use the mates and crew of the blockade runner to assist Schley and twelve navy men. Ordered to keep his own men on deck and the Southerners aloft, Schley did so and delivered the ship to Philadelphia. He then reported to the naval commander, who granted Schley a leave of absence to visit his family in Maryland. That summer the young officer was promoted to acting master and then to the regular master's rank and ordered to the *Potomac,* a frigate assigned to the Western Gulf Blockading Squadron under Flag Officer David G. Farragut.[6]

Schley came under hostile fire for the first time in a small boat rushing to capture a burning schooner that had been set afire by her pro-Southern crew in Mobile Bay. Confederate guns on Fort Morgan kept Schley's craft at a distance until the schooner was destroyed. Schley and his men assisted another boat crew in the capture of the brig *Wilder,* but they were disappointed when their efforts did not lead to a share of the prize money.[7]

Concerns about prizes and the blockade were temporarily put aside when the *Potomac* was ordered to Vera Cruz to investigate the intervention of British, Spanish, and French naval forces in Mexico for debt collection. This duty put the final strain on the old ship; she had to be laid up in Pensacola and her officers assigned to other duties. For Schley the change brought a promotion to the rank of lieutenant and orders to join the steam gunboat *Winona* off Mobile, as her executive officer. When he reported on board, Schley found that his fellow officers were much concerned about the conduct of their skipper, Lieutenant Commander James S. Thornton. Several times Thornton had taken his ship in front of Fort Morgan and fired at it. The fort was outside the range of the *Winona*'s guns, but the ship was well within the range of the cannons in the fort. The *Winona*'s officers thought that their lives were being jeopardized for no reason. When Thornton made another foray in the direction of the fort, Schley ordered the ship's surgeon to examine Thornton and to write a report on his condition. The surgeon reported that the captain was suffering from delirium tremens, presumably due to excessive alcohol consumption. Schley reported these facts to Commander James Alden, the senior officer present, who relieved Thornton and ordered a court-martial, which resulted in Thornton's dismissal from the squadron. Thornton harbored no bitterness toward Schley, telling him that he had done his duty. Later Schley was happy to learn that Thornton had redeemed himself by performing good service in the *Kearsarge.*[8]

Under a new commander the *Winona* was assigned to patrol duty on the Mississippi River between Port Hudson and Donaldsonville, where the ship was in almost daily conflict with Confederate batteries or infantry. When the captain of the *Monongahela* was severely wounded in an attack on Port Hudson, Schley was sent to that ship as her acting commander. The stage was now set for an incident that would leave a strong impression on Schley for the rest of his career. Schley was ordered to attack a Confederate citadel that was a part of the defenses of Port Hudson. While engaged in this fight, the *Monon-*

gahela's quartermaster informed Schley that Farragut's flagship had hoisted a signal, but that a lack of wind and the smoke of battle made the signal impossible to read. The attack continued until the citadel was silenced. Schley then moved the ship downstream to her regular position, anchored, and went to the flagship to report his success. After returning Schley's salute, Farragut said: "Captain, you begin early in your life to disobey orders. Did you not see the signal flying for near an hour to withdraw from action?" Stunned by the accusation, Schley stammered a reply to the effect that weather conditions and the smoke of battle made it difficult to see and to interpret the signal. He added that in view of his orders to destroy the citadel, he did not think that the signal was meant for him.

Farragut then alluded to an incident in the battle of Copenhagen in 1801 when British vessels were ordered to withdraw from an attack. In one of the ships, Captain Horatio Nelson put a telescope to his blind eye and told his officers that he did not see the signal. He then went on to destroy the Danish fleet. Farragut said that he wanted none of that Nelson business in his squadron. He then invited Schley into his cabin.

Once the door was closed, Farragut smiled and became friendly. He told Schley: "I have censured you, sir, on the quarter-deck for what appeared to be a disregard of my orders. I desire to commend you and your officers and men for doing what you believed right under the circumstances. Do it again whenever in your judgment it is necessary to carry out your conception of duty." Farragut then invited Schley to join him in a glass of wine.[9]

In the years that followed, Schley often recalled the words of Farragut. They reinforced his belief that "the secret of all important success was dependence upon the responsible judgment of an officer on the spot. If circumstances compelled him to disobey his orders to achieve signal success for his country, such constructive disobedience becomes a virtue."

Farragut continued to inspire Schley as well as other officers, such as George Dewey, throughout their careers. Whenever they faced a difficult situation, they asked themselves: "What would Farragut do?" They were convinced that such reflections produced proper answers.

After his interview with Farragut, Schley returned to his ship in a highly satisfied state. But he did not have many more days to enjoy his command. The *Monongahela's* captain returned from the hospital, and Schley was transferred to the sloop *Richmond*. In that ship he participated in at least twenty engagements with Confederate batteries, the damage from which made it necessary to send the ship to New York for repairs. Schley was given a month's leave while the work on the ship went forward.[10]

Hurrying to Annapolis, he married his sweetheart, Annie Rebecca Franklin, to whom he had been betrothed for two years. Their love had been tested by war, separation, and distance, and it remained strong. On 10 September 1863, the couple were married in St. Anne's Episcopal Church in Annapolis, and they proceeded to Washington for their honeymoon.

While in Washington, Schley called at the Navy Department to try to determine what his next assignment might be. There he met Commander Henry A. Wise, with whom he had served in the *Niagara,* and who at that time was the navy's chief of ordnance. Wise said that in the midst of the war, it was difficult to request any specific duty, but if Schley wished, Wise would have him assigned to the ordnance factory at the Washington Navy Yard while his ship was undergoing repairs. Schley readily assented to this arrangement.

Duty at the navy yard gave Schley the opportunity to become acquainted with the workings of the Navy Department, but he was happy to be returned to sea in December 1863. His appointment was as executive officer in the experimental ship *Wateree,* a double ender, or one whose bow and stern were of the same shape. These vessels were designed to operate in narrow rivers where there was not enough room to turn, and the Navy Department was interested in learning how they would perform at sea. Consequently, the *Wateree* was ordered to sail around South America to Mare Island, California. The assignment proved to be a rather unpleasant one.[11]

Rolling and flooding were constant problems, along with shortages of fuel. Men had to be sent ashore to cut logs for the boilers on one occasion, to buy wood on another, and to borrow five to six tons of coal from a coastal steamer in a third instance. At one place they could find only coal dust for fuel. Their fortunes improved when they reached the coal mining region of Chile, where they purchased enough coal to take them to California. The whole experience underscored for Schley how vulnerable ships were when their fuel supplies were not adequate.[12]

In Panama, Schley was detached from the ship and sent home in April 1866. A brief furlough enabled him to spend some time with his wife and family. With the end of the Civil War in 1865 and the resultant reduction in the size of the U.S. Navy, Schley wondered what his next assignment would be. In July 1866, he was promoted to lieutenant commander and ordered to the Naval Academy as a member of the Department of Discipline. This duty provided an occasion for Schley to consider the things that ought to be a part of the training of a naval officer. His own years as a midshipman were still fresh in his mind, and he had the experiences of the war to draw upon. Some of his own assignments made him conscious of the value of foreign languages. He had a chance to make a small contribution toward better language training during his second and third years at the Academy when he was assigned to the Department of Modern Languages.[13]

Schley left the academic environment in 1869, assigned to the newly completed steam sloop *Benicia* as her executive officer. A winter cruise was ordered between Portsmouth and New York to test the sailing and steaming qualities of the ship. Frostbitten hands and general discomfort were the order of the day for officers and men on this duty, but it gave Schley experience in handling a ship in a winter environment.

Returning to Portsmouth, the *Benicia* received orders to proceed to China by way of the Cape of Good Hope, and she departed from Portsmouth on 2 March 1870. In the Indian Ocean, winds rose to hurricane force, and the seas became so heavy that for a time it looked as though the ship would founder. But the storm gradually abated, and the *Benicia* survived, without a loss, what Schley would remember as the fiercest gale in his naval career.

When the *Benicia* reached Shanghai, the Americans discovered a great concern in the foreign community for its own safety following the recent massacre of a group of French nuns by antiforeign Chinese. Missionaries retreated from the interior regions to Shanghai and other treaty ports. Westerners were organizing themselves for defense and collecting arms. The arrival of the *Benecia* and later that of Admiral John Rodgers, the commander of the Asiatic Squadron, in his flagship *Colorado* brought a sense of security to the foreign community.

When the crisis passed, the *Benecia* carried missionaries to North China, and then proceeded to Japan where she was ordered to join Admiral Rodgers's Asiatic Squadron. The force proceeded to Korea to investigate the circumstances surrounding the loss of a merchant ship, the *General Sherman,* known to have ventured into prohibited waters in search of trading opportunities. Traveling with Rogers's squadron was Frederick F. Low, the U.S. Minister to China, accompanied by two Chinese interpreters. Admiral Rodgers opened communication with the Korean authorities by requesting permission to survey the territorial waters of that country, desiring to find for the squadron a secure anchorage against the threat of a typhoon. The Koreans made no apparent objection to this request, and the work began. Everything went well until the survey ships reached the lower end of Kangwha Island, where there stood a line of forts connected by a wall and facing the Salee River. While two survey ships were examining a channel at the mouth of the river, the Korean forts commanding the waterway fired upon them. The American ships returned the fire, silencing the batteries. The local Korean authorities informed their king of the incident, noting that even Korean vessels were not allowed to venture beyond the contested point without a pass. Because the intentions of the foreign warships were not known, the forts had tried to prevent them from going any farther. From the point of view of Admiral Rodgers and Minister Low, however, ships engaged in peaceful work had been attacked without provocation. They decided to allow the Korean authorities ten days within which to apologize for the attack. If no apology was forthcoming, the forts would be assaulted.

During the ten days allotted for a reply, the squadron was the scene of intense activity. Battalions from the various ships were formed into a division. Rations were prepared, as well as guns and ammunition. On 11 July 1871, a force of 651 officers and men were landed under the leadership of Commander L. A. Kimberley with Schley serving as his adjutant. As the landing force moved against the forts, its flanks were protected by two ships of the squadron. Fire from the *Monocacy* surprised the Korean defenders of the first fort, who fled, and the men of the landing force then dismantled the fort's guns. The column moved next against the main fort, and while fighting his way toward it, Schley was slightly wounded in the left arm by a spear. The main fort was finally taken, and before returning to their ships, the Americans dismounted its guns and destroyed its magazines and storehouses. The operations of the landing force had cost the lives of 3 Americans and 243 Koreans. Another six or seven Americans were wounded, as were an undetermined number of Koreans. Schley emerged from the experience convinced that shows of force could have highly useful effects. As far as he, Rodgers, and other Americans were concerned, an insult to the flag had been avenged. It never occurred to them that the Koreans were within their rights in defending their territorial waterways.

In any case, the hopes of signing a treaty similar to that negotiated by Commodore Matthew Perry with Japan in 1854 were doomed to disappointment. The fate of the *General Sherman* and her crew was also unresolved. These questions would be settled by others at a later date. For Schley and the men of the *Benecia,* however, the events of Korea were the most exciting highlights of a memorable cruise, which ended in San Francisco in August 1872. A month later the ship was out of commission, and Schley was back at the Naval Academy.[14]

This time Schley took over the direction of the Department of Modern Languages. His own experiences convinced him that too much time was spent on learning the rules of grammar and memorizing vocabulary instead of learning to speak a language. Accordingly he put a new emphasis on practicing conversation. At the same time he recognized that with all the other subjects that the midshipmen had to master, there was all too little time for foreign languages.

The deficiency in the teaching of languages was but one of many problems affecting the navy. Young officers had grown discouraged about the drastic reductions in the size and efficiency of the service since the end of the Civil War. A small group of them decided to do something about the situation, and in 1873 formed the U.S. Naval Institute. Schley became a charter member of the private, non-profit professional organization, and he supported professional, literary, and scientific knowledge in the U.S. Navy through lectures and the publication of a periodical that would serve as a forum for discussions and criticisms.[15]

If the navy was not progressing as fast as some officers thought it should, Schley's own career was moving along satisfactorily. In June 1874, he was promoted to commander; two years later, he was assigned to the screw steamer *Essex* as her captain. From August 1876 to October 1879, Schley's command of the ship took him to Mexico, Africa, South America, and the Falkland Islands.[16]

These years at sea were followed by a pleasant tour as a member of the Lighthouse Board under Commander George Dewey. Assigned to the Second District, extending from Newburyport, Massachusetts, to Newport, Rhode Island, Schley had to see that all lighthouses, ship lights, and buoys within the area were in good working condition and ready for all kinds of weather. From his headquarters in Boston, he made periodic tours of inspection of the installations under his jurisdiction. During these tours, Schley met lighthouse keepers and their families as well as seafaring people, and he formed warm friendships that lasted until the end of his life. His duties also brought him into contact with business people, from whom he learned the ways of the commercial world and gained valuable experience that he would draw on in subsequent assignments.

Schley left the lighthouse service a lasting reminder of his tour with it. Believing that a simple and neat uniform would give a sense of organizational identity to lighthouse keepers as well as improving discipline, Schley designed such a garb and sent it to Washington. It was a source of pleasure to him that the uniform he proposed was later adopted.[17]

While engaged in his lighthouse duties, Schley read newspaper accounts of the departure of a polar exploring expedition in the steam whaler *Proteus* under Lieutenant Adolphus Greely, USA, and he remarked prophetically that one day some poor naval officer would have to rescue the members of the expedition. The newspaper stories stimulated curiosity about the polar regions, and Schley began to read about past expeditions, especially that of the Englishman Sir George Nares, who in 1875 had followed virtually the same route that Greely was now taking.

In the fall of 1883 word reached the War Department that the *Proteus* had been crushed by ice and sunk, but that the members of the expedition had made their way to the Uppernavik region of northern Greenland. After the U.S. Army made two unsuccessful attempts to rescue Greely and his party, President Chester A. Arthur convened a group of military officers and charged them with formulating a plan to save the explorers. Three plans were proposed. Subsequently the president decided that it would be an all-navy expedition, and Congress stipulated that it be composed of volunteers. The secretary of the navy offered Schley command of the expedition, and Schley accepted, provided that he could pick his own officers—a condition that was agreed to. Meanwhile special ships were acquired and strengthened for Arctic duty. On 21 April 1884, Schley departed from New York in the *Thetis,* accompanied by the *Bear* and the *Alert.* By the time the ships had reached Godhaven on the island of Disco on 22 May, Schley and his companions had acquired valuable experience in dealing with icebergs, cold, and fog. But the real challenge lay ahead.

From the governor of north Greenland, Schley obtained useful information on the conditions generally prevailing in the area. As the Greely Relief Expedition moved northward, it was followed by whalers from St. John's, Newfoundland, who were attracted by a reward of $25,000 authorized by the U.S. Congress to any person not in the military or naval service who discovered and rescued Greely and his companions. The captains of these whalers had frequent gatherings or "mollies" on one or another of their ships, where they exchanged stories of their experiences in the northern regions. Schley made it a point to attend these "mollies," but said very little. He preferred to listen and to absorb what lessons he could. The whaling captains inferred that Schley would fail in his mission because he was inexperienced, but Schley thought otherwise. He considered that their information about adventures, escapes, and sufferings would be pertinent if the goal were to catch whales. But his mission was to rescue Greely and his men; so risk, not caution, was the rule of action. Schley believed that in this particular case, the value of experience could be overestimated and lead to an overly conservative outlook. Schley later wrote that "they who know nothing fear nothing. This proved to be the dominant factor in the expedition's work."

This attitude did not mean that Schley was reckless. Weather conditions changed quickly in the Arctic, and one had to be constantly on the alert for danger or opportunity. Schley spent as much as twenty hours at a time in the crow's nest of the *Thetis,* studying the ice for passages or for breaks that could be exploited. It was a test of endurance for men and for ships. Several of the more conservative whaling captains turned back to the safety of the Duck Islands. Only three of the whalers remained with the relief ships.

At Brevoort Island, records were discovered indicating that Greely and his party would be found at Cape Sabine. The relief ships pressed on. At 10:00 p.m. on 22 June 1884, the *Bear* reached the survivors. Eighteen of the party had died; Greely and the remaining six lay in sleeping bags amid a violent gale. Schley was convinced that in another 48 hours all would have died, and so believed that his strategy of pressing forward constantly had been the right one. As for the expedition as a whole, it was successful because its leader had been able to absorb and synthesize a great deal of unfamiliar information. Schley made his own judgments about what was feasible and worth the risk. He did not spare himself from the cold, discomfort, and long hours, and his example inspired his crew. The rescue of Greely and his men was the high point of Schley's professional career.[18]

Upon his return to the United States, Schley found himself a national hero. President Arthur came to New York personally to thank the members of the relief expedition, and later received Schley in his hotel room. Here the chief executive informed Schley that he would soon become the chief of the Bureau of Equipment and Recruiting in Washington, D.C. Two weeks after he took up his new duties, Schley received a letter from Secretary of the Navy William C. Whitney asking him what changes should be made in the interests of the public and of efficiency. In his reply, Schley described the various duties of the bureau and wisely concluded that no change should be made until he had observed his staff at work. A year later, he suggested the replacement of his aging chief clerk, and this was done. Schley had shown that he was a careful and a humane administrator. In other areas it was hard not to make some people unhappy.

The Greely Relief Expedition. Rescued army personnel sit on the deck with their rescuers behind them in this photograph taken on board the USS *Thetis* at Upernivik, Greenland, in July 1884. Schley is third from the right among the naval officers standing immediately behind the seated group. *Courtesy of the Naval Historical Center.*

Knowing that the Navy Department was trying to hold down costs, Schley had the unhappy task of telling his fellow officers that they must use up old canvas and rope, and keep aging furniture, carpeting, and fixtures in place for yet another year. To do otherwise would be to risk the curtailment of expenditures that were currently allowed.

To some extent this effort to make all possible savings was dictated by the fact that other expenses were being incurred in connection with the construction and outfitting of ships for the New Steel Navy. The new navy had its beginning in 1883 when Congress authorized the construction of three steel cruisers and one dispatch boat. In 1886, Congress provided funds for a cruiser, two ironclads, and a torpedo boat. A gradual transformation of the U.S. Navy was in progress, and no one connected with it wanted to see it delayed or stopped.

From Schley's point of view, it was time to do something to improve the conditions of service of the enlisted men so that the new ships would have the best possible crews. This involved taking a critical look at the organization and functioning of the naval apprentice program and of the way in which meat and vegetables were preserved and prepared for use on ships. Schley wanted better-trained men, and he wanted them to have a more nutritious, varied, and palatable diet. One of his plans to achieve that goal was to enlist two experienced civilian cooks for one year and have them train a cadre of naval cooks who would then teach others. Schley was able to carry out some of his experiments because in June 1885 President Grover Cleveland asked him to perform the duties of the chief of the Bureau of Provisions and Clothing in addition to his other bureau responsibilities. The dual authority gave Schley the opportunity to get new uniform regulations adopted for the officers and enlisted men. He felt that the manpower in the new navy needed a new look and better-quality clothing.

Schley's efforts to improve the daily lives and morale of the enlisted men came at a time when other officers were struggling to establish the curriculum of the Naval War College, which opened in Newport, Rhode Island, in September 1885. His priorities for the bureaus he headed tended to put him in opposition to Commodore Stephen B. Luce, the president of the War College, partly because both the apprentice training for enlisted men and the advanced course for officers were to be carried out at the same base. It is also possible that Schley doubted that the art of war could be taught, an outlook possibly reinforced by his own experiences under Farragut and Rodgers.[19]

Schley also had no experience with a modern warship, a deficiency he set about to remedy by applying for command of the new cruiser *Baltimore* even before her keel was laid. When the ship was completed in 1889, Schley, who had since been promoted to captain, was given her command.

Accompanied by his executive officer, Lieutenant Commander Uriel Sebree, with whom he had served in the *Thetis,* Schley went to Cramp Shipyards in Philadelphia to take command of the ship. Before doing so, the two donned overalls and inspected the ship from stem to stern. They familiarized themselves with the workings of the engines, pipes, fittings, and other features. This was in keeping with Schley's philosophy that no ship could be effectively commanded unless the captain knew the vessel thoroughly.

After an initial shakedown cruise, the *Baltimore* carried the body of John Ericsson, the inventor of the *Monitor,* back to Sweden for burial. There followed a series of visits to European ports before Schley returned to the United States for the wedding of his daughter.

Schley was in Washington on a brief visit in January 1891 when news arrived of an uprising in Chile. Concerned about the protection of American interests in that country, the secretary of the navy cabled Rear Admiral W. P. McCann, the commander of the South Atlantic Squadron, to proceed to Valparaiso. To Schley the secretary remarked that he would like to have another warship on the Chilean scene. The captain responded that while his ship, the *Baltimore,* was then in the Mediterranean, she could be transferred to South America as soon as Schley returned to Europe. The secretary approved of this suggestion, and Schley rejoined his ship, had her hull inspected, took on fresh supplies, and departed from France on 22 March. The ship reached Valparaiso on 7 April, and later in that month Admiral McCann transferred his flag to the *Baltimore.*[20]

Meanwhile, Chilean–American affairs had reached a very strained state, due in part to unneutral actions by the American minister to that country and to diplomatic problems relating to the shipment of American arms in a ship chartered by Chilean rebels. Hostile feelings toward the Americans increased as a result of the misinterpretation of various events by the rebels. One such misunderstanding involved the activities of American ships moving up and down the coast in an effort to establish which areas of the country were under rebel control. To the Chilean rebels, this looked suspiciously like the collection of intelligence information for the benefit of the government in power. Also, when the insurgent army captured Valparaiso, one hundred bluejackets and marines were landed to protect the U.S. consulate. Then Admiral George Brown (who replaced McCann) sent Chilean refugees from his ship to the *Baltimore,* and ordered Schley to land them in neutral territory. Some of the Chilean rebels interpreted these acts as American interference in their affairs. The *Baltimore* became a symbol of that unwanted involvement, thus setting the stage for a violent reaction.

A conscientious commander, Schley was concerned about the morale of his crew. Many of the men had not had any shore leave since the ship left Europe. When order seemed to prevail in Valparaiso, Schley asked the local intendente if there would be any objection to his granting shore leave to his men. Told that there was no reason why his sailors could not enjoy the same privileges as those from other foreign ships, Schley, on the afternoon of 16 October 1891, granted liberty to 115 men of the *Baltimore.* By late afternoon, officers returning from the city reported that the men were neat and orderly, and that they were saluting both their own and foreign officers on the streets.

A few hours later all this had changed. About 8:00 p.m. a merchant captain, accompanied by a young Chilean, reported to Schley that American sailors were being attacked in various parts of the city, their assailants being longshoremen, boatmen, and other Chileans. One sailor had already been killed, and others were wounded. According to the merchant officer, in some instances policemen had participated in the assaults, and in other cases they had taken no steps to restrain the mob. These attacks were unprovoked, said the merchant officer, who suggested that Schley turn his guns on the city. Schley responded by pointing out that such an action would injure or kill many people, including women and children, who were in no way responsible for what happened to the sailors. Instead, Schley opted for a more mature response.

He appointed a three-member court of inquiry to ascertain the facts and to make a report. This group took the testimony of a number of persons. It was established that the trouble began in the True Blue Saloon when a Chilean spat in the face of an American sailor. In the brawl that followed, two American sailors were killed by bayonet and knife wounds, seventeen others were injured, and other men were beaten and imprisoned. The investigation established that Americans were attacked in widely separated parts of the city, a find-

Schley on board the USS *Baltimore*. The appointments of Schley's cabin illustrate the relative splendor in which a ship commander could live in the late nineteenth century. *Courtesy of the Library of Congress.*

ing that suggested some sort of coordination by the Chileans. The testimony of foreigners and of the Chilean Sisters of Charity, from the hospital to which the wounded Americans had been taken, agreed on the point that the sailors were not drunk. The probe also revealed that some Chileans and a few policemen tried to help the Americans. In other instances, a lack of cooperation on the part of the Chilean police was brought out.[21]

When the court of inquiry finished its investigation, and the *Baltimore* was relieved of her duty at Valparaiso, Schley steamed for California. At San Francisco, Schley received orders from the secretary of the navy directing him to Mare Island, where a court of inquiry was held on the *Baltimore* incident. The judge advocate general of the U.S. Navy was sent to the West Coast to conduct the inquiry.

Seventy-two witnesses were examined, and their testimony was sent to President Benjamin Harrison. It was a source of pride for Schley that this testimony agreed in all particulars with the results of his own investigation in Valparaiso.[22]

Establishing the facts was only a part of the procedure used to demand an apology from Chile. War fever was running high in both countries. Secretary of State James G. Blaine sent Chile an ultimatum drafted by President Harrison. The Chileans capitulated and subsequently paid $75,000 to the injured sailors and to the families of the two men who died.

Before this was accomplished, Schley turned over the command of the *Baltimore* to his successor, and proceeded by train across the continent to take up new duties with the Lighthouse Board. He carried with him a gold-headed cane, a gift from the men of the *Baltimore* as a token of their esteem, which he would treasure for the rest of his life. It was reassuring to Schley that his own views on how to lead the men of the navy were appreciated by the men themselves.[23]

A different brand of leadership was required for Schley's new assignment as an inspector of the Third Lighthouse District, which extended from Narragansett Bay to New Jersey and included Lake Champlain as well as the Thames and Hudson rivers. Schley found that his duties were routine, and that he was able to delegate and to simplify some of the procedures. This left him time for more challenging activities, such as devising a plan to light the waterfront of the Columbian Exposition at Chicago. Schley conferred with the manufacturers of various types of specialized equipment as well as with business leaders, and oversaw the installation of a highly successful system. The experience gained at this exposition led the Lighthouse Board to use alternating current through submarine cables to improve the lighting of New York Bay.[24]

Another matter, which also involved consultative work for the navy, led to Schley's recommendation that wood not be used in the ceilings and bulkheads of the new steel warships. The space thus saved could be used to increase the area for the coal supply as well as for enlarging the spaces allotted to accommodate personnel and supplies. Thus Schley was physically removed from a command at sea, but adequate coal and better living conditions for the men were never far from his mind.[25]

After a brief (March to October 1895) assignment to the Navy Department's Board of Inspection, Schley was given command of the battleship *New York*. Following an uneventful two years of squadron maneuvers, Schley returned to shore duty as a member of the Lighthouse Board in Washington, and was elected its chairman.

In the midst of his duties, Schley was ordered to appear before an examining board of officers in Washington, after which he was promoted to the rank of commodore, effective 6 February 1898. By the time Schley had received his new commission, the battleship *Maine* had been destroyed in the harbor of Havana, Cuba, and the United States was moving rapidly toward war with Spain.[26]

When war came, Schley was given command of the Flying Squadron based at Hampton Roads, with the USS *Brooklyn* as his flagship. The Flying Squadron had been created to reassure northeastern politicians and civic leaders who were worried that Spanish ships would bombard coastal cities; in theory, the squadron would move rapidly to any point on the coast that was threatened. Schley, its commanding officer, had been well known to the public for his resourcefulness and courage since the rescue of Greely. His being given this command over at least a dozen admirals and more senior commodores was probably due to the influence of Assistant Secretary of the Navy Theodore Roosevelt. Not surprisingly, Schley's elevation stimulated feelings of envy and jealousy in some naval circles.[27]

There was also the matter of how the Flying Squadron was supposed to function in relation to the North Atlantic Squadron under Captain William T. Sampson. On 8 April, Sampson asked Secretary of the Navy John D. Long to clarify the assignment given to Schley's squadron. Long declined to do so. As the things turned out, the two forces were not unified under Sampson's control until 24 May. By that time a series of confusing orders and movements had taken place.[28]

Sampson was promoted to an acting rear admiral on 21 April; and when war was declared against Spain four days later, Sampson disposed his forces for blockade of northern Cuba. A report that a Spanish squadron under Admiral Pascual Cervera y Topete was en route to the West Indies induced Sampson to move his ships to Puerto Rico in an effort to intercept Cervera. Finding no Spanish naval vessels in Puerto Rico, Sampson sailed for Key West where he expected to have access to the latest news. Meanwhile, the sighting of Cervera's squadron off Martinique prompted the Navy Department to order Schley's squadron to Key West to await further instructions. Upon his arrival there, the secretary ordered Schley to blockade Havana, Cuba. But before he left for this duty, Sampson returned from Puerto Rico to confer with Schley.

Sampson did not believe that Cervera would head for Havana, thinking it more likely that the Spanish destination would be the Cuban port of Cienfuegos. He therefore ordered Schley to that point. As for the orders of the Navy Department, Sampson took the position that his arrival at Key West had modified the previous orders to Schley.[29] Accordingly, Schley moved his squadron to Cienfuegos, for a time believing that Cervera was in that port. He did not learn otherwise until 24 May. Meanwhile, the Navy Department had learned from a Cuban agent on 20 May that Cervera was in Santiago. On 25 May, Sampson ordered Schley to proceed to Santiago and to blockade that port.[30] Having been reinforced by the battleship *Iowa,* the unprotected cruiser *Marblehead,* the converted yachts *Vixen* and *Eagle,* and the collier *Merrimac,* Schley arrived off the city a day after he received his orders.[31] No sooner was he in place than doubts were cast on the accuracy of the information about the Spanish navy.

Both Captain Charles Sigsbee, the commander of the *St. Paul,* and a Cuban harbor pilot informed Schley that the Spanish fleet was not in Santiago harbor. Schley wondered if the reported arrival of Cervera was not a ruse. Schley reasoned that when the Spanish squadron reached its destination it would need several days in port for rest and refueling before it ventured out again. Once the Spanish were in port, the maintenance of the blockade would be a constant drain on the coal supplies of the American squadron; so if it was likely that Cervera was not yet in Santiago, it might be wise for Schley to take advantage of the delay to replenish the coal supplies of his ships.[32] Some of his ships were already low on coal, but the projecting sponsons on the *Texas* and the *Marblehead* made it dangerous to refuel them from the squadron's colliers when seas were high. The task might be done quickly and efficiently in the calmer waters off Key West. Accordingly, Schley notified the Navy Department that he was proceeding to Key West to recoal. This message caused Secretary Long and Sampson some concern, as it seemed to them that Schley was leaving his post at a critical time. The secretary had no doubt that Cervera was in Santiago as reported. Both Long and Sampson were anxious that Schley's forces be back in place before Santiago. As things turned out, Schley did not have to travel to Key West for fuel. While he was en route there, the weather moderated, and Schley was able to recoal at sea and return to Santiago on the night of 28–29 May.[33]

On the morning of 29 May, the Spanish armored cruiser *Cristóbal Colón* was discovered at anchor about 1,000 yards inside the mouth of the harbor of Santiago. Using a Spanish pilot to make contact with the Cuban rebels, Schley was then able to confirm that Cervera's entire fleet was in the harbor, and he imposed a close blockade on that port.[34]

Mindful of an order of the secretary of the navy not to risk his ships against land fortifications, Schley shifted his flag to the *Massachusetts* and led his three largest ships in a reconnaissance of the forts at the mouth of the harbor. At a range estimated at 7,000 yards, the American ships fired at the *Colón* without effect, drawing fire from the Spanish forts and ships. Although the Spanish gunfire did not hit any of the American ships, Schley concluded that there were some well placed long-range guns protecting the harbor. Therefore, when some of his officers wanted to move in closer so that they could hit the *Colón* with their guns, Schley was against it for fear of damaging his ships in advance of the naval battle and violating the instructions of the secretary. Schley believed that his reconnaissance had fulfilled its purpose in locating the Spanish squadron and in ascertaining the locations and strength of the shore batteries. He apparently also believed that the Spanish defenses were stronger than they appeared to some of the other officers in the squadron.[35]

When Sampson and his squadron arrived off Santiago on 1 June, Schley explained the situation to him, and Sampson expressed no disapproval of the blockade or of Schley's other actions up to that time. Sampson imposed a semicircular blockade around Santiago. Within a six-mile radius, the ships' bows were pointed to the land, with Sampson's flagship, the *New York,* in a position on the east quadrant and Schley's *Brooklyn* posted on the west. As the commander on the scene, Sampson presented to his officers his plan for defeating Cervera.[36]

Believing that the narrow entrance to the harbor, the land fortifications, and possibly mines posed a hazard to the American ships, the Navy Department had forbidden Sampson to risk his vessels in an attack inside the harbor as Dewey had done at Manila. Therefore, Sampson's strategy was based on closing in on the Spanish as they emerged from Santiago. To do so, the ships of the blockading squadron had to keep up their steam at all times. With the U.S. Army gradually closing in on Santiago by land, it was only a matter of time before Cervera would be forced to face a capture by land or a battle at sea.

On Sunday, 3 July, Sampson signaled the squadron to "disregard movements of the commander-in-chief" and set off to the east at high speed without explanation. Only six months later did Schley learn that Sampson planned to confer with the army commander ashore. At the time he was mystified, but he realized that Sampson's departure left him in command of the squadron.[37]

The Spanish noted that the blockade was weaker than usual that day, and Cervera made his move. Sampson's flagship had gone to the east accompanied by a torpedo boat and an armed yacht. Also one battleship, two cruisers, and a converted tender had gone to Guantanamo for coal. The *Brooklyn* was the fastest and most powerful American warship off Cuba and thus a major target from the Spanish point of view; and this Sunday she was anchored farther out than usual, leaving a gap in the western end of the blockade. This disposition led Cervera to decide on a sortie to the west toward Cienfuegos. With his flagship the *Infanta María Teresa* in the lead, Cervera hoped to ram the *Brooklyn* and thereby help the other Spanish ships to escape.[38]

To give himself the best possible view of the coming battle, and at the same time to be near Captain Francis A. Cook, the commander of the *Brooklyn,* Schley had a wooden platform built around the outside of the armored conning tower forward in the ship. When the signal was received that the Spaniards were attempting to escape, Schley raced to his platform, binoculars in hand; and the officers and crew of the *Brooklyn* rushed to their stations. Similar scenes took place throughout the squadron. The Americans had only small amounts of steam power in reserve for such a contingency, but they got under way quickly. The Spanish ships were steaming under full power. Cervera's flagship was heading directly toward the *Brooklyn* and concentrating her firepower on the big American ship. But the *Teresa* was also coming under heavy fire herself, and Cervera abandoned the attempt to ram. The *Teresa* suddenly turned westward, leaving a small gap between herself and the *Vizcaya.*[39] When the *Teresa* turned, Schley ordered the *Brooklyn* to swing rapidly and continuously to port, or a little more than half of her tactical diameter, a controversial maneuver that Schley never adequately explained to critics. When the turn was completed, the *Teresa* was ahead on the *Brooklyn*'s starboard bow. The *Vizcaya,* which had also intended to ram the *Brooklyn,* now followed the *Teresa* to the westward. The movement of the *Brooklyn* took the captain of the *Texas* by surprise, and he backed his engines to avoid what seemed to be the threat of a possible collision.[40] The *Brooklyn* straightened out, taking her place at the head of the American line paralleling the Spaniards. The *Teresa* was soon disabled by American firepower and ran ashore on the beach. The

Americans now turned their attention to the rest of the Spanish squadron.

One by one the Spanish ships emerged from the harbor, at eight-to ten-minute intervals, and headed west, each coming under the bombardment of the American ships. During the pursuit, Schley ordered that the men below decks in the *Brooklyn* be kept informed of the progress of the battle. So every few minutes a report came through the voice tube that was greeted with cheers from down below. By such means Schley could give all his men a sense of identification with the work at hand and enlarge upon the concept that all of the ship's company was part of a unified team.[41]

As the battle raged, a Spanish shell tore the head off Yeoman George Ellis, who was using a stadimeter to keep Schley informed on the range of the target. Immediately two officers picked up the body and prepared to throw it over the side, but Schley ordered them to stop, stating that Ellis had fought bravely and deserved a Christian burial. The body thus was covered until it could be attended to after the battle.[42]

Each of the Spanish ships was pursued in turn as they headed west. The cruisers *Vizcaya, Cristóbal Colón,* and *Oquendo,* as well as the destroyers *Furor* and *Pluton,* were shattered and run aground. At 1:15 p.m. the last of the Spanish ships struck her colors, and Schley ordered a cease-fire. Sampson, to the east in the *New York* when the battle began, headed for the scene of the action, but he did not arrive until firing had ceased. When the *New York* was within signal range, Schley sent a message that a great victory had been won. Five minutes later Sampson signaled: "Report your casualties." Schley, disappointed for himself and his men that there was no note of congratulation, dutifully reported that one man had been killed and two were wounded. It was a remarkable record for the whole squadron.[43] Subsequently it was learned that the Spanish had lost 260 men. Later that afternoon one of Sampson's officers sent a message to Washington in his name, proclaiming the victory to be a Fourth of July present to the nation. No mention was made of the fact that technically Schley was in operational command during the battle. This action set the stage for a long argument between partisans of Sampson and of Schley over which officer should have the credit for the victory at Santiago: the one who planned the action or the one who carried it to execution.[44]

Most of the daily newspapers gave credit to Schley for the victory and ignored the *New York.* When Schley received copies of their articles on 10 July, the embarrassed officer drafted a message to Secretary Long that said: "Feel some mortification that the newspaper accounts of July 6th have attributed victory on July 3rd almost entirely to me. Victory was secured by the force under command Commander in Chief, North Atlantic Station (Sampson), and to him all honor is due." He then showed the message to Sampson, who responded: "Schley, this is kind and generous: I will transmit it at once."[45] That same day Sampson also sent a secret message to the secretary, in which he, for the first time, complained about Schley's conduct in locating and blockading the Spanish fleet before the battle. On the matter of credit for the victory, Sampson wrote to Long on 10 July that he preferred to let the Navy Department decide the issue. Sampson said that in his opinion as well as those of other officers, Schley's conduct before the battle, particularly his decision

The Spanish cruiser *Oquendo*. The Spanish flagship, the *Infanta María Teresa*, drew most American fire as she led Cervera's squadron out of the harbor at Santiago. The next two ships, the *Vizcaya* and *Cristóbal Colón*, received little initial fire; but as the *Oquendo* emerged, American fire was so concentrated that she was struck by 57 of the 123 American hits on the four Spanish vessels and was forced to turn toward shore and run aground to avoid sinking. *Courtesy of the National Archives.*

to leave his post and head for Key West to recoal, was "reprehensible," and he could not separate this from Schley's achievement at Santiago. He asked Long to give Schley "ample justice."[46]

In their relations with each other, Sampson and Schley were courteous and correct. For his part, Schley knew that the Navy Department had been highly agitated about his movements prior to 1 June, but he assumed that his conduct at Santiago had more than compensated for any errors of judgment prior to the battle. This view of things had seemingly been corroborated by the fact that at a victory celebration in New York he walked arm in arm with Sampson and was greeted by Long and other members of the cabinet. Schley was given a hero's welcome in Washington, where he was received by President McKinley. When Schley's supporters later read about Sampson's secret criticism of his subordinate's actions prior to the battle of Santiago, they felt that Sampson had been guilty of duplicity. Resentment and hard feelings grew on both sides of the issue.[47] Meanwhile, on 3 March 1899, Schley was promoted to rear admiral and appointed as a member of the Puerto Rican Commission.[48]

This duty and that on various naval boards gave Schley time to respond to requests for public appearances. For nearly a year he traveled to various parts of the country as the guest of state legislatures, cities, and other organizations, from which he received a variety of loving cups, special medals, and other awards. Meanwhile, much to Schley's chagrin, the Sampson–Schley controversy continued to rage. Secretary Long had helped to keep it alive when he proposed that, along with promotions for both officers, Sampson be advanced eight numbers on the navy list and Schley six. This action would have put Sampson one number ahead of Schley. It set off a series of arguments in Congress on the merits of the two officers, which went on intermittently for two years. When Schley was given command of the South Atlantic Squadron in November 1899, some of his partisans charged that the Navy Department had exiled him. While Schley was out of the country, the unfortunate controversy reached a new and ugly stage.[49]

The tumult began when Edgar Stanton Maclay, a clerk in the Brooklyn Navy Yard, published the third volume of his history of the U.S. Navy, which covered the Spanish–American War. Maclay's account of the battle of Santiago and the events that preceded it were extremely critical of Schley. Maclay wrote: "Schley's contribution to naval strategy, as too plainly shown by his conduct throughout the campaign, was, 'Avoid your enemy as long as possible, and if he

makes for you, run.' " If this were not bad enough, the volume had
been adopted as a textbook at the Naval Academy. Friends of Schley
sent him clippings and reviews of the book. Stung by what he considered to be a perversion of facts as well as abuse and defamation,
Schley requested a court of inquiry on his conduct. The navy fired
Maclay, Congress forbade the use of his book at the Academy, and
the publisher recalled the volume, issuing a new and drastically revised account of the role of Schley. As soon as his duties with the
squadron were completed, Schley was ready for the investigation.[50]

Acting on Schley's request, Secretary Long ordered Admiral George
Dewey, the ranking officer of the U.S. Navy, to convene a court of
inquiry in order to examine and to reach conclusions on ten specific
questions, as well as any other matters relating to the case. Subsequently the court set forth fourteen points to be investigated. Basically a series of charges, these items may be summarized as follows:
(1) At Cienfuegos Schley failed to maintain a close blockade; did not
locate the Spanish fleet or open communications with the Cuban
rebels; did not coal his ships when he could have and should have
done so. (2) When informed that the Spaniards were not at Cienfuegos, Schley did not promptly act on this information or proceed to
Santiago where the Spanish fleet was known to be. (3) After receiving
orders to proceed to Santiago, Schley moved slowly, failed to establish an effective blockade, took no steps to locate the enemy, left his
station in defiance of orders, and falsely alleged that his squadron
was short of coal and could not coal at sea. (4) Once he reached
Santiago, Schley did not do his utmost to destroy the *Cristóbal Colón*,
and he falsely reported that the defenses of Santiago were formidable,
a conclusion that was disputed by other officers, with subsequent
investigation showing that the defenses were feeble. (5) During the
battle of Santiago, Schley did not follow Sampson's plan for the U.S.
fleet to close in on the harbor, and thus allowed the Spaniards to
escape. His actions made it possible for the Spanish ships to be run
ashore and be destroyed instead of being captured. And, in turning
his ship during the battle, Schley endangered the *Texas* and, to a
lesser extent, the *Iowa*. (6) Schley's bearing in battle fell short of the
standards of activity and obedience required of a naval officer.[51]

On 12 September 1901, the court of inquiry opened at the Washington Navy Yard. It was attended by large crowds, including many
prominent women, and its proceedings were covered by reporters
from all over the country. A number of navy men of all ranks gave

testimony, as did a few civilian experts. But the scope of the inquiry was so limited that only testimony that directly concerned Schley was admitted. Schley's lawyers fought this ruling without success, as the court ruled that Sampson's conduct was not under review. Because the official connections and actions of both officers were related, the ruling was unfair. Sampson himself was in poor health and unable to give testimony, thus further limiting the value of the proceedings. After forty days the hearing came to an end. The court's ruling was mixed. It described Schley's campaign prior to 1 June 1898 as being characterized "by vacillation, dilatoriness, and a lack of enterprise." It also said that during the battle of Santiago, he was "self possessed" and by his example encouraged his subordinate officers and men to fight courageously.

The report did not credit Schley with victory in the battle, but Admiral George Dewey, the president of the court, filed a minority report that not only disagreed with most of the findings of the majority, but concluded that Schley had been in absolute command and was entitled to the credit for the victory.[52] Dewey's gesture of support for his old friend helped to assuage Schley's great disappointment in the verdict of the court.[53] Schley's lawyers called attention to the shortcomings of the court in their appeal to President Theodore Roosevelt for a reversal of the findings. But Roosevelt reviewed the evidence and narrowed the scope of criticism, hoping to end this entirely unhappy chapter in the history of the navy.[54]

Schley's years of active service came to an end on 9 October 1901 when he reached the age of sixty-two and was placed on the retired list. Three years later he published his autobiography, setting forth the events in his long and active career in a fair and detached way. His wife and members of his family knew, however, that the verdict of the court of inquiry had hurt him deeply. About 1909 he began to show symptoms of declining health, and in the early part of 1911 signs of heart trouble. On 2 October 1911, the Admiral and Mrs. Schley, returning from a vacation, stopped in New York City. Schley left his wife at a hotel and crossed the street for a brief visit at the Yacht Club. From there he intended to walk to the office of his younger son, Dr. Winfield Scott Schley, Jr.; but as he reached the curb, he staggered and fell. Taken to a hospital, Schley failed to regain consciousness and soon died. His body was transported to Washington for funeral services. All government workers who were veterans of the Spanish–American War were given a half day's leave to attend the services, and Schley was buried in Arlington Cemetery with full military honors. So passed from the scene a warm-hearted, generous, resourceful, and courageous officer.[55]

To many of his contemporaries Schley was something of an anachronism. In the Civil War his courage, patriotism, and dedication to duty were never in doubt. He was a fine young officer. What set him apart from his fellows was that he had many dimensions. Possibly his early dealings with the French and Spanish, and perhaps an interest in his own Huguenot ancestry, stimulated in him a desire to know more about the language and culture of those nations. Many of Schley's contemporaries had a dislike of the French and/or of Emperor Louis Napoleon because of the latter's sympathy for the Confederacy and his intervention in Mexico. Although Schley did not approve of these actions, he had a great admiration for Empress Eugenie and for French culture.

At a time when few naval officers had any interest or proficiency in foreign languages, Schley was adept in French and fluent in Spanish. He practiced speaking those languages at every opportunity. When many of his countrymen tended to look down on anything Spanish, Schley came to believe that he understood the Spanish mind and temperament.

From his parents, Schley seems to have inherited a rich sense of humor and a love for people. As a young man he attracted followers. During his long naval service he demonstrated the ability to inspire his men. He was quick to praise his subordinates for their prompt and efficient responses to duty. He believed that praise made the crew feel appreciated, and that their own sense of worth made for an efficient ship. His men had an affection for him and he reciprocated their feelings. Schley placed high value on knowing the enlisted man and his problems. It was a source of surprise and disappointment to him that few officers were really interested in the concerns of the enlisted men, whom Schley saw as a vital resource that needed to be cultivated and inspired if the demands of modern war were to be met.

As a man of culture, intelligence, and wit, Schley made friends easily both in and out of the navy. Those who knew him socially found him a marvelous raconteur whose interesting and funny stories were repeated by others. Some of his less gifted or lucky contemporaries in the navy resented him and the opportunities that he had to advance professionally. To some in the navy he seemed vain and eager for publicity; yet it seems clear that if other officers had had similar opportunities to advance themselves, they would have done so.

On the professional level, Schley grew to maturity in a time of lean naval budgets. Officers were enjoined to think small and economically. Schley learned something from every assignment, and frequently the lesson was applied to another circumstance. While doing one job, Schley was always preparing himself psychologically for the next. It was his custom to keep a bag partially packed to narrow the time necessary to set out for his next assignment. Most of his professional career was spent in wooden ships powered by sails and steam, but he welcomed the arrival of the New Steel Navy and mastered the technology associated with it.

Schley was an admirer of Farragut, and may well have thought that the ingredients that made Farragut a great commander did not come from classroom experience. There is no indication that Schley was among the anti-intellectual naval officers who opposed the Naval War College, but it would not be surprising if he doubted that it was practical. In both Civil War and peacetime assignments, his combat experience was on a small scale. The strategy was elementary: the enemy is over there; go and get him. The Korean forts affair gave Schley some experience in ground combat and in the coordination of units. The situation was unique, however, and the officers adapted themselves to the condition they faced. Likewise the rescue of Greely was a special operation. In carrying it out, Schley showed a healthy skepticism for the opinions for some experts, and relied on his own judgment. He was willing to take risks based on his own calculations. And he was lucky.

But Schley did believe that lessons could be learned from history. While he was with the *Baltimore* off Chile, he found time to write a congratulatory note to Alfred T. Mahan on his book *The Influence of Sea Power on History,* which became a text at the Naval War College. Schley's memoirs also indicate an awareness of historical precedents and parallels.

The good luck that characterized most of Schley's professional life began to run out during the Spanish–American War. He was older and more cautious, operating under the command of an officer who had been his junior at the Naval Academy. It was a command relationship that required diplomacy and tact on both sides. Schley had been trained to believe that the man on the scene must make judgments about the enemy and his own capabilities, even if they were at variance with the views of a distant commander. This method of command had won the respect of his superiors in the Civil War; now it got him into trouble. His enemies put the worst possible interpretation on his actions. For people who knew Schley or who were familiar with his career, and especially his rescue of Greely, any suggestion of cowardice in the turning of the *Brooklyn* or neglect of duty at any time was unconscionable. Eventually the verbal and written slurs forced Schley to request a court of inquiry. To his enemies and to those who believed that he had received more credit than he was due, it was a golden opportunity to disparage Schley publicly. Many of those who observed the tenor and the restrictive nature of that inquiry believed that Schley did not get a fair hearing. The verdict of the court and the failure to get it reversed hurt Schley deeply, even though the pain was partly mitigated by Dewey's statement and by much public support for his cause. For Schley's family, the verdict brought sadness to the admiral's later years and accelerated the decline in his health. This dedicated officer with a long record of service to his country deserved a happier fate and a remembrance of his finest qualities.

FURTHER READING

The basic source of information on Schley's life and work is his autobiography, *Forty-five Years under the Flag*. This should be supplemented by a series of magazine articles that Schley wrote just before he died, entitled "Admiral Schley's Own Story," *Cosmopolitan Magazine* 52 (December 1911–May 1912). The material is especially useful on Schley's early life down through the Naval Academy years. The articles contained photographs that have since been lost. There is a very good account of Schley's career in Richard S. West, Jr.'s *Admirals of the American Empire*. This work consists of the combined lives of George Dewey, Alfred Thayer Mahan, William T. Sampson, and Schley. Brief accounts of Schley's life were published in *The National Cyclopedia of American Biography*, IX:8–9, and by Allen Westcott in the Allan Johnson et al., eds., *Dictionary of American Biography*, XVI:437–39. There is a brief memoir, mainly of principal assignments and dates, in Schley's own hand in the Franklin D. Roosevelt Library at Hyde Park, New York. Although there is no body of personal papers, there are manuscript materials that are helpful for various phases of his life. Schley's official dealings with the Navy Department may be traced in various records in the National Archives. These include Officers' Letters, Commanders' Letters, Captains' Letters, and Letters Sent by the Secretary of the Navy to Officers, all in Record Group 45. At the Nimitz Library at the Naval Academy is a volume entitled Personal Correspondence of W. S.

Schley, Chief of the Bureau of Equipment and Recruiting, March 12, 1885–November 3, 1891. This library also has Schley's letterbooks for the period when he was in command of the USS *Baltimore,* 14 August 1891 to 22 February 1892, and two volumes of incoming letters to the USS *Essex,* for September 1876 to October 1879.

Secondary sources with information on aspects of Schley's career include Park Benjamin, *The United States Naval Academy;* Jack Sweetman, *The U.S. Naval Academy: An Illustrated History;* Charles Todorich, *The Spirited Years: A History of the Antebellum Naval Academy;* Robert Seager II, *Alfred Thayer Mahan: The Man and His Letters;* Robert Seager II and Doris D. Maguire, eds., *Letters and Papers of Alfred Thayer Mahan,* 3 vols.; The American Japan Society, *The First Japanese Embassy to the United States of America;* Lewis W. Bush, *Seventy-seven Samarai: Japanese Embassy to America;* K. Jack Bauer, "The Korean Expedition of 1871"; H. A. Gosnell, "The Navy in Korea, 1871"; Robert Erwin Johnson, *Rear Admiral John Rodgers, 1812–1882;* A. B. Johnson, "The Light House Establishment"; John B. Hattendorf et al., *Sailors and Scholars: The Centennial History of the U.S. Naval War College;* Ronald Spector, *Professors of War: The Naval War College and the Development of the Naval Profession;* and Peter Karsten, *The Naval Aristocracy.* For an overview of the policies and practices of the Navy Department during the years when Schley was active, see Paolo E. Coletta et al., eds., *The American Secretaries of the Navy,* 2 vols. Additional information on the development of the Steel Navy may be found in Walter R. Herrick, Jr., *The American Naval Revolution;* and in two books by Benjamin Franklin Cooling, *Benjamin Franklin Tracy* and *Gray Steel and Blue Water Navy: The Formative Years of America's Military–Industrial Complex, 1881–1917.* For the best source on the details and the drama of the Greely Relief Expedition, see Winfield Scott Schley and J. R. Soley, *The Rescue of Greely.*

The problems with Chile and the *Baltimore* incident are explored in documents published in U.S. Department of State, *Foreign Relations of the United States, 1891,* and the inquiry at Mare Island Navy Yard is printed in U.S. Congress, *House Executive Document No. 9,* 52nd Cong., 1st Sess. A critical view of Schley's approach to the problem is found in Robley D. Evans, *A Sailor's Log: Recollections of Forty Years of Naval Life,* and Edwin A. Falk, *Fighting Bob Evans.* It should be borne in mind, however, that as Schley's successor on the scene in Chile, it was not in the interest of Evans to endorse the actions of his predecessor. Evans was also among the anti-Schley officers before and after Santiago. Also, it is apparent from the way that Evans dealt with sailors on leave during the cruise of the fleet around the world, 1907–9, that he had little confidence in a policy that trusted enlisted men. Although the fleet had been purged of malcontents and unhealthy men before the cruise, Evans made liberal use of shore patrols to get his sailors back on board the ships. See Robert A. Hart, *The Great*

White Fleet, 80–81, 83, 226, 252. Insights into the Chilean view of the *Baltimore* incident may be found in Frederick B. Pike, *Chile and the United States, 1880–1962,* and Joyce S. Goldberg, *The Baltimore Affair.*

On the Spanish–American War see Margaret Leech, *In the Days of McKinley,* for a view from Washington. This should be supplemented by Lewis L. Gould, *The Spanish–American War and President McKinley,* and Gerald F. Linderman, *The Mirror of War: American Society and the Spanish–American War.* David F. Trask's *The War with Spain in 1898* has been widely praised for its use of a wide range of Spanish and American sources and for its objectivity, but it refers to only a single page of Schley's autobiography, and that relates to his decision to remain off Cienfuegos. The author does cite archival copies of Schley's messages, and the published accounts by Evans and Secretary of the Navy John D. Long, and French Ensor Chadwick's *The Relations of the United States and Spain: The Spanish–American War,* 2 vols., but the search for objectivity should have involved a greater effort to establish Schley's point of view. Without it, Trask's account is unfair to Schley. Secretary Long's attitudes may be studied in Lawrence Shaw Mayo, ed., *America of Yesterday as Reflected in the Journal of John Davis Long;* in Margaret D. Long, ed., *The Journal of John D. Long;* and in John D. Long, *The New American Navy,* 2 vols. See also the Long Papers in the Massachusetts Historical Society.

An account of Schley's activities including the battle of Santiago, as described by a reporter on board the *Brooklyn,* is George Edward Graham's *Schley and Santiago.* The proceedings of the court of inquiry may be found in U.S. Congress, *Record of Proceedings of a Court of Inquiry in the Case of Rear Admiral Winfield Scott Schley, U.S. Navy,* 2 vols. A pictorial account of the court is in the Washington Post, *Pictorial History of the Schley Court of Inquiry.* For two critiques of the inquiry see Charles E. Grinnell, "A Legal View of the Inquiry Granted to Rear Admiral Schley and Other Inquiries by Military Courts," and H. W. Wilson, "The Schley Court of Inquiry." Trophies, medals, and other signs of public affection for Schley are in the Armed Forces History Division, National Museum of American History, Smithsonian Institution.

NOTES

1. Winfield Scott Schley, *Forty-five Years under the Flag,* 1–2 (hereafter cited as Schley, *Forty-five Years*); *Washington Post,* 3 October 1911. Schley discusses his youth through Naval Academy years in the last articles he wrote, "Admiral Schley's Own Story."

2. Schley, *Forty-five Years,* 2–5; Schley, "Admiral Schley's Own Story," 4–14. Of his youthful environment Schley wrote late in life that "everything around and about me, though peaceful and beautiful to see, was reminiscent of venture and had come about from warfare." Schley's father,

although trained as a lawyer, admired the military skill of Napoleon, and had a porcelain inkstand on his desk modeled in the bust of the emperor.

3. Schley, *Forty-five Years*, 5–10; Schley, "Admiral Schley's Own Story," 188–90; *New York Times*, 3 October 1911; Robert Seager II, *Alfred Thayer Mahan: The Man and His Letters*, 26–27; Robert Seager II and Doris D. Maguire, eds., *Letters and Papers of Alfred Thayer Mahan*, I:8, 33, 48, 54. For insights into life at the Naval Academy at this time see Park Benjamin, *The United States Naval Academy*, 210–26; Jack Sweetman, *The U.S. Naval Academy: An Illustrated History*, 45–59; and Charles Todorich, *The Spirited Years: A History of the Antebellum Naval Academy*, 101–32.

4. Schley, *Forty-five Years*, 11–20. For an account of the mission see The American Japan Society, *The First Japanese Embassy to the United States of America*, and Lewis W. Bush, *Seventy-seven Samarai: Japanese Embassy to America*.

5. Schley, *Forty-five Years*, 20–23.

6. Ibid., 24–27; U.S. Navy Department, *Official Records of the Union and Confederate Navies in the War of the Rebellion*, Series I, V:629 (hereafter cited as *ORN*).

7. Schley, *Forty-five Years*, 28–29. Confederate records identify the ship as the schooner *Andrieta*, formerly the *J. W. Wilder*. See *ORN*, I, XVII:57–66. Schley's report is on 61–62; Schley, "Admiral Schley's Own Story," 198.

8. Schley, *Forty-five Years*, 31–36; Schley, "Admiral Schley's Own Story," 367–68.

9. Schley, "Admiral Schley's Own Story," 368–69; Schley, *Forty-five Years*, 37–46. For reports of the *Winona*'s activities on the Mississippi see the *Annual Report of the Secretary of the Navy for 1862*, 404–5, 418–20.

10. Schley, *Forty-five Years*, 47–52; Schley, "Admiral Schley's Own Story," 369–70.

11. Schley, "Admiral Schley's Own Story," 370; Schley, *Forty-five Years*, 52–53. From Schley's marriage three children were born: Thomas Franklin, later an infantry officer in the Spanish–American War; Winfield Scott, Jr., who became a physician and surgeon; and Mary Virginia, who became the wife of an Englishman, the Honorable Ralph Montagu Stuart Wortley.

12. The *Wateree*, officially designated as a sidewheel gunboat, was commissioned at the Philadelphia Navy Yard on 20 January 1864 and departed for the Pacific Squadron soon after this. Under the command of Commander Francis Key Murray, the ship reached San Francisco in mid-November 1864 in a damaged condition. She was repaired and had her hull scraped at the Mare Island Navy Yard. In late February 1866, she left Mare Island for patrol duty on the coast of South America. See U.S. Navy Department, *Dictionary of American Naval Fighting Ships*, VIII:159. With a company of bluejackets and a Gatling gun, Schley guarded the American property and customs house in San Salvador during a period of revolution in El Salvador. See Schley, *Forty-five Years*, 58–60; Schley, "Admiral Schley's Own Story," 370–72.

13. Schley, *Forty-five Years,* 63–66. Both discipline and academic pursuits were affected by the changes introduced during the superintendency of Rear Admiral David D. Porter at the Naval Academy, September 1865 to December 1869. The Academy changed from a high school level of education to one of college. Classes were designated by the year of graduation instead of the year of appointment, as heretofore, and each class had its own badge and colors. The first yearbook, called *Shakings,* was published in the spring of 1867. Porter ended a system of espionage on the midshipmen and introduced an honor system. Midshipmen were treated as gentlemen and were expected to act in that way. A man's word was accepted as the truth. Demerits could be worked off by tours of guard duty. Porter introduced recreational sports, theatricals, and weekly dances. Attached to the Academy at this time were Lieutenant Commander Stephen D. Luce, the commandant of midshipmen, and Lieutenant William T. Sampson, an instructor in the Department of Physics and Chemistry. See Park Benjamin, *The United States Naval Academy,* 261–81, 298, and Sweetman, *The U.S. Naval Academy,* 83–89.

On the matter of foreign languages, the Board of Visitors made the following statement in 1868: "It is also deemed important that increased attention should be given to the acquisition of French and Spanish, as spoken languages [and] therefore recommended that every means be used to perfect the instruction in these branches. . . ." *Annual Report of the Secretary of the Navy for 1868,* 80.

14. Schley, *Forty-five Years,* 66–105; Schley, "Admiral Schley's Own Story," 374–78; K. Jack Bauer, "The Korean Expedition of 1871"; H. A. Gosnell, "The Navy in Korea, 1871"; Robert Erwin Johnson, *Rear Admiral John Rodgers, 1812–1882,* 305–33. The official report of the expedition is in the *Annual Report of the Secretary of the Navy for 1871.*

15. Schley, *Forty-five Years,* 106–7. While Schley was at the Academy this time, he served under two superintendents, Commodore John L. Worden, 1869–74, and Rear Admiral Christopher Raymond Perry, 1874–78. Worden represented the Old Navy's school of thinking, and his administration was conservative. To some extent the disciplinary and morale gains under Porter were eroded. In the case of Perry, he believed that the midshipmen were capable of reaching much higher attainments. Unfortunately the economy wave in naval expenditures meant that new officers would have to spend much of their careers in obsolete ships and expect slow promotions. Benjamin, *The United States Naval Academy,* 284–306; Sweetman, *The U.S. Naval Academy,* 102–11.

16. Schley, *Forty-five Years,* 107–37. Two volumes of incoming letters to the *Essex,* covering the period September 1876 to October 1879 and reflecting the variety of assignments of the ship, are in the Nimitz Library, U.S. Naval Academy.

17. Schley, *Forty-five Years,* 137–40. For an insight into the functioning of the Lighthouse Service at this time, see A. B. Johnson, "The Light House Establishment," in *The Naval Encyclopedia,* 430–41.

18. Schley, *Forty-five Years*, 40–181. The story is told in more detail in Winfield Scott Schley and J. R. Soley, *The Rescue of Greely*.

19. Schley, *Forty-five Years*, 182–92. For details of Schley's plans and accomplishments, see The Personal Correspondence of W. S. Schley, Chief of the Bureau of Equipment and Recruiting, March 12, 1885–November 3, 1891, Nimitz Library, U.S. Naval Academy. On the War College and its problems, see John B. Hattendorf et al., *Sailors and Scholars: The Centennial History of the U.S. Naval War College*, 25. Alfred T. Mahan believed that Schley was the inspiration for Secretary Whitney's decision to transfer the War College from Coaster's Harbor to the Torpedo Station on Goat Island. See Seager and Maguire, *Letters and Papers of Alfred Thayer Mahan*, II:655, 664, 716. Subsequently Whitney placed the college under Commander Caspar F. Goodrich, the commandant of the Torpedo Station, who was in sympathy with the goals of the college and who obtained funds for new quarters for it. See Walter R. Herrick, "William C. Whitney," I:410.

In later years, one of Schley's fondest recollections of his years in the bureau was his advocacy of an "open door" from the forecastle to the quarterdeck for enlisted men. He urged that after a competitive examination by graduated apprentice seamen, a certain number be chosen each year for the rank of ensign. The navy was not ready for such a proposal then, but it came about after the Spanish–American War. Schley, "Admiral Schley's Own Story," 616.

20. Schley, *Forty-five Years*, 192–212. Schley's official report on the behavior of the *Baltimore* in European and South American waters was published in the U.S. Naval Institute *Proceedings* 18 (1892): 235–49. He was very enthusiastic about the ship and had only a few suggestions for improvements. One of them was to reduce the size of the officers' quarters to give more room to the men. Another was to create three classes of petty officers. On the matter of coaling, he had this to say: "It has been found that the rolling swell in all these ports (in Europe and South America) sends the heavy lighters so violently against the ship's side that the stages are unshipped, ash-shutes are smashed, and much time is lost in waiting and watching for smooth times, when working, to pass coal safely or surely from lighters to men on the stages, and so into side ports to the bunkers." Ibid., 236. Schley's letterbooks for the period when he was in command of the *Baltimore*, 14 August 1891 to 22 February 1892, are in the Nimitz Library, U.S. Naval Academy.

21. Schley, *Forty-five Years*, 212–31. For a critical account of Schley's handling of the affair by the officer who succeeded him at Valparaiso, see Robley D. Evans, *A Sailor's Log: Recollections of Forty Years of Naval Life*, 258–64. See also Edwin A. Falk, *Fighting Bob Evans*, 145–65. Documents relating to the diplomatic and political preliminaries in Chile, as well as to the *Baltimore* incident, are in U.S. Department of State, *Foreign Relations of the United States, 1891*, 90–352; and in U.S. Congress, *House Executive Document No. 9*, 52nd Cong., 1st Sess. For the diplomatic background of American relations with Chile, see Frederick B. Pike, *Chile and the United*

States, 1880–1962, 71–85, 141–87, 332–34. The most recent study is Joyce S. Goldberg, *The Baltimore Affair.* Both Pike and Goldberg used Chilean sources as well as American, Goldberg visited the site of the saloon, and both tend to be pro-Chilean in their treatment of the incident. The present writer believes that insufficient attention has been paid to the fact that on 22 September 1891 a sailor from the German warship *Nemman* was stabbed while on liberty because he was mistaken for an American. Also, when the men from the *Baltimore* were en route to the shore, they passed the Chilean warship *Esmerelda,* and members of her crew made threatening gestures. Once on shore, the American sailors received warnings from several sources that there would be trouble after dark and to get a room for the night. At the True Blue Saloon, Bosun Mate Charles W. Riggin asked his shipmates not to drink because they might all have to stick together in a fight. Several sailors testified that they decided not to drink, or in a few instances to have only one or two beers, in anticipation of trouble from Chilean sailors. Riggin and coal heaver William Turnbull were killed in the fighting between Chileans and Americans.

22. Schley, *Forty-five Years,* 232–34. For the record of the inquiry at Mare Island, see U.S. Congress, *House Executive Document No. 9,* 52nd Cong., 1st Sess., 341–610.

23. Schley, *Forty-five Years,* 234–36, 238–39; Goldberg, *The Baltimore Affair,* 139–43.

24. Schley, *Forty-five Years,* 235–38, 240–43.

25. Ibid., 239–40. Schley made similar recommendations in the case of the *Baltimore;* see footnote 20.

26. Ibid., 244–55.

27. Ibid., 256–59; Richard S. West, *Admirals of American Empire,* 173, 222–25, 227. West states that Schley's appointment was due primarily to political considerations, and that Assistant Secretary Theodore Roosevelt was probably the main force behind it. See also Margaret Leech, *In the Days of McKinley,* 197.

28. West, *Admirals of American Empire,* 227.

29. Ibid., 225–34; Schley, *Forty-five Years,* 261–62; Leech, *In the Days of McKinley,* 219–21; David F. Trask, *The War with Spain in 1898,* 118–21. Captain Alfred T. Mahan, who was a member of the Naval War Board, considered it improbable that Cervera would go to Santiago because, unlike Cienfuegos, it was inaccessible by land. See "Narrative Account of the Work of the Naval War Board of 1898," 29 October 1906, published in Seager and Maguire, *Letters and Papers of Alfred Thayer Mahan,* III:627–43.

30. Schley, *Forty-five Years,* 262–74; West, *Admirals of American Empire,* 234–40; Trask, *The War with Spain in 1898,* 121–23. When the Flying Squadron left for Cuba, it consisted of the cruiser *Brooklyn,* the battleships *Massachusetts* and *Texas,* and the armed yacht *Scorpion.* When off Cienfuegos, Schley saw lights on the shore whose meaning he did not understand. Captain Robley Evans of the *Iowa* knew that arrangements had been made to have the Cuban insurgents signal to the American squadron,

but he did not tell Schley this because he presumed that the commodore also had this information and knew what to do. It was not until the cruiser *Marblehead,* under Captain Bowman H. McCalla, joined the squadron on 24 May that Schley learned of the signal arrangements; but the only signals seen were on the night of 23 May. Sampson's orders to proceed to Santiago were received on 23 May.

31. The Flying Squadron left Cienfuegos as a unit about 7:00 p.m. on 25 May and moved as a unit to Santiago; its speed was geared to that of the slowest vessel. Schley, *Forty-five Years,* 274–75; West, *Admirals of American Empire,* 238–40.

32. A memorandum from Sampson to Schley, sent with his order of 21 May to move to Santiago, stated: "It is thought that the Spanish squadron will probably still be in Santiago as they must have some repairs to make and coal to take." In his memoirs, Schley noted that subsequent information showed that the Spanish squadron could not leave Santiago because of a lack of facilities for getting coal and water and other needed supplies. Also, repairs were not within the capability of the port. See Schley, *Forty-five Years,* 270, 275–77, 279.

33. This was the famous retrograde movement that caused so much concern. Secretary Long described Schley's message as "one of the most infelicitous in history." For both the president and himself, wrote Long, the news that Schley was leaving Santiago was the darkest day of the war. See Leech, *In the Days of McKinley,* 222.

In his memoirs Schley says that the engine of the collier *Merrimac* broke down shortly after the squadron arrived off Santiago, and she had to be towed by the converted cruiser *Yale.* Twenty-four hours elapsed before her engines could function at a reduced speed. The vessel was not completely repaired until the squadron returned to its position off Santiago. Schley, *Forty-five Years,* 275, 278. Between mechanical breakdowns, efforts to coal, and a zigzag course, the squadron was only about fifty miles from Santiago when it returned. West, *Admirals of American Empire,* 349. In the subsequent court of inquiry, Schley was accused of exaggerating the shortage of coal in his squadron and the need for replenishment, but these concerns did not begin at Santiago. While at Hampton Roads, prior to going to Key West and to Cuba, Schley had coaled his ships every day. He was fearful of running out of coal while chasing the Spaniards. West, *Admirals of American Empire,* 234–35.

34. Schley, *Forty-five Years,* 281–92; West, *Admirals of American Empire,* 247–49. Speaking of the movements of the *Yale, Harvard, St. Paul,* and *Minneapolis* off Santiago between 21 and 24 May, David Trask says: "It is surprising that none of the American cruisers ordered stationed off Santiago de Cuba established Cervera's presence there." Trask, *The War with Spain in 1898,* 124.

35. Schley, *Forty-five Years,* 283–84; Trask, *The War with Spain in 1898,* 128–29. Trask pointed out that the *Colón* lacked its main battery of 10-inch guns.

An Associated Press correspondent attached to the *Brooklyn*, noting that Schley was transferring his flag to the *Massachusetts*, asked to go along. He quotes Schley as replying: "We are not going to do any real scrapping, but I want to find out what those fellows have, and we'll simply run in and locate the batteries." George Edward Graham, *Schley and Santiago*, 167–68. In his efforts to hit the *Colón*, Captain Evans gave the guns of *Iowa* so extreme an elevation that he temporarily disabled them. West, *Admirals of American Empire*, 250.

36. Schley, *Forty-five Years*, 283–84. In his memoirs, Schley points out that after Sampson arrived on the scene he did nothing about the *Colón*, which did not change its position until 10:35 a.m. The *New York* reached Santiago at 6:00 a.m. In the last article that he wrote, Schley described the differences between his and Sampson's type of blockade as follows: "The form of blockade which I established was in line of battle, cruising before the port about four miles off shore, with the *Marblehead* and *Vixen* on the flanks at night, closer in shore and ready for instant action. Its advantage was that the heavy broadside fire of the squadron was always concentrated upon the entrance. . . . Under [Sampson's] arrangement only the bow guns could be brought effectively to bear on the entrance, and if the enemy in a sortie should have charged down through our squadron so arranged we would probably have suffered considerably from our own fire." See "Admiral Schley's Own Story," 756.

37. Schley, *Forty-five Years*, 286–97; West, *Admirals of American Empire*, 251–58; Trask, *The War with Spain in 1898*, 132–39, 257–61; Schley, "Admiral Schley's Own Story," 758.

38. Schley, *Forty-five Years*, 298–99, 322; West, *Admirals of American Empire*, 258–62; Trask, *The War with Spain in 1898*, 261–62.

39. Schley, *Forty-five Years*, 300–302; Trask, *The War with Spain in 1898*, 262–63.

40. At the subsequent court of inquiry, Schley was asked why the *Brooklyn* made her controversial turn or "loop." Each time the question was asked, he gave a different answer. The first time he replied: "Simply for the reason that it would have carried us into a dangerous proximity to the torpedo attack, the broadside torpedo attack, of the enemy's vessels." At that stage of the fight he thought that the *Brooklyn* ought not to be sacrificed. The second time the matter came up, Schley said: "The movement, of course, had two purposes—first to avoid [the cross fire of the battleship] and second, to continue the action." On the third occasion, Schley stated that the turn was made so "that the ship might continue in the action and beat the enemy, as we did. That was the controlling one of all." He also noted that while the controversial turn had been ordered by Captain Francis Cook of the *Brooklyn*, it was a proper movement, and he would have ordered it himself. Schley claimed that the helm was put hard to port when the *Vizcaya* was about 1,000 yards away. The commodore also noted that he never heard of the *Texas* incident until six months after the battle. Also he claimed that the *Texas* was never closer than 500 to 600 yards to the *Brooklyn*, and

that there was never any danger of collision. See U.S. Congress, *Record of Proceedings of a Court of Inquiry in the Case of Rear Admiral Winfield Scott Schley, U.S. Navy*, II:1397, 1512, 1517, 1521 (hereafter cited as *Schley Inquiry*). Although the court took no notice of it, it is apparent from the testimony that the controversial loop confused the Spanish gunners as well as Captain Evans.

41. Schley, *Forty-five Years*, 302–4; West, *Admirals of American Empire*, 263–64; Trask, *The War with Spain in 1898*, 263–65.

42. Schley, *Forty-five Years*, 305.

43. Schley, *Forty-five Years*, 304–10; Trask, *The War with Spain in 1898*, 265–66.

44. The wording of the message to Washington bothered some people because they thought it a conscious effort to imitate William T. Sherman's message to Lincoln on the surrender of Savannah. Schley's report to the secretary of the navy on the battle was returned to him because one from Sampson's staff was sent instead. The text of both these messages as well as Schley's report to Sampson on the battle are printed in Schley's memoirs. Schley, *Forty-five Years*, 317–20. For the reaction of President McKinley and Secretary Long, see Trask, *The War with Spain in 1898*, 267–68. Trask points out that Long did all that he could to minimize the contribution of Schley to the victory. For the reaction of the public to the victory, see Leech, *In the Days of McKinley*, 258–59, and West, *Admirals of American Empire*, 287–88.

45. See, for example, the 6 July 1898 *Baltimore American* account of the battle, which said that Schley was the real hero and that Sampson lacked the grace even to mention his name. Schley, *Forty-five Years*, 335.

46. Ibid.; West, *Admirals of American Empire*, 288–89.

47. Schley and his supporters did not know about Sampson's 10 July message to Long until it was published by the Senate on 6 February 1899. Schley, *Forty-five Years*, 341–44; West, *Admirals of American Empire*, 292, 296–98.

48. Schley, *Forty-five Years*, 344–52, 376.

49. Ibid., 376–406. On 15 September 1898, Captain Robley Evans of the *Iowa* told Secretary Long about "the inefficiency of Commodore Schley when he was in command of the squadron off Santiago. . . ." Lawrence Shaw Mayo, ed., *America of Yesterday as Reflected in the Journal of John Davis Long*, 208. When the Senate confirmed the promotions of Sampson and Schley, Long sent a copy of the official word to Sampson with a letter in which he said that if the admiral wanted to write anything and have it placed in the file, the secretary would be happy to have him do so. Long also wrote to Schley on 17 March 1899 and made reference to the suggestions in some newspapers that an injustice had been done to Schley in the matter of his examination for promotion. The secretary said that he was sure that Schley did not feel that way, but he would be glad if Schley would inform him if he was in error in that respect, and if so, what could be done to make the examination more satisfactory. See Long to Sampson

15 March 1899 and Long to Schley 17 March 1899, Letterbook, Personal-Official No. 24, Long Papers, Massachusetts Historical Society. When Senator Louis E. McComas of Maryland told Long that he was bringing a delegation from Baltimore to see him about the "persecution" of Schley, the secretary wrote to McKinley on 3 July 1899 outlining the facts in Schley's case after he took command of the Flying Squadron. This letter is published as appendix III in vol. 3 of Edgar Stanton Maclay's *History of the Navy.*

50. Maclay, *History of the Navy,* III:365. In a letter of 3 July 1899 to McKinley concerning the alleged persecution of Schley, Long said: "It is inconceivable that any self-respecting naval officer would for a moment rest under criticism, much less the persecution, of a superior authority and not demand at once a hearing of a court of inquiry." The fact that Schley had not requested a court of inquiry was to Long "conclusive evidence" that the actions of the department were entirely satisfactory to him. Ibid., III:453. The tone of the Maclay book and its adoption by the Naval Academy seem to be clear indications that Schley's enemies intended to force him into demanding a court of inquiry.

Schley's letter to Long of 22 July 1901, complaining about the Maclay book and requesting a court of inquiry, Long's letter to Dewey setting forth the ten questions to be decided, and the court's list of questions to be decided are printed in *Schley Inquiry,* I:2–4.

51. *Schley Inquiry,* I:2–3.

52. The *Washington Post* presented extensive coverage of the court of inquiry including sketches of the participants, which later were reprinted in book form. The court is briefly discussed in West, *Admirals of American Empire,* 301–2. West calls it "the most famous and perhaps the most unsatisfactory court of inquiry in American history. . . ." The opinion of the court on the questions and Dewey's opinion and recommendation are in *Schley Inquiry,* II:1829–30.

53. The court's report settled little. A critique in a legal periodical concluded: "If it be correct that the president of the court concurred in what he did not express dissent from, then a comparison of opinions seems to show that all the members of the court at least agreed in finding that the retrograde movement should not have been made, that the order of 25 May [to investigate Santiago] should have been promptly obeyed, that the *Colón,* at least, should have been attacked to the utmost on 31 May, that the reports covering coaling were inaccurate and misleading. . . ." All members of the court also agreed about Schley's self-possessed conduct during the battle and that he encouraged his subordinate officers to fight courageously. Charles E. Grinnell, "A Legal View of the Inquiry Granted to Rear Admiral Schley and of Other Inquiries by Military Courts," 113. A British critique of the inquiry defended Schley's controversial "loop" and added that it was "a little strange that the Commodore should have been condemned for it." The author went on to say that: "Yet we do not think that posterity, when it reviews his career, will disagree with the general

tendency of the majority verdict. Schley showed too much hesitation and indecision at critical moments to claim the proud fame of a great admiral." The author goes on to defend Schley's conduct in battle and says: "There is no foundation whatever for the imputation of cowardice, and it is a thousand pities that it was ever made." For those who argued that Sampson should get credit for Santiago because he planned the dispositions, the author says: "But rarely will the Anglo–Saxon mind believe that the brain which plans is as much entitled to renown as the hand which executes." H. W. Wilson, "The Schley Court of Inquiry," 788–800.

54. Schley and his lawyers sent a letter to Secretary Long on 18 December 1901 and to President Roosevelt on 21 January 1902. Long had the judge advocate and his assistant prepare a reply for the president that was forwarded on 25 January 1902. Roosevelt replied to Schley's appeal on 18 February 1902. The president's position was that most of the actions that the court condemned took place five or more weeks before the action at Santiago. Because Sampson did not call Schley to account for them, he, in effect, condoned them. If Schley's actions were censurable, he should not have been left as second in command. Therefore Roosevelt dismissed all points of the appeal except those relating to the battle. As he saw it, five-sixths of Schley's appeal dealt with command and credit for the victory, points that the court did not consider. So Roosevelt got statements from the five commanders of ships (other than Sampson and Schley) who were in the battle. From these he concluded that technically Sampson commanded the fleet and Schley the western division, but the battle itself was a captain's fight. Roosevelt saw no excuse from either side to keep the controversy alive. To do so would damage the navy and the country. See *Schley Inquiry,* II:1899–1936.

At a cabinet meeting on 14 January 1902, the president made a reference to the Sampson–Schley controversy that led Long to send him a copy of the secretary's letter to President McKinley of 3 January 1899. In a cover letter to Roosevelt, Long said: "The occasion for writing was not one in which I felt like calling attention to the fact 1st that Sampson, who first knew of the facts, did not take any disciplinary measures, and 2d that, he failing to do so, the Department was justified, inasmuch as the war was over, in presuming that the promotion of both men, the Commander-in-Chief first and the second in command next, was the best disposition of the case." Long to Roosevelt, 14 January 1902, Letterbook, Personal-Official No. 24, January 8–April 10, 1902, John Davis Long Papers, Massachusetts Historical Society.

55. *New York Times,* 3 October 1911; *Army and Navy Journal,* 7 October 1911.

GEORGE DEWEY:
ADMIRAL OF THE NAVY

VERNON L. WILLIAMS

He had compiled a good record, but one that lacked distinction. He had spent very little time at sea during the previous twenty years, played only a minor role in the development of the New Navy, and was not considered a member of that brash new group of scientific officers determined to modernize the navy; nor was he a contributor to the school of naval theorists led by Stephen B. Luce and Alfred T. Mahan. There was little in George Dewey's record to suggest that he had much hope for further promotion and leadership opportunities in the emerging navy of the twentieth century.[1] His prospects changed markedly, however, in the early morning hours of 1 May 1898 when Dewey turned to the captain of the *Olympia* in Manila Bay and said quietly, "You may fire when ready, Gridley." From that fateful moment on, Dewey's star ascended dramatically as the nation sought to recognize this new hero of America's war of manifest destiny. Some might debate the degree of Dewey's contribution to the modernization of the U.S. Navy, but no one can ignore Dewey's administrative presence in that modernization process from the turn of the century until his death in 1917.

George Dewey was born in Montpelier, Vermont, on 26 December 1837. His father, Julius Y. Dewey, was a well-to-do physician whose entrepreneurial pursuits led him to found a successful insurance venture that later would give Dewey a more than comfortable life-style in the navy. Dewey spent his childhood with two older brothers and a younger sister, as his mother, Mary Perrin Dewey, had died early in his life, leaving the four children and the widowed doctor to fend for themselves. According to Dewey, his relationship

George Dewey. Photograph taken in 1899. From the collection of Mabel Croft Graham. *Courtesy of the Naval Historical Center.*

with his father was close and remained so throughout the remainder of the elder Dewey's life. Much in the character of George Dewey seems to have been drawn from his father: "He was one of those natural leaders to whom men turn for unbiased advice. His ideas of right and wrong were very fixed."[2]

Of the years before he attended the Naval Academy, Dewey left very little behind to indicate what kind of boyhood he had enjoyed. After his fame was won at Manila Bay, all kinds of wonderful stories were published in the newspapers and popular histories that exploded on the scene in 1898 and 1899. As Dewey biographer Ronald Spector has suggested, "Old residents of Montpelier, at the urging of eager newspapermen, found little difficulty in 'remembering' many colorful and prophetic incidents from Dewey's early years."[3] Earlier biographers noted that "it is curious how the wording of many passages in the autobiography follows so closely the phrases of eulogistic volumes on Dewey published in 1899."[4] From all indications it appears that Dewey was no shy, withdrawn boy, but one who was active and, at times, difficult to control. Later, as a young cadet at the Naval Academy, Dewey would be hard-pressed to refrain from mischievous pranks.

Dewey entered the Naval Academy in 1854 despite his desire to go to West Point. No appointments were available to either West Point or Annapolis, but a last-minute change of heart by a Naval Academy appointee gave Julius Dewey the opportunity to use his influence with Senator Solomon Foote to name George as the substitute.[5] During the next four years, Dewey compiled a solid academic record while leaving behind a handsome list of demerits, eventually graduating fifth in a class of fourteen.[6]

Emerging from four years of "hell and discipline,"[7] Dewey was assigned to the USS *Wabash,* flagship of the Mediterranean Squadron. With no opportunity for leave, Dewey sailed with the *Wabash* on 22 July 1858 en route to her station in the Mediterranean. Despite bouts of homesickness, Dewey came to appreciate the Mediterranean and the opportunity to observe European politics at each port of call. Impressionable and idealistic, Dewey spent the next three years in the region developing his maritime skills and attending to his naval and diplomatic duties, serving successively in the *Wabash,* the *Powhatan,* and the *Pawnee.* In 1861 he was ordered back to the Academy to take the examination for lieutenant.[8]

Dewey stood third in his class on the examination and would be commissioned lieutenant in April 1862. Immediately after taking the exam, however, he went home to Montpelier on leave. When word reached Dewey that hostilities had begun at Fort Sumter, he proceeded to a new assignment, the steam frigate *Mississippi.* The ship had had a distinguished career, having fought in the Mexican War and having accompanied Matthew C. Perry to Japan in 1853; but the introduction of screw propulsion had rendered her obsolete, and she was not expected to play an important role in the impending conflict. In the middle of May 1861, the *Mississippi,* with Lieutenant Dewey on board, left Boston and steamed down the Atlantic coast to Key West. During the rest of 1861, Dewey participated in blockading activities and support of the Union Army along the southern Gulf Coast.[9]

Following the indecisive battle at Bull Run and a series of naval successes at Cape Hatteras and Port Royal, Secretary of the Navy Gideon Welles and Assistant Secretary of the Navy Gustavus Fox convinced President Lincoln that the Union must secure control of the mouth of the Mississippi River and that David Glasgow Farragut was the man to command the naval forces sent there.[10] Dewey considered, years later, that the New Orleans campaign was the most important training he received as a young officer: "Valuable as the training at Annapolis was, it was poor schooling beside that of serving under Farragut in time of war."[11]

Shortly before beginning operations against New Orleans, the *Mississippi* received a new commander, Captain Melancthon Smith. Because of transfers and a lack of trained officers, the *Mississippi* had only four line officers on board, including the captain, and, by a process of elimination, Dewey was the second ranking officer. Farragut informed Smith "that there was complaint on the part of some officers on the Navy list" that Dewey, who was very low on the list, held a "position higher than theirs." Although Smith had the reputation of being a difficult captain to serve under, Dewey apparently worked well with him and won his trust. Smith persuaded Farragut to let Dewey remain as his executive officer, saying, "Dewey is doing all right. I don't want a stranger here."[12]

Formidable obstacles stood between Flag Officer Farragut and his objective, the most important being two forts, Jackson and St. Philip. The forts were located midway between New Orleans and the mouth of the Mississippi, and the Confederates had built a boom of cypress logs and chain at Fort Jackson to block passage upriver. Ordered to use his gunboats to bombard the forts into submission before attacking New Orleans, Farragut doubted that he had the ammunition or the manpower to capture them. In spite of repeated warnings from his commanders that attacking New Orleans without control of the forts would bring disaster, Farragut proposed to bypass the forts and move against New Orleans.[13]

The first problem facing Farragut was getting all his vessels—including the *Mississippi,* to which Dewey was still assigned—across the bars at the entrance to the river. On 18 March 1862, using shallow-draft mortar boats, Farragut began towing his ships across the bar at the deepest point in the streams leading into the Mississippi River. For eight laborious hours the *Mississippi* was pulled through mud until she finally cleared the bar on the other side. A month later, on 17 April, the mortar boats opened fire on Forts Jackson and St. Philip; and on the twentieth, two gunboats forced an opening through the boom that was wide enough for Farragut's ships to pass through, one at a time.[14]

On board the *Mississippi* on 24 April, Smith received orders to begin an early morning cruise past the two Confederate forts. His ship, the *Mississippi,* was assigned to the first division, behind the *Cayuga* and the *Pensacola.* Farragut was hoping to get as many ships as possible past the two forts before the rebel gunners noticed his intention to bypass the gun positions and attack New Orleans. Explaining that his night vision was poor, Smith ordered young Lieutenant Dewey to take the helm while he supervised fire control.

According to Dewey, the *Pensacola* stopped as she came abreast of each fort to fire a broadside, each time causing Dewey, just behind with the *Mississippi,* to reverse engines to prevent a collision. Dewey later remarked that "for a man of twenty-four I was having my share of responsibility." All during this time, the *Mississippi* was "under fire and returning it." To complicate matters, the Confederate ram *Manassas* appeared, and Dewey, seeing an opportunity to run the ironclad down, quickly maneuvered the ship toward the ram. The rebel commander reacted in time to avoid the crush of the *Mississippi,* and at the last minute, "sheering in, he [the captain of the ram] managed to strike us a glancing blow just abaft the port paddlewheel." The damage to the *Mississippi* proved not to be fatal, and Dewey continued on past the forts out of range of the Confederate guns.[15]

As dawn was breaking, the *Manassas* was spotted astern of the fleet bearing down on Farragut's ships in a second attempt to disrupt the Union attack. Smith was back in command on the bridge of the *Mississippi,* and reacted swiftly to the sudden appearance of the ram. He was in the act of requesting permission to attack when Farragut appeared on the scene; hanging out of the rigging of the *Hartford,* he cried out to Smith to "run down the ram."

Turning to Dewey, Smith asked if he could turn the ship around. Dewey replied that he could, but later admitted that "I did not know whether I could turn her or not, but I knew that either I was going to do so or else run her aground." On the first try, the *Mississippi* came around and faced the ram. Realizing that the cruiser bearing down on his ship would inflict a fatal blow, the Confederate captain evaded the collision and ran aground on the river bank. With a stationary target, the *Mississippi* "so riddled her [the *Manassas*] with shot that she was dislodged from the bank and drifted below the forts, [where] she blew up and sank." In his report to Farragut, Smith praised Dewey for his "efficient service," which "kept the vessel in her station during the engagement, a task exceedingly difficult from the darkness and thick smoke" that crowded the scene.[16]

Dewey's initial battle experience indelibly influenced him. The unforgettable image of Farragut hanging on the rigging of the *Hart-*

ford with blood in his eyes and screaming for attack remained with Dewey the rest of his life. Dewey confided later that when hard-pressed for a difficult decision, he often thought of Farragut and what he would do in the same situation. ". . . I confess that I was thinking of him the night that we entered [Manila] Bay. . . ." In those early morning hours of 1 May 1898, Dewey was confident that he was doing exactly what Farragut would have done, striking boldly and aggressively at the enemy.[17]

In the spring of 1863 two events occurred that almost cut short Dewey's naval career. At 10:00 p.m. on 13 March, the *Mississippi* began the approach to Port Hudson with Farragut, in order to co-operate with Farragut's plan to cut Confederate naval support of Vicksburg. As the Union fleet attempted to pass Port Hudson, Con-federate guns opened fire. Because of a critical mistake by her civilian pilot, the *Mississippi* grounded near the ninety-degree turn in the river at the base of the rebel fortifications. Despite repeated efforts to back off the sandbar, heavy fire concentrated upon the disabled vessel forced Smith to order his crew to abandon ship. Using the few undamaged boats still able to float, Dewey, brandishing his pistol, made a reluctant boat crew return to the burning ship to rescue the remaining ship's crew and the captain. Although under fire since the grounding, Dewey was not one of the sixty-four casualties. In his report after the action, Smith wrote the secretary of navy that "I should be neglecting a most important duty should I omit to men-tion the coolness of my executive officer, Mr. Dewey. . . ." In de-scribing the event to his father, Dewey wrote that "such scenes make people Christians."[18]

If Fortune was smiling on him that day, Dewey got a special dispensation a few weeks later. With the loss of the *Mississippi,* he briefly served as prize commissioner at New Orleans before being transferred to the *Monongahela* to continue the river campaign. While he was serving as executive officer in the steam sloop, a rebel shell "came through the bulwarks on the port quarter" mortally wounding her captain, who was standing next to Dewey on the bridge. Dewey emerged from the incident unscathed and in command of the ship.[19]

On 10 July, Dewey received orders for the *Monongahela* to proceed with the *Essex* to White Hall Point to assist the *New London,* which had been disabled by shell damage to her boilers. On the trip upriver, enemy batteries shelled the vessels without effect. At White Hall Point, Dewey was able to pull the *New London* off the bank, "took her in tow on the port side," and moved her out into the river. He then attached tow lines from the *Monongahela* to the port side of the *Essex,* so that "thus sheltered," the *New London* could be towed downriver past the enemy batteries, kept to the starboard of the two ships. According to Commander Robert Townsend, captain of the *Essex,* Dewey "displayed coolness, skill, and judgment" in rescuing the *New London,* and he used his guns effectively on enemy batteries.

A few days later Dewey was transferred to blockade duty on board the *Brooklyn* off Charleston, then was sent to the *Agawam* in the James River Squadron, and finally reported to the *Colorado,* in which he took part in the capture of Fort Fisher in North Carolina. During this period, Dewey had an opportunity to return to the Gulf, but he wrote to his father of his reluctance to accept such an assignment, saying, "if I go to the Gulf I shall have fighting and I have had quite enough of that."[20] He ended the war as a lieutenant commander on board the *Kearsarge.*

Dewey spent the decade after the Civil War taking advantage of friendships to obtain preferred assignments, such as serving as flag lieutenant to Admiral L. M. Goldborough while he commanded the European Squadron and teaching at the Naval Academy; and he courted his future wife, Susan Boardman Goodwin, daughter of the governor of New Hampshire.[21]

The postwar era left much to be desired for naval officers eager for a career of promotions and leadership. Dewey was doomed, as were others, to endure service in an increasingly obsolete fleet with an overcrowded officer corps. Dewey's service during these long years of stagnation was somewhat moderated, however, by his rank at the end of the war and his financial position. His war experience gained Dewey promotion to lieutenant commander in 1865, giving him a jump on other officers of his age. Many of his classmates were still lieutenants and lieutenant commanders in the 1890s when Dewey had reached flag rank. Dewey was also fortunate to have a good income from his share of his father's insurance business. This insulated Dewey from the financial problems that plagued many officers and allowed him to take advantage of the social life of Washington during his several tours of duty there.

During the years before Manila Bay, Dewey slowly ascended the career ladder, taking advantage of his friendships in and out of the navy. In 1875, he moved to Washington, D.C., to serve as a member of the Lighthouse Board. For seven years he enjoyed the social seasons and developed his contacts within the Navy Department. "I found myself in Washington social life, with its round of dinners and receptions, which were a new and enjoyable experience to me, if exhausting physically."[22]

In 1882, Dewey returned to sea, commanding the sloop *Juaniata* bound for the Asiatic Station. As he traveled to the East, his health took a turn for the worse, resulting in his hospitalization at Malta where it was feared that he might not survive. His full recovery took almost two years. In 1884, Dewey was assigned command of the *Dolphin*, one of the U.S. Navy's first steel ships, still under construction. Growing frustrated at delays in the commissioning of the new ship, Dewey accepted transfer to command of the old steam-sloop *Pensacola*, flagship of the European Squadron, the following March, and would remain with the ship throughout her four-year cruise before again returning to Washington for service at Navy Department headquarters.[23]

In 1889, Dewey succeeded Winfield Scott Schley as chief of the Bureau of Equipment. In his autobiography, Dewey took great pains to convince his readers that before his attempt to capture the flag of the Asiatic Squadron in 1897, he had never used political influence to further his career. Obviously this was not true. Dewey had used his father's influence to gain acceptance to Annapolis, continued to use the good offices of friends for choice assignments in the postwar years, made use of Vermont political clout through his brothers to obtain the equipment post, and eventually would employ every means available to obtain the flag of the Asiatic station in 1898.[24]

Dewey's service in the Bureau of Equipment coincided with the emerging new steel-hulled, steam-powered navy. The United States was beginning to retire the outdated ships of the Civil War in favor of ships equipped with the new, modern technology. It was Dewey's responsibility to ensure that the fleet could steam at will wherever American foreign policy dictated. It is perhaps here that Dewey's administrative abilities begin to mature and to presage his later contributions to the navy in the post-Philippines era.

Under Dewey, the bureau fitted the new ships with many of the inventions that the scientific officers were designing for the modern navy. Although not a producing member of that group, Dewey was not only receptive to progressive change, but enthusiastically endorsed many of their improvements. Dewey biographer Ronald Spector assesses Dewey positively, saying that he had "done a creditable job in a rather routine assignment [and] had established a reputation as an energetic administrator and a friend of innovation," but rejects the thesis that Dewey's three years as head of the bureau "marked" him for later advancement. Certainly Dewey's performance reflected the role he would later play as Admiral of the Navy. As a facilitator of creativity, Dewey acted as a buffer to the more reluctant traditionalists who found new ideas difficult to accept.[25]

After his term in the Bureau of Equipment expired, Dewey remained in Washington as president of the Board of Inspection and Survey from 1895 to 1897. During this time he won promotion to commodore, a rank that "entitled [him] to the command of a squadron as soon as there was a vacancy." The first such vacancy occurred in the Asiatic Squadron. By the fall of 1897, Dewey knew of the impending vacancy and knew that he and Commodore John A. Howell were the two contenders for the position. The appointment became more important in the context of American foreign policy decisions arising out of concern for Spanish depredations in Cuba. In any war with Spain, the Philippines would figure prominently with American success or failure. President William McKinley and Secretary of the Navy John D. Long wanted a reliable commander on the Asiatic who could supply the aggressive action necessary to prevent the Spanish fleet in the Philippines from reinforcing Spanish forces in the Caribbean region. It was up to Dewey to persuade them that he was their man.[26]

Once again Dewey turned to his political contacts for support. To one he complained that Arendt S. Crowninshield, the influential head of the Bureau of Navigation, disliked him and would "hardly recommend me to any command; and his advice had great weight with . . . the secretary of the navy." Dewey turned to his friend Theodore Roosevelt, then assistant secretary of the navy. Roosevelt supported Dewey for the command, informing him of a political letter already on file in support of Howell and urging that Dewey use all the political leverage he had to combat Howell's apparent advantage. Dewey next turned to Vermont Senator Redfield Proctor, a close family friend, and with his support obtained the assignment.[27]

Before leaving Washington to assume his command, Dewey studied everything he could find on the Philippines. In early January 1898, he reached Japan and broke his flag on the *Olympia*, arriving on station at a time of increasingly strained relations between the United States and Spain. Knowing that any war with Spain would mean instant action for his small squadron, Dewey began preparing for operations against the Spanish Philippines. His first move was to shift his base of operations to Hong Kong because "it was evident that in case of emergency Hong Kong was the most advantageous position from which to move to the attack." By the time Dewey established his headquarters at Hong Kong, the *Maine* had been sunk in Havana harbor, and war appeared imminent. Theodore Roosevelt, briefly acting as secretary of the navy, sent him orders to "keep full of coal. In the event . . . of war . . . , your duty will be to see that the Spanish squadron does not leave the Asiatic coast, and then offensive operations in Philippine Islands."[28]

No such instructions were necessary. Dewey understood the strategic setting and was already preparing his fleet for hostilities. He knew a state of war with Spain would cut him off from supply by the neutral British at Hong Kong. To assure that he had enough coal and provisions, Dewey had purchased the *Zafiro* and the *Nanshan* to serve the fleet as supply ships. By April he had his warships, four protected cruisers, two gunboats, and a small revenue cutter prepared for battle, their hulls cleaned and their white peacetime paint covered with gray. Crews drilled daily under Dewey's personal inspection; and, leaving as little to chance as possible, Dewey sent a spy to Manila to report on the Spanish fleet and fortifications and another into Hong Kong to obtain what information he could from travelers recently arrived from the Philippines.[29]

On 23 April 1898, the British at Hong Kong ordered Dewey to remove the American fleet from their waters, according to the rules of neutrality. Though this was the first notice Dewey had that a state of war existed between the United States and Spain, he had anticipated the order to leave and arranged for a temporary anchorage in Chinese waters at Mirs Bay. Dewey ordered his squadron to move there the next day, and a day later, on 25 April, he received a cable from Long stating that war had been declared. Dewey was ordered to "proceed at once to the Philippine Islands. Commence operations at once, particularly against Spanish fleet. You must capture vessels or destroy. Use utmost endeavors."[30]

Dewey immediately cabled the American consul at Manila, Oscar F. Williams, asking for the location of the Spanish fleet and the general situation in the archipelago. Williams quickly left for Mirs Bay with intelligence that the Spanish commander, Rear Admiral Patricio Montojo, planned to oppose Dewey at Subig Bay north of Manila on the west coast of Luzon. On 27 April, Dewey set a course for Luzon, exercising his men en route in day and night battle drills, firefighting, and damage control. All unnecessary woodwork was stowed below or thrown overboard to reduce the fire hazard.[31]

Arriving off the coast of Bataan and Corregidor on the thirtieth, Dewey ordered the *Boston* and the *Concord* to reconnoiter Subig Bay to locate the enemy's fleet. When they returned without seeing any

Spanish ships, Dewey concluded that Montojo had elected to position his ships near the city of Manila. Dewey was correct; the Spanish commander knew that his ships were no match for the Americans in a battle involving maneuvering, and had deployed his ships in an east–west line across Canacao Bay near Cavite, the Spanish naval base opposite the city of Manila. Montojo wanted to fight at anchor and use the shore batteries to support his ships while not putting the city of Manila in the line of fire.[32]

Manila was regarded by many as the "Gibraltar of the Far East," and mining of the passages into the bay was rumored to make it impregnable. Dewey was undeterred. Reasoning that the Spanish lacked the expertise to properly mine the deep channel into the Bay, Dewey ordered his ships to enter Boca Grande Passage at 11:30 p.m. on 30 April. Slipping past the gun emplacements on Corregidor, the fleet steamed into Manila Bay in column on a course for Manila. Before reaching the city, Dewey sent the two supply ships and the revenue cutter "into an unfrequented part of the bay in order that they should sustain no injury and that they might not hamper the movements of the fighting-ships."[33]

Once he was safely through the mouth of the bay, Dewey slowed the fleet down to four knots, to delay its arrival at Manila until he had daylight to assist him in determining the location of the Spanish fleet and identifying gun positions along the shore. At daybreak, Dewey's ship came into range of the shore guns. As he steamed in a slow arc across the Manila waterfront, it was apparent that no warships were at anchor there; so Dewey adjusted his course farther to the south and west and soon found the Spanish line of battle. At 5:40 a.m. he came within 5,000 yards of the enemy and told the commander of his flagship to open fire. The little American fleet steamed across the line of Spanish ships, firing first from the port side and then, reversing its course, from the starboard. Dewey pressed his attack on the beleaguered defenders in a series of five passes in all, three to the west and two to the east, pouring a rapid fire into the hapless Spanish ships. Throughout the early morning hours, the Spanish fire was inaccurate while the Americans laid in a "continuous and precise fire at ranges varying from [5,000 to 2,000] yards, countermarching in a line approximately parallel to that of the Spanish fleet."[34]

At 7:30 a.m. Dewey received a report that his gunners were low on ammunition and quickly moved the fleet beyond the range of the Spanish guns at Cavite. The artillery from Manila continued to fire from emplacements along the shoreline near the city. Dewey sent word that unless the firing stopped, he would order his captains to shell the city. The guns soon fell silent. The atmosphere was tense in the *Olympia*. Smoke engulfed the Spanish ships, but the Americans did not know the extent of the damage.[35] Dewey sent the men to breakfast while he investigated the problem of ammunition and considered what to do next. At 8:40 a.m. he called a meeting of his captains and was much relieved to learn that none of his ships had been seriously damaged, and the report of an ammunition shortage was erroneous. Luckily he also had sufficient coal to continue the battle; otherwise, there would have been serious complications. With neutral Hong Kong closed to American warships, the nearest fuel stocks were thousands of miles away. Fortunately, the supply of coal on board would prove to be adequate.

As soon as the men finished eating, Dewey once again moved in for the attack. It was 11:16 a.m. Just over an hour later, his victory was complete. Several days later Dewey was to recall that "by this time the flagship and almost the entire Spanish fleet were in flames, and at [12:30] p.m., the squadron ceased firing, the batteries being silenced and the ships sunk, burnt and deserted."[36] Spanish casualties numbered seven warships and 370 men killed. Dewey was able to report that no American ships were lost, no sailors killed in the action, and only eight wounded.[37] The battle was a resounding success—a success secured by careful preparation, daring, and no small measure of luck. For the rest of his life, when moved to reminisce, Dewey would often remark that the Battle of Manila Bay was won in Hong Kong harbor where he prepared his squadron for battle.[38] Perhaps therein lies the best explanation for his master stroke.

For the time being, Dewey had accomplished his mission. No Spanish fleet from the Philippines could threaten the American coast or reinforce Cuba. He waited for the U.S. Army to bring sufficient troops to take and hold Manila and for the Navy Department to transfer additional ships and supplies to his small fleet off the coast. During the interim, Dewey used his guns to maintain control of the Manila region. One Hong Kong correspondent reported that "Commodore Dewey has exercised consummate judgement and rare ability in maintaining a distance at once safe for his fleet and deadly to the Spaniards."[39]

During the summer, as the American presence began to increase, Dewey established a blockade patrol to bottle up the Spaniards, dealt with problems arising out of a German plan to outmaneuver the Americans for the islands, and organized a system of supply for his meager force.[40] He maintained a limited line of communications with

Battle of Manila Bay. Contemporary lithograph showing the USS *Olympia* leading the U.S. Asiatic squadron against the Spanish squadron at Cavite, Manila Bay. *Courtesy of the Naval Historical Center.*

Washington. Some critics suggest that Dewey failed his superiors by not supplying adequate intelligence on the mood of the Filipinos regarding independence or acceptance of the United States as a colonial control. This failure was not one of communication, but of analysis; he could not discriminate between information sources and simply did not recognize accurate information regarding the Filipinos' position on independence. Although he was on the scene, Dewey relied on unsubstantiated reports and the advice of many individuals who were not privy to Filipino attitudes and plans. Further, he ignored available documents that clearly stated the Filipino position on the American role in the post-Spanish period and the question of independence; and he failed to provide Washington with assessments of these documents. Thus, Dewey contributed little to the formulation of a viable policy for the islands.[41] His greatest failure in the Philippines was not his failure to communicate information, but his inability to correctly identify and rely on sources of intelligence that certainly were available to him.

By August 1898, just four months after Dewey's destruction of Montojo's fleet, American military power had increased enough to pressure the Spanish into surrendering Manila.[42] By the end of the year, the war was won, and the Treaty of Paris transferred ownership of the islands to the United States.

But by that time the Americans had new opponents to subdue. During the fall of 1898, following the surrender of Manila, tensions between the Americans and the Filipinos led to open conflict. Dewey suggested later that the insurrection occurred because long-term tension had been allowed to develop that altered the Filipinos' earlier acceptance of some kind of American government for the islands. Whatever the error of earlier intelligence, in November 1898 Dewey received a report that began to change his original assessment of Filipino attitudes. Two naval officers, Paymaster W. B. Wilcox and Naval Cadet Leonard R. Sargent, traveled into the interior of Luzon on a fact-finding mission. There they found firm resistance to the idea of American control, and military preparations were under way for an insurrection should the United States attempt to establish a colonial government for the islands. Dewey dutifully reported this intelligence to Washington, but by that time it was too late to change the minds of President McKinley and the War Department. They were convinced of the rightness of the acquisition of the Philippines.[43] On 4 February 1899, shots were fired, and the Philippine Insurrection began. Shortly thereafter, Dewey's service in the Phil-

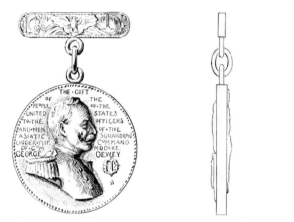

Dewey Medal. Daniel Chester French's drawing for the Dewey Medal, which was awarded to all participants in the Battle of Manila Bay. *Courtesy of Tiffany Archives.*

ippines ended. When he sailed for the United States on 20 May, he was grateful to leave behind the problems of dealing with the insurrection. "It is the responsibility that kills," he wrote. "A year is long enough in this climate for an old man, and I am glad to be permitted to rest."[44]

Dewey left the Philippines as Admiral of the Navy, a new rank created for him by Congress a week after the Battle of Manila Bay. His meteoric rise from commodore was due primarily to the wave of Deweymania that swept the United States following his success at Manila. Awaiting him at home were celebrations and the adulation of an adoring public, and even the opportunity to run for president in 1900.

Long before Dewey's departure from the islands, there were Dewey-for-president "booms," led by men such as Joseph Pulitzer of the *New York World* and others who sought to transform Dewey's sudden fame into political leverage. Dewey would have none of it, saying he was "unfitted for it [the presidency], having neither the education nor the training." Even during the triumphal voyage from Manila he refused to consider the possibility, with public curiosity beginning to build as the *Olympia* sailed closer to home.[45]

When Dewey arrived in New York in October 1899, public celebrations began, and the interest in his political future intensified. During the next six months Dewey refused to discuss politics, to commit himself as a candidate, or to take advantage of the political opportunities presented him. Instead he watched as the crowds began to dwindle and his popularity waned, never fully understanding what was happening. His refusal to accept many of the invitations to local Dewey celebrations dampened the enthusiasm of many of his fans. Dewey committed the ultimate example of "ingratitude and ill-taste" when he gave his wife the house that public subscription had purchased for him in Washington. What once had been effusive and adoring oratory began to degenerate into disparagement and amusement.[46] In April 1900, Dewey's resolve to avoid politics wavered, and he issued an ill-timed statement indicating his willingness to become a candidate:

> If the American people want me for this high office, I shall be only too willing to serve them.
> It is the highest honor in the gift of this nation; what citizen would refuse it?
> Since studying this subject, I am convinced that the office of the President is not such a very difficult one to fill, his duties being mainly to execute the laws of the Congress. Should I be chosen for this exalted position I would execute the laws of Congress as faithfully as I have always executed the orders of my superiors.[47]

The response from the press was to attack and ridicule the admiral's candidacy and his view of the presidency. In May the attacks were becoming more personal and biting until, on 18 May 1900, Dewey announced that he was no longer a candidate, saying, "I don't understand how I got the idea in the first place."[48] The brevity of the people's infatuation with him and the failure of his tentative move to enter politics left Dewey bewildered. His venture outside the confines of the U.S. Navy illustrated a certain naïveté that was ridiculed by some but admired by others, and did not retard his naval career.

Plans to reorganize the navy had been hotly debated for over a decade. The most popular plan, advanced by Captain Henry C. Taylor, championed the establishment of a general staff that would control naval planning. The proposal met with opposition from the Democratic Secretary of the Navy Hilary A. Herbert and some hesitation from his Republican successor John D. Long, both fearing a shift of authority from civilian to military leaders.[49] Dewey distanced himself from the debate, but could not avoid direct involvement in it when, in March 1900, Long established the General Board as an in-house advisory mechanism for the secretary. The board was established by executive order, had no basis in law, and was always controversial. Most civilians believed it fulfilled the need for a body of serving officers to advise the secretary on policy and coordinate the work of the navy's bureaus, but many officers considered it only the first step in the establishment of a true general staff that could determine policy and direct operations. As senior ranking officer in the navy, Dewey was appointed president of the board and in that position could exercise great influence on the membership of the board and its staff. Careful to include the brightest of the new young officers on the staff, Dewey brought together the best minds the navy had to offer.[50]

In the early years, Dewey and the board focused on the new empire so recently won from Spain. In a detailed communication to Dewey on 30 March 1900, Long ordered the General Board to make plans for all possible contingencies of war for the United States.[51] With Long's instructions in mind, Dewey and the board established a series of operational strategies and plans designed to protect the Philippines, Puerto Rico, and other American possessions and bases. At the heart of these plans was Germany. Dewey's distrust of Germans, at least partially due to his experiences with them in the Philippines, reflected the mood of many in the navy. The United States was emerging as a major naval power at the turn of the century and encountering stiff competition from Germany. It was natural for both German and American naval planners to anticipate war between the two countries. Much has been made of Dewey's personal dislike of all things German, and certainly his influence on the board carried great weight. However, the settlement of most Anglo–American disputes and the aggressive actions of Germany would have made that nation the primary target of the U.S. Navy's war plans had Dewey not served on the board.[52]

Soon after Dewey's appointment to the General Board, the death of McKinley brought Theodore Roosevelt, a friend of the navy, to the White House. His presidency changed Dewey's professional and personal life. In 1902 Secretary of the Navy Long was forced into retirement and replaced with William H. Moody, a strong proponent of the Big Navy and a logical selection by Roosevelt. As a capable and respected ex-congressman from Massachusetts, Moody performed a variety of political duties for the president while managing "to stay on top of his work [in the Navy Department]." Moody played an important role in pushing for "additional naval and coaling stations, more ships, and an increase of officers and men."[53] Unlike Long, Dewey's new superior was receptive to his counsel, and during the two years Moody served in the top naval post there existed a "harmonious" spirit of cooperation between civilian and naval leadership.

Contributing to Dewey's increased influence was the departure of his long-standing nemesis Arendt S. Crowinshield, who left the Bureau of Navigation and was replaced with Henry C. Taylor, now a rear admiral. Compared to their predecessors, Dewey was perhaps more comfortable with Moody and Taylor, who shared his ideas regarding deficiencies in the navy and what was required to establish the United States as a naval power second only to Great Britain.[54]

Facing Dewey and the General Board in the immediate future were important questions relating to the developing American empire and the emerging navy assigned to protect it. Naval construction, personnel expansion, naval bases and a strategy for the Pacific, and the role of naval power in American foreign policy were all on the agenda for Roosevelt's General Board.

In 1902 the board was forced to deal with its first important crisis when Britain, Italy, and Germany sent naval forces to blockade the coast of Venezuela and force it to pay some long-standing debts. Roosevelt responded by shifting the site of previously scheduled naval maneuvers in the Caribbean to demonstrate his concern and to pressure the Europeans into negotiating a peaceful solution to the crisis. To further impress the blockaders with the gravity of the situation, he ordered Dewey to take personal command of the American forces. Dewey's reputation for unilateral action and his success in the Philippines had the desired effect. His well-known dislike for Germany was designed to place additional pressure on the nation Roosevelt considered most responsible for the crisis. Tempers eventually cooled, and a settlement was reached in which Germany gained no territory. Dewey's contribution to the resolution is difficult to pinpoint. His presence in the general area caused some concern for the Germans, but it is doubtful that Roosevelt used Dewey as anything more than a veiled threat. Through it all, the U.S. Navy received some favorable publicity, the public's perception of Dewey's reputation in battle was revived, and Roosevelt's role as a policeman in the hemisphere was more clearly defined.[55]

Much more came from the naval exercises than a resolution to foreign policy problems. The maneuvers brought home the alarming fact that the Atlantic, European, and South Atlantic squadrons were unable to perform acceptably when brought together to form a single fleet. The exercises pointed to "defects in fundamental organization of the squadrons, such as the want of homogeneity among vessels on the same station." Before fleet maneuvers could begin at Culebra, the three squadrons had to be broken into groups of similarly classed vessels. The squadrons' organization prevented them from drilling as a unit during fleet-level maneuvers, to the detriment of their efficiency and achievement of battle objectives. The lessons learned at Culebra led to the reorganization of the U.S. fleet. In peacetime, cruisers would make up the squadrons in the Caribbean, Europe, and other distant stations, with the battleships divided between the Asiatic and North Atlantic fleets. In time of war, the cruisers would be reassigned from their squadrons to act as "auxiliaries to the battleships."[56]

Stationing similar ships together allowed the commanding officers to conduct maneuvers and coordinate gunnery practice. The Spanish–American War had demonstrated the need to keep the battle fleet together, but the Bureau of Navigation, which controlled the assignment of ships, refused to do so. Instead it argued that the "specific" requirements of the various squadrons dictated the dispersal of ships to widely separated stations. The effect of this policy was to reduce the ability of the ships to function as a single unit and thus to reduce their power. The Venezuelan crisis did not end the debate, but it did force a compromise on the General Board between those who wanted all the battleships assigned to a single "strategic" location and those who wanted them dispersed. The solution also represented a compromise between those factions on the General Board that saw the greatest danger in the growing Japanese navy and German imperialism in the Far East, and those that believed the greatest threat to American interests was in the Caribbean. This division of opinion continued until after World War I, and the argument over the stationing of battleships was not solved until the United States developed a two-battle-fleet navy.[57]

Both sides on the battleship deployment debate agreed that the future required a battleship construction program that would enable the United States to field a full battleship fleet in both the Atlantic and the Pacific. Although there was some difference of opinion as to the number of battleships needed, in February 1903 the General Board submitted a request to Secretary Moody calling for construction of one battleship for each of the forty-eight states, one armored cruiser for every two battleships, and one scout cruiser and one large, seagoing, quick-turning torpedo destroyer for each battleship added to the fleet. In addition, the board recommended increases in the auxiliary fleet and naval personnel as needed for each year's appropriation.[58]

Congress, in the midst of enormous appropriations for domestic reforms, refused to accept the ambitious naval building program. In 1904 Congress authorized only one new battleship, and in 1905 only two, in contrast to the navy's plan of four per year until all forty-eight had been funded. Even Roosevelt seemed to waver by 1905, suggesting that the twenty-eight battleships and twelve armored cruisers currently in the fleet or under construction placed the United States "second only to France and Great Britain." Dewey and the General Board did not agree with his estimation on two grounds: first, because Roosevelt's assessment did not take into account Germany's plan for future construction, and, second, because the president's estimate included seven ships completed before the Spanish–American War whose combat effectiveness was at best "debatable."[59]

In July 1904, the death of Henry C. Taylor deprived Dewey of a close ally in his program of orderly change within the navy. Taylor had continued to push for a general staff after the formation of the General Board, but with his death, leadership in the movement was assumed by a group of more radical officers who clashed with the traditional leadership in the bureaus.[60] These young officers considered the navy's poor administrative organization and its lack of a general staff to be the cause of all of its problems. As the "insurgents" grew more vocal and aggressive, and the gap between the reformers and their conservative opponents widened, Dewey found it increasingly difficult to effect compromise and, in his caution, edged closer to the conservative officers and their allies in the navy's bureaus.

His first clash with the insurgents came when the young officers presented their plan for a general staff to the General Board without first discussing the plan with Dewey. As chairman of the board, Dewey thought he should have been consulted and considered their action a personal attack upon his reputation and position. Even though the plan was similar to Taylor's of 1902, Dewey refused to support the proposal or even to attend meetings of the board, and some of his closest associates feared that he would resign. With Dewey so strongly against them, the insurgents backed down, and the plan died.[61]

Later in 1909 plans for Navy Department reorganization were advanced from a different direction. As Roosevelt's attempts to get changes through Congress had failed, George von Lengerke Meyer, secretary of the navy in the new Taft administration, decided to act on his own authority and ordered the department divided into four divisions, each to be headed by a senior naval officer answerable only to the civilian secretary. Although this reorganization did not fully satisfy the insurgents, it did reduce the power of the bureau chiefs, and it brought more centralized control to the service. When congressional critics began to question Meyer's authority to make such major changes within the department, Dewey lent his support to the reorganization, and it was put into effect.[62]

Another issue facing Dewey during his tenure as president of the General Board was the placement of a major naval base in the Pacific. Since the acquisition of the Philippines, the location of such a base had been an integral part of naval war planning. In 1900, the board "unanimously recommended" the establishment of the base at Iloilo in the Central Philippines, but Dewey must have had second thoughts because he later urged the formation of a commission to study both Iloilo and Subig Bay. At the same time, Dewey pushed the government to secure another base somewhere on the Chinese coast even though this violated the American Open Door policy. No consideration was given to Dewey's proposal for a Chinese base, however, and he soon took the lead in supporting the navy's choice of Subig Bay, rather than Manila Bay, which the army demanded in order to concentrate all military and naval bases at Manila "to facilitate their defense." The navy countered that the channels in the approach to Manila were too wide and deep to "be defended securely by either guns, mines or torpedoes or all of them," whereas the Army placed great emphasis on the ability of its Coast Artillery Corps to use Corregidor to defend Manila against any enemy approach. Dewey responded to this argument by suggesting that any such plan would leave "all the outworks and the natural base of the fleet, Subig, for the comfort and security of the enemy operating against Manila."[63]

The debate continued for over three years, and ultimately neither group won. Little building was done anywhere because Congress refused to appropriate funds. Thus Dewey failed to obtain for the navy a base he considered crucial to its fulfillment of its role in American defense.

During the same period, plans were being developed to defend American interests against Japan and Germany. Code-named War Plan Orange, the plan for war with Japan predicted possible defeat for the United States if Japan struck in the Pacific while the fleet was in the Atlantic. The plan for war with Germany (War Plan Black) predicted similar results if the fleet were in the Pacific when Germany struck. There were only two solutions to the problem; either a two-ocean navy had to be built, an unlikely event in the near future, or a mechanism had to be developed to accurately predict the location of a war long enough in advance to allow the concentration of the fleet in the area. Dewey rejected a Naval War College proposal that called for a council made up of civilian heads of the services, members of Congress, and military leaders because he doubted its ability to accurately assess the possibility of war. Instead he continued to stress the navy's ability to meet any enemy if it were given proper resources.[64]

Preparedness was the best guard against a future war, and Dewey was convinced that Germany, which he believed posed the greatest threat, would not dare strike if the battle fleet were stationed in the Atlantic. This remained his view until the California legislature precipitated a war scare with Japan by debating a bill that would prohibit Oriental aliens from owning land in that state. The year was 1913, the eve of World War I, but even such a Germanophobe as Dewey admitted that "it looks as if the Japanese are determined to find a reason for declaring war on us, perhaps they want the Philippines and Hawaii."[65] In time the crisis passed, but from that point on Dewey saw Japan in a different light and took the threat of Japanese aggression more seriously.[66]

The timing was ironic. Only a year later, World War I engulfed Europe. Beset by health problems and weakened by old age, Dewey realized that his influence was beginning to decline, but he remained a defender of the navy against outside detractors as well as against those reformers within the service who he believed did the navy a disservice by publicizing its shortcomings in order to gain support for changes they deemed necessary.

In a 1916 interview published in the *New York World,* Dewey refuted charges that the U.S. Navy was inefficient, demoralized, in need of a general staff, and wholly inadequate. In a statement reflecting his pride, he told reporter George Creel: "The attacks that have been made upon the navy are as false as many of them are shameful. . . . There is no demoralization. Both in material and personnel we are more efficient today than ever before. Our ships are as good as any, our officers are as good as any, and our enlisted men are the finest in the world."[67]

It was Dewey's last broadside at what he perceived to be the enemies of the navy. On 11 January 1917, five months almost to the day after the interview, the Admiral of the Navy lost his final battle. Nearly two decades had passed since his victory at Manila Bay, a

Dewey unveiling statue of John Paul Jones. As Admiral of the Navy, Dewey (note the braid on his sleeve) participated in numerous ceremonies, including the 17 April 1912 unveiling of a statue of John Paul Jones in Washington, D.C. *Courtesy of the Naval Historical Center.*

victory made certain by his thorough preparations and aggressive leadership. As a result the United States had gained an empire, and its navy immense new responsibility. Dewey remained firmly in control of what could be described as a moderate course of change using traditional avenues to accomplish modernization and improvements in the navy. He was often seen as an obstacle to progress by more radical and impatient officers, but more often than not, he supported their aims and goals. Dewey perhaps lacked the vision of other more capable men, allowed himself to be persuaded by personal bias along the way, and stretched the limits of his talents. He had done his duty as he understood it and served his nation and his service well.

FURTHER READING

The major George Dewey manuscript collections are located in the Library of Congress, the Naval Historical Center, and the Vermont Historical Society. Additional Dewey material is included in scores of collections in scattered repositories, much of it correspondence to or from the admiral. There are valuable records in the National Archives relating to the navy during Dewey's tenure in the Philippines and later on the General Board. Record Group 45, Naval Records Collection of the Office of Naval Records and Library, is an especially rich source.

Of the published works on the life of Dewey, only four rate a second look. Dewey's *Autobiography* was ghost-written by Frederick Palmer and relied heavily on secondary sources. It does, on occasion, provide important clues to attitudes and the perspective of the admiral. Of the three biographies published in recent times, Ronald Spector's *Admiral of the New Empire* is the best. Its section on Dewey's seventeen years on the General Board is the high point of all Dewey scholarship. Laurin Hall Healy and Luis Kutner's *The Admiral* and Richard S. West's *Admirals of the American Empire* are also of value. Based on more limited sources than Spector, both include more detail in earlier periods of Dewey's career, drawing often on the many popular accounts published soon after Manila Bay. Spector makes it a point to exclude many of these "Dewey stories."

Other works containing important Dewey material include "The U.S. Navy in the Philippine Insurrection and Subsequent Native Unrest, 1898–1906," a dissertation by Vernon L. Williams, which discusses Dewey's encounters with the Spanish and the Germans and details his strategy for blockade and early operations against the Spanish and the Filipino insurgents. Philip Y. Nicholson's "George Dewey and the Transformation of American Foreign Policy," another unpublished dissertation, provides an interesting look at Dewey in the context of public policy, the Philippines, and his service on the General Board. A third dissertation, Daniel Costello's "Planning for War: A History of the General Board of the Navy, 1900–1914," contains the best account of the General Board.

The U.S. Naval Institute *Proceedings* of the era include a host of articles on various Dewey topics. Many relate to the Battle of Manila Bay, whereas others deal with the attempts at naval reorganization. Other articles of note include Thomas A. Bailey, "Dewey and the Germans at Manila Bay"; James K. Eyre, "Japan and the American Annexation of the Philippines"; William R. Braisted, "The Philippine Naval Base Problem, 1898–1909"; and Paul T. Heffron, "Secretary Moody and Naval Administrative Reform."

NOTES

1. This assessment of Dewey's career before the Spanish–American War reflects the view of Ronald Spector, whose opening chapter in his biography of Dewey is entitled "Obscurity." Ronald Spector, *Admiral of the New Empire: The Life and Career of George Dewey,* 1–39, esp. 39.

2. George Dewey, *Autobiography of George Dewey: Admiral of the Navy,* 4.

3. Spector, *Admiral,* 4.

4. Laurin Hall Healy and Luis Kutner, *The Admiral,* 23. Dewey's *Autobiography,* ghosted by the noted journalist Frederick Palmer, relied on many questionable anecdotes found in the immediate post–Manila Bay press.

5. Dewey, *Autobiography,* 12–13.

6. Ibid., 14–15.

7. Healy and Kutner, *The Admiral,* 39.

8. Dewey, *Autobiography,* 23–36; George Dewey to Julius Y. Dewey, 13 June, 19 June, 8 July, and 11 August 1858, Dewey Papers, Vermont Historical Society (hereafter cited as VHS).

9. Dewey, *Autobiography,* 47–479; Navy Department, *Official Records of the Union and Confederate Navies in the War of the Rebellion,* Series I, 16:519–22, 525–26, 530–33, 540–51, 560–66, 574–75, 646–49, 676–77 (hereafter cited as *ORN*).

10. John Niven, "Gideon Welles, 5 March 1861–4 March 1869," in *American Secretaries of the Navy,* ed. Paolo E. Coletta et al., I:336–37.

11. *ORN,* I, 18:57; Dewey, *Autobiography,* 50.

12. Dewey, *Autobiography,* 50–51.

13. *ORN,* I, 18:135, 139, 159–60.

14. William N. Still, Jr., "David Glasgow Farragut: The Union's Nelson," in *Captains of the Old Steam Navy,* ed. James C. Bradford, 169; Dewey, *Autobiography,* 54; *ORN,* I, 18:361.

15. Dewey, *Autobiography,* 60–64; *ORN,* I, 18:151, 156, 171–72.

16. Dewey, *Autobiography,* 68–71; *ORN,* I, 18:142, 154, 157, 206.

17. Dewey, *Autobiography,* 50.

18. *ORN,* I, 19:681, 684, 692; George Dewey to Dr. Julius Y. Dewey, 29 November 1864, VHS.

19. Dewey, *Autobiography,* 106–12; *ORN,* I, 20:133, 145, 360–61. Ronald Spector lists four officers killed in his account of the *Monongahela* firefight on 7 July. Dewey mentions only one death, that of Commander Abner Read. In a casualty report three weeks later, Navy Surgeon David Kindleberger listed one officer killed, one officer wounded, one enlisted killed, and three enlisted wounded. The log of the *Monongahela* confirms Kindleberger's report. Spector, *Admiral,* 18; Dewey, *Autobiography,* 111–12; *ORN,* I, 20:335, 360.

20. *ORN,* I, 20:339, 361; George Dewey to Julius Y. Dewey, 18 January 1865, VHS.

21. Dewey, *Autobiography,* 113–49.

22. Ibid., 150–51.

23. Ibid., 153–60, 163–64.

24. Dewey, *Autobiography,* 164, 167; George Edmunds to Charles Dewey (this letter was forwarded to George Dewey with a brief note from his brother Charles), 9 March, Dewey Papers, Manuscript Division, Library of Congress (hereafter cited as DPLC); Charles Dewey to George Dewey, 23 March 1889, DPLC; Redfield Proctor to Edward Dewey (this letter was forwarded to George Dewey with a brief note from his brother Edward), 18 March 1889; DPLC; George Edmunds to George Dewey, 4 April 1889,

DPLC. Senator Edmunds offered little assistance other than to "vouch" for Dewey if asked by the Navy Department. Edmunds explained that "in the last 12 years," he had found that offering references only when requested by the appropriate agency had been beneficial to the "public interest." He suggested that Dewey or "his friends" use his name as a reference. Edmunds concluded his letter by stating that "Vermont is handicapped by having been given the Secretaryship of War which . . . should close our expectations [for Dewey's appointment]." William E. Chandler to George Dewey, 18 March 1889, DPLC; Eugene Hale to George Dewey, 19 March 1889, DPLC.

25. Dewey, *Autobiography*, 164–66; Spector, *Admiral*, 30.

26. Dewey, *Autobiography*, 166–67.

27. Ibid., 167–69. Again Proctor was called upon (see note 24) to bring political pressure to bear for Dewey. Proctor's letter of support as senator contained none of the hesitancy exhibited by George Edmunds eight years earlier. Redfield Proctor to George Dewey, 16 October 1897, DPLC. It appears that Theodore Roosevelt was aware of Dewey as early as 1889, but their friendship did not develop until Roosevelt's appointment as assistant secretary of the navy in 1897. Dewey and other army and naval officers became a part of Roosevelt's circle at the Metropolitan Club in Washington, where Dewey had enjoyed membership for some years. Theodore Roosevelt, *An Autobiography*, 210–11; Leonard Wood, "Introduction," in Theodore Roosevelt, *The Works of Theodore Roosevelt*, XI:xiii.

28. Dewey, *Autobiography*, 169–72, 174, 178–79; *Annual Report of the Secretary of the Navy for the Year 1898*, 4–5 (hereafter cited as *Annual Report, 1898*); Roosevelt, *Autobiography*, 214.

29. Dewey, *Autobiography*, 180, 186–95; E. B. Potter, *Sea Power: A Naval History*, 178.

30. Dewey, *Autobiography*, 193–96; *Annual Report, 1898*, 6.

31. George Dewey to John Long, 4 May 1898, R.G. 45: Naval Records Collection of the Office of Naval Records and Library, Area 10 File, National Archives (hereafter cited as R.G. 45: Area 10 File).

32. Ibid.

33. Dewey, *Autobiography*, 211–12.

34. Dewey to Long, 4 May 1898, R.G. 45: Area 10 File. "Precise fire" was an overstatement. American fire was woefully inaccurate, registering fewer than 200 hits out of almost 6,000 fired. Luckily the Spanish were even poorer, registering only fifteen hits.

35. Ibid. Joseph L. Stickney, "With Dewey at Manila," 476, said that "as we hauled off into the bay, the gloom on the bridge of the *Olympia* was thicker than a London fog in November."

36. Dewey to Long, 4 May 1898, R.G. 45: Area 10 File.

37. Annual Report, 1898, 6. Dewey lost one man to heatstroke during the earlier passage into Manila Bay. Philip Y. Nicholson, "George Dewey and the Transformation of American Foreign Policy," 90.

38. Nathan Sargent, comp., *Admiral Dewey and the Manila Campaign*, 48.

39. *New York Times,* 9 May 1898.

40. For a description of naval operations in the Philippines following the battle, see Vernon L. Williams, "The U.S. Navy in the Philippine Insurrection and Subsequent Native Unrest, 1898–1906," 94–131. For Dewey's encounter with the Germans in the Philippines, see ibid., 17–24; Lester B. Shippee, "Germany and the Spanish–American War," 764; Thomas A. Bailey, "Dewey and the Germans at Manila Bay," 61; T. F. Brumby, "Synopsis of Interview with Vice Admiral Von Diederichs on board the *Kaiser* at Manila," 7 July 1898, R.G. 45: Area 10 File; Henry V. Butler, "Memorandum," 16 November 1930, ibid. For a discussion of the affairs of the navy's occupation in the Philippines under Dewey's leadership, see Williams, "U.S. Navy," 24–35, 65–95.

41. Examples of Filipino statements forwarded by Dewey without comment include Emilio Aguinaldo, "Amados Paisanos Mios," 24 May 1898; "Filipinos," 24 May 1898, R.G. 45: Subject File VD, Box 2, National Archives.

42. For a discussion of the events surrounding the surrender of Manila, see Williams, "U.S. Navy," 39–43.

43. Ibid., 50–54; W. B. Wilcox and Leonard R. Sargent to George Dewey, 23 November 1898, R.G. 45: Subject File OH, Box 2, National Archives.

44. Murat Halstead, *Life and Achievements of Admiral Dewey: From Montpelier to Manila,* 446.

45. Healy and Kutner, *The Admiral,* 263; Adelbert Milton Dewey, *The Life and Letters of Admiral Dewey from Montpelier to Manila,* 426.

46. Dewey later explained that he transferred ownership of the house to his wife for legal reasons. He wanted to ensure that his son would inherit the property. Dewey's explanation did not appease the disaffected public. Frederick Palmer, *With My Own Eyes,* 127.

47. *New York World,* 4 April 1900. As quoted in Healy and Kutner, *The Admiral,* 266.

48. *New York Times,* 18 May 1900.

49. The General Board did not abolish the authority of the bureaus or establish a centralized authority within the Navy Department. Taylor saw the board as a start toward a general staff similar to that of the German navy. Taylor and Dewey continued to push for such a general staff until Taylor's death in 1904. For an account of the history of the General Board see Daniel J. Costello, "Planning for War: A History of the General Board of the Navy, 1900–1914."

50. Charles O. Paullin, "Half Century of Naval Administration," Part X, 111, 116.

51. John D. Long to George Dewey, 30 March 1900, R.G. 80: Records of the General Board, 1900–1902, National Archives, Washington, D.C. (hereafter cited as R.G. 80: General Board).

52. See Spector, *Admiral,* Chapter 6, for a good analysis of the anti-German perspective of many officers in the U.S. Navy at the turn of the century.

53. Paul T. Heffron, "William H. Moody, 1 May 1902–30 June 1904," in Paolo E. Coletta et al., eds., *American Secretaries of the Navy*, 1:461–62.

54. Ibid., 462.

55. Seward W. Livermore, "Theodore Roosevelt, the American Navy, and the Venezuelan Crisis of 1902–1903," 453–56, 470–71.

56. *Annual Report of the Secretary of the Navy for the Year 1903*, House Document No. 3, 58th Cong., 2nd Sess., 1903, 478, 648–49.

57. Harold Sprout and Margaret Sprout, *The Rise of American Naval Power 1776–1918*, 246; Robert Albion, *Makers of Naval Policy, 1798–1947*, 327–28.

58. General Board Minutes, 31 January 1903, 1:237–38, R.G. 80: General Board; Dewey to Secretary of the Navy William H. Moody, 9 February 1903, and Frank Marble to the Chief Clerk, Navy Department, 2 March 1903, ibid.

59. Sprout and Sprout, *Naval Power*, 260–61.

60. The young naval reformers included such officers as Bradley A. Fiske, Albert L. Key, William Sims, and Philip Andrews. Other more senior officers taking the radical position were such men as Stephen B. Luce, William J. Barnette, and William Swift. Spector, *Admiral*, 156.

61. Mildred Dewey Diary, 27 January 1906, Box 86, DPLC.

62. Meyer's term as secretary of the navy is briefly discussed in Paolo E. Coletta, "George von Lengerke Meyer, 6 March 1909–4 March 1913," in Paolo E. Coletta et al., eds., *American Secretaries of the Navy*, 496–98; M. A. De Wolfe Howe, *George von Lengerke Meyer*, 466–70; George Dewey to George A. Loud, 31 January 1910, DPLC.

63. Secretary of the Navy Long to William McKinley, 12 July 1900, General Board No. 25, R.G. 80: General Board. It was probably the prohibitive cost and certain geographical disadvantages of Iloilo that caused Dewey to shift his support for Subig early in the debate. For a discussion of the investigation of the Iloilo site and the General Board's early approval, see Williams, "U.S. Navy," 236–43; Dewey to Long, 27 June 1900, General Board No. 25, R.G. 80: General Board; Dewey to Long, 10 October 1900, ibid.; William R. Braisted, "The Philippine Naval Base Problem, 1898–1909," 24.

64. Dewey to Theodore Roosevelt, 4 August 1904, R.G. 80: General Board. Although this letter was written in 1904, Dewey stated in the letter that Subig Bay had been the desired site of the General Board (and his) for several years, and he outlined in concise terms the navy's objections to Manila.

65. George Dewey to President, Naval War College, 19 June 1912, R.G. 80: General Board.

66. George Dewey to George Goodwin Dewey, 19 April 1913, George Goodwin Dewey Papers, Naval Historical Center.

67. *New York World*, 20 August 1916.

U.S. Fleet in the Straits of Magellan, 1908. The round-the-world cruise of the Great White Fleet in 1907 reflected America's pride in its navy and its desire for recognition as a world power. This photograph, taken from the USS *Georgia*, shows the battleships entering the Straits of Magellan. *Courtesy of the Naval Historical Center.*

A NAVY SECOND TO NONE

HENRY T. MAYO:
LAST OF THE INDEPENDENT
NAVAL DIPLOMATS

JAMES C. BRADFORD

Shortly before noon on 9 April 1914, Assistant Paymaster Charles C. Copp and a party of eight enlisted men left the USS *Dolphin* and headed up the Pánuco River in a whaleboat to pick up drums of gasoline. The party was unarmed; the American flags flying from the bow and stern of the whaleboat were deemed sufficient protection even in revolution-torn Mexico. Copp found the designated warehouse, and his men had nearly completed stowing the gasoline drums when a party of Mexican soldiers appeared, ordered the Americans out of their boat at gunpoint, and led them away. The merchant selling them the gasoline went immediately to the *Dolphin* and informed her captain of the altercation. The captain, Ralph K. Earle, reported the incident to Admiral Henry T. Mayo, commander of American naval forces off the port, who responded by ordering Earle ashore to demand release of the Americans.

So began the Tampico Incident, the first in a series of events that would lift Mayo from obscurity to the world headlines, precipitate a division within the American government, and ultimately bring to a close the era of American naval history in which officers operating away from home and trusting in their superior knowledge of events acted on their own responsibility. For an officer such independent action could bring glory or censure; for the nation the result could be a diplomatic imbroglio or war. Nineteenth-century officers were forced to operate in such conditions; twentieth-century officers were prohibited from doing so. This shift, as much as changes in technology, marked an important part of the transition from the Old Navy to the New.

Henry T. Mayo. Post–World War I portrait in oil of Mayo by Marvin Julian. *Courtesy of the Naval War College.*

It has been the fate of most naval officers, both before the turn of the century and since, to live lives of relative anonymity. They move from duty to duty, serving in a succession of ships and shore billets, and, if they perform their jobs acceptably, they advance through the grades and retire. Such was the lot of Henry T. Mayo for a quarter of a century before two events combined in less than a year to remove him from the ranks of typical officers. Of these events, the Tampico Incident is the more dramatic one; but Mayo would not have become involved in it had it not been for a chance meeting with an influential figure only a year before, while Mayo was serving as commander of the Mare Island Navy Yard near San Francisco. Newly appointed Secretary of the Navy Josephus Daniels was touring America's West Coast naval facilities when he visited Mare Island and met Henry T. Mayo for the first time. Daniels, still in the process of filling his staff, was immediately impressed by the middle-aged Mayo, and before leaving offered to appoint him his aid for personnel in the Navy Department and have him transferred to Washington. Precisely what impressed the secretary about Mayo is unknown. There was little in his career to set him apart from dozens of his contemporaries.

Mayo was born in 1856, the fourth son and eighth of nine children of Elizabeth Eldredge Mayo and her husband, Henry Mayo, captain of a Lake Champlain steamboat. Educated in public schools, the young Mayo held a variety of jobs. His habit of reading probably helped him win an appointment to the Naval Academy when he was only fifteen. Though young, and physically one of the smallest members of his class, Mayo enjoyed Academy life and was an above-average student. His class standing fluctuated in all subjects, but he usually stood highest in seamanship, ordnance, and navigation and lowest in the humanities, history, composition, and French. Mayo may have had some trouble adapting to military life; during his first two years he was given significantly more demerits than average. Most were for inattention during drill, skylarking, "cutting up and disturbing class," "loitering in doorway during study hours," tardiness, writing on the bathroom wall, visiting during study hours, laughing in ranks during formation, and offenses of a similar nature. Near the end of Mayo's first year, the midshipman officer-of-the-day caught him smoking in his room. Mayo later recalled that the upperclassman decided not to report him when Mayo explained that he already had 240 demerits and reporting him would certainly lead to his expulsion. Mayo appears to have learned from this experience because the number of demerits he received dropped to just above average during his final years, though the nature of his offenses remained the same. His overall standing in the order of merit slipped from seventeenth of one hundred five students in his first year at the Academy to twenty-first out of the forty-eight students in his depleted class a year later. He must have recovered academically because he stood fourteenth in a graduating class of forty-two when he left Annapolis in 1876.[1]

Graduation brought with it the rank of passed midshipman and assignment to the Asiatic Station. Mayo had requested the posting and enjoyed journeying by train across the United States and by steamer across the Pacific to Japan, where he joined the screw sloop-of-war *Kearsarge*. Letters home show that he liked duty in the Far East despite homesickness and that his salary as an officer helped keep him in the service. "I would like above all things to live ashore, having enough money to support two," he wrote, but "if I could only earn enough to support one I would rather be at sea." From the *Kearsarge* Mayo transferred briefly to the sidewheel gunboat *Monocacy* and then to the monitor *Tennessee,* in which he sailed home via the Suez Canal in 1878. After three months leave in Burlington, Mayo took the qualifying examination and was promoted to ensign. Further promotion was as slow for Mayo as for all officers of the era, and it would be seven years before he became a lieutenant (jg), five more until he was promoted to lieutenant (1890), and another nine until he made lieutenant commander (1899).[2]

Billets in naval ships were scarce during the 1880s and 1890s, and Mayo spent most of the time assigned to the Coast and Geodetic Survey. His first duty with that organization involved surveying Puget Sound in the schooner *Earnest.* After two years on the West Coast, Mayo was granted leave to visit his ill mother in Vermont. By the time he reached Burlington, his mother had practically recovered; but the journey took on new meaning when, before returning to duty, Mayo wed Mary Caroline "Carrie" Wing. Mayo decided not to take his bride with him to the West Coast because he expected transfer back to the East within a year, and so the couple experienced the first of many separations. Mayo hoped for assignment to a warship next, but when he returned East, it was to the *Eagre,* a survey vessel charting the coast of Maine. Such duty allowed the young officer to indulge his interest in science but provided little of the excitement he might have expected in joining the navy.

After a year in the *Eagre,* Mayo was able to return to the regular navy with an assignment to the bark-rigged, screw sloop *Yantic* of the North Atlantic Squadron. Upon reporting to his new ship, Mayo was immediately put to work as a watch officer and in September promoted to the command of a division. He believed that this promotion should bring with it mess privileges and quarters in the ship's wardroom, but the captain denied him these amenities, and Mayo appealed the decision to Admiral Cooper, commander of the North Atlantic Squadron. Cooper upheld the captain, pointing out that "the Ward Room of the *Yantic* is very small, and if Ensign Mayo's request is granted, Ensign Benson, of the *Yantic,* has the same claim. . . . The transfer of these two officers to the Ward Room will crowd it very much and cause much inconvenience and discomfort." Still not satisfied, Mayo wrote to the secretary of the navy, citing the applicable section of navy regulations. Secretary William Chandler referred the matter to the judge advocate general. The final disposition of the appeal is unknown, but the fact that while an ensign Mayo would pursue such an appeal all the way to the secretary of the navy is indicative of his character.[3]

Mayo was still serving in the *Yantic* when she participated in the Greely Relief Expedition and went to Panama to protect American interests during the Prestau Rebellion. After passing the examination for lieutenant (jg) and spending 1886 at the Naval Observatory in Washington, Mayo returned to Puget Sound and more survey work in the *Earnest*. Like most other officers, he sought appointment to one of the navy's new steel ships but was sent instead to the apprentice training ship *Jamestown*. After three years he was again returned to the West Coast, this time to open a new branch hydrographic office at Port Townsend, Washington, where he served from 1892 to 1895. By now Mayo had acquired a reputation for being a "coaster," that is, preferring duty ashore to that at sea. This epithet was perhaps unfair, and in 1895 he was finally able to secure duty in one of the U.S. Navy's modern ships as executive officer of the gunboat *Bennington*. His pleasure at the appointment was marred by the outbreak of the Spanish–American War and his inability to get transferred to the war zone. "For the first and only time in my Naval Career—I tried to obtain political influence to get ordered to some ship in the Atlantic," Mayo later admitted, saying that he "wrote to the Senators and Representatives from Vermont asking their aid [but] of course it was useless. . . ."[4] Thus it was not Mayo's fault that he missed the opportunities for laurels brought by the war. Everything seemed to indicate that he was destined for a respectful but uneventful career. Mayo's only distinction, conducting the first hydrographic survey of Pearl Harbor, was small consolation for his failure to see action in the Philippines or Cuba.

America's victory in the War with Spain and Theodore Roosevelt's assumption of the presidency heralded an era of great naval expansion. Mayo, by then a lieutenant commander, was ordered to the Union Iron Works in San Francisco to inspect the equipment of the new battleship *Wisconsin*. In 1900 he joined the ship's company, and a year later became first her navigator and then her executive officer during a cruise to the Asiatic Station.

There followed a year ashore as the assistant equipment officer at the Boston Navy Yard and three years at San Francisco as lighthouse inspector of the Twelfth Naval District before Mayo finally, at age 51, received his first command at sea, the protected cruiser *Albany*. He was stationed off the west coast of Central America, and his tour, like his entire career to date, was uneventful. So was his year as secretary to the Lighthouse Board, 1908–9, and his subsequent command of the armored cruiser *California* on the West Coast.

In 1911 Mayo took command of the Twelfth Naval District and the navy yard at Mare Island near San Francisco. This appeared to be another routine appointment in his long string of uneventful assignments; but it would be the turning point in his career because Josephus Daniels, Woodrow Wilson's secretary of the navy, decided to visit the yard during an orientation tour. Impressed with Mayo, the new secretary brought him to Washington to serve as his aid for personnel at the Navy Department. (The aid system had been established by Secretary of the Navy George von L. Meyer, and four aids— one each for operations, material, personnel, and inspection—functioned as a kind of cabinet to the secretary, who used them to counter the influence of the various bureau chiefs.) Mayo, now a captain, assumed his new duties in April 1913, and only two months later Daniels arranged his promotion to rear admiral over several older, more senior officers. Perhaps this preferment increased Mayo's desire for the professional advancement that he knew could come only through command at sea. Prior to this time his assignments had been fairly typical, if not career-enhancing. Now, for the first time, Mayo was in a position to influence his duty assignments at the highest level. Only a few months after reporting to Washington he asked for, and received, command of the Fourth Division, Atlantic Fleet, then stationed in the Caribbean. Before reporting for duty there, he attended the Naval War College for a six-week course of study.

Mayo's new tour, like his previous ones, promised to be routine. His unit's main function was to patrol the Mexican coast and show the flag when necessary to protect American interests. Conditions appeared relatively quiet; and, with war threatening in Europe, virtually all European naval vessels had been recalled from the area. In February 1913, Victoriano Huerta had seized control of the Mexican government. To Woodrow Wilson, who less than a year before had vowed that he would "teach the South American republics to elect good men," Huerta represented everything he despised.[5] When opposition groups organized in various parts of the country, Wilson turned a blind eye to the arms and supplies being shipped to them from the United States. By the spring of 1914, three Constitutionalist armies were moving south against Huerta. A major target in their path was Tampico, the center of Mexico's lucrative oil industry and its second most important port; a city of nearly 30,000, it was

defended by an army of 2,000 under the command of General Ignacio Morelos Zaragoza. These Federals, as supporters of Huerta were
called, were backed by an undetermined number of state guardsmen
and the Mexican navy gunboats *Veracruz* and *Saragoza.*

By March a Constitutionalist attack on Tampico appeared imminent. The large American community in the city appealed to the
U.S. Navy for protection, and Mayo, stationed off the city, responded by delineating a neutrality zone in Tampico and warning
both the Federals and the Constitutionalists to refrain from hostile
activities within the zone.[6] Mayo's command, the Fifth Division of
the Atlantic Fleet, consisted of the old battleships *Connecticut* and
Minnesota, and the cruisers *Chester* and *Des Moines,* the mine depot
ship *San Francisco,* the collier *Cyclops,* and the hospital ship *Solace.*
The battleships both carried detachments of marines to which sailors
could be added to form landing parties, but neither of the battleships
could cross the bar and anchor near the city itself. Thus, on 28
March, Mayo wrote to Rear Admiral Frank F. Fletcher, commander
of the First Division of the Atlantic Fleet, which was then at Vera
Cruz, to apprise him of the situation. Mayo asked Fletcher to send
the gunboat *Dolphin* to serve as his flagship in the harbor at Tampico
because Mayo's larger ships could not cross the bar at the mouth of
the Pánuco River.[7] Two weeks later, as conditions worsened, Clarence Miller, the American consul in Tampico, requested that the
State Department send an army transport or charter a commercial
ship for the evacuation of American civilians from the city. Denial
of that request by officials in Washington may have led Mayo to
conclude that he understood the gravity of conditions in Tampico
better than officials in Washington did, and thus may have increased
his willingness to take action without first consulting his superiors.[8]

At the time of Mayo's dispatch to the area, Bradley Fiske, the
highest-ranking officer in the U.S. Navy, asked Fletcher his opinion
of his new associate. Fletcher responded by saying that, when operating under conditions like those in Mexico, "the man on the spot
has only his judgment for a guide. I am pleased that Mayo is here
now."[9] Fletcher, though not Mayo's commanding officer, was the
senior officer in the area. The radios in Mayo's ships were too short-
ranged to communicate directly with the United States, but the ones
in two of Fletcher's ships were powerful enough to reach the U.S.
naval base at Key West, Florida, which was in telegraph contact
with Washington. Fletcher could also use the cable office at Vera
Cruz, though its staff was Mexican and its security therefore suspect.

The difficulty of communication with Admiral C. J. Badger, who as commander in chief of the Atlantic Fleet was superior to both Fletcher and Mayo, and with officials in Washington also may have influenced Mayo's decision to act upon his own responsibility when the Tampico Incident occurred.

Mayo's reaction at the start of the incident—demanding the release of the American boat party—was probably reflexive, but his subsequent actions were not. Perhaps the entire affair might have ended right after it began had someone else been the American commander on the scene. Mayo's actions were due not only to career-long conditioning to uphold the honor of the American flag and a bellicosity typical of many American naval officers, but also to his own assessment of the situation and a determination and a self-assurance already apparent to his fellow officers.

The American sailors had been taken to a Mexican regimental headquarters only a few blocks from their boat, where they were released by the colonel in command and allowed to return to the dock and continue loading the drums of gasoline. Meanwhile, Captain Earle and Clarence Miller, the American consul at Tampico, arrived at the headquarters of the Federal commander in the city. When confronted by the Americans, General Ignacio Zaragoza apologized, sent orders that the party should be allowed to return to the *Dolphin,* and asked Earl to convey his "regrets" to Mayo.

The original confrontation had been caused by a member of the state guard who was unfamiliar with international law, it had happened in an area away from the center of the city, and the Americans had not been injured in any way. Zaragoza probably considered the incident trivial and of no more importance than a misunderstanding that had occurred the day before, when a U.S. Marine courier was held briefly by Mexican authorities until he explained that he was carrying messages from the American consulate and had lost his way. But to Mayo there was a crucial difference between the two events. The sailors had been ordered out of a vessel flying the American flag and that, in Mayo's eyes, constituted an assault on sovereign American territory, an insult compounded by the marching of the sailors through the streets at gunpoint. Thus Mayo did not consider Zaragoza's apology sufficient reparation for such a blatant act. Only an equally public show of contrition could remove the stain that Mayo thought perpetrated against his nation's honor.

Without consulting Fletcher or contacting higher authority, Mayo wrote to Zaragoza, saying that "I do not need to tell you that taking men from a boat flying the American flag is a hostile act, not to be excused." Mayo rejected the explanation that the captors had acted from ignorance, and stated:

> In view of the publicity of this occurrence, I must require that you send me, by suitable members of your staff, a formal disavowal of and an apology for the act, together with your assurance that the officer responsible for it will receive severe punishment. Also that you . . . hoist the American flag in a prominent position on shore and salute it with 21 guns, which salute will be duly returned by this ship.
>
> Your answer to this communication should reach me and the called for salute be fired within twenty-four hours from 6 p.m. of this date.[10]

To impress Saragoza with the gravity of the situation, Mayo had the message delivered by Commander William A. Moffett, the senior American officer on the river. Zaragoza received the message and asked for an extension of twenty-four hours to give him time to consult with authorities in Mexico City.

Mayo reported his ultimatum to Fletcher, stating that:

> The arrest of this officer and these men, some of whom were taken from a United States boat flying the United States flag, and the marching of these men through the streets publicly, under armed guard; was, I consider, such a humiliating and gross insult to them and to the flag of the United States that such public apology and reparation as I ask for in my letter to General Zaragoza should be insisted upon.

Fletcher forwarded the report to Secretary of the Navy Josephus Daniels, saying he agreed with Mayo's ultimatum and adding that "retaliatory measures, even to the seizing of a Mexican gunboat, would not be excessive under the circumstance."[11] Daniels sent a copy of the report to Secretary of State William Jennings Bryan, who sent it to the president, writing, "I do not see that Mayo could have done otherwise." Wilson, unsurprised by the report, said that "I have known for months that some such thing could happen—it was inevitable, in fact," and backed Mayo without further investigation.[12] When news of the incident reached Mexican President Victoriano Huerta, he was equally quick to reject the demand for the salute.

Communications between Mexico and the United States were so poor that it took several days for officials in the capital cities to fully understand the gravity of the situation. In Washington, Secretary of State Bryan told news reporters that there was no crisis. "I am inclined to believe," he said, "that Admiral Mayo, who after all has this whole matter in his hands, will regard the apology as sufficient. The greater includes the less, and if the federal commander at Tampico should not actually salute the flag, Admiral Mayo will pass by the matter, satisfied with what Huerta has said of the incident." [13] In this assessment Bryan had seriously misjudged the situation. Mayo was anything but ready to compromise, and once Wilson and Huerta had made up their minds, neither man would retreat. Thus the stage was set for a confrontation, if not a war.

Off Tampico, Mayo prepared for combat. On 11 April, he stationed the *Des Moines* close to the shore with her decks cleared for action. "The moral effect [of positioning the ship close to shore] would be beneficial," he wrote Fletcher. On the next day, he and his officers completed work on "Campaign Order No. 1," a plan for seizing Tampico that called for the *Chester, Des Moines,* and *San Francisco* to anchor close to shore and provide cover for the *Dolphin,* which would seize the fiscal wharf and its custom house. If the Mexican gunboats attempted to interfere, they would be sunk by the cruisers. [14] All of this could be accomplished with a minimum of danger to the Americans, but it would be quite different if a larger landing force had to be employed. If men had to be brought from the battleships outside the river, the whaleboats used to ferry them would be in great danger from enemy fire as they crossed the wide area between the sandbar and the shore. Such an opposed landing would almost certainly lead to expanded hostilities, and Mayo thought about shelling the city instead of occupying it if the salute was not rendered, but rejected the idea because Tampico was not fortified, and international law banned the shelling of unfortified cities.

Sir Christopher Cradock, the commander of the British cruiser squadron off Tampico, was not favorably impressed by Mayo at this time. "I fear the Admiral is in a high state of nervous tension," Cradock wrote, when noting that on 14 April Mayo had promised to inform him "if violent action was likely to take place." [15] Nervous or not, Mayo weighed the possible consequences of a landing or shelling and decided that he would neither shell the city nor seize the fiscal wharf, but that he would withdraw his ships from the river and leave the entire matter to the diplomats. Before Mayo could do so, Admiral Fletcher and officials in Washington rejected Mayo's plan and ordered him to keep his ships in the river. President Wilson was in no mood to back down, and on the same day that Cradock met with Mayo, Wilson informed his cabinet that he was determined to "back up" Mayo. The president told reporters in Washington that "the salute will be fired" even though he knew that Mexican President Huerta had declared Zaragoza's apology and the arrest of Hinojosa, the man who had detained the American sailors, to be sufficient reparation for the indignity suffered by the United States. A week of diplomatic maneuvering in both capitals failed to produce an acceptable settlement to the situation. Visited by a congressional delegation, Wilson told its members that more was involved than the seizure of the *Dolphin*'s boat crew. The real issue was the "studied and planned exhibitions of ill-will and contempt for the American government on the part of Huerta." [16]

While the diplomats talked, Wilson began preparations for military action, should it be necessary. Army troops began gathering in Texas, and on 14 April, the same day that he met with his cabinet and the press, Wilson ordered Rear Admiral Charles J. Badger to concentrate his Atlantic Fleet on Mexico's eastern coast. When Secretary Daniels learned of Mayo's reluctance to act with the forces available to him, he immediately sent the transport *Hancock* and the 800-man First Marine Regiment as reinforcements. After the marines, led by Colonel John A. Lejeune, arrived on 19 April, Mayo reported to Fletcher that he was confident he could control events in Tampico until Admiral Badger and the Atlantic Fleet reached Tampico in a few days. On 20 April, Mayo received orders from Navy Secretary Josephus Daniels to remove all American merchant ships from the Pánuco River. Observers in the city considered this a sign that military action was imminent. [17]

Within hours, Wilson changed his plans. On 18 April, the State Department had learned that a ship carrying arms and ammunition was expected to dock at Vera Cruz on the twenty-first. Wilson was convinced that this had to be prevented; so, on 20 April, Secretary Daniels sent orders through Fletcher that Mayo and all but one of his ships should proceed to Vera Cruz and be ready upon arrival to occupy the city and prevent unloading of the cargo. Admiral Fletcher had only two battleships and a gunboat off the more important port, and officials in Washington believed that he would need the help of Mayo's larger force if a confrontation developed. Alarmed by the orders he received late on the twentieth, Mayo sent Fletcher a message citing his "fear that our ships leaving Tampico will result in much loss of American life and property due to intense anti-American feeling prevailing. Position of USS DESMOINES and Americans in vicinity will be untenable, therefore request repetition and full verification of order before ships leave here." When Mayo told Clarence Miller of his orders, the consul was so concerned that he sent a message to the State Department protesting the withdrawal of Mayo's ships from Tampico.[18]

Fletcher did not inform Washington of Mayo's fears, but asked for and received confirmation of his orders. When that confirmation was relayed to him on the night of the twentieth, Mayo reluctantly began withdrawing his ships from the harbor at Tampico, a maneuver slowed by Consul Miller's refusal to obtain a pilot. So delayed was Mayo that, midway through the withdrawal, he received a message from Fletcher saying that he needed only two of Mayo's ships, the *San Francisco* and the *Chester*, at Vera Cruz, and Mayo could "retain *Connecticut, Dolphin, Des Moines, Cyclops, Solace* to look out for American and other foreigners' lives until other provision is made." This change in plans presented Mayo with a problem: he wished to remain at Tampico but feared that the Mexicans in the city might view the return of his ships across the bar as the start of landing operations. Thus he kept his ships outside the bar, a position that would not precipitate hostilities, but also one from which he could render little assistance to Americans in the city should the need arise. Woodrow Wilson would not have been upset by this decision because he did not believe it was the duty of his government to protect U.S. citizens and their property in Mexico. The State Department had earlier advised them to leave the country, advice that Secretary Bryan ordered the American consul general in Mexico to repeat on 21 April, the same day that Fletcher gave Mayo permission to remain at Tampico and sent his men ashore at Vera Cruz.[19]

When news of the landing at Vera Cruz reached Tampico the following day, rioting broke out in the city. Consul Miller immediately asked Mayo to send forces to protect Americans, but Mayo hesitated. Fearing that the return of his ships to the harbor might do more harm than good, he signaled Miller: "Present force inadequate and cannot be effective. Any move on our part now would increase disorder and aggravate situation. Have urgently requested increased force. [signed] MAYO." During the night of 21–22 April, additional reports convinced Mayo that he would have to reenter the river, but this step was avoided when the commander of the British cruiser in the harbor offered to transport American refugees out of the city. Mayo readily agreed, and the Americans were brought out. Most thought that they would be returned to their homes in a few days, however, and reacted angrily when Mayo refused to allow this and sent them to Galveston, Texas, instead.[20] When many of the refugees protested to Congress that they had been prevented from returning to their homes in Mexico, Secretary Daniels released a statement to the press putting blame on Mayo, saying that he had made the decision to move his ships out of the harbor at Tampico to avoid hostilities. Both Mayo and Admiral Badger, his superior as commander of the Atlantic Fleet, protested to Daniels about this statement privately, but they did not air their complaints publicly.[21]

Such discreet behavior was typical of Mayo. He always worked within the system, and though supportive of the goals of many of the naval reformers of the era, he certainly was not a leader. The Philadelphia *Public Ledger* noted that Mayo had been "wholly unknown to the great majority of Americans" at the start of the Tampico Incident; yet less than a month after his demand for a salute to the American flag, the paper speculated about his career:

> [Though Mayo] is the baby of his rank in the naval service. . . . It is dollars to doughnuts that if Congress enacts the proposed law enabling the President to designate a limited number of flag-officers as vice-admirals, Mayo will get one of the prizes on account of his conduct in the Tampico incident, even if the trouble with Mexico does not develop proportions that will give him greater opportunity for the display of his genius as a fleet commander.[22]

The paper's prediction proved to be basically accurate. Relations with Mexico continued tense, U.S. Army troops replaced the U.S. Navy's bluejackets and marines in Vera Cruz, and American warships remained in Mexican waters until November, but Mayo did not receive additional opportunities to distinguish himself. None were needed. His actions at Tampico had assured his advancement in the service. In October, just after the opening of hostilities in Europe, Mayo was promoted to command of the First Division of the Atlantic Fleet. The following June, he became second in command of the Atlantic Fleet with the rank of vice admiral.

The tenuous balance of naval power in the early stages of World War I lent urgency to the training exercises that occupied the Atlantic Fleet after its withdrawal from Mexican waters. Each winter the fleet would sail to the Caribbean for maneuvers. In December 1915, Lieutenant Commander Ernest J. King joined Mayo's staff while planning for the training cruise was under way. One of Mayo's chief strengths as a commander was his ability to delegate authority, and King later remembered gaining Mayo's confidence when he (King) opposed an operational plan drawn up by the staff that included detailed instructions for its destroyer scouts. King suggested instead that the senior destroyer captain be given only general guidelines, and that operational details be left to him.[23]

When Admiral Fletcher ended his command of the fleet in July, Mayo was chosen to replace him. Since 1912, naval administration had become increasingly centralized, so that by 1916 even routine matters such as requests for leave reached the desks of fleet commanders. Mayo refused to operate in such a fashion; he preferred to discuss matters with his staff and issue general guidelines, leaving them to work out the details. Ernest King, who continued to serve on Mayo's staff for much of the war, fully approved of Mayo's system and remembered that when even admirals "turned to Admiral Mayo for detailed instructions, he would quite calmly tell them, 'That is your own job,' and let them" work out problems for themselves. King also remembered Mayo as a leader who "possessed the ability to look at situations fairly and squarely, with hard sense and a dry humor that confounded the pompous"; and to illustrate this, he recalled the time when the chief of naval operations, Admiral Benson, told Mayo that because he was commander in chief of the Atlantic Fleet, Mayo's chief of staff should be a flag officer. In reply, King remembered: "Mayo stuck his hands in his hip pockets, looked Benson over, and said very slowly, 'Benson, I agree with you. You can arrange to make [my chief of staff, Captain] Jackson a flag officer this very day.' But Benson did nothing about it!"[24]

Although Mayo's official duties were limited to operational command of the Atlantic Fleet, he was often called upon by Secretary Daniels for advice on a variety of topics. Late in 1916, for example, Daniels asked him to review the report of the Helm Board, calling for the building of submarine and air bases along the East Coast. Mayo strongly opposed the board's recommendations, proposing instead that the money should be used to purchase submarines and aircraft, which would prove more useful should the United States enter the war. The bases were not really needed, Mayo argued, as submarine and airplane tenders could provide support as easily as shore installations and had the advantage of mobility because they could be shifted from the Atlantic to the Pacific if necessary. Mayo also opposed the establishment of a separate naval air corps, fearing that such an organization would divide the officer corps, much like the old division between engineering and line officers, and that men whose service was limited to flying would have to be retired when

Josephus Daniels, Thomas A. Edison, and Mayo on board the USS
New York. Mayo, commander of the First Division of the Atlantic Fleet,
welcomed Thomas A. Edison, chairman of the U.S. Navy's Consulting
Board (left), and Secretary of the Navy Daniels (center) to his flagship in
1916. *Courtesy of the Naval Historical Center.*

they became too old to fly. Daniels also sought Mayo's advice on
matters of less importance, such as a proposal for the use of "moving
picture photographers."[25]

During the 1916 election, Wilson's opponents publicized charges
made by refugees from Tampico that when Mayo was ordered to
leave the city, Americans were forced to depend on foreign navies for
their protection. The fact that the British navy transported many
Americans from the city to the American ships waiting outside the
bar lent credence to these charges, but Mayo was quick to counter
such statements, saying: "It is a misrepresentation to say that American citizens in Tampico were deserted in an hour of imminent danger [and] compelled to seek refuge under the colors of a foreign flag."
Josephus Daniels believed that Mayo's reputation for political impartiality led most Americans to accept his refutation of these claims.[26]

Though responsive to the political needs of the administration, Mayo was not reluctant to argue with Daniels when he thought it necessary, and did so over both major and minor matters. On one occasion, for example, Mayo and Chief of Naval Operations Benson protested, albeit without success, against Daniels's decision to replace the choker collar on officer uniforms with a more comfortable one that lay flat. On another, perhaps equally trivial, matter, Mayo was quick to let the secretary know that he resented it when Daniels refused his requests to entertain a retired admiral at dinner on board his flagship.[27]

Demands on Mayo increased as the United States edged closer to war in early 1917. In January, the Atlantic Fleet was recalled from its usual winter exercises in the Caribbean. Late in March, Mayo was ordered to withdraw his ships from Hampton Roads to the York River where they could be protected by torpedo nets. America entered the war two weeks later. On 10 April, four days after Wilson signed the congressional declaration of war, Mayo attended the first of what would become a succession of conferences with other Allied naval leaders, when British Vice Admiral Sir Montague Browning and French Rear Admiral Maurice Ferdinand Albert de Grasset met with Mayo and Benson on board Mayo's flagship to present their views on the proper role of the U.S. Navy in the war. When newsmen from Allied countries requested statements from Mayo and permission to visit his ships, he was cooperative when possible, but probably resented taking time from what he considered his more important task of preparing the fleet to contribute to the war effort.[28]

The task was made more difficult by a command structure that Secretary Daniels initiated without consulting Mayo. After conferring with Mayo and Benson in Virginia, Admiral Browning went to Washington where it was agreed that the U.S. Navy would assume responsibility for patrolling the east coast of North America and the Caribbean Sea. Within a month, Captain J. K. Taussig and a division of American destroyers were sent to Queenstown, Ireland, to operate under British command. Rear Admiral Albert Gleaves, commander of Atlantic Fleet destroyers, protested against the move, and Mayo supported him. In July, Gleaves was made "Commander United States Convoy Operations in the Atlantic," and like Taussig was told to consider his command to be part of Mayo's fleet even though their orders came directly from Washington rather than through Mayo. Mayo opposed such a command structure and asked to be transferred to Europe. His request was denied on the grounds that such a high-ranking American was not needed in Europe, and the Atlantic Fleet must be prepared to operate independently of other Allied navies should the balance of the naval war shift significantly. Mayo was promoted to full admiral on 22 May 1917 but remained distressed by the command structure and thought it necessary to visit Washington at approximately three-week intervals to keep abreast of developments, such as a proposal to transfer several battleships and cruisers from the Atlantic Fleet to the Pacific.[29]

During those visits, Mayo quickly learned that Secretary Daniels and CNO Benson were reluctant to accede to the requests that William Sims, Commander United States Naval Forces Operating in European Waters, was forwarding from London; and Mayo suggested that he be sent to London to assess the naval needs of the Allies. Daniels presented the recommendation to President Wilson, "who rather thought it wise" and ordered the State Department to propose a naval conference with Britain. When this proposal led to a meeting of all the Allies in London in September, Wilson designated Mayo "principal United States representative." On 16 August, Mayo, Daniels, and Benson met with President Wilson, who "impressed upon [the naval officers] the need [for a naval] offensive." When Mayo expressed his hope that "The President would not expect too much," Daniels noted, "No, but . . . he expected plans by which America could lead & be the senior partner in a successful naval campaign." Although it was unrealistic for Wilson to think that the British would accept American leadership in the naval war, Daniels shared his belief, and in his diary asked, "Is Mayo hopeful enough?"[30] Two days later, Mayo and his staff sailed for Britain. En route Mayo and his staff compiled a list of topics they wanted to discuss with British officials, and upon arrival in Britain gave the senior British naval officer, Admiral Jellicoe, a short memorandum saying that Mayo had come to England:

1. To learn more fully what has happened and what has been done.
2. To get more clearly in touch with what is being done, and *then*
3. Discuss what it is proposed to do.

Mayo also assured the civilian head of the Admiralty that he sought to "ascertain in what possible way the Americans can more fully come into naval warfare."[31]

The two-day formal meetings of the naval leaders provided the opportunity for an exchange of views, but, Mayo reported to Benson, "it [was] extremely difficult to reach any conclusions other than those of a very general nature." After the conference adjourned on 5 September, Mayo toured bases at Portsmouth and Southampton, visited the Grand Fleet at Leith, and traveled to France, where he met with officials in Paris, visited the front near Amiens, inspected American facilities and forces at Brest, and joined Admiral Jellicoe in the *Broke* to watch the British bombard Ostend. The flags of both Jellicoe and Mayo were flown on the last occasion, marking the first time the four-star flag of an American admiral had flow in a British warship. After a brief visit to American forces at Queenstown, Mayo sailed for the United States, where he made a series of recommendations to the navy, his suggestions including the immediate implementation of a North Sea mine barrage, the dispatch of a division of battleships and additional destroyers to Europe, and the establishment of naval air stations in Britain and France. If Wilson and Daniels had hoped that Mayo would supply them with an independent assessment of the naval war, they were not disappointed. Mayo, far more critical of the British than Sims, criticized the lack of planning and analysis on the part of the Admiralty. Nevertheless, Mayo was essentially optimistic, and if the president hoped that Mayo would provide support for pressing the British to take more offensive action, he was disappointed when Mayo explained the difficulties involved in launching such an operation.[32] Mayo's recommendation that battleships be sent to join the Grand Fleet was not acted upon until CNO Benson visited London a short time later.

Mayo had returned to the Atlantic Fleet by the end of October and spent the remainder of the year and the first half of 1918 readying its men and ships for action. Still troubled by the unorthodox command structure, he sent a paper to the Navy Department entitled "Estimate of the Situation with Regard to the Efficient Development of the Operations of the Atlantic Fleet" on 2 February 1918, proposing that he and his flagship be sent to Europe to facilitate cooperation among the Allies, and that the next highest-ranking officer in the fleet remain in home waters to direct training and preparations there. When rumors reached England that Mayo might be transferred to Europe, William Sims protested to CNO Benson: "I do not know what there might be in these rumors, but I think you will realize that in case Admiral Mayo should be sent over here that my position would become impossible."[33] Sims had nothing to fear, as Daniels ignored Mayo's February request the same way he did earlier proposals by Mayo that he be transferred to Europe and his August

1918 proposal to send the U.S. Navy's newest battleships to Brest, where they could reinforce the British fleet should the Germans attempt to seize control of the English Channel and interrupt the flow of men and supplies to France.

In late August 1918, Mayo left the United States for a second trip to Europe, this time to inspect American installations, ships, and personnel. He was again received with great warmth by the British, and dined and spent a night with King George V at Windsor Castle before moving on to France, where he again visited the front, and to Italy, where he was dining with the commander in chief of the Italian army when news arrived of the Armistice. Mayo and his party returned to Paris, where they were entertained lavishly to celebrate

Inspecting a naval railway battery in France, 1918. During World War I, a variety of U.S. Navy units were stationed in Europe. These units included ships ranging in size from battleships to 110-foot-long submarine chasers, planes flying from twenty patrol bases in England, France, and Italy, the Fourth Marine Brigade on the Western front, and five naval railway batteries. During the fall of 1918, Mayo visited each type of unit. *Courtesy of the Naval Historical Center.*

the end of the war. After passing through Britain, Mayo finally reached New York on 1 December.[34] Three days later, Mayo was turned around and on his way to Europe again, this time escorting President Wilson on his journey to take part in the Paris peace talks.

Mayo and his staff spent much of the winter of 1918–19 completing reports on wartime activities. During the spring, the Atlantic Fleet resumed its peacetime practice of holding maneuvers off the coast of Cuba. Mayo was particularly interested in working with aircraft, which accompanied the fleet for the first time. A squadron of flying boats attached to the converted minelayer *Shawmut* conducted search operations and simulated bombing raids against the fleet, and land planes took off from beams placed on the battleships *Texas* and *Mississippi* to spot gunfire. As usual Mayo followed the basic principle of command set down in his first report as commander in chief of the Atlantic Fleet:

> The general principle . . . was a proper coordinating of the various forces comprising the Fleet so that the Fleet should be in a true sense of the word a "Fleet" and not a collection of more or less independent forces. To accomplish this end the Commander in Chief endeavored to instill into the Fleet a proper realization of "decentralization of authority" and "initiative of the subordinate." The principle was followed of passing down the chain of command the handling of all details to the lowest link in the chain which could properly handle them and, on the other hand, gathering in and coordinating into the high command the control of all policies and matters of major importance from all the units of the Fleet.[35]

The 1919 cruise was to be Mayo's last command at sea. On 30 June 1919, he hauled down his flag as commander in chief, Atlantic Fleet, and reported to Washington for duty as a member of the General Board. The duty was not particularly pleasant for Mayo because much of his time was devoted to defending the navy's conduct of the war, which was being investigated by a subcommittee of the Senate Committee on Naval Affairs.

The investigation resulted from criticisms of the Navy Department made by William Sims, who told members of Congress that the navy had been unprepared for war in 1917 and as a result had performed poorly. Sims estimated that the navy's lack of trained personnel and its failure to prepare adequate war plans resulted in the unnecessary loss of 500,000 Allied lives, the sinking of 2,500,000 tons of Allied shipping, and the expenditure of $15 billion. Daniels prepared his defense of the Navy Department by asking all bureau chiefs and other high-ranking officers to prepare reports of their activities prior to and during the war. He met personally with a number of congressmen and talked with most of the naval officers before they testified. His conversations with Mayo made him a bit apprehensive: "Talked with Mayo. Said he wished to be fair. . . . Too judicial & had not recovered his difference with Benson." Daniels's fears proved unfounded. When Mayo testified before Congress, he decried Sims's "unwarranted attack upon the Navy Department and the Navy" and flatly declared that his statements were "not at all susceptible of proof," though he admitted that the "Fleet was lacking in types of vessels essential to efficiency, such as battle cruisers, scout cruisers, light cruisers, and fleet submarines [i.e., that it was unbalanced]."[36] The Senate hearing started in January with great fanfare but passed from the public consciousness soon after it ended in May. It was an election year, and most Americans came to view the investigation as a partisan ploy by Senate Republicans to embarrass the outgoing Democratic administration.

Mayo reached the statutory retirement age of sixty-four in December 1920, but his service was extended so that he could complete work as a member of the court of inquiry appointed in October 1920 to investigate the conduct of the Marine Corps in Haiti. The Mayo Board, as it became known, was in a difficult position. A marine brigade had been sent to Haiti in 1916 with orders to impose order on the country in the midst of a guerrilla war. One of the methods used to fight the rebels was the establishment of a Gendarmerie of Haitians commanded by Marine Corps officers. The Gendarmerie was charged with conducting summary executions, brutalizing prisoners, and oppressing civilians. When stories of the atrocities reached the United States, Secretary Daniels ordered George Barnett, the commandant of the Marine Corps, to investigate. Dissatisfied with Barnett's report, Daniels sent his successor as commandant, John A. Lejeune, and Brigadier General Smedley Butler to Haiti to make an additional report. Upon their return, the two marine generals told Daniels they had found indications that the atrocities were continuing to occur in defiance of orders to end them. By now the presidential election of 1920 was in full swing, with the Wilson administration defending its military and foreign policies. Mayo was widely respected as being above partisan politics, and so was appointed to a third and, Daniels hoped, last inquiry into conditions in Haiti.

The Mayo Board sifted through the various accusations but concluded that it could not tell what constituted an atrocity. It pointed out that Herman Hanneken, a marine enlisted man, had been awarded a medal by President Wilson for infiltrating the headquarters of the Haitian rebels and shooting their commander, but Hanneken was at the same time denounced in the press as a murderer. The Mayo Board identified twenty incidents of unjustifiable violence against Haitians, but noted that in each case the American perpetrator had been punished. It also reported that such incidents were no longer taking place, that conditions in Haiti were relatively calm by 1921, and that press reports of brutality and systematic torture were "ill considered, regrettable, and thoroughly unwarranted." His report complete, Mayo was relieved of all active duty in February 1921 and reverted to his permanent rank of rear admiral. After victorious Republicans took office a month later, they launched a Senate investigation of both the Haitian and Dominican occupations, which reached conclusions similar to those reported by the Mayo Board.[37]

As in the Senate's naval investigations, Mayo acted in a completely nonpartisan manner. His continued good standing with leaders of the Wilson administration was reflected by Edward House's invitation to him to take part in a series of lectures. Mayo spoke on "The Atlantic Fleet in the Great War" in March 1921 and reviewed with pride his service's accomplishments.[38] Three years later, Republicans indicated their faith in Mayo by recalling him to be governor of the Naval Home at Philadelphia. Mayo served in that sinecure for four years, after which he and his wife returned to Burlington, Vermont. In 1929 the Bureau of Navigation invited Mayo to become a member of the Board of Visitors of the Naval Academy. Mayo telegraphed back that he was "pleased to accept" the appointment. He must have been equally pleased when the six regular navy officers, five members of the House of Representatives, and two senators who comprised the board unanimously elected him its chairman in both 1929 and 1930. Records of the board indicate that its work was routine during those years, and Mayo must have enjoyed the spring weather in Annapolis. It was fitting that he should end his naval service at the Academy almost fifty-eight years after he first entered its gates in 1872.[39] That same year he was promoted to admiral on the retired list. Getting on in years, Mayo and his wife moved to Portsmouth, New Hampshire, to be near their son, Chester G. Mayo, a captain in the navy's supply corps. It was at his home in Portsmouth that Admiral Mayo died of a heart attack on 23 February 1937.

Mayo's name is not well known to modern Americans, but his legacy for the U.S. Navy remains important. He was the last naval officer given orders with enough latitude that he could, while acting within those orders, precipitate a war on his own. Colonel Edward House, Woodrow Wilson's personal advisor, was appalled by the Tampico situation. The introduction of radio communications should have made it unnecessary for commanders to act on their own judgment. "Such things were as obsolete as the duelling code," said House.[40] Secretary of the Navy Josephus Daniels fully agreed, and indeed sought to make impossible the repetition of such an incident. In his memoirs, Daniels described the cabinet discussions held after Mayo issued his ultimatum to the Mexicans, saying that he had

> expressed the opinion that no ultimatums should be sent by a Naval officer without the approval of the Commander in Chief when time permitted obtaining his views. . . . A long time after (September 16, 1916) when it would not be construed as a rebuke to Mayo, I changed U.S. Navy Regulations by inserting in Article 1648 the following:
> "Due to the ease with which the Navy Department can be communicated with from all parts of the world, no commander in chief, division commander, or commanding officer, shall issue an ultimatum to the representative of any foreign Government, or demand the performance of any service from any such representative that must be executed within a limited time, without first communicating with the Navy Department, except in extreme cases where such action is necessary to save life."[41]

Thus Mayo, without realizing it, was extremely influential in bringing about an alteration in the powers conferred upon naval officers by civilian leaders.

He was probably equally unaware of having another, more subtle, influence—leadership by example. This is an important role of any commanding officer, and Henry T. Mayo's fulfillment of it is admirably attested to by Ernest J. King, who was subsequently chief of naval operations and commander in chief, U.S. Fleet, during World War II. Having served as Mayo's assistant chief of staff, King acknowledged his debt to Mayo in his memoirs, saying that he "had learned much from [their] association [especially by] observ[ing] the methods by which Admiral Mayo worked." In a speech delivered in 1936, King described Mayo's style of leadership:

> His judgment was sound—based on his native capacity—confirmed by his long and varied experience. . . . He had the capacity so important to the holder of high naval position, to decentralize, and not only trust his subordinates, but to require of them due performance of their proper responsibilities. . . . [He] had a gift for using his

staff to work for him, and that was largely because they were made truly to feel that they were working with him.

King's memoirs, written with Walter Muir Whitehill, state that "Mayo's influence upon King's career was more decisive than that of any other officer that he had encountered," and that "to King, Admiral Mayo seemed the best, the ablest, and the most competent of all the flag officers of the United States Navy down to the end of World War I." Such accolades are high coming from one of the leading American naval officers of the twentieth century.[42]

Mayo never gave any hint that he ever had any regrets about his actions at Tampico, nor was he ever critical of the way officials in Washington handled the affair. Had Mayo lived another decade, he probably would have been pleased to learn of his influence on King, but he would not have considered it extraordinary. It simply resulted from his having fulfilled his duty, which to Mayo was what being a naval officer was all about. He sought neither fame nor glory, and one suspects that he read with some pride a newspaper's description of him at the time of the Tampico Incident, calling Mayo "a plain, every-day American sailor, who knows his business and lets it go at that."[43] This was certainly an accurate assessment, but Mayo was much more. His actions at Tampico, his command of the Atlantic Fleet during World War I, and the influence he exerted on younger officers place him among those officers who were makers of the American naval tradition.

FURTHER READING

Most of what is known about Mayo's early life comes from his autobiography and letters he wrote to family members from his postings overseas. No extended biography has been published, but sketches appear in such works as the *Dictionary of American Biography,* edited by Johnson et al., and Clark Reynolds's *Famous American Admirals.*

The best general account of the Tampico Incident and the subsequent occupation of Vera Cruz is Robert E. Quick's *An Affair of Honor: Woodrow Wilson and the Occupation of Vera Cruz.* He and Paolo Coletta, *William Jennings Bryan: Progressive Politician and Moral Statesman, 1909–1915,* agree that "all of the American principals concerned . . . supported Mayo's demands, with Wilson desirous of using the Tampico incident to force the showdown with Huerta he had long sought." Kendrick Clements, "Woodrow Wilson's Mexican Policy, 1913–15," presents a positive view of the president's policy, arguing that he was attempting to expel all foreign economic domination, including American, from Mexico and to let the Mexican people choose their own government. Jack Sweetman's *The Landing at Vera Cruz* contains additional details of operational aspects of the campaign. Mayo's style of leadership and his World War I activities are described by an admiring Ernest J. King, *Fleet Admiral King: A Naval Record,* who served as Mayo's assistant chief of staff from December 1915 through the spring of 1919. Mayo's role in the various naval conferences is analyzed by David Trask in *Captains and Cabinets: Anglo–American Naval Relations, 1917–1918,* and his relations with CNO William Benson are described in Mary Klachko, *Admiral William Shepherd Benson.* Captain C. G. Mayo lent his father's papers (now in the Library of Congress) to Walter Muir Whitehall, who collaborated with King on his memoirs and planned an extended biography of Admiral Mayo.

NOTES

1. An autobiography prepared by Mayo in collaboration with a family friend provides information on his early life, including the fact that he outscored nine other applicants to gain entry into the Naval Academy and the story of his encounter with the upperclassman. Mayo, Autobiography, Henry T. Mayo Papers, Library of Congress, 14, 19. Mayo stood at the sixteenth percentile his first year (first percentile being the top of the class), at the forty-fourth percentile his second, nineteenth his third, and thirty-third at graduation. Annual Register of the United States Naval Academy, 1873, 13; 1874, 19; 1874–75, 19; 1875–76, 14; 1876–77, 12. Register of Delinquencies, vols. 377–79, 381, R.G. 405: Records of the U.S. Naval Academy, National Archives, Washington, D.C.

2. Mayo, Autobiography, 74; "Henry Thomas Mayo," Service Records, Military Personnel Records Center, St. Louis, Mo. Mayo's career is outlined in Lewis Randolph Hamersly, comp., *The Records of Living Officers of the U.S. Navy and Marine Corps,* 5th ed., 227, and 7th ed., 247.

3. The Ensign Benson who did not insist upon wardroom privileges was William Shepherd Benson, who became the U.S. Navy's first chief of naval operations while Mayo commanded the Atlantic Fleet. Mayo to William B. Chandler, 18 October 1882. Henry T. Mayo File, Biographical Files, Operational Archives, Naval Historical Center, Washington, D.C. Mayo made no mention of the incident in his autobiography.

4. Mayo, Autobiography, 196.

5. Wilson made his statement to Sir William Tyrrell, secretary to Great Britain's ambassador to the United States. Quoted in Harley Notter, *The Origins of the Foreign Policy of Woodrow Wilson,* 274.

6. "Mayo at Tampico," *Literary Digest,* 2 May 1914, 1060.

7. Mayo to Fletcher, 28 March 1914, R.G. 45: Naval Records Collection of the Office of Naval Records and Library, section 659 (henceforth R.G. 45:659.)

8. Robert E. Quick, author of the most complete examination of the Tampico Incident and the subsequent occupation of Vera Cruz, does not

assess Mayo's motives, but does conclude that throughout the era "both [Secretary of State William Jennings] Bryan and [Woodrow] Wilson showed a curious lack of concern for the safety of American nationals throughout Mexico." Quick, *An Affair of Honor,* 18.

9. Fletcher to Fiske, 3 February 1914, Josephus Daniels Papers, Library of Congress, Box 39 (henceforth DLC).

10. Mayo to Zaragosa, 9 April 1914, R.G. 45:659. A copy of the letter, with minor changes, including the insertion of "publicly," is printed in *Papers Relating to the Foreign Relations of the United States* [1914], 448–49 (henceforth *Foreign Relations Papers, 1914*). For the commander of the arrested boat party's report see "Statement of Charles C. Copp to Ralph K. Earle," 9 April 1914, R.G. 45:659.

11. Mayo to Fletcher, 9 April 1914, R.G. 45:659. Fletcher to Daniels, 11 April 1914, *Foreign Relations Papers, 1914,* 451–52.

12. Bryan to Woodrow Wilson, 10 April 1914, *Foreign Relations Papers, 1914,* 449. Wilson is quoted in Josephus Daniels, *The Wilson Era: Years of Peace—1910–1917,* 189. In his memoirs Daniels also says that "I found that in the State and Navy Departments I was almost alone in feeling that Mayo, when apologies were promptly offered, should have accepted them [and that he] expressed the opinion that no ultimatums should be sent by a Naval officer without the approval of the Commander in Chief when time permitted obtaining his views." No contemporary evidence has been found to corroborate these statements or Daniels's statement that Wilson was at first reluctant to support Mayo. Ibid.

13. *New York Times,* 12 April 1914.

14. Mayo to Fletcher, 11 April 1914, and Mayo, "Campaign Order No. 1," 12 April 1914, R.G. 45:659.

15. Sir Christopher Cradock, "Second Attack by Rebels in Tampico 26 March to 14 April and their subsequent retirement. Incident of Demand by United States Rear Admiral Mayo for Salute to the United States Flag," 14 April 1914, Admiralty File 1/8374, quoted in Jack Sweetman, *The Landing at Vera Cruz,* 43.

16. *New York World,* 14 April 1914. Quick, *An Affair of Honor,* 48–68, describes the diplomatic maneuvering. Wilson's statement is quoted in Arthur Link, *The Papers of Woodrow Wilson,* 29:441.

17. Frank F. Fletcher, "Seizure and Occupation of Vera Cruz, April 21–30, 1914," 13 May 1914, R.G. 45:659 (henceforth Fletcher, "Seizure of Vera Cruz"). Mayo's message, Flag *Dolphin* [Mayo] to Flag *Florida* [Fletcher], 20 April 1914, is quoted in Mayo to Daniels, 29 June 1916, Daniels Papers, DLC.

18. Fletcher, "Seizure of Vera Cruz." Daniels to Mayo, 20 April 1914, Daniels Papers, DLC. Miller reported that Mayo was "almost broken hearted [and] almost in tears when he informed me of his orders." Clarence Miller, "Political Conditions at Tampico," 21 May 1914, R.G. 59: General Records of the Department of State, Post Records (Tampico), National Ar-

chives (henceforth Miller, "Political Conditions"). The confusion resulting from poor communications between the Navy Department in Washington and its ships off Mexico is best described in Sweetman, *Landing at Vera Cruz,* 45–47.

19. Fletcher, "Seizure Vera Cruz," R.G. 45:569. The Secretary of State to Consul General Shanklin [Telegram], 21 April 1914, *Foreign Relations Papers, 1914,* 477. When Senator Henry Cabot Lodge told Wilson that American lives and property needed to be protected in Mexico, Wilson told him that Americans had to leave Mexico or take their chances because intervention to defend them might lead to war. Henry Cabot Lodge, *The Senate and the League of Nations,* 13–14.

20. Mayo to Fletcher, 23 April 1914; H. M. Daughty to Mayo, 23 April 1914; and Mayo to Badger, 23 and 30 April 1914; R.G. 45:659. Mayo quoted the significant messages with Miller in Mayo to Daniels, 29 June 1916, Daniels Papers, DLC.

21. Mayo to Badger, 23 and 30 April 1914, R.G. 45:653 and 659. *New York Times,* 8 May 1914. Charles Badger, Report on the withdrawal of the U.S. Naval ships from Pánuco River, 9 May 1914, Daniels Papers, DLC.

22. Quoted in *Literary Digest,* 2 May 1914.

23. King preferred Mayo's style of leadership, which emphasized delegation of authority, to that of William S. Benson, "who felt compelled to run everything himself." Ernest J. King and Walter Muir Whitehill, *Fleet Admiral King: A Naval Record,* 99, 103.

24. Ibid., 106–7.

25. Ibid., 108–9. Daniels to Mayo, 25 May 1917, Daniels Papers, DLC.

26. Daniels discussed events at Tampico with Mayo when he visited his flagship in June 1916, and Mayo, probably at his request, sent him a letter quoting pertinent messages received and sent at the time Americans were evacuated from Tampico. Mayo also stated he and the commander of the British cruiser at Tampico had agreed that the British would help evacuate the Americans before, not after, Mayo removed his ships from the harbor. Mayo to Daniels, 29 June 1916, Daniels Papers, DLC; Daniels, *The Wilson Era,* 188–89.

27. Daniels, *The Wilson Era,* 270–71; Mayo to Daniels, 28 December 1916, Daniels Papers, DLC.

28. See, for example, Daniels to Mayo, 4 April 1917 (forwarding a request for a statement), and Mayo to Editor, *Sunday Pictorial,* 6 April 1917 (declining his "invitation" to make a statement), Daniels to Mayo, 5 May 1917 (informing Mayo that six British writers were coming to visit the fleet), and Daniels to Mayo, 11 May 1917 (telling him that Winston Churchill would also be visiting the fleet), Daniels Papers, DLC.

29. Mayo coupled his support with a recommendation that Gleaves be promoted to vice admiral, a recommendation Daniels recorded in his diary followed by the word "Never." David Cronon, ed., *The Cabinet Diaries of*

Josephus Daniels, 1913–1921, 143. For Mayo's opposition to the transfer of ships, see William V. Pratt to William Sims, 27 May 1917, Sims Papers, DLC.

30. Cronon, *Cabinet Diaries of Josephus Diaries,* 191–92.

31. Mayo described his preparations for the conference in his Report, 11 October 1917, R.G. 45: Area Files, D—Navy Department.

32. For Mayo's report to Benson at the close of the conference, see Mayo to Benson, 6 September, R.G. 45: Subject Files QI—International Naval Conference. For an analysis of its results see David Trask, *Captains and Cabinets: Anglo–American Naval Relations, 1917–1918,* 149–53. Mayo's official report was dated 11 October 1917, R.G. 45: Area Files, D—Navy Department. Mayo's 13 October briefing of Daniels and 19 October meeting with Wilson are described in Cronon, *Cabinet Diaries of Josephus Daniels,* 220, 223. The European trip is described by a member of Mayo's staff in King and Whitehill, *Fleet Admiral King,* 116–23.

33. Sims to Benson, 15 February 1918, Benson Papers, DLC.

34. Mayo's second European trip, particularly the social aspects, is described in King and Whitehill, *Fleet Admiral King,* 133–41.

35. Quoted in ibid., 144.

36. The call for reports was contained in a memorandum dated 22 January 1920, Benson Papers, DLC. For Daniels's notes on his meeting with Mayo see Cronon, *Cabinet Diaries of Josephus Daniels,* 511. His reference to a break between Mayo and Benson is unfounded, as the two worked together harmoniously and appear to have gotten along equally well on a personal basis. See Mary Klachko, *Admiral William Shepherd Benson,* 195, for an account of a testimonial dinner for Benson attended by Mayo, and for the warm exchange of letters that followed, including Mayo's expression to Benson of his "appreciation of our long and close associations in the Service." Mayo's testimony and that which supported his view of Sims is in U.S. Congress, Senate, *Naval Investigation: Hearings before the Subcommittee of the Committee on Naval Affairs, United States Senate,* 66th Cong., 2nd Sess., 1920, II:585, 2181–89.

37. U.S. Senate, Select Committee on Haiti and Santo Domingo, *Inquiry,* 434–35, 1642–43, quoted in Lester D. Langley, *The Banana Wars,* 164, 239.

38. Mayo's speech was published in Edward Mandell House and Charles Seymour, eds., *What Really Happened at Paris: The Story of the Peace Conference, 1918–1919,* 348–69, 490–94.

39. Mayo's correspondence concerning the appointment is in the Board of Visitors Records, Bureau of Navigation, U.S. Naval Academy Archives, Annapolis, Md. For the actions of the board see *Report of the Board of Visitors of the United States Naval Academy, Annapolis, Maryland, May 1, 1929* and *May 1, 1930.*

40. Diary of Edward House, 15 April 1914, quoted in Link, *Papers of Wilson,* 29:448.

41. Daniels, *The Wilson Era,* 191. Historians have been less critical of Mayo than of officials in Washington. The author of the most complete study of the entire conflict with Mexico states that "the mismanagement of Mayo's forces at Tampico was indicative of the lack of any coherent plan in Washington for handling the Mexican situation. Woodrow Wilson seemed content to let each day be sufficient unto itself, so that policy was made, not by the president or the Department of State, but by the events themselves." Quick, *Affair of Honor,* 73. One of Bryan's biographers is equally critical of the secretary of state, saying of Bryan: "rather than exercising leadership he neither directed Mayo to lessen his demands nor suggested that Wilson direct Mayo to do so." Paolo Coletta, *William Jennings Bryan: Progressive Politician and Moral Statesman, 1909–1915,* 162.

42. King, *Fleet Admiral King,* 144–45. Mayo's influence is evident in other places in the memoirs; e.g., "In establishing headquarters in Washington, many basic policies that King had learned from Admiral Mayo . . . were applied to the new emergency," "One of the things that King had absorbed from his service with Mayo . . . ," and "This was in keeping with ideas King had learned from Admiral Mayo. . . ." Ibid., 345, 574, 637; cf., 274, 314–15, 641.

43. "Mayo at Tampico," *Literary Digest,* 2 May 1914.

WILLIAM SOWDEN SIMS:
THE VICTORY ASHORE

DAVID F. TRASK

Admiral William Sowden Sims ought to have commanded a battle fleet. An aggressive personality in the Nelsonian tradition, he should have become a swashbuckling seafighter, but he never gained the opportunity to do so. He missed the War with Spain in 1898 because he was serving in Paris as a naval attaché, and during World War I he commanded a desk in London. Sims exercised only one responsibility at sea of special significance, the leadership of a destroyer flotilla (1913–15). He captained two battleships, the *Minnesota* (1909–11) and the *Nevada* (1915–16), before the United States intervened in World War I; and in January 1917 he became the president of the Naval War College at Newport, Rhode Island.

Sims suffered from an unfortunate accident of birth: he was born while his American parents, Alfred William and Adelaide Sowden Sims, were living in Port Hope, Canada, in 1858. His pro-British bias was often ascribed to this circumstance, certainly an unfair accusation. He spent most of his childhood in Pennsylvania and often lived in Washington, D.C., thereafter.

Sims was a domineering presence, forthright to a fault, leaving no doubt about his views, although reticent in at least one respect, postponing marriage until he reached his forty-eighth year. His bride, Ann Hitchcock, was the daughter of a prominent politician, Ethan Allen Hitchcock, a former diplomat who had served as secretary of the interior.

After graduating from the Naval Academy in 1880, Sims grew up with the "New Navy" that came into existence during the next decade. Although the United States built a modest steel fleet powered

William Sowden Sims. In this 1907 photograph Sims wears his uniform as naval aide to President Roosevelt. *Courtesy of the Naval Historical Center.*

by steam, and later enlarged it somewhat, the frustrations of life in the U.S. Navy were certainly considerable. Promotions came slowly, and challenging assignments were rare. To escape sea duty in old wooden vessels, Sims spent a year on leave in Paris studying French (1888–89), and developed a facility for the language that would serve him well later in his career. The "free security" that the United States enjoyed across the nineteenth century after the War of 1812 made construction of a great navy unnecessary and inhibited the professional development of the naval service as a warfighting institution. The navy concentrated on peacetime missions, notably protection of the nation's limited overseas commerce and defense of unchallenged coastlines. The activist Sims more than once contemplated resignation from the navy in order to pursue more challenging civilian opportunities.

During the 1890s, however, Sims recaptured his commitment to the naval profession, especially while serving in the Pacific in some of the new steel ships. When assigned to the cruiser *Charleston,* he developed a strong interest in the application of modern technology to naval warfare. He soon identified himself as one of the so-called reformers in the naval officer corps who advocated increases in the size and efficiency of the navy to meet changing responsibilities in an era of revolutionary scientific and political change.

When the brief War with Spain took place in 1898, Sims was once again in Paris, serving the American embassy as the naval attaché. The Navy Department's need for information about Spanish naval movements led to the development of a network of American espionage agents in Europe. Sims proved energetic in this respect, receiving valuable information from a number of agents whom he employed to spy in Madrid and elsewhere. The Naval War Board in Washington, whose leading member was none other than the influential naval writer Captain Alfred Thayer Mahan, made good use of the information that Sims and other attachés in Europe sent to the Navy Department about the movements of two naval squadrons deployed from Spanish ports during the war: that of Admiral Pascual Cervera, who steamed to a disastrous defeat at Santiago de Cuba, and that of Admiral Manuel de la Càmara, who progressed no farther than the Suez Canal in an abortive effort to challenge Admiral George Dewey at Manila Bay.[1]

The War with Spain led to the acquisition of a little American empire in the Caribbean Sea and the Pacific Ocean, notably Puerto Rico and the Philippines, along with the annexation of the Hawaiian Islands and the creation of a protectorate over Cuba. This short-lived burst of expansion was part of a stimulus to a measurable enlargement of the U.S. Navy, the other influence, more significant, being a great naval armaments race between Great Britain and Germany that reflected a dangerous destabilization in western Eurasia.

These circumstances encouraged the reformers within the naval officer corps, of whom Sims was one of the most vocal, to advocate an improved naval force, fully professionalized and equipped, that could rival those of such nations as Great Britain, France, Germany, and Japan. Sims agreed with such officers as Rear Admiral Bradley

Fiske who urged extensive naval building programs and favored creation of a naval general staff to guide the navy. The latter step would diminish civilian interference with those measures required to build a great fleet of the kind that Captain Mahan advocated—one prepared to defeat any opponent and able to achieve general and lasting command of the sea.

Sims was certain that senior officers, wedded to the status quo, were the bane for those junior officers who, like himself, advocated enlightened progress. To a fellow officer, William S. Benson, also interested in naval efficiency, he wrote in 1908: "If you can imagine a service in which all of the upper officers would carefully study and easily comprehend all criticism, and cheerfully and openly acknowledge all defects for which they were either actively or passively responsible, then there could be no such condition as that which we deplore." His naval heroes, courageous senior commanders with vision such as Commodore Robert Stockton and Admiral Richard Wainwright, were "always a small minority."[2]

Sims first came to the attention of the nation as a persuasive advocate of improved gunnery in the fleet. During the War with Spain, despite the successes of Admiral Dewey at Manila Bay and Admiral William T. Sampson at Santiago de Cuba, the shooting of the navy had proved woefully deficient. For example, Dewey's ships fired 5,859 shells but made only 142 hits, a success rate of only 2.42 percent. While serving in the Pacific after the war, Sims became acquainted with the gunnery reforms that Sir Percy Scott had initiated in the Royal Navy. Forceful, even overbearing in manner, Sims fought effectively for the adoption of Scott's methods in the U.S. Navy as inspector of target practice from 1902 to 1909. More an advocate than a creative intellect, Sims did not add much to Scott's techniques; his energies went toward breaking resistance to changes in the fleet. In 1916, when he was asked to guide the gunnery of the fleet once again, he declined, noting: "I did not initiate any part of it [gunnery training]. It was taken bodily from Sir Percy Scott. . . . I was never anything of an expert in the development of the details of gunnery training."[3] Sims's naval career received a distinct boost when President Theodore Roosevelt, a patron of naval expansion, assigned him to additional duties as his naval aide in November 1907, although Sims was disappointed when Roosevelt failed to support the more radical elements in the program of the naval reformers.

However progressive his outlook, Sims's advocacy of reform carried a sharp edge, reflecting inner turmoil that led him on occasion to immoderate and unprofessional behavior. A most notable example of this tendency to excess was an unguarded and unauthorized endorsement of Anglo–American solidarity during a speech delivered in London during 1910, an indiscretion that earned him a reprimand from President William Howard Taft. Sims had the knack of engaging the loyalty of younger officers, among them Dudley Knox, later to become a leading naval historian, and William V. Pratt, who eventually served as chief of naval operations, but he demanded total fidelity, a requirement that sometimes alienated him from close associates who presumed to differ on one or another professional matter. In any event, Sims's behavior did not prevent his promotion to rear admiral on the eve of the American intervention in World War I, an event that gave him an opportunity to contribute importantly to American naval history.

After President Woodrow Wilson decided to declare war on the Central Powers but before Congress acted, Sims was called to Washington and asked to represent the U.S. Navy in Great Britain. Early Anglo–American naval cooperation was imperative. Germany had resumed unrestricted submarine warfare against noncombatant and neutral commerce with no concern about the prospect of American belligerency because German leaders assumed that undersea warfare would knock the Allies out of the war before the United States, largely unprepared, could hope to influence the outcome.

When Admiral William Shepherd Benson, the chief of naval operations, gave Sims this assignment, he took note of Sims's reputation as an Anglophile by cautioning against undue pro-British behavior. "Don't let the British pull the wool over your eyes. It is none of our business pulling their chestnuts out of the fire. We would as soon fight the British as the Germans." These were representative views then, especially in the navy, reflecting the sturdy, bumptious nationalism of the era, often suspicious of British motives, and concern about the possibility that Germany might defeat the Allies, leaving the United States to fight on alone; but they conflicted with Sims's conception of sound inter-Allied relations.

Proceeding to London, Sims immediately discovered the extent of the submarine crisis. About 540,000 tons of shipping had gone to the bottom in February, the first month of unrestricted submarine operations. In March the bag rose to over 600,000 tons, and in April to 875,000 tons. German naval leaders predicted that losses of this magnitude would force a decision upon the Allies within six months. Sims soon began a series of dramatic reports to the Navy Department in which he described the danger of Germany's successes against Allied merchant ships and endorsed various naval measures advocated by the British Admiralty, some of which did not conform to inclinations in Washington. He agreed with the Admiralty's view that the United States should make an early entry into the naval war by supporting British antisubmarine operations to protect sea lines of communication between the Allied nations, especially naval escort of merchant ships gathered in convoys. This course would require the United States to postpone construction of a balanced battle fleet and concentrate instead on building antisubmarine craft, especially destroyers, and merchant ships. Moreover, to all intents and purposes it would commit American ships and crews to service under the command of British senior officers.

Some historians erroneously maintain that Sims pressed the adoption of the convoy system upon the Admiralty, but modern scholarship has demonstrated that this measure came about when advocates of this tactic convinced Prime Minister David Lloyd of its practicality, in April 1917. In this case, as in most others, Sims adjusted his views to conform with those of British naval authorities.[4]

As Sims conducted his initial investigations in London, a series of missions from the Allied nations, most importantly from Britain and France, visited Washington to arrange wartime cooperation with the United States, including naval coordination. British naval representatives reinforced the recommendations that came from Sims. The Royal Navy believed that the Grand Fleet, maintaining a distant blockade in the North Sea, could contain the German high sea fleet in port, thus commanding the surface of the sea. This effort, however, limited the number of naval vessels available for antisubmarine operations. To augment the antisubmarine force, the head of the British mission, Foreign Minister Arthur James Balfour, urged the immediate dispatch of American destroyers to European waters.[5]

Admiral Benson and others opposed so much subservience to British desires, worried about larger British motives, and were concerned about the consequences should the Germans force the Allies out of the war. Benson was anxious to protect the long-term naval interests of the United States, which might well diverge from those of Great Britain at some future time. Sims discounted views of this type, convinced that British and American interests were complementary and would remain so indefinitely.

Sims's ideas prevailed, if only because President Wilson had no choice. The grave threat of the German U-boats limited his freedom

British and American naval officers on board the USS *New York*.
Photo taken when the U.S. World War I Battleship Division Nine was
dispatched to Scapa Flow to strengthen the British Grand Fleet. The Division's flagship, the *New York,* was frequently visited by Allied leaders.
From left to right in this photograph stand Admiral David Beatty, commander in chief of the Grand Fleet; Rear Admiral Hugh Rodman, commander of Battleship Division Nine; King George V; Sims; and the
Prince of Wales, later Edward VIII. *Courtesy of Treasure Island Museum.*

of action; America must do what it could as soon as possible to help
keep Germany from achieving victory through sea power before the
U.S. Army could deploy to Europe and make a significant contribution to Germany's defeat.[6]

Sims's position in London was in many respects unique in the
nation's naval experience. Given the decision to place American antisubmarine craft under European commanders, he did not exercise
direct operational command over ships at sea. Instead he transferred
his authority to British officers such as Vice Admiral Sir Lewis Bayly,
who commanded the naval base at Queenstown, Ireland, from whence
destroyers sortied to protect convoys entering the submarine danger

zone. Sims's energies during 1917 were almost entirely devoted to urging the Navy Department to deploy all available antisubmarine reinforcements to Europe and to ensuring their effective use against the German U-boats. In constant contact with the Admiralty in London, which he considered the center of inter-Allied coordination, he generally supported British initiatives, a course that aroused growing irritation in Washington. Sims tried to allay such suspicions, on one occasion telling Secretary of the Navy Josephus Daniels that he realized his opinions might be considered suspect but that "It should be unnecessary to state that I have done everything within my ability to maintain a broad viewpoint." Such protestations proved useless.[7]

However equivocal his standing in Washington, Sims gained unrivaled prestige in Europe. He enjoyed the full confidence of his British associates, establishing the closest possible day-to-day contacts. At the same time, he built an efficient staff that provided effective support for expanding American naval activity, not only in the waters surrounding Great Britain but increasingly in other regions of the Atlantic Ocean and in the Mediterranean Sea where merchant ships and troop transports were exposed to enemy attacks. Sims's personal qualities and his professional skills served him well during 1917–18. He was the right man in the right place at a supreme moment in the naval history of his country.

Benson and others were concerned about the defense of home waters, but Sims discounted this problem. He argued correctly that submarines would not operate frequently in waters so distant from bases. The long voyage across the Atlantic Ocean would keep U-boats that undertook it out of action for an extended time; they could spend only a short time on station. Moreover, Sims believed that "the most effective defence which can be afforded to our home waters is an offensive campaign against the enemy which threatens these waters . . . the place for protection of home waters is . . . where the enemy is operating and must continue to operate in force."[8]

President Woodrow Wilson and Admiral Benson, disdainful of what they believed to be undue British preferences for defensive measures, both pressed for offensive action against bases that harbored the German submarines, such as those on the Belgian coast; but Sims supported British naval opinion, which during 1917 was decidedly resistant to such operations because they were deemed impractical and liable to disturb some of the Allies. Belgium, for example, opposed raids on German bases at occupied places such as Ostend because they might do extensive damage. These arguments caused much irritation in Washington, but Wilson and others lacked sufficient leverage to coerce the Admiralty to U.S. views.[9]

Like Admiral Benson, the General Board of the Navy was especially anxious to preserve the great naval building program of 1916, which envisioned a battle fleet capable of operating along Mahanian lines—one that could gain general and lasting command of the sea. Opposition to this course appeared to contradict Mahan's views, but Sims argued for the need to consider that the naval forces of the entire Allied coalition constituted an inter-Allied battle fleet, to which the United States was making an important contribution. Moreover, in sending antisubmarine craft to European waters, the American fleet was merely maneuvering its screen to a position at a considerable distance in advance of its capital ships. If necessary the heavy vessels could close up later.[10]

Sims was anxious to build a staff in London prepared to cope with the many administrative responsibilities that developed there. Seeking officers with whom he had developed close relations in the past, especially the "band of brothers" who had served in the torpedo flotilla, Sims found his desires frequently set aside. The Navy Department had good reasons for its reluctance. Experienced officers were in great demand; their assignments were intended to provide some leaven of experience in the much-expanded navy. Sims, however, characteristically chose to interpret his difficulties as the result of personal animosity or incompetence. Disputes over personnel were among the many incidents that fueled his growing alienation from officials in the Navy Department, especially Josephus Daniels and to a considerable degree also the chief of naval operations, Admiral Benson. Fortunately, Benson's assistant, Captain William V. Pratt, was one of Sims's most valued associates in the navy. Pratt managed to mediate effectively, explaining the ways of each admiral to the other and providing Sims with information about the basis of the Navy Department's views on disputatious issues.[11]

Although the president and the Navy Department accepted Sims's arguments about the need to concentrate on antisubmarine operations, there was a considerable difference of opinion about their character. Sims believed that the prime consideration was protection of commerce supplying the Allies, whereas the Navy Department interpreted its first responsibility as the escort of transports ferrying the American expeditionary force to Europe. During 1917, this difference did not create tensions because few troops were as yet ready to go to France; but when the American reinforcement began in earnest during the early months of 1918, it became a serious bone of contention. The Allies' need for manpower proved so extensive that eventually Great Britain was forced not only to accede to the American desire for strong escorts to guard troop convoys but also to a demand that Britain provide vessels for use as transports.[12] To cover the arrival of American troops in 1918, Admiral Benson sought to develop a great base at Brest, adjacent to the route of American transports, an action that would inhibit the expansion of submarine operations out of Queenstown intended to guard convoys of merchant ships bound for British ports.

By the outset of 1918, it had become clear that the Allies had succeeded in containing the undersea offensive sufficiently to maintain effective maritime communications, thus frustrating the German attempt to achieve a decision at sea. About 300,000 tons of merchant shipping were destroyed per month during 1918, but new construction, averaging about 500,000 tons per month, more than offset this loss. The failure of the maritime gambit forced Germany's high command to seek a decision on land before American help could flow to Europe in large quantities. A great German offensive materialized on the Western Front, lasting about four months from March to mid-July 1918. Although the Germans gained a great deal of ground, the assault fell short of decisive objectives. Marshal Ferdinand Foch then launched an inter-Allied counteroffensive that finally forced Germany to accept an armistice on 11 November. These land battles in France obscured the growing success of the Allied navies during the final year of the war.[13]

During 1918, Admiral Sims gave much of his attention to the frustrating question of naval warfare in the Mediterranean Sea. He shared the British view that the Italians were entirely too inactive in dealing with the Austro–Hungarian fleet, and with naval bases at Pola and Cattaro in the Adriatic Sea that harbored German submarines. After the western coalition formed an Allied Naval Council in December 1917, Sims represented the United States during its sessions. The council dedicated much of its energy to Mediterranean affairs. Making use of an American planning section that he had managed to establish in London, Sims busied himself with all manner of schemes to wage an effective antisubmarine campaign in the Mediterranean Sea where maritime losses remained at a high level. He came to appreciate the political tensions between the French, the Italians, and the British that precluded action. Sims's failure to achieve much in the Mediterranean was perhaps the principal setback that he encountered during his wartime service in Europe, although he and others largely ignored the subject in postwar writings.[14]

Two petty but highly irritating developments contributed to Sims's growing disgust with the Navy Department. The British government sought to make him and Benson honorary members of the Board of Admiralty, an unprecedented honor to foreigners, but Secretary Daniels and Admiral Benson were definitively opposed to it, and they decided the matter. When Sims, seeking to boost the morale of his command, proposed that European governments be allowed to present decorations to American sailors, Daniels objected.[15]

When the war suddenly approached a most unexpected end late in 1918, Admiral Sims went to Paris for meetings of the Allied Naval Council that were called to determine the naval terms of armistice. Unfortunately for Sims, Admiral Benson had journeyed to Paris with Edward M. House, the president's principal representative at pre-armistice discussions concerning inter-Allied policy. At House's insistence, Benson displaced Sims as the American representative on the Allied Naval Council, and Sims returned to London. After the

Sims in Paris. Sims and his aide view captured German guns on exhibit at the Place de la Concorde. The Hotel Crillon in the background served as headquarters for American naval personnel in Paris. *Courtesy of the Naval Historical Center.*

Armistice of 11 November 1918, Benson remained in Paris as the naval adviser to the American peace commissioners, thereby preventing Sims from taking part in important naval negotiations that occurred during the postwar peace conference. Sims privately betrayed his disappointment. After noting that General Pershing also had not been appointed a plenipotentiary, he confided snidely to a close friend: "As for our naval advisor [Benson] with the peace delegates he is exactly the kind of man they want; of course you know why!" Sims here adverted to the conviction of his circle that Benson, lacking independent views and special talents of his own, was a yes-man who kowtowed to civilians.[16]

Sims's accumulating frustration with the Navy Department surfaced on several occasions during the war and shortly afterward. On 13 August 1918, he commented portentously to Captain Pratt: "When the history of this war comes to be written there will be a number of features that will not be very creditable to the United States Navy. If hearings are held on the conduct of the war, a number of rather disagreeable facts must inevitably be brought out." He mentioned especially the Navy Department's failure to bring the most experienced naval officers to Europe. Much more devastating was his reaction to a report that Captain Pratt drafted shortly after the Armistice, detailing the navy's accomplishments during wartime. To Sims this report indicated that the Navy Department claimed "to have always foreseen everything, planned everything and supported us up to the handle," thereby depreciating the accomplishments of the navy overseas. To the contrary, he concluded that "the cablegrams exchanged between the Department and me during the first four months of our participation in the war will be, I think, pretty damaging testimony to the game played by the Department, and will make this Departmental letter . . . look pretty sick."[17]

Sims returned to the United States in high dudgeon. Maneuvering successfully for reappointment as president of the Naval War College, he resettled in Newport to write a memoir of his wartime service. Negotiating a lucrative contract with Doubleday, Page & Company, and arranging for the collaboration of the talented Burton J. Hendrick, an editor at Doubleday, Page, Sims prepared a detailed report of his activities that appeared initially as a series of articles in *World's Work*, a well-known magazine of the day, and later as a book entitled *The Victory at Sea*. Hendrick drafted the entire text of this cogent account, which faithfully reflected Sims's criticisms to the degree that he cared to express them. Naval regulations prevented

Sims from venting his spleen extensively in this publication; he dealt with his tormentors by ignoring them, hardly mentioning Daniels and Benson. *The Victory at Sea* did not sell as well as Sims and his publishers had hoped, but it achieved a succès d'estime, the award of the Pulitzer Prize for 1920, and it became the accepted comment on the navy's participation in the war, however unfair it was in its failure to give due credit to the Navy Department.[18]

Meanwhile, Sims took advantage of opportunities to provoke a congressional investigation of naval policy during the war. In so doing he redeemed a pledge to Admiral William Fullam, another naval reformer of the day: "You may be sure . . . that at the proper time I will tell the whole truth as I understand it." In another communication, he added: "You know I entirely agree with you that the country has got to be informed as to the condition of the Navy in the immediate past and its condition now." Those responsible who had "camouflaged the subject cannot escape very long." The basis for a public controversy developed when Sims angrily refused to accept a postwar decoration, the Distinguished Service Medal, in December 1919 because he felt that the list of those honored did not fairly reflect the contributions of various officers during the war. On 7 January 1920, after the Senate decided to examine the list of decorations, Sims wrote to Secretary Daniels, outlining his indictment of the Navy Department. He stressed the department's failure to respond immediately to his recommendations from London during 1917, when the crisis over the U-boat campaign was at its height. Thus Sims fulfilled a vow he made to his collaborator, Hendrick: "You may be sure that if in the course of these hearings I can pry the lid off I will do so. I am prepared to go to the limit." [19]

When he appeared before the Senate subcommittee that conducted the naval investigation, Sims provided a detailed exposition of the complaints that he had made in 1917 and of the Navy Department's alleged failure to respond appropriately. Daniels, Benson, and others had not prepared for the war properly, and the navy had not been able to meet its responsibilities: "We pursued a policy of vacillation, or in simpler words, a hand to mouth policy, attempting to formulate our plans from day to day, based upon an incorrect appreciation of the situation." Sims maintained that the Navy Department had cost the Allies a half-million lives, two and a half million tons of shipping, and $15 billion in expenditures. His testimony included extensive reference to the cable exchanges that he had conducted with the Navy Department during 1917 over the nature of the American naval contribution.[20]

In response, the Navy Department offered a spirited defense of its actions, as Daniels, Benson, Pratt, and others testified at length. They admitted that the navy had been less than fully prepared at the beginning of hostilities in 1917, but they offered explanations of the reasons why the Navy Department had responded as it did to Sims's requests.

Benson made the most explicit rejoinder to the burden of Sims's charges. As to prewar unpreparedness, he noted that he had desired readiness, but "this was not the attitude of the people of the United States and not the attitude of the Administration." Political decisions, to which he was subject, accounted for naval unpreparedness in April 1917. During the war he had acted in terms of the national interest, emphasizing his duty "to safeguard American interests regardless of any duty to humanity or anything else." Nevertheless the United States had responded handsomely to the desires of the Allies and in some ways had urged more ambitious measures than had been recommended from Europe.

Benson left no doubt of his views in a sweeping conclusion: The Navy Department met its obligations "with efficiency and success; . . . the policies we adopted and our plans in accordance therewith were thoroughly justified by events." He, his colleagues, and the entire navy had "performed well a difficult task; cooperating from beginning to end with the Allies and rendering them every assistance in our power, and contributing very materially to the general result." This rosy evaluation surely overstated a generally reasonable case, thereby further obscuring the whole truth about the navy's wartime record.[21]

Sims hoped that the hearings would catch the imagination of the American public, but the outcome proved a great disappointment to him. The Republican majority on the Senate subcommittee supported Sims, but the Democratic minority defended the Navy Department. No action was taken against Daniels or Benson, and the investigation was soon forgotten, although it caused a long-term rift within the navy between Sims's advocates and his enemies. Instead of reviewing wartime events, during 1921 the nation engaged in a discussion about future security in the Pacific Ocean that led to naval disarmament, one aspect of the treaty system that emerged from the Washington Naval Conference.

Various circumstances account for Sims's discomfiture. Above all, the naval war had ended in a great victory, whatever problems might have emerged along the way. Sims's charges appeared to many as simply to reflect a quarrel among admirals, reminiscent of the Sampson–Schley controversy that followed the War with Spain. Second, the public had already tired of the war. Postwar exhaustion and disillusionment, reflected in the failure of the Senate to accept the Treaty of Versailles, certainly worked against Sims's efforts to arouse the American people. Finally, Sims overplayed his hand. His proclivity to overpersonalize issues and to tendentiousness caught up with him in this climactic episode. After all, Sims's general views about the centrality of the inter-Allied antisubmarine effort and the need to postpone the American naval building programs had prevailed over those of Benson; and good reasons existed for the delays and modifications that the Navy Department made in response to Sims's strident demands in 1917. Sims fell victim to a common error: theater commanders all too often view their activities from the narrow perspective of their own situations, insufficiently mindful of the larger considerations that motivate higher authority. Perhaps also Sims's admiration of Great Britain and the Royal Navy affected his judgment in some respects, and surely he erred in identifying too closely with the Republicans during the hearings, allowing his critics to accuse him of partisanship. During the presidential campaign of 1920 he sought an audience with the Republican candidate, Warren G. Harding, to press his views on naval matters, but he was unsuccessful. Any interest he may have had in becoming secretary of the navy went glimmering when President Harding appointed a loyal Republican rather than a naval expert.

Sims retired from the U.S. Navy in 1922 in the rank of rear admiral, taking up residence in Newport, from where he occasionally attempted to influence naval policy until his death in 1936. Noteworthy was his strong support of naval aviation, which led to a brief recall to active duty in 1925. Advancing age did not moderate the inveterate intemperance that dogged Sims through most of his naval career and in the end compromised his success. Perhaps this failing was consistent with his performance as a naval reformer before the war. He failed to weigh his views carefully against those of his antagonists or to give them due consideration, in the process alienating many who otherwise might have rallied to him.[22]

In evaluating Sims's naval career it is important neither to underestimate nor to exaggerate its significance. Sims's reputation benefited greatly from his book, *The Victory at Sea,* and especially from an excellent biography, written by his son-in-law Elting E. Morison, that glorified the admiral as the exemplar par excellence of the modern American navy and fixed him in the minds of naval historians and others as the leading prophet of the naval future after World War I.[23] A modern finding must deplore Sims's intolerance of those who disagreed with him, an unlovely trait that eventually compromised his advocacy of naval reform. It must also identify some significant negative characteristics of his outlook, especially his unwillingness to give sufficient recognition to the principle of civilian supremacy over the military establishment. Like many other officers of his day, Sims failed to come to terms with the constraints that a democracy necessarily places upon its naval officers. Perhaps, finally, an accounting must recognize that often Sims was more a publicist than an originator of the reforms he pressed so energetically.

In the end, however, Sims stands in the foremost ranks of those who led the U.S. Navy during the transitional years from the age of free security in the nineteenth century to an era of great international destabilization, a shift that forced the nation to create a powerful steel fleet that met Woodrow Wilson's criterion—a navy second to none. More than most others, Sims discerned the basic security requirements of the new age. Most important, whatever his failing, he served with the greatest distinction in London during 1917–18, steadfast in attention to duty and remarkably successful in the conduct of his enormous responsibilities as executor of the American naval contribution to the victory at sea in European waters. No other officer in the navy of his time could have matched his performance in the crucible of total war.

FURTHER READING

For general accounts of the naval war, the most informative works are Arthur J. Marder's *From the Dreadnought to Scapa Flow: The Royal Navy in the Fisher Era*, 5 vols., especially the last two volumes, which cover 1917–18; Thomas G. Frothingham, *The Naval History of the World War*, 3 vols.; Paul G. Halpern, *The Naval War in the Mediterranean, 1914–1918;* Robert M. Grant, *U-Boats Destroyed: The Effect of Anti-submarine Warfare, 1914–1918,* and *U-Boat Intelligence, 1914–1918;* and Holger H. Herwig and David F. Trask, "The Failure of Imperial Germany's Undersea Offensive against World Shipping, February 1917–October 1918."

Articles on the role of the U.S. Navy include Dean C. Allard, "Anglo–American Naval Differences during World War I"; and David F. Trask, "The American Navy in a World at War, 1914–1919," in *In Peace and War: Interpretations of American Naval History, 1775–1978,* ed. Kenneth J. Hagan.

For the views of Admiral William S. Sims, see his *The Victory at Sea,* ed. David F. Trask, in *Classics of Naval Literature,* ed. Jack Sweetman, a reprint of the original 1920 edition. See also the magisterial biography by Elting E. Morison, *Admiral Sims and the Modern American Navy;* Dean C. Allard, "Admiral William S. Sims and United States Naval Policy in World War I"; and David F. Trask, *Captains and Cabinets: Anglo–American Naval Relations, 1917–1918.*

For other personalities see Gerald E. Wheeler, *Admiral William Veazie Pratt, U.S. Navy: A Sailor's Life;* Mary Klachko with David F. Trask, *Admiral William Shepherd Benson: First Chief of Naval Operations;* Paolo Coletta, "Josephus Daniels: 5 March 1913–5 March 1921," in *The American Secretaries of the Navy,* ed. Paolo Coletta; and E. David Cronon, ed., *The Cabinet Diaries of Josephus Daniels, 1913–1921.*

For the record of the congressional inquiry into the navy after World War I, see U.S. Congress, Senate, *Naval Investigation: Hearings before the Subcommittee of the Committee on Naval Affairs.*

NOTES

1. For biographical information, see Elting E. Morison, *Admiral Sims and the Modern American Navy.* A striking short sketch by Jeffery M. Dorwart is in Roger Spiller et al., *Dictionary of American Military Biography,* III:1003–6. Dorwart measurably modifies Morison's highly favorable evaluation of Sims, an approach that is extended in this essay. For naval intelligence during 1898, see David F. Trask, *The War with Spain,* 87–89, 143.

2. Quoted in Mary Klachko with David F. Trask, *Admiral William Shepherd Benson: First Chief of Naval Operations,* 18.

3. Quoted in ibid., 43.

4. See David F. Trask, *Captains and Cabinet: Anglo–American Naval Cooperation, 1917–1918,* 72, 79–80, an interpretation first advanced by Arthur Marder.

5. For information about the Allied missions see ibid., 62–64, 74–77.

6. A convenient collection of Sims's messages to the Navy Department during this critical period is found in the admiral's memoir of the war, entitled *The Victory at Sea,* edited with an introduction by David F. Trask and reprinted in the Naval Institute's series *Classics of Naval Literature,* 374–99. For accounts of the discussion between Sims and the Navy Department, see Trask, *Captains and Cabinets,* 61–101; Klachko, *Benson,* 70–81.

7. Sims to Daniels, 16 July 1917, reprinted in Sims, *Victory at Sea,* 398.

8. Ibid., 396.

9. Trask, *Captains and Cabinets,* 131–32.

10. David F. Trask, "The American Navy in a World at War, 1914–1919," in *In Peace and War: Interpretations of American Naval History, 1775–1978*, ed. Kenneth J. Hagan, 209–10.

11. For information about Captain Pratt and his dealings with Benson and Sims, see Gerald Wheeler, *Admiral William Veazie Pratt, U.S. Navy: A Sailor's Life*, especially 71–126.

12. For this subject, see two articles by Dean C. Allard, "Admiral William S. Sims and United States Naval Policy in World War I," and "Anglo–American Naval Differences during World War I."

13. For information on the course of the submarine war, see Holger H. Herwig and David F. Trask, "The Failure of Imperial Germany's Offensive against World Shipping, February 1917–October 1918," 611–36.

14. A recent book by Paul G. Halpern finally provides an up-to-date study of the tangled naval situation in the Mediterranean area during World War I. See his *The Naval War in the Mediterranean, 1914–1918*.

15. Trask, *Captain and Cabinets*, 193–96.

16. Klachko, *Benson*, 121, 131–32.

17. For the quotations and information concerning Sims's irritation, see Wheeler, *Pratt*, 147–48. Sims, of course, had complained regularly. Wheeler notes one such comment made to Pratt on 21 November 1917: "My great fear is that this war may be lost or that the Allies may be forced into a very unsatisfactory peace and that the subsequent examinations as to the causes of this condition may reveal the fact that we have not done our utmost to prevent it and that our military decisions in many cases have been unsound." Sims here reflected the plenary fears that emerged in the Allied nations as the Germans began preparations for their great offensive of March 1918, but it may be of some significance that already he was thinking about the possibility of a postwar investigation of the American naval effort. Ibid., 147.

18. For the story of the writing of *The Victory at Sea*, see Trask, "Introduction" to *The Victory at Sea*, xx–xxvii.

19. For the preliminaries to the hearings of 1920, see Klachko, *Benson*, 170–71. Sims's comment to Hendrick is quoted in Trask, "Introduction" to *The Victory at Sea*, xxiii.

20. Klachko, *Benson*, 172–73. For the hearings, see U.S. Congress, Senate, *Naval Investigation: Hearings before the Subcommittee of the Committee on Naval Affairs, United States Senate*, 2 vols., 66th Cong., 2nd Sess., 1920. A spirited redefinition of Sims's views is in Tracy B. Kittredge, *Naval Lessons of the Great War: A Review of the Senate Naval Investigation of the Criticisms of Admiral Sims of the Policies and Methods of Josephus Daniels*.

21. See for this information Klachko, *Benson*, 176, 178–79.

22. Sims along with a number of other officers, including Admiral Benson, was restored to his wartime rank of full admiral in 1930.

23. Elting E. Morison's biography is *Admiral Sims and the Modern American Navy*.

WILLIAM SHEPHERD BENSON: NAVAL GENERAL STAFF AMERICAN STYLE

MARY KLACHKO

The shot that felled Archduke Francis Ferdinand of Austria threw Europe into a turmoil that in little more than a month evolved into World War I. On 4 August 1914, the same day Great Britain declared war on Germany, President Woodrow Wilson proclaimed the neutrality of the United States. For more than two and a half years he sought to mediate the conflict and to realize his ambition to become a great peacemaker.

Naval officers shared Wilson's interest in the war, but viewed it from a different perspective. Many believed that American involvement was inevitable. Thus the General Board of the Navy met at the Naval War College to explore measures to be taken to enhance the readiness of the American navy to fight the war, should America enter the conflict. On 1 August 1914, the board sent a series of proposals to Secretary of the Navy Josephus Daniels. Knowing that Wilson feared that the belligerents would construe martial improvements as unneutral behavior, Daniels ignored these recommendations.

Discussion of the navy's preparedness for possible participation in the conflict did not become public until mid-October 1914 when Augustus P. Gardner, chairman of the House Committee on Military Affairs, called for an investigation to determine whether the naval forces of the United States were ready for war. Insurgent naval reformers led by Rear Admiral Bradley A. Fiske, at that time aid for operations, saw this as an opportunity to establish a naval general staff. When Gardner's committee recommended such a body, President Wilson denounced the proposal, and the *New York Times* reported on 20 October that the "President Is Calm To Our War Needs." Secretary Daniels held that the creation of a general staff for the navy was inconsistent with the principles of the country. Like his predecessors, he opposed such a staff because it could place control of the navy in the hands of uniformed line officers instead of civilian policymakers. Daniels had the support of the bureau chiefs because they feared that a strong naval general staff would weaken their autonomy and lessen their chances of contact with the secretary of the navy. Fiske wrote in his diary, "I think a fight will start on the subject very soon." [1]

When Congressman Richmond P. Hobson, in an amendment to the 1915 naval construction bill, proposed the establishment of an office of naval operations with fifteen assistants who would be responsible for readiness of the navy and its general direction, Secretary Daniels said that should it pass, he "would go home." However, upon realizing that the Fiske–Hobson proposals might lead to the creation of a powerful naval staff, Daniels outmaneuvered the reformers with a proposal of his own. He introduced an amendment to the naval construction bill creating an office of naval operations whose chief would be charged with overseeing operations of the fleet and preparing plans for its use in war, but would not have authority to issue orders except through the secretary of the navy.

Daniels's plan passed on 3 March 1915, leaving control of naval policy in the hands of civilian authority. The effectiveness of the chief of naval operations would depend upon the ability of the appointee to maintain a good working relationship with the civilian superior. To ensure such a relationship, Secretary Daniels passed over twenty-six rear admirals and five captains and appointed Captain William Shepherd Benson to the position.

Benson, an "unassuming" officer, was neither well known to the public nor influential in Washington politics. But he was not without qualifications. At the age of sixty, Benson, son of a Southern plantation owner and one of the first Southerners to enter the Naval Academy after the Civil War, had thirty-eight years of naval service and a record of solid accomplishments. During his wide gamut of sea and land duty, Benson had witnessed the evolution of ships from wood to steel, from sail to steam, and from communication by carrier pigeon to radio transmission. His service gave him a broad understanding of the needs of the American navy and difficulties that must be faced in meeting them. Now it became his responsibility to develop the newly created office at a time of intense debate among

William Shepherd Benson. Rear Admiral Benson as chief of naval operations, 1915. *Courtesy of the Naval Historical Center.*

naval officers concerning the best procedure to follow in leading the American navy toward preparedness for war.

Announcing Captain Benson's appointment to the press, Secretary Daniels spoke of Benson's "ripe experience of varied character." His first tour of sea duty had been in the old historic screw sloop *Hartford* back in 1877. He had sailed the historic frigate *Constitution,* still under sail, on her last cruise. His most recent tour of sea duty was in the *Utah,* the newest battleship of the Atlantic Fleet, whose construction he had overseen. In that vessel he had achieved a reputation as "one of the most capable and resourceful captains of the Navy."[2] At the time of his appointment as CNO, Benson was commandant of the Philadelphia Navy Yard. By his tact and discretion in this capacity, he had gained the cooperation of Secretary Daniels and earned his respect.[3]

Fiske, then aid for operations, had hoped that he would be appointed chief of naval operations, a logical expectation. However, his frequent clashes with Secretary Daniels as well as his perception of the role of a naval staff did not serve him well. Daniels did not want the newly created office held by anyone who had a "consuming passion . . . to confer all power on the head of Operations." He wanted an officer of "practical judgment who believed in the American system."[4]

Fiske's disappointment at not getting the appointment was revealed first of all in his diary entry. Then he vented his frustration upon the appointee even though he and Benson had not been adversaries before then. Both had been in naval service during the same period of its development. They also had a common interest in the installation of range finders—so much so that, on 13 April 1909, Benson had written to Secretary of the Navy George von Lengerke Meyer strongly urging their development. On 28 August 1910, Fiske had written to Benson that he remembered Benson's coming on board the *Tennessee* and suggesting that range finders be built in turrets. Benson had not taken part in the recent drive for creation of a naval general staff, but he favored one, as is seen by his letter of 3 September 1906 to Assistant Secretary of the Navy Truman H. Newberry, in which he wrote, "A properly selected and organized General Staff once established most, if not all, the vexing and disturbing questions now arising will disappear and cease to come up."[5]

Fiske also showed his disappointment at not being named chief of naval operations in an address he delivered at the annual alumni dinner at the Naval Academy. In his remarks he recognized the establishment of the Office of Naval Operations as a step in the right direction, and then by insinuation cast an aspersion against Benson by criticizing naval officers who would not publicly take issue with the secretary of the navy. He said, "If we fear to do this, less we incur displeasure and spoil our individual career, we are unworthy of the uniform we wear and we fail our country in her hour of need, just as effectively as if we deserted her flag in war."[6]

This was the beginning of a campaign of slurs against Benson that persisted in some circles throughout his term as CNO and robbed him of much deserved recognition. After Fiske's speech, Sims wrote to him: "At exactly the right time, you said exactly the right thing, and it will do a heap of good to our poor Navy. . . . Our trouble has always been that the politicians have been able to find naval officers to say what they wanted them to say." This was quite a turnabout from the response he had sent to Benson back in 1906, after Benson had written to congratulate him on his accomplishments in the area of accuracy of gunfire during his term as inspector of target practice. Then Sims had lamented "the scarcity of such officers as Remey, Stockton, Wainright and Benson," adding that the situation could not be expected to be otherwise because "Remeys, Stocktons, Wainrights, and Bensons, are always a small minority."[7]

Fiske once again revealed his bitterness at being bypassed in favor of Benson in his autobiography, in which he wrote that Benson had never shown interest in strategy, nor had he "even taken the summer course at the War College."[8]

Both these statements are inaccurate. In the summer of 1906, Benson was one of seventeen naval officers who attended the only course given at that time at the Naval War College—a two-month summer session. Regular twelve-month courses were not offered until 1914. Moreover, in 1910 Benson presented a series of lectures at the same institution on strategy in the Pacific.

All this is indication that the insurgent reformers were critical of Benson not because he lacked qualifications or ability for his office, but because of his behavior in dealing with Secretary Daniels. Benson was a reformer in principle but not a supporter of the aggressive tactics sometimes utilized against higher civilian authority. He had deep respect for the principle of chain of command. Benson considered it his duty to assist his civilian superior in formulating policy, but through proper channels and not by public criticism. As the first CNO, he faced the task of developing the newly created office and preparing the American navy for the eventuality of war at a time of intense debate among naval officers about the best procedure to follow to accomplish these undertakings.

Upon assuming office as chief of naval operations, Benson confronted a multitude of problems because of inadequate accommodations, equipment, professional naval staff, and clerical help. He was assigned Fiske's former office—a main room in the old State, War, and Navy Building near the White House and two smaller rooms beyond it. The main room was just large enough for a flattopped desk and a few chairs. There was no clerical staff in the office. Benson assumed office with a naval staff of three officers he chose upon being appointed CNO—Captain Volney Chase, Lieutenant Byron McCandless, and Lieutenant Wilson Brown.

The organizational setup of his office was not conducive to dealing quickly with naval problems, whether they involved administration or strategic planning. The CNO lacked authority commensurate with his responsibilities. Benson could not issue orders except through Secretary Daniels. To get anything done, it was necessary for him first of all to gain the respect, the confidence, and then the cooperation of his civilian superior. He set out to do so. Benson also faced a number of autonomous sectors in the Navy Department, which jealously guarded their independence: the General Board and the bureau chiefs, all vying with each other to gain Secretary Daniels's attention and his support for their respective suggestions or requests. There was little coordination of plans among them. To achieve any centralization of the bureaus with the Office of Naval Operations, Benson depended upon the cooperation and goodwill of their chiefs. Only some of the existing sectors within the Division of Operations automatically came under Benson's domain, including the Office of Naval Intelligence, the Naval War College, the Office of Target Practice and Engineering Competitions, the Naval Radio Service, the Office of Naval Aeronautics, and the Board of Inspection and Survey.

Under the existing organizational setup in the Navy Department, it was difficult for Benson's office to function as a naval general staff and deal with strategy, operations, and commands. The General Board was the agency to which policymaking had been entrusted, and its plans were subject only to the approval of the secretary of the navy. Being an ex officio member of the General Board, Benson on the very day of his installation as CNO attended a meeting of its executive committee and continued to do so regularly, and thus participated in planning strategy. He worked very closely with the General Board throughout his term of office as CNO with great success.

Benson's tactics in dealing with Daniels, in light of the "get Daniels" atmosphere, exposed him to the criticism of insurgent reformers, which did not, however, convince him to act otherwise. He cautioned critics of Secretary Daniels not to place blame for unpreparedness at any one person's doorstep. Asserting that preparedness was the best guarantee for peace, he pointed out that everything possible had not been done with the existing resources and stated that it was his aim under the new setup "to get every unit in the best possible shape," for then "we will be in a position to go to Congress and ask for more."[9]

Benson worked quietly but diligently during his first year as CNO to widen his narrow role in strategy formulation by what may be termed a strategic reorganization of the Navy Department; he for the most part succeeded in limiting its various sectors to administrative functions. He began by taking measures to ready the American navy for possible involvement in the ongoing conflict in Europe. In his characteristically low-key manner, he drafted an order for Secretary

Daniels's signature implementing the shelved "General Plan," which Fiske had submitted on 13 March 1915 but on which Daniels had not acted. Now, Daniels quickly signed it and sent it to the bureau chiefs, directing them to submit their reports and recommendations to the Navy Department through the CNO's office, which would then submit them to the General Board. Benson received the first batch of these documents in late June. On 10 August, he discontinued the annual three-month overhaul of ships because he considered the practice both harmful to the morale of the fleet and uneconomical in administration. Vessels would not be ordered to yards until all plans and material were ready for beginning actual work.

To foster improved cooperation among the bureau chiefs, Benson convinced Daniels to create an advisory council, a measure that worked out to the great satisfaction of both. On 24 June, Daniels remarked that the system of bureau chiefs had never been so universally recognized as "masters of the professional work under their special direction." Benson gleefully wrote: "Idea of the Council is meeting with even better results than were anticipated." Benson ran into a problem with Daniels when the secretary was unwilling to name a successor to Rear Admiral Albert G. Winterhalter for the post of aid for matériel. He solved the situation by convincing Daniels that the functions of this bureau should be performed by an assistant for matériel, to be assigned to the office of the CNO. He explained that this arrangement would end "separation of matériel preparation of the fleet from its operation" and make for "the highest efficiency of the fleet." On 23 June, Captain Josiah S. McKean was named assistant for matériel, an appointment that was well received by Benson's critics.[10]

One of the provisions of the General War Plan was for the inspection of the American merchant vessels to determine the possibility of their use as naval auxiliaries in time of war. To hasten this procedure, Benson won an increase in the personnel of the Board of Inspection. The inspection was done separately by the army and by the navy, but Benson considered this duplication a waste of effort. Upon the reestablishment of the Joint Army and Navy Board at Benson's suggestion, President Wilson named him its naval member. Benson then initiated a conference to explore the possibility of a joint program of inspection, which resulted in the establishment of a joint Army and Navy Inspection Board. After inspection the merchant ships would be assigned to either the War Department or the Navy Department for the necessary adjustments.[11]

The General Board had under consideration a plan for the reorganization of the fleet. Desiring to "advance the development of fleet tactics" and provide "increased opportunity for the exercise of flag commands," Benson on 24 May submitted a plan on the "Organization of the Active Battleship Fleet" to both Secretary Daniels and the General Board. The board suspended deliberation on the plan it had been studying, and on 2 June accepted Benson's recommendation for a battleship fleet with three squadrons of three divisions, each of which would have three ships.

Benson considered organization of the fleet to be a "technical question" and did not expect objections to his plan from Secretary Daniels, but he was mistaken. Daniels considered the term "Force"—as in Cruiser Force, Destroyer Force, and Battleship Force—too antagonistic and did not want to use it. Benson stood his ground; after considerable delay his plan was accepted, and flag officers were detached to command each division. A year later, Benson proudly claimed that the fleet was completely and thoroughly organized for the first time.[12]

Well acquainted with the setup of naval districts because of his service as supervisor of the Third, Fourth, and Fifth Naval Districts when in command of the Philadelphia Navy Yard, Benson considered the existing organization of naval districts "nominal." At his suggestion a board was formed to review the existing system. This board recommended the establishment of a separate Office of Naval Districts to undertake the establishment of a uniform organization with a general plan. Secretary Daniels issued an order transferring the Office of Naval Districts from the Division of Naval Militia Affairs in the Bureau of Navigation to the Office of Naval Operations.

The deterioration of gunnery in the American fleet since Sims had left the post of director of target practice was of great concern to Admiral Benson. He requested his "old friend" Sims to accept this detail again. Benson was disappointed at Sims's refusal to do so but showed him no ill will. On the contrary, he acted on Sims's suggestion that Captain Charles P. Plunkett be appointed to the position.[13]

Benson's drive to reorganize the Navy Department and improve the efficiency of the navy was conducted against the backdrop of Germany's successful submarine warfare. Considering the submarine an integral part of the fleet, Benson arranged a conference with Secretary Daniels to consider development of this new weapon. Afterward the announcement was made that a "determined effort would be made" to put every unit of the submarine flotilla in first-class condition to perform all the functions for which it was designed. The appointment of Captain Albert W. Grant to command the Atlantic Submarine Flotilla was, in itself, a major step forward in this field. Pleased with Grant's early improvements, Benson wrote to Secretary Daniels: "Already the success of this new policy has been gratifying."[14]

The development of aviation also lagged in the United States. Benson planned to "dig it out to the foundation" and establish an effective organization. At a meeting of the Council of Aids, he proposed placing jurisdiction over aviation under the Matériel Division. The abolition of an independent Office of Naval Aeronautics has been criticized, but critics overlook the fact that bureau chiefs as well as the majority of line officers considered aviation an "element of sea power" rather than a separate source of it. Benson appointed Captain Mark L. Bristol Commander of Air Service with additional duty to supervise all aircraft and aircraft stations for further development of aeronautics.

Unfortunately Bristol had difficulties with Lieutenant Commander Henry C. Mustin, whom he had chosen to be the "key man" in the new aviation setup. Their differences became so significant that Benson found it necessary to intervene and limit Bristol's wide supervisory duties, leaving him in charge only of development of tactics and use of aircraft afloat and putting Mustin in charge of work at the single aeronautic station in the United States, located at Pensacola, Florida. At that time it had only fourteen aircraft, none of them ready for regular service. The armored cruiser North Carolina was the only aeronautical vessel in the fleet. Despite its humble and difficult beginning, by the end of the war naval aviation had grown to a force of 6,716 officers and 30,693 enlisted men in naval units with 2,107 aircraft. Of this force 18,000 officers and men and 570 aircraft had reached foreign lands.[15]

The ongoing war in Europe greatly stimulated technological developments. To mobilize the scientific and technical expertise of the nation on behalf of naval improvements, a Naval Consulting Board was established in July 1915 with Thomas A. Edison as chairman. Benson drafted the rules and regulations of the group, which played an important role in keeping the navy abreast of the technological innovations of the day.

When Benson became CNO, the Office of Naval Radio Service under the jurisdiction of the Bureau of Navigation handled naval communications, but the existing facility was grossly inefficient. On

28 July 1916, the Naval Radio Service was replaced by the Naval Communications Service in the Office of Naval Operations, which operated day and night, providing telephonic and telegraphic communication to ships at sea.[16]

The Office of Naval Intelligence had a personnel roster of only eight people at the beginning of Benson's term as CNO. Holding that "complete and correct information is the first requisite for judicious decision and intelligent action," Benson recommended an organizational change to provide better machinery for securing information from sources abroad. A War Information Service was established in the Office of Naval Intelligence.[17]

By the end of his first year as CNO, Benson had made considerable progress in strengthening the Navy Department. He reported that the work was being conducted under five categories: intelligence, education, planning, inspection, and execution. His staff now occupied nine renovated and properly equipped rooms; essential data about the U.S. Navy and the principal navies of the world had been gathered and filed; weekly meetings of the Advisory Council had secured a closer contact with Secretary Daniels; a rapport had been established between the bureau chiefs and the General Board; and the CNO had created a more cordial and cooperative atmosphere between himself and the bureau chiefs. A major accomplishment was Benson's success in convincing Secretary Daniels to accept the preparedness plan proposed by militant reformers.

Seven months from his appointment as CNO, Benson became eligible for regular promotion to the rank of rear admiral. In his report to the Naval Examining Board, Secretary Daniels wrote that under Benson's leadership Operations had set a "new pace in naval preparedness and strategy." Promoted to regular rank of rear admiral as of 26 November 1915, Benson felt justifiable pride in his achievements. The office of CNO had demonstrated that it was an "effective means of coordinating the complex work of the Navy in harmony with maturely considered plans."[18]

Paralleling Benson's preoccupation with reorganization of the Navy Department was his involvement in formulation of the naval expansion program. Congress debated the naval appropriation bill for 1916 under dubious circumstances. While both Great Britain and Germany were violating the doctrine of freedom of the seas and curbing the neutral rights of the United States, President Wilson was "devoted to peace. His master passion was the hope of an opportunity to end the war." Secretary Daniels was extremely devoted to the president. The secretary's loyalty, along with public apathy and a Congress divided on the type of legislation to be passed for naval expansion in 1916, inhibited efforts of professional policymakers to determine what and how much to build.

These were the circumstances that influenced Benson's procedure to win the support of the Wilson administration for an adequate naval construction program. Years later, Benson wrote that it was unfortunate that in the early days of the war Secretary Daniels was "honestly and firmly of the opinion that we could not be drawn into the war, [and] consequently when requests were made upon him for increased appropriations, more officers or material, he often could not see his way clear to give full and wholehearted cooperation and sometimes even refused consent. He was at times suspicious of changes in reorganization." [19]

Besides Benson's tactful approach to Secretary Daniels, developments in the international arena such as an increase in the intensity of German submarine warfare, the sinking of the *Lusitania,* and the possibility of a German–Japanese alliance were all factors in convincing President Wilson to seek "professional advice" about an "adequate program" to propose to Congress. Considering that about two months earlier he had maintained that soldiers or sailors had nothing to do with the formulation of national policy, and that the duty of the military was to support whatever policy the president developed, this was quite a turnaround. [20]

When Secretary Daniels requested that the General Board draft a program, it recommended that the U.S. Navy should "ultimately be equal to the most powerful maintained by any other nation in the world and [that it] should attain this position not later than 1925." Benson provided Secretary Daniels with a detailed description of the ships to be built and a justification for the particular vessels to be constructed. He continued to send Daniels memoranda expounding the need to accept the General Board proposal.

After a study of the board's proposal, Daniels asked Benson to request that the board formulate a program with an expenditure of about $100 million each year for five years for strictly new construction. In principle Daniels's proposal was in agreement with that of the General Board, but it limited the spending allocation for the first year of construction. Nevertheless the General Board went along with it, undoubtedly because in two ways it was a definit departure from the policies observed to that time. This was the fiᵣ t occasion when a secretary of the navy had proposed a continuous naval program. It was also a departure from the standard in force since the presidency of Theodore Roosevelt of maintaining a navy second to that of Great Britain. It held forth the promise of unprecedented naval expansion.

The proposal encountered difficulties in a Congress sharply divided between a Republican minority that favored a larger program and a Democratic majority split over the size of the program. A further impediment was the introduction by Admiral Fiske of a provision to augment the Office of Naval Operations. The deadlock was not broken until after the Battle of Jutland, which convinced American legislators of the need to build battleships because such vessels had saved the day for the British navy.

A revision of the stalled naval appropriations bill was initiated on 27 June 1916, and President Wilson not only supported the original program of naval construction but favored its completion in three years. Admiral Benson exerted no small influence in winning passage of the naval construction bill. After the Battle of Jutland—when the outlook seemed promising for the passage of a construction program that would provide for many capital ships to face a possible coalition of the naval forces of Germany and Japan, should Great Britain be defeated in the ongoing struggle—Benson did not hesitate to urge Secretary Daniels to add four proposals to the bill to strengthen the Office of Naval Operations. He proposed granting the CNO the rank of full admiral, authorizing him to issue orders to the fleet in the name of the secretary of the navy, designating a certain number of officers as assistants to the CNO, and stipulating retirement of the CNO at his permanent lineal rank. Teaming with Benson, Daniels conceded a great deal to the professional naval sector. He even incorporated Benson's suggestions into the appropriations bill, a turn of events that astonished Benson's critics.[21] The Naval Appropriations Act of 1916 heralded the construction of an American navy that in a few years would be second to none.

International developments during the autumn of 1916 and the early winter of 1917 did nothing either to clarify or to stabilize American policy toward the belligerents. Sentiment in the United States certainly favored the Allies, but continued British action against American commerce taxed American benevolent neutrality toward Britain. President Wilson continued his efforts to avoid belligerency after German resumption of submarine warfare in accordance with prize rules. This left naval policymakers in the dark as to American foreign policy—a determining factor in proceeding with naval expansion.

After both Kaiser Wilhelm's and President Wilson's peace initiatives fell on the deaf ears of David Lloyd George, who had just assumed control of the British government and was committed to a knockout blow, Germany resorted to unrestricted submarine warfare. Circumstances compelled President Wilson to sever relations with Germany, but he still entertained the hope of keeping the United States out of the war.

Recognizing the possibility that the United States might be drawn into the conflict, Admiral Benson sent Secretary Daniels a number of memoranda on the existing situation. The first pointed out that belligerents and neutrals, as partners to The Hague Convention of 1907, were governed by its provisions. Otherwise local neutrality regulations govern them. He explained that this made it possible for the United States to take some measures short of war, among them the adoption of the convoy, to protect its shipping on the high seas.[22]

In a second memorandum, Benson explored the pros and cons of instituting a convoy of American naval vessels to protect American shipping. Then he sent Daniels a thirty-one page memorandum prepared by his staff on "The Possibility of War." It suggested eleven measures that could be taken immediately in preparation for war, and maintained that American naval policy should serve a threefold purpose: *"(1) To develop the full military and naval strength of the United States as fast as possible, (2) To employ our forces in war so as best to build up our fighting power as an independent nation, (3) To render the maximum possible support now to the enemies of the Central Powers."* It held that the United States must "not only act quickly" but with the realization that eventually it "may have to act alone." Upon failure to adopt the convoy system and the decision of shippers and shipping agencies to keep their vessels in port, Benson pressed for arming merchant ships.[23] On 9 March 1917, President Wilson approved such a measure. Ten days later, news came that within twenty-four hours three American merchant ships had been sunk by German submarines.

The United States, though the world's third-ranking naval power, was unprepared for even a conventional war, let alone one in which a weapon heretofore unutilized was enabling the second-ranking German fleet to diminish the ability of the Mistress of the Seas to keep open supply lines, thereby threatening her with defeat. The unprecedented American naval expansion program passed in 1916 did little to prepare the United States for Allied war partnership. President Wilson was slow in implementing the provision for an increase of enlisted personnel. Officers were in short supply, and ships and naval offices were greatly understaffed. For example, Benson by January 1917 had only seventy-five officers on his staff. The navy yards were not ready for the unprecedented shipbuilding program that had been authorized. There was also a shortage of merchant ships.

Prior to President Wilson's declaration of war against Germany, Benson was limited to taking essentially defensive actions. These included augmenting the Caribbean Squadron with armored cruisers and destroyers drawn from the Pacific Ocean to ensure the security of the Panama Canal, concentrating the American battle fleet in the Chesapeake Bay, and giving orders to the commandants of the eight naval districts to ensure effective coastal defense. Only after Wilson called a special session of Congress on 21 March, to report on "grave questions of national policy which should be taken immediately under consideration," could American policymakers take definite action to prepare for the entry of the United States into war. They had to "adjust to a truly remarkable political reversal," something that could not be done overnight.[24] President Wilson finally asked Congress for a declaration of war, which he signed on 6 April 1917.

The first effort to consult with the Allies came after President Wilson wrote to Secretary Daniels: "The main thing is no doubt to get into immediate communication with the Admiralty on the other side (through confidential channels until the Congress has acted) and work out the scheme of cooperation." Upon the suggestion of Admiral Benson, Admiral Sims was ordered to London with his aide, Lieutenant Commander John V. Babcock.

Undoubtedly Benson chose Sims for this assignment because he was likely to gain the confidence and cooperation of the British. But aware of Sims's unauthorized pro-British statement in his Guildhall speech in December 1910, Benson gave him oral instructions that Sims later reported as: "Don't let the British pull the wool over your eyes. It is none of your business pulling their chestnuts out of the fire."[25] Benson did not deny that he said something to that effect, but, in quoting his words out of context, Sims did him a great disservice. He created the impression that Benson was an Anglophobe and Sims an Anglophile, an oversimplification that clouded the basic reasons for the deep conflict that developed between the two during 1917–18.

As Sims and Babcock neared the shores of England, Admiral Benson and Rear Admiral Henry T. Mayo, commander of the Atlantic Fleet, accompanied by their aides met on 10 April at Hampton Roads with French Rear Admiral Maurice F. A. de Grasset, commander of the West Indies Division, and Vice Admiral Montague E. Browning, commander in chief of Britain's North America and West Indies Squadron, to confer on the existing situation and explore the possibility of American aid. The most important item on the agenda was a British request that American destroyers be sent to the war zone. At the second session, held in Washington the next day, chaired by Secretary Daniels and attended by Assistant Secretary of the Navy F. D. Roosevelt and members of the General Board, it was decided to send six destroyers to England. This step was contrary to the accepted Mahanian precept of keeping the fleet intact—a practice adhered to by Great Britain in retaining two destroyers with each battleship in its fleet. During this two-day session British officers did not reveal the drastic situation confronting the Allies, and mutual naval planing was not considered.[26]

Meanwhile in London, Sims met with Sir John R. Jellicoe, First Sea Lord of the Admiralty, and others. In his first cable to Secretary Daniels, Sims revealed the staggering losses suffered from German submarine warfare and warned that naval forces were strained to the point that operations by all the forces except the Grand Fleet neared disruption.

British and American priorities differed at this time. The naval policy of the United States had for its goal the construction of a navy second to none, with emphasis on capital ships to enable a full-fledged engagement between battle fleets. The United States was preparing to act alone or even to face an enemy coalition in both oceans to protect its national interests should Germany defeat the Allied Powers. Washington policymakers also focused their attention on making the American navy an instrument of foreign policy in postwar peace negotiations. British leaders were most interested in gaining immediate assistance for their battle against the U-boats.

From London, Admiral Sims's recommendations reflected British views as he pressed for the immediate dispatch of all available antisubmarine ships, particularly destroyers, to the submarine zone, favored suspending construction of capital ships, and urged a concentrated effort to construct antisubmarine vessels.

In subsequent reports, Sims revealed that after facing German submarine warfare for two and a half years the British had not initiated a convoy system. Vessels needed for escort were not available. Britain depended on speed and zigzagging to protect its ships; there seemed to be no plans other than to outrun the enemy submarines and confine the German fleet to the North Sea. This latter measure forced the British fleet to remain in a narrow area—a policy criticized not only by naval authorities in Washington but also in Great Britain. Nevertheless Sims was supportive of British naval practices.[27]

A British mission headed by Arthur J. Balfour came to the United States on 22 April 1917 to press for additional American destroyers, and urged the United States to stop building the capital ships in favor of destroyers.[28] American naval policymakers proved responsive to the British request. Admiral Benson accompanied Rear Admiral Sir Dudley R. S. de Chair, who was the naval spokesman for the Balfour mission, to Capitol Hill, where he appeared before congressional leaders and urged them to make changes in construction plans.

Because such a course would leave the U.S. Navy unbalanced after the war, Colonel House suggested that Great Britain show good will by giving the United States an option to buy British capital ships in sufficient numbers to make up the deficiency. This proposal was unacceptable to the British representatives, who suggested instead a six-power alliance, including Japan, to which the Americans demurred. Both sides showed concern for postwar interests. Nevertheless, given the extreme emergency, the United States subordinated long-range naval plans to the immediate needs of the Allied war effort by revising its naval construction program to emphasize construction of destroyers rather than capital ships.[29]

While these negotiations were in progress, Admiral Benson continued his efforts to learn about Allied plans of "water strategy and tactics."[30] The information was not forthcoming—a source of American annoyance in Washington. Sims's cables and letters from London did nothing to alleviate existing dissatisfaction.

American plans to send a vast number of troops to France "in time to beat the German armies before they could gain a decision over the Allies" heightened American concern about British naval operations.[31] Both Great Britain and the United States gave serious consideration to the convoy system, and both instituted its use. Its adoption, and later the undertaking of the United States to transport a large number of American troops to Europe, sowed seeds of additional friction between Sims and Washington policymakers. The impelling British reason for the use of the convoy was protection of food and war supplies, whereas the American reason was protection of the country's military forces crossing the seas. Thus, two kinds of convoys were instituted—both requiring destroyers. As nominal commander of American destroyer forces in Europe, which were placed under Vice Admiral Sir Lewis Bayly at Queenstown, Sims held a point of view that reflected England's position. He manifested the concerns of a theater commander, whereas Benson represented those of a naval general staff of the United States with broad politico-military problems. Despite this difference, by July 1917 there were thirty-four American destroyers in England. In the words of Vice Admiral Browning "just 6 times as numerous" as the U.S. government representatives had agreed to provide, and they were "simply a Godsend."[32]

Naval policymakers in the United States became increasingly dissatisfied with what seemed to them the unduly defensive posture of the British Admiralty—which Sims supported—and the lack of mutual naval planning. During his visit to the Atlantic Fleet on 11 August, President Wilson expressed this feeling publicly in his "hunting for hornets" speech, in which he was critical of the British naval policy of chasing German submarines in the Atlantic rather than attacking them while they were still in their bases. One week later, the decision was made to send Admiral Henry T. Mayo, commander in chief of the Atlantic Fleet, to England to confer with Allied representatives about formulating more aggressive naval policies.

On 4–5 September, such a conference—to which French, Italian, and Russian ministers of marine were invited—was held in London. At its conclusion, Mayo reported to both Secretary Daniels and Admiral Benson that although the conference was very useful, it was "extremely difficult to reach any conclusions other than those of a very general nature.[33] Perhaps the most important result of the conference was that Admiral Jellicoe took advantage of Admiral Mayo's presence to begin a correspondence with Admiral Benson.

Admiral Mayo was still in London when suggestions were made to send an American mission to London.[34] Such a mission, headed by Colonel Edward M. House and including Admiral Benson and General Tasker H. Bliss, the army's chief of staff, sailed for Europe 28 October 1917. On 8 November, accompanied by Sims, Benson paid an official call on the First Lord of the Admiralty Sir Eric Geddes and the First Sea Lord of the Admiralty Admiral Jellicoe. Expressing an understanding of the need for the "defensive–offensive" measures used to the time, Benson said that he did not consider them suffi-

En route to Europe, 1917. Army Chief of Staff Tasker H. Bliss, delegation leader Edward M. House, and CNO Benson on board the USS *Huntington* on the way to Britain in November 1917. *Courtesy of the Naval Historical Center.*

cient and pressed for stronger offensive action. Sims, impressed with Benson's procedure, praised him lavishly.[35]

Admiral Benson made important decisions while in London. Upon learning why the British earlier had requested four American battleships to reinforce the Grand Fleet, he recommended that the request be fulfilled. He convinced the British that it was necessary to establish a mine barrage in the North Sea and the Strait of Dover, which, though unfinished before the end of the war, exercised a strong psychological impact on the Germans conducting submarine attacks on

Allied shipping. Benson also arranged for Sims to take on the additional duty of naval attaché in London, and authorized a planning section in London that would work closely with the British Admiralty. He assisted in drafting plans for the creation of the Allied Naval Council "to coordinate the naval operations of the Allied and Associated powers, a counterpart of the Supreme War Council that earlier had been created, to offer expert counsel on land warfare." Benson would be a member of the council, and Sims would substitute for him in his absence. Benson also proposed a plan to close German submarine bases and their points of exit from German waters by naval bombardment—something he had suggested back at the Hampton Roads conference. British representatives had reservations: they argued that in more than three years of war Germany had gained ample opportunity to fortify the coastline and harbors, making such a measure almost foolhardy. Under pressure the proposal finally was accepted, but it never was fully undertaken.

The House mission next went to France for an inter-Allied conference. A general session held 29 November erected a formal facade of unity to convey an impression of Allied solidarity and avoid a public review of differences. The real work was tackled in small committee meetings of experts. The creation of the Inter-Allied Naval Council was the greatest accomplishment of the naval authorities.

While in France, Benson met with naval and military representatives and made field trips to evaluate the readiness of French facilities to accommodate the vast numbers of soldiers the United States was planning to transport to Europe. He was unhappy with existing conditions, seeing the adverse consequences of the Navy Department's failure to establish an American naval command in France—a measure that he had recommended in May but one that was not implemented because Secretary Daniels had bowed to Sims's objections. Benson convinced Daniels to reverse his decision, and on 3 January 1918 sent Sims a cable explaining the reorganization plan. Rear Admiral Henry B. Wilson was named "Commander, U.S. Naval Forces in France," with Sims remaining "Commander, U.S. Navy Forces in European Waters." Upon returning to Washington, Colonel House told President Wilson that he had realized for some time that "there was a man in the Navy who was doing things," and now he discovered "that man was Benson."[36]

Benson left London with hope for greater understanding and cooperation between the Navy Department and the Admiralty and increased support from Sims for plans originating in Washington, but things did not work out so positively. Sims continued to support British policy and delayed transfers of destroyers from England to France. Annoyance in Washington with his procedure made him bitter, nurtured his insecurity, and intensified his fear of being either replaced or superseded by Admiral Mayo or even Admiral Benson.

Conflict arose with Great Britain over the vastly increased need for vessels to transport American troops to France. The dispute was "never resolved to the satisfaction of all parties," but it was tempered sufficiently to enable the United States to send over two million men to France by the summer of 1918. Forty-eight percent of the men were transported in British ships, with the U.S. Navy providing eighty-three percent of the convoy escorts. Rear Admiral Sir Lionel Halsey acknowledged: "Any impression that may have existed in the minds of some Britishers that the Americans were vain talkers (and I think I may say it to you without offense that *such* an impression *was* current) has been entirely dissipated, and everyone now, both high and low, is lost in admiration and respect at the businesslike way in which America has taken up her responsibilities."[37]

Much of the American military success in France stemmed in no small measure from close cooperation between the U.S. Army and U.S. Navy. Secretary of War Newton D. Baker wrote that "as proud as Admiral Benson was of the Navy, he was prouder still of his country and . . . no question of mere prestige for his service was to be allowed for a moment to stand in the way of the best thing for the country's cause." Baker found in Benson an "ideal of patriotic loyalty, wisdom, and tireless devotion." He thought it was not too much to say that throughout the participation of the United States in war, the cooperation between the army and the navy was ideal. As far as the navy was concerned, this outcome was "directly due to the broad, tolerant, and devoted wisdom of Admiral Benson."[38]

Despite the desperate military situation in France that developed during the spring of 1918, the British government undertook a number of initiatives that indicated to the United States a postwar intention to maintain commercial and naval primacy. One of the earliest signs was the trade mission led by Sir Maurice de Bunsen to South America, an obvious attempt to ensure the recapture of Britain's prewar commercial markets there. Another was the British request for an option to purchase merchant ships built in the United States as a way to compensate Great Britain for its inability to build such ships during the war, because of that nation's considerable maintenance of America naval vessels. When these efforts seemed unlikely to succeed because the United States had paid for the service, First Lord of the Admiralty Sir Eric Geddes pursued British purposes by another means. He proposed to negotiate an agreement with the United States to ensure that the ratios between warships and merchant ships built by Great Britain and the United States after the war would be the same.[39]

These British initiatives suggested to American naval policymakers in Washington the possibility that the United States would face an "overwhelming preponderance" of naval power in the postwar era, should the wartime alliance between Great Britain, France, and Italy continue, and should the Anglo–Japanese alliance due to expire in 1921 be renewed. Such an alignment of powers in the face of Japan's possible retention of the Marianas, Carolines, and Marshall Islands (which Japan had captured from Germany during the war) would strongly enhance Japan's strategic position in the mid-Pacific and weaken the position of the United States by placing a "potential antagonist squarely athwart the Navy's main lines of communication with the Far East."[40]

This concern, along with the need to compel acceptance of peace on the basis of President Wilson's Fourteen Points program, laid the foundation for the position Benson assumed in the armistice and peace negotiations.

When in October 1918 it became apparent that surrender of Germany was imminent, Admiral Benson once again accompanied Colonel House to Europe, this time on a peacemaking mission. As Colonel House's naval adviser, he had the responsibility to advise on "steps to be taken from a naval standpoint, with the enemy fleet during the armistice." The questions of freedom of the seas and the disposition of the German fleet immediately became sources of tension between Great Britain and the United States. With an eye to recent British initiatives intended to preserve British supremacy on the oceans, Benson was determined to prevent any agreements—political or naval—that might give undue advantage to the Royal Navy. He strongly defended the principle of freedom of the seas and just as firmly opposed distribution of the German fleet among the victors. To strengthen the position of the American negotiators, Secretary Daniels recommended to Congress a three-year naval construction program in addition to the one authorized in 1916 but revised to meet the wartime need for destroyers.

During Benson's second trip to Europe, an incident occurred that aroused Sims's resentment. The Allied Naval Council was scheduled to meet in Paris to consider naval terms of the armistice. While

Benson was in Washington, Sims attended the council meetings. After Admiral Benson arrived in Paris, Sims wanted to accompany him to the meetings of the Allied Naval Council and the Council of Ministers. Because Colonel House did not want Sims to attend these meetings, Benson suggested to Sims that he might as well return to London, a step that engendered displeasure and bitterness.[41]

The Allies were forced to accept President Wilson's principles for peace, the Fourteen Points and associated pronouncements, but they had reservations about a number of specific points, among them the disposition of the German fleet, the establishment of a League of Nations, and recognition of the Monroe Doctrine. Having decided to head the American peace delegation in Paris, President Wilson said that he wanted to go to the peace conference armed with as many weapons as his pockets would hold. After the signing of the armistice, Benson remained in France as the technical adviser for naval affairs to the president, spending a good part of his last year as CNO in Europe helping to make peace.

Admiral Benson held that President Wilson's best weapon during peace negotiations would be a naval construction program intended to give the United States a navy at least equal to Britain's. He maintained that to stabilize the League of Nations, it was "vitally necessary that no one power included in it should dominate in military or naval strength"; there should be at least two powers of equal naval strength. Therefore, he strongly urged passage of a bill that would give the United States the strongest navy in the world—a position he maintained throughout peace negotiations.

Before sailing for Europe, President Wilson asked Congress for a naval construction program, submitted by Secretary Daniels, that had the earmarks of Benson's advice. This program, which placed Great Britain and the United States on a diplomatic collision course, came to be known as the "Naval Battle of Paris." An impasse was avoided when the issue was taken out of the hands of naval authorities and entrusted to civilian negotiators, Lord Robert Cecil and Colonel House. Great Britain acquiesced to recognition of the Monroe Doctrine in the covenant of the League of Nations, in return for American postponement of the proposed naval construction program, which would have given the United States the strongest navy in the world.[42] Benson did not take part in these negotiations, but the agreement reflected his desire to preserve the naval construction program of 1916, completion of which would give the United States virtual naval parity with Great Britain.

President Wilson and Secretary Daniels did not always completely understand Benson's position. For the most part, however, they had concurred in his recommendations, even to the extent that the president considered leaving the conference because of British opposition to the Monroe Doctrine. Josephus Daniels later wrote: "Wilson was fortunate in having so levelheaded a Naval adviser in Paris as Benson, one whose Americanism was undiluted." Captain Pratt, who some years later himself became CNO, noted that "few people realize how many sound decisions" originated with Benson.[43]

When Benson began to feel that he was no longer useful in Paris, he requested President Wilson's permission to return to Washington, and he sailed from Brest on 11 June 1919. Back in Washington, he expended much of his time on demobilization and reorganization. Ironically, on Benson's first full day in Washington upon his return from Europe, attention centered on a problem left unsolved in Paris— the disposition of the German fleet. The Germans scuttled their interned fleet at Scapa Flow just forty-eight hours before the Allies were to take it over. In Paris, Colonel House recorded in his diary: "It is all to the liking of Benson and myself who wanted the boats sunk."[44]

High on Admiral Benson's agenda upon his return from Europe were the two items on which he could take action without congressional involvement: reorganization of the fleet and reorganization of the Office of Naval Operations.

Benson had transmitted his plans for the reorganization of the fleet to Secretary Daniels back in December 1918. Japan's acquisition of the Marshall, Caroline, and Mariana islands between the Philippines and Hawaii had greatly improved its strategic position in the mid-Pacific, and potential difficulties that could result from this expansion led Benson to propose the creation of two equally powerful fleets for Atlantic and Pacific duty. He recommended that Admiral Henry B. Wilson be named to command the Atlantic Fleet and Admiral Hugh Rodman the Pacific Fleet. On 25 June 1919, Secretary Daniels announced the creation of two fleets and, much to the disappointment of Sims and Fullam, named the admirals whom Benson suggested. Sims disliked Wilson, and William F. Fullam had had hopes of being appointed to command the Pacific Fleet.

As CNO, Admiral Benson, by creating various channels of communication among segments of the Navy Department, had broken down barriers to cooperation among them. This enabled coordination of action and accelerated accomplishments. He established a rela-

Secretary of the Navy Daniels and Benson. Shown together in Paris in 1919, the two naval leaders worked together with a minimum of disagreements for four years. *Courtesy of the Naval Historical Center.*

tively mature system of administration in the department. Considering Secretary Daniels's negative attitude toward the CNO office, Benson looked at this accomplishment with pride. He tried to establish further improvement by issuing a new organizational plan, under which two main entities within his office were created: the Planning Division and the Division of Operating Forces. The revised orders for the new divisions were issued on 1 August 1919. The Planning Division was given the responsibility for making war plans and plans for current administrative work; its members had no administrative functions. Sections within this division considered policy, strategy, tactics, education, submarines, aviation, logistics, and administrative plans. Its recommendations were to be submitted to the chief of naval operations for action. The Division of Operating Forces was made responsible for movements of all naval craft, be they surface, subsurface, or air "not specifically designated for training and experimental purposes exclusively." Officers assigned to supervise the movements of ships were to report to the CNO or his assistant.[45] This arrangement strengthened the role of the Office of Naval Operations as a centralized command post.

Having reached his sixty-fourth birthday, the statutory age for retirement, Secretary Daniels informed Benson on 24 September 1919 that, having been put on the retired list of officers, he was detached from duty as chief of naval operations. In an official memorandum, the secretary congratulated Benson on his service, noting that the U.S. Navy "was largely responsible for the final and overwhelming defeat of the enemy," and he also paid tribute to Benson for his counsel during peace negotiations as the principal naval advisor to the president of the United States.[46]

Benson automatically reverted back to his linear rank of rear admiral—just as Sims and others had after vacating their wartime posts. However, Benson did not disappear from the national scene, as President Wilson appointed him chairman of the United States Shipping Board. However, his satisfaction in remaining in government service was dampened by the naval hearings instigated by Sims with the cooperation of Fiske and Fullam in 1920, as the hearings had strong overtones of personal vindictiveness. Failing to produce affirmative measures to improve the Office of Naval Operations, this naval investigation helped rob the American navy of due credit for the part it played in bringing about an Allied victory. It distorted Admiral Benson's image, and aroused much bitterness among outstanding personalities of the time, traces of which can be felt to this day among some naval officers and naval scholars. A comment of Secretary of War Baker to Benson seems highly appropriate: "The fact is, that we have treated our War leaders shabbily. England gave her's Earldoms and fortunes, we hardly know the names of ours! Your case is peculiarly impressive since you have never said a word or nodded a hint in your own behalf."[47]

After these hearings, Benson continued to serve on the Shipping Board during the Republican administration of Presidents Warren G. Harding and Calvin Coolidge. Not until 1928, at the age of seventy-three, after almost a half century of service to his country, did Benson become a private citizen. He died on 20 May 1932, his full brevet rating having been restored to him in 1930, and he was buried in the Arlington National Cemetery with full military honors.

Admiral William Shepherd Benson merits recognition as one of the outstanding American naval officers who have played an important role in the development of the navy of their country. Appointed chief of naval operations by a secretary of the navy who at first was against such a post, Benson made the office an effective administrative organ. He was instrumental in the passage of the first naval construction program of continuity, aiming to build an American navy second to none; he prepared his country's navy to serve as an instrument of defense, and then used it at the Paris Peace Conference as an instrument of diplomacy to gain support for President Wilson's peace program. During the war he achieved unprecedented cooperation between American military and naval authorities. He had great success in enabling the Office of Naval Operations to function as a naval general staff in the face of the fact that a civilian held the highest authority over it. Benson created a naval general staff American style, and it performed well. The Office of Naval Operations that he revised remained much as he left it until 1942.

FURTHER READING

After World War I a number of participants in the events of that period, among them Secretary Josephus Daniels, Admirals Bradley A. Fiske and William S. Sims, and General John J. Pershing, wrote their memoirs. They all make a valuable contribution to American naval history and perpetuate the memory of their personal achievements as they saw them. Admiral William Shepherd Benson wrote neither his memoirs nor an autobiography. In consequence he is remembered as others portrayed him. The post–World War I hearings did not do much to rectify some of the false impressions of him.

It has been only in recent years that a number of scholars have begun to question the accuracy of the pro-Sims and anti-Benson interpretations, which do neither of these two admirals justice, as both did much toward winning the war, Benson in a position comparable to that of chief of a naval general staff and Sims as a theater commander. Among these authors are Dean C. Allard, Jr., in "Admiral William Sims and the United States Naval Policy in World War I," and "Anglo–American Naval Differences during World War I"; David F. Trask, "William Shepherd Benson," in Robert Love Jr., ed., *The Chiefs of Naval Operations;* and Mary Klachko with David F. Trask, *Admiral William Shepherd Benson: First Chief of Naval Operations,* which is the first full-length biography of Benson. The detailed analysis of the creation and functioning of the Inter-Allied Supreme War Council and pre-armistice negotiations given in Trask's *The United States in the Supreme War Council, 1917–1918* and his *Captains and Cabinets* contributes greatly to an understanding of postwar Anglo–American friction and the positions maintained by Benson in Washington and Sims in London.

The first principal in the period under study to publish his memoirs was Admiral Fiske, and his autobiography, *From Midshipman to Rear Admiral*, is helpful in acquiring an insight into his relationship with both Secretary Daniels and Admiral Benson after the latter became CNO.

Next Admiral Sims wrote his *The Victory at Sea*. Originally published in 1920, it is a review of the operations of American naval forces in Europe from the point of view of a disappointed theater commander who planned on writing it before the war was over. Sims gives ample credit to the officers engaged in various naval actions but does not acknowledge that they performed the duty to which they were ordered by Secretary Daniels and Admiral Benson. These officers did not act on their own or under Sims's actual command, but under Admiral Sir Lewis Bayly from Queenstown. In 1984 Sims's book was reprinted in the series *Classics of Naval History* under the editorship of David F. Trask, whose introduction goes a long way in rectifying the shortcomings of the original publication.

Elting E. Morison, Sims's son-in-law, wrote *Admiral Sims and the Modern American Navy*, a prolonged effort at maximizing services performed by Sims and minimizing those of Washington naval policymakers.

Understandably the most detailed account of the period from 1910 to 1923 is given by Secretary of the Navy Josephus Daniels in his two volumes: *The Wilson Era: Years of Peace, 1910–1917* and *The Wilson Era: Years of War and After, 1917–1923*. They are studies more of political strategy and diplomacy than of naval action. A valuable supplement to them is E. David Cronon's *The Cabinet Diaries of Josephus Daniels, 1913–1921*.

Paolo E. Coletta has two works of interest to this period. One is his full-length biography *Admiral Bradley A. Fiske and the American Navy* and the other a biographical essay on Josephus Daniels in *American Secretaries of the Navy*. Fiske's biography is based on official naval records and his personal diary. It is a valuable review of his accomplishments as an inventor and engineer and is a good portrayal of the transition of the American Navy from the "Old Navy" of the nineteenth century to the new one of the twentieth. In this book Coletta gives an interesting presentation of Fiske's "parting the ways" with Secretary Daniels and his resultant negative attitude toward Admiral Benson after he became CNO. It establishes Fiske's cooperation with Sims in preparation for the postwar naval hearings. Coletta's biographical essay on Daniels is, for the most part, an unbiased account of Josephus Daniels's performance as secretary of the navy. It is helpful in correcting some existing distortion about Daniels and to a lesser degree about Admiral Benson.

An important personality in Benson's Washington office was William V. Pratt, at that time in the rank of captain serving as assistant CNO. Gerald E. Wheeler's biography, *Admiral William Veazie Pratt, U.S. Navy. A Sailor's Life,* gives deserved credit to Pratt for his service to his country during very difficult circumstances. Surprisingly, however, after consulting both Benson's and Pratt's papers and knowing of Pratt's switch of admiration and loyalty from Sims to Benson, the author of this work still shows lingering misinterpretations about Benson.

There are many other studies about various phases of the period but space permits the mention of just one more: William R. Braisted, *The United States in the Pacific, 1909–1922.* The main concern of this thoroughly researched book is with the American navy's involvement in the Pacific, but Braisted makes a significant contribution to the understanding of Admiral Benson's naval policy by the association of military policy with economic considerations and foreign policy with Japan, as important factors in its determination.

NOTES

1. Bradley Fiske Diary, 20 October 1914, Library of Congress. See Mary Klachko with David F. Trask, *Admiral William Shepherd Benson: First Chief of Naval Operations,* 27–30, for the establishment of the office of the Chief of Naval Operations.

2. "Captain Benson is Appointed Chief of Naval Operations," *Philadelphia Inquirer,* 29 April 1915.

3. Klachko, *Admiral Benson,* 24–26.

4. Josephus Daniels, *The Wilson Era: Years of Peace, 1910–1917,* 243. Negotiations for the establishment of the general staff and the Office of Naval Operations are presented in Bradley A. Fiske, *From Midshipman to Rear Admiral,* 569–76; Paolo E. Coletta, *Admiral Bradley A. Fiske and the American Navy,* 149–62.

5. All letters in Benson Papers, Library of Congress.

6. Fiske's speech at the annual Naval Academy alumni dinner was reported in the *New York Times,* 15 May 1915.

7. Sims to Fiske, 10 June 1915; Sims to Benson, 26 June 1909, Sims Papers, Library of Congress.

8. Bradley Fiske, *From Midshipman to Rear Admiral,* 585. This entire passage is in italics in original.

9. "Prepare for War to Assure Peace, Advice of Admiral Benson," *North American,* 6 June 1915.

10. For the establishment of the Advisory Council, including Daniels's comment, see memorandum "Advisory Council Created in June 1915"; also Benson to Secretary of the Advisory Commission, 4 August 1915; both in Josephus Daniels Papers, Library of Congress. For Sims's assessment of McKean's appointment see Sims to Assistant for Operations (Chase), 7 July 1915, Sims Papers.

11. 3 August 1915, File No. 422, General Board Papers, Naval Historical Center; *Annual Reports of the Secretary of the Navy,* 1915, 10; *Annual Reports of the Secretary of the Navy,* 1916, 87.

12. For Benson's suggestion and its final acceptance see Admiral Benson's Notes, 28 December 1919, Benson Papers; for Benson's firmness with Secretary Daniels, see Klachko, *Benson,* 42.

13. Benson to Sims, 8 September 1915, Sims to Benson, 10 September 1915, Sims Papers.

14. See address delivered by Benson in Philadelphia and reported in *North American,* 29 April 1915; Benson, "Memorandum for the Secretary," 30 September 1915, Benson Papers.

15. See U.S. Congress, *Naval Investigation,* 1920, 1:1725. For the development of naval aviation see Reginald Wright Arthur, *Contact: Careers of U.S. Naval Aviators Assigned Numbers 1–2000.* Mark L. Bristol to Navy Department via Chief of Naval Operations, "The Organization of our Air Fleet," 8 June 1915, Daniels Papers; Archibald D. Turnbull and Clifford L. Lord, *History of United States Naval Aviation,* 21, 69; Chief of Naval Operations to Chief of Bureau of Navigation, 25 February 1915, Benson Papers.

16. "Statement by the Chief of Naval Operations," *Annual Reports of the Secretary of the Navy,* 1916, 89.

17. Memorandum for the Secretary, 22 August 1916, Benson Papers.

18. For Daniels's evaluation of Benson's accomplishments see Fitness Reports, 11 May–22 November 1915, Record Group 125: Naval Examining Board Records, National Archives. For Benson's remarks as to the achievements see "Statement by the Chief of Naval Operations," 12 October 1916, *Annual Reports of the Secretary of the Navy,* 1916, 86.

19. For Benson's role in the passage of the 1916 naval construction bill see Klachko, *Admiral Benson,* 46–51. Benson, Memorandum, 3 March 1927, Benson Papers.

20. President Wilson to Secretary Daniels, 21 July 1915, Woodrow Wilson Papers, Library of Congress. See also President Wilson's address at the Baltimore Hotel, 17 May 1915, Ray S. Baker and William E. Dodd, eds., *The Public Papers of Woodrow Wilson: The New Democracy (1913–1917),* I:331.

21. For Benson's proposals see Benson to Daniels, 26 June 1916, Benson Papers. For the provision in the appropriations bill relating to CNO see *U.S. Statutes at Large, 1915–1917,* 39:558.

22. Benson Memorandum, "Regarding Belligerents in Neutral Jurisdiction," 2 February 1917, Daniels Papers.

23. Three mentioned memoranda are: "Situation: The United States being at peace, and Germany having declared zones as per present information. Required: An Examination of the question of convoy by vessels of the United States Navy," 2 February 1917; "The Possibility of War," February 1917; and "On Arming Merchant Vessels," 14 February 1917; all in Daniels Papers.

24. David F. Trask, "William Shepherd Benson," in Robert William Love, Jr., *The Chief of Naval Operations,* 10.

25. Wilson to Daniels, 24 March 1917, Daniels Papers. For Benson's remarks to Sims, see Elting E. Morison, *Admiral Sims and the Modern American Navy,* 338.

26. Admiral Browning to Secretary of the Admiralty, 13 April 1917, Admiralty Papers, 137/1436, Public Record Office.

27. Sims's cable to Secretary of the Navy through State Department, 14 April 1917, Daniels Papers. See also Morison, *Admiral Sims,* for a detailed analysis of Sims's views of the situation in Great Britain.

28. War Cabinet Minutes, 10 April 1917, Cab. 23/2; Records of the War Cabinet, Public Record Office.

29. For this question, see David F. Trask, *Captains and Cabinets: Anglo–American Naval Relations, 1917–1918,* Chapter 3, 102–25; also William R. Braisted, *The United States Navy in the Pacific, 1909–1922,* 297–325.

30. Pratt to Sims, 15 May 1917, Sims Papers.

31. John J. Pershing, *My Experiences in the World War,* 1:49.

32. Pratt, "Autobiography," 216; about the "paramount duty of the destroyers in European waters" see cable, Daniels to Sims, 28 July 1917, quoted in Daniels, *Years of War and After,* 95. Browning to Benson, undated [July 1917], Benson Papers. Number 6 is underlined twice.

33. For President Wilson's speech and origin of the Mayo visit see Klachko, *Benson,* 76–78. For Mayo's report to Daniels and Benson of 8 September 1917, see Benson Papers.

34. Lloyd George to Colonel House, 4 September 1917, House Collection, Yale University Archives; Ambassador Page to President Wilson, 25 September 1917, Walter Hines Papers, Houghton Library, Harvard University; and later Sims to Pratt, 15 October 1917, Sims Papers.

35. Quoted in Klachko, *Benson,* 91–92, 94.

36. For the purposes of the Supreme War Council and the Allied Naval Council, see Trask, *Captains and Cabinets,* 175–79. For Colonel House's comment on Benson, see Klachko, *Benson,* 103.

37. Pershing, *My Experiences in World War,* 1:48, 52, 95, 288–89. Trask, *Captains and Cabinets,* 171–72; see also Dean C. Allard, Jr., "Anglo–American Naval Differences during World War I," 20. Halsey's acknowledgment is from his letter to Sims, 16 June 1918, Subject File 1911–1927, Admiral Sims's Personal File, Record Group 45: Naval Records Collection of the Office of Naval Records and Library, National Archives.

38. N. D. Baker to Patrick R. Duffy, C.S.C., 25 August 1932; see also Baker's letter to Duffy, 16 August 1932; both in Benson Papers.

39. For a detailed analysis of the de Bunsen mission see Mary Klachko, "Anglo–American Naval Competition, 1918–1922," 26–32. The Geddes mission to the United States is discussed in detail by Trask in *Captains and Cabinets,* 283–312. For de Bunsen's and Geddes's activities, see also Klachko, *Benson,* 115–18.

40. Stephen Roskill, *Naval Policy Between the Wars, I: The Period of Anglo–American Antagonism*, 72; Braisted, *The United States Navy in the Pacific*, 441.

41. Klachko, *Benson*, 121–32.

42. On the question of the Armistice and the Paris Peace Conference see: Braisted, *The United States Navy in the Pacific*, Chapter 24; Klachko, *Benson*, Chapters 11–12; Trask, "William Shepherd Benson," in *The Chiefs of Naval Operations*, ed. Love; Roskill, *Naval Policy*, Chapter 1; and Harry R. Rudin, *Armistice, 1918*.

43. Daniels, *Years of War and After*, 370; Pratt to Benson, 5 July 1927, Benson Papers.

44. Edward M. House Diaries of 23 June 1919, Yale University Archives, quoted in Klachko, *Benson*, 163.

45. *Revised Organization Orders of the Office of Naval Operations* (1 August 1919). For a concise, more readily available source see Klachko, *Benson*, 163–65.

46. 24 September 1919, Benson Papers.

47. 25 September 1926, ibid.

MARK LAMBERT BRISTOL: NAVAL DIPLOMAT EXTRAORDINARY OF THE BATTLESHIP AGE

WILLIAM R. BRAISTED

Mark Lambert Bristol was the quintessential line officer of the U.S. Navy's battleship age, an officer trained to address and command in any situation that might confront him at home or abroad, at sea or ashore. Bristol early identified with such other energetic line officer reformers as William S. Sims and Bradley Fiske, when to command a battleship was every aspiring young line officer's dream. Indeed, even as Theodore Roosevelt's Great White Fleet of sixteen battleships completed its world cruise in early 1909, Bristol conceived of an American navy of seventy-two battleships composed of three fleets of sixteen battleships each, one for the Atlantic, one for the Pacific, one for service in either ocean, and a reserve of one-third (twenty-four) of the active fleets.[1] It is primarily as a naval diplomat, however, that this omnicompetent line officer will be remembered. First as high commissioner to Turkey, 1919–27, and then as commander in chief of the Asiatic Fleet, 1927–29, Bristol listened sympathetically to the nationalist aspirations of Turks and Chinese at a time when Western naval men and diplomats were all too inclined to regard nationalism as a phenomenon of the Western world.

Bristol was born in 1868 in Glassboro, New Jersey, to a farm family that claimed descent from Henry Bristol, who had migrated from England to New Haven in the mid–seventeenth century. Young Mark attended public schools before winning an appointment to the Naval Academy from Democratic Congressman Thomas F. Ferrol of New Jersey. At the Academy, Bristol demonstrated ability and independence, finishing fifth among the forty-four graduates in the class of 1887. Academy records reveal that during his upper class

Mark Lambert Bristol. *Courtesy of the Naval Historical Center.*

year Bristol scored first in seamanship, second in shipbuilding, third in navigation, and thirty-eighth in conduct.[2] Most of his first ten years out of Annapolis, Bristol spent in modest assignments such as deck officer in ships of the Old Navy of wood and sail, which took him around the Horn, cruising on the China Coast, or surveying off Oregon. As a member of the gunnery crew of the first battleship *Texas,* he fought at Santiago in the Spanish–American War, a war that for him was evidence of the enlightened motives that lay behind U.S. actions.[3]

Like other progressive line officers of his day, Bristol earnestly supported the principle of line officer (military) direction of the navy and something comparable to a naval general staff. He viewed as entirely inadequate the decision by Secretary of the Navy John D. Long in 1900 to establish the General Board of the Navy with power only to advise the secretary. What was needed, Bristol insisted to Rear Admiral Henry C. Taylor, was a *"Military Executive"* with "power and responsibility." Bristol himself would never avoid "power and responsibility" even when afforded the opportunity to do so. In the later bitter controversy between line and staff officers, Bristol urged that line officers be designated by law to advise the civilian secretary, as they alone were qualified to view matters impartially.[4] Bristol never doubted his own ability to deal squarely and impartially.

Bristol moved increasingly into ordnance after the Spanish–American War, as fleet gunnery officer for the European Squadron, in the Bureau of Ordnance working on mines and torpedoes, and on the staff of Rear Admiral Robley D. ("Fighting Bob") Evans when the latter commanded the Atlantic Fleet. Impressed by his junior's unremitting efforts to design and install new gun sights before an upcoming target practice, Evans declared that Bristol's work was "enough to breakdown half a dozen men, but fortunately he was not of the breaking down kind."[5] From his orders, it seems that Bristol was constantly on the move during these years to confer with the General Board or with the inspector of target practice (Sims), to visit the Du Pont gun factories, to inquire into the manufacture of torpedoes, or to devise rules with the U.S. Army for joint army and navy maneuvers.[6]

1909 was a banner year for Bristol, bringing him promotion to commander, assignment as ordnance inspector in charge of the naval torpedo station at Newport, Rhode Island, and marriage to the intelligent and charming Helen Beverly Moore of Mobile, Alabama. The Bristols were a superb team. She accompanied him to every station except to Europe during World War I; and before the war, they bought a home at the lower end of Washington's famed Massachusetts Avenue embassy row, a clear statement of their design for living. Years later a sailor was heard to comment: "Mrs. Bristol is the real admiral, and Admiral Bristol is the loud speaker."[7] During Bristol's tenure at the torpedo station, the factory doubled its work force and increased its output fourfold. The modified Whitehead torpedo adopted during Bristol's time served the navy through World War II.[8] At the end of his Newport shore duty, Bristol was ordered to England to inspect the Whitehead Torpedo Company at Weymouth and then to visit arms factories on the Continent. His European tour ended at Genoa, where he and his wife caught the North German Lloyd steamer *Princess Alice* bound for the Asiatic Station.[9]

Bristol's two years with the Asiatic Fleet were also the first years of China's 1911 republican revolution. First in command of the old monitor *Monterey* and then of the protected cruiser *Albany,* Bristol called at south and middle Chinese ports, befriending local American missionaries and businessmen as well as the Chinese. The revolution involved Chinese against Chinese, and he found the Chinese entirely friendly toward his protection of American lives and property.[10] All was going well until the *Albany,* Bristol on the bridge, struck a rock off the South China coast. At the court of inquiry, Bristol apparently engaged in an acrimonious debate with the ship's navigator as to whether he (Bristol) had ordered a S 84°E or a N 84°E course. Fortunately for Bristol, he had friends in high places.[11] Copies of the inquiry papers were simply filed in his personnel jacket without further action. The incident evidently cost Bristol the opportunity to command the Asiatic Fleet flagship *Saratoga.*[12] It did not interfere, however, with his promotion to captain the following year (1913) or his orders to an important assignment at the Navy Department.

When Bristol reached Washington in late 1913, Rear Admiral Bradley A. Fiske, the aid for operations, pressed him to take over organization of a naval air service. A recent convert to aviation, the ever active Fiske clearly recognized in Bristol just the man to move naval aviation off the ground and out to sea. Bristol was not too anxious to enter the new field, but loyal line officer that he was, he was persuaded by Fiske to accept a job that had not yet been created.[13]

In 1913, U.S. naval aviation was still in its early, heroic age. Most aviation histories of the period tell of the exploits of young daredevil naval flyers and of shoestring enterprising by the pioneer plane builder Glenn Curtiss. Since 1911, aviation at the Navy Department had been the primary concern of the noble Captain Washington T. Chambers, who had a desk under a stairway in the State–War–Navy Building, the power to write letters, and a budget of perhaps $25,000. Pressed by Fiske, the General Board with Admiral Dewey presiding had warned Secretary of the Navy Josephus Daniels in August 1913 that a "complete and *trained* air fleet" had become "a necessary adjunct" to the navy. To press building of a naval air fleet, the board also recommended establishment of an air department within Fiske's Operations Division headed by a director of at least captain's rank and provided with assistants and authority. Daniels responded by appointing a special board headed by Chambers that asked for an appropriation of $1,297,700 for the construction of fifty planes, a fleet dirigible and two balloons, and a naval aeronautic center and flying school at Pensacola, Florida.[14] Chambers having been passed over for rear admiral, presumably for want of sea service as captain, the directorship of the new service went to the dynamic Bristol.

Without any specific appointment to his new job, Bristol was given the far side of Fiske's commodious desk and one drawer in the desk for his official correspondence file. Most of his letters Bristol wrote in longhand until he was finally assigned a regular clerk on 1 August 1914. He could look for strong support from Fiske and from Rear Admiral David W. Taylor, the new chief of the Bureau of Construction and Repair, who fought successfully for a wind tunnel and an aerodynamic laboratory at the Washington Navy Yard.[15]

Bristol moved quickly in early 1914 to transfer seven of the navy's nine pilots and nine planes to the prospective air station at Pensacola, to secure the misfit battleship *Mississippi* for experimental aeronautical work at the station, and to designate Lieutenant Commander Henry C. Mustin as skipper of the *Mississippi* and senior officer in charge. Bristol and Mustin were both men of independent disposition, and their relations were not always smooth, as Bristol, with practically no funds, sought to regulate from Washington nearly every detail at Pensacola. Work at Pensacola, however, was abruptly halted in April 1914 when planes, airmen, and the *Mississippi* were ordered to Vera Cruz and Tampico to deal with crisis in Mexico. Bristol was able to get his precious airmen, planes, and ship back to Pensacola within two months only to lose the *Mississippi* through sale to Greece. Airmen and equipment were then hardly loaded on the armored cruiser *North Carolina,* the *Mississippi*'s replacement, before the *North Carolina* too was dispatched to Europe, to assist Americans caught abroad at the outbreak of World War I. She carried with her a good part of the navy's airmen, the cooks from the Pensacola station, and the pay records for the airmen left behind. Only gradually did Bristol retrieve his airmen. The *North Carolina* did not return to Pensacola until September 1915.[16]

The harassed air chief, meanwhile, had to do much with very little. On 1 July 1914, Bristol proudly bestowed Navy Air Pilot Certificates on six naval airmen. President Wilson approved regulations for an Office of Naval Aeronautics in July 1914, but Bristol himself was only named director of naval aeronautics and given his own office the following November, when the facility at Pensacola was finally designated a naval aeronautical station. He tried to interest plane manufacturers in the navy's business with an estimated allowance of about $250,000 donated by the Navy Department's bureaus for fiscal year 1915. Secretary Daniels approved Bristol's recommendation that two planes be purchased as models from Europe, but their delivery was indefinitely postponed by the war.[17]

Bristol's pressing need was for funds budgeted specifically for naval air. Appealing to Fiske in September 1914 for support in the General Board, Bristol mourned that, whereas the Chambers Board a year earlier had recommended an air fleet of fifty planes and three dirigibles, the navy then possessed but twelve planes, none of them suited for war. Dewey and the General Board agreed that the situation of naval air was "truly deplorable," as the fleet without aircraft would be blind in scouting, unable to detect enemy submarines, and helpless against enemy aircraft. To establish an efficient air service, the General Board wanted Daniels to ask Congress for at least $5,000,000.[18]

Bristol himself wanted $1,187,000 to build essentially what the Chambers Board had recommended the previous year. To the House Naval Affairs Committee, he compared planes to torpedo boats in their ability to scout for the enemy's fleet, submarines, and mines; and he likened dirigibles to wide-ranging battleships capable of dropping "aerial torpedoes." His vision of an air service of 200 planes and 400 officer pilots was severely shaken, however, when he discovered that the prospective naval appropriations bill provided but $150,000 for naval air.[19] Probably under prodding from Fiske, Congress finally set aside $1,000,000 of previously unexpended balances to acquire and maintain aircraft and carry out experiments during fiscal year 1916. This money was specifically designed for the Naval Air Service, not subject to cuts at the discretion of the Navy Department's bureaus. Congress also approved the munificent sum of $5,000 for the prestigious new Aeronautic Advisory Board, on which Bristol would serve as one of the navy's members.[20] The prospects for naval air dimmed, however, when Secretary Daniels shipped Admiral Fiske to a quiet desk at the Naval War College. The new chief of Naval Operations would be Rear Admiral William S. Benson, an upright officer without Fiske's vision of naval air power.

Bristol's impatience to move ahead is clearly reflected in his letters to Mustin, who was safely back at Pensacola by the spring of 1915. "Don't stand for any foolishness among the men," the exasperated air director admonished from Washington. "Soft heartedness in that respect as well as in all others generally leads to all kinds of disagreeable complications."[21] Still, naval aviation moved ahead, if only slowly, in 1915 as the $1,000,000 funding by 1 July became a certainty. The first class of ten student pilots arrived that day at Pensacola, the first step in Bristol's program to induct new classes of ten students each quarter. Bristol pushed through orders for new engines in his search for a motor adequate for naval purposes as well as to replace those that had failed. A wind tunnel was in operation at the Washington Navy Yard by the end of the year, and an engine testing laboratory opened a short time later. Bristol was especially proud of a large experimental plane, with an estimated lifting capacity of 6,000 pounds, that Naval Constructor Holden C. Richardson started building at the Washington Navy Yard in the autumn of 1915. Other evidences of achievement were the establishment of air units in the Naval Militia, Bristol's adoption of the modified deperdussin system for controlling aircraft by the pilot with a stick and pedals, and the installation of a catapult (flawed as it turned out) on board the *North Carolina*.[22]

In August 1915, the irrepressible air director presented Secretary Daniels with a "Proposed Program for Further Development of an Air Fleet." Bristol declared that "command of the air is the one thing to strive for," as this command would provide "security of information," the first requirement for victory. Whereas the navy's air service then boasted but twenty officer pilots (thirteen with naval air certificates) and thirteen planes (none of them fit for more than training), Bristol wanted a fleet of 180 planes, four kite balloons, two dirigibles, and two "aircraft ships," the ships to cost some $3,000,000 each. Bristol wanted no less than $17,076,000 for fiscal year 1917, of which $4,000,000 should be made immediately available. Such an expanded air service would require the organization of four sections—for administration in the Office of Naval Operations, for the fleet, for advanced bases, and for coast defense. These sections, together with the aeronautic station at Pensacola, would in Bristol's plan all be placed under a single "Commanding Officer of the Air Service," undoubtedly the captain himself.[23]

With Fiske at Newport, the prospects for Bristol's ambitious program were not bright. An indication of hard times ahead was the announcement by Secretary Daniels in October 1915 that the director of naval aeronautics would be replaced by an officer in charge of aeronautics in the Office of Naval Operations, with funding provided by the secretary upon recommendation by the bureaus.[24] The General Board recommended an expenditure for naval air of $7,000,000 over five years, with $3,000,000 to be available in fiscal 1917. From Assistant Secretary of the Navy Franklin D. Roosevelt, Bristol learned that the $6,000,000 for "aircraft ships" would be deleted. And Daniels, apparently without even informing his naval air director, asked Congress for an appropriation of but $2,000,000 for 1917 and $1,000,000 for each of four years thereafter.

In a stellar all-day performance before the House Naval Affairs Committee in early 1916 shortly before his departure for sea, Bristol appealed for the full $13,000,000, this time without the "aircraft ships." He insisted that this large sum was essential to encourage private manufacturers and to provide advanced eyes for the fleet. He conceded that the navy had not yet acquired aircraft suitable for service with the fleet, but he remained confident of success if only Congress would vote the money.[25] With Bristol at sea, Congress in the famed Naval Expansion Act of 1916 approved expenditures of $3,500,000 for aircraft and the Pensacola air station during fiscal year 1917, $25,000 for clerical and messenger services connected with naval air, and a Naval Flying Corps of 150 officers and 350 men.[26]

A Naval Flying Corps, separate from the regular navy, was *not* what Bristol wanted. Because an airplane was to him no less a "vessel" than floating or submarine craft, officers of the air service—just like officers of other vessels—were necessarily "qualified by the most complete technical training, both theoretical and practical that it is possible to give them, beginning the training at an early age, and continuing it practically throughout a lifetime." To place them in "a separate corps for air vessels" would thus violate long established principles for the development of naval line officers. Bristol conceived air duty to be primarily for young line officers, as "the importance of the duty is not commensurate with the rank of high officers." It probably never occurred to Bristol that he, a fully trained line officer, should qualify for a naval air pilot's certificate![27] On the issue of a separate air corps, Bristol parted with Mustin and some of the navy's younger air enthusiasts. The Naval Flying Corps died in 1917 as line officers in the Office of Naval Operations found unworkable this mandate by Congress.[28]

Perhaps to avoid the unhappy fate of the passed-over Captain Chambers, Bristol secured orders for sea duty in early March 1916 to command the experimental aviation station ship, the cruiser *North*

Carolina, with the title of commander of the Naval Air Service. His job at the Navy Department was abolished, as Lieutenant C. K. Bronson was designated to take charge of aeronautics in the Division of Matériel of the Office of Naval Operations, and much of aeronautics reverted to the bureaus.[29] Bristol presumably envisioned an expanding role for himself as supreme commander of naval air ashore and afloat; but the captain fell into an ugly debate with Mustin over the alleged failure by the latter to prepare the *North Carolina* for sea, and Admiral Benson, perhaps to keep peace, removed naval air ashore from Bristol's command on 1 June.[30]

For nine months, Bristol sought to move naval air to sea on board the *North Carolina* with a defective catapult, two unsafe planes, and some spirited young airmen. In late July, Benson ordered the *North Carolina* to join an exercise with a group of destroyers on the southern drill ground that was actually a cover for a check on the conduct of the Allies in the Caribbean. "Particularly keep quiet," Benson cautioned his air commander.[31] Bristol remained at sea until December, when control of naval air at sea without the title was shifted to Rear Admiral Albert Gleaves, the commander of destroyers with the Atlantic Fleet. Gleaves's flagship, the armored cruiser *Seattle* (formerly the *Washington*), was furnished with planes and an improved catapult. The *North Carolina* was ordered to the navy yard at Portsmouth, New Hampshire, for a new catapult and other improvements. The somewhat disappointed Bristol moved to the Naval War College in the expectation that the Bureau of Navigation would eventually give him a battleship.[32]

Bristol would never again hold an important air job. He had given to naval air the vigorous leadership that was his duty as a dedicated line officer. Naval air, he believed, was essential to provide the fleet with "security of information." Given the state of air technology, he could not visualize planes as truly offensive weapons, certainly not as threats to battleships. Bristol failed in his most important objective—to create a large service under strong, unified direction. This failure must be attributed to the circumstances of the times, not to the efforts or the ambitions of the man.

Less than two months after his arrival at the Naval War College, the Navy Department sent Bristol orders to hold himself in readiness to resume command of the *North Carolina* should war break out with Germany. His clothes packed, Bristol managed to finish a thesis at the college in which he extolled the high principles of American foreign policy derived from the Declaration of Independence.[33] Joining Admiral Gleaves's Cruiser and Transportation Service, the *North Carolina* under Bristol's command escorted four troop convoys to Europe between 31 July 1917 and 18 February 1918. Her mission was to deal with any German raider that might break out into the Atlantic. Bristol's general orders reminded his crew of the high principles for which they were fighting as well as the urgent necessity for saving coal, as the ship had to complete the round trip across the Atlantic and return without refueling. On her last crossing under Bristol's command, the cruiser arrived back at Hampton Roads with just thirty-seven tons in her bunkers.[34]

Bristol's battleship command, the USS *Oklahoma,* finally came through in March 1918. The *Oklahoma* was ordered in the summer of 1918 to take station with two other American battleships at Berehaven on the Irish Coast shortly before Bristol's selection for the rank of temporary rear admiral. His new rank brought him a new job as commander of the U.S. naval base at Plymouth, England, where he was just settling when the war was halted by the Armistice on 11 November.[35] Sims then ordered Bristol to serve with British Admiral Roger Keyes on the Allied commission that accepted surrender of German naval forces in Belgium.[36] That job completed, Bristol was expecting early return to the United States when Sims recommended to Admiral Benson that he be sent as senior American naval officer in Turkish waters.[37] Little did Bristol appreciate that he was embarking on an assignment that would keep him abroad, except for a visit to the United States in 1925, for another eight years.

Bristol went to the Near East with only the most general instructions to deal with conditions that neither he nor his superiors could possibly anticipate. Turkey had fought with the Central Powers against the European Allies in World War I, but had only broken relations with the United States after the latter declared war on Germany. The United States was thus not party to any of the complex and sometimes contradictory agreements by which the European Allies proposed to reward themselves by practically dismantling the Ottoman Empire. President Wilson, on the other hand, had proposed in the twelfth of his famed Fourteen Points that the Turks should be assured sovereignty in the clearly Turkish portions of the empire and that non-Turkish people should enjoy unfettered autonomous development.

Bristol was initially given the title of senior U.S. naval officer present in Turkey, with his command embracing the Mediterranean

Bristol in Turkey, 1919. Bristol (second from right) and his staff out-side their headquarters in Constantinople. *Courtesy of the Naval Historical Center.*

east of the 21st meridian east of Greenwich and "territory known as the Near East." His task, as outlined by Admiral Sims, was to "safe-guard and assist American citizens and interests" by such actions as he deemed necessary. He was also to work cordially with Allied rep-resentatives at Constantinople and keep in close touch with Lewis Heck, the former Turkish secretary at the embassy who was return-ing to Constantinople with the title of Commissioner. Bristol was promised immediately only the USS *Scorpion,* a former yacht that had served as station ship at Constantinople before the Turks interned her during the war.[38]

En route to his new command, Bristol stopped at Paris to confer with Admiral Benson and other luminaries at the Peace Conference. The chief of naval operations warned Bristol of delicate problems ahead. Bristol was to provide all practicable aid to American government agencies, but he was to avoid being dominated by "any nationality" even as he cultivated friendly relations with all.[39] From Paris, Bristol made his way by train to Taranto, and from Taranto the destroyer *Schley*, only one of her propellers operating, conveyed him to his primary base at Constantinople, where he raised his flag on board the *Scorpion* on 28 January 1919.

Bristol quickly made himself the focus of American activities in the Near East. Finding the *Scorpion* inadequate, the admiral soon established himself at the embassy where, through seniority and force of personality, he achieved primacy over the other resident officials. Step by step, he labored to demonstrate his usefulness, if not his indispensability, until President Wilson appointed him American high commissioner at Constantinople in early August 1919, thereby according him equality with the high commissioners of the victorious Allies. Responsible both to the State Department and to the navy (through the commander U.S. Naval Forces, Europe), Bristol assumed a variety of roles on behalf of the Shipping Board, the Food Administration, various relief bodies, missionaries, and businessmen. The absence of official relations between the United States and Turkey clearly did not prevent him from cultivating the trust and friendship of the Turks.[40]

In addition to the *Scorpion*, Bristol's command initially included two other converted yachts, the *Nahm* and the *Noma*, and four subchasers. The *Nahm* and the *Noma* were soon sold off with the arrival of four destroyers. The number of ships was gradually increased as the situation became more critical. These destroyers and others added later were kept moving by Bristol on individual missions to eastern Mediterranean and Black Sea ports, providing communication between these points and Constantinople, affording transportation to Americans, rendering other assistance where practical, and showing the flag in a nonbelligerent sort of way. Bristol never got a flagship he deemed appropriate, but to support his ships he was able to assemble a considerable staff ashore at Constantinople and a cluster of backup facilities such as the large oil storage plant maintained by Standard Oil Company of New York (SOCONY).[41]

Bristol began an investigation of his area beyond Constantinople by visiting South Russia in the *Nahm* in April. He observed the first

Bolshevik capture of Odessa after the European backers of the White Russians (mostly Greeks, Moroccans, and a few French under French command) withdrew from the city, practically without warning. Odessa was then host to perhaps 130,000 refugees, only about a third of whom escaped by land or sea. The *Nahm*'s launch and her personnel worked with the American consul to assist withdrawal of proven anti-Bolsheviks. Bristol then called at Sevastopol in the Crimea, where HMS *Marlborough* had just evacuated the Dowager Tsarina Dagmar and the Grand Duke Nicholas with their large entourages. The admiral believed that the United States could best win friends in Russia by assisting the peasants, not by restoring a reactionary Old Order.[42]

With an upturn in White Russian fortunes in 1919, Bristol recommended that his good friend and classmate, Rear Admiral Newton A. McCully, be sent as commissioner to the so-called Volunteer Army of White General Anton D. Denikin, then operating in South Russia. McCully was a superb choice to head any new mission to Russia, as he had learned Russian and developed genuine affection for the Russian people while serving as naval attaché in Petrograd during the war. With unusual speed, McCully was ordered to South Russia as an observer, there to establish an "informal connection" with Denikin.[43]

Bristol's destroyers provided transportation and other support for McCully as the latter moved from point to point along the northern Black Sea littoral, observing the civil war and devising futile schemes of economic assistance until the collapse of the last White regime in November 1920.[44] Bristol then ordered the cruiser *St. Louis,* five destroyers, and a merchantman to Sevastopol even as he cautioned McCully that "measures for the sake of humanity" should not involve the Americans with the Bolsheviks. The heartsick McCully on his own initiative worked with American sailors to load some 150,000 Russians in ships bound for Constantinople.[45] Bristol then provided assistance for the thousands of Russians stranded and unwanted in the Turkish capital.[46]

Bristol sensed from the outset of his mission that the Near East, particularly Turkey, was torn by "racial" and religious antagonisms that might explode at the slightest provocation. He was wholly opposed to the Armenians who agitated for a Christian Armenian state carved from Turkish and Russian territories in which Armenians resided. And he equally rejected Greek aspirations to build a greater Greece by seizing Smyrna and other remnants of the Ottoman Empire. Armenians and Greeks, Bristol insisted, were only minorities that risked their own extermination if they provoked Turkish retaliation by pushing their separatist designs. Armenians, Greeks, and Turks being equally unprepared to rule themselves, and still less others, Bristol wanted in 1919 to place the entire Ottoman Empire under a single mandatory power, preferably the United States, charged with pushing reforms that would eventually prepare the various peoples for self-rule.

The explosion Bristol feared came in mid-May 1919 when, under the authority of the Supreme Council at the Paris Peace Conference and supported by naval units of the European Allies, Greek forces occupied Smyrna with considerable bloodshed, and began moving into the countryside. To Bristol it was "a calamity to let the Greeks take anything in this part of the world." He confessed to regard the Turks as the best in the Near East, but he also held "the Turk, the Greek, the Armenian, the Syrian, etc., if shaken up in a bag, you would not know which would come out first."[47]

Violence in Smyrna led to the appointment of an Inter-Allied Commission of Inquiry on which Bristol served with three senior European officers. The commission agreed with Bristol that Greek actions were wholly unjustified, and that the Turks would never accept alienation of an area in which the majority of the population was Turkish. To ease the crisis, the commission recommended that Smyrna be occupied by a small Allied force until the Turks, with Allied assistance, could restore orderly Turkish rule. To Bristol's distress, the commission's report was quietly shelved at the Paris Peace Conference.[48] Four days after the Greek landing at Smyrna, Mustapha Kemal disembarked at Samsun in eastern Anatolia to begin a nationalist struggle for the liberation of Turkey.

A counterpart to the Greek landings in western Anatolia was Armenian agitation for an independent Christian Armenia in the East. Well-publicized massacres of Armenians by Turks during the war had generated enormous sympathy for the idea of an independent Armenia among American church groups. Congress supplemented large voluntary contributions to fund a Near East Relief organization headed by James L. Barton, foreign secretary of the American Board of Commissioners of Foreign Missions. Missionaries, Armenian agitators, and many of Near East Relief thus formed a powerful lobby for the independent Armenia Bristol opposed. Estimating that there were but 2,000,000 Christian Armenians among the 25,000,000 inhabitants in the Ottoman Empire, Bristol insisted that no Armenian Christian state could be created without employing wholly unacceptable foreign force to overcome the Moslem majority.[49] The admiral felt vindicated by the findings of a commission under Major General James G. Harbord, USA, that an American mandate would cost $756,104,000 over five years, and by the conclusion of the so-called King–Crane Commission favoring assignment of the Ottoman Empire, except Mesopotamia, as a mandate to the United States.[50] These commission reports were also buried beyond public view.

Bristol's destroyers assisted the operations of Near East Relief by maintaining communication between Batum and Constantinople, even as the admiral complained that Near East Relief had been politicized by its pro-Armenian stance.[51] Bristol pressed his views of Armenia on the American government, which had been all but immobilized by President Wilson's incapacitating stroke and by the subsequent impasse between the president and the Senate on foreign policy. After the Soviet Union and the Turkish nationalists in 1919–20 divided Armenia between themselves, Bristol concluded that, as he had predicted, the Armenians were the ultimate victims of the animosities they had provoked among the Moslem Turks.[52] Nevertheless, a free Christian Armenia remained the dream of such unreconstructed friends as James Barton of Near East Relief, who tried unsuccessfully in 1922 to have Bristol removed as high commissioner.[53]

Bristol was also outraged by European powers that played with dividing up the Ottoman Empire among themselves. The admiral warned loud and clear that predatory European powers, especially Britain and Greece, would provoke an outbreak among the "Moslem races" against the "Christian races" that would endanger 500 Americans scattered through the Near East. Instead of driving the Turks out of Europe, the Europeans should be driven out of Turkey, in Bristol's opinion.[54] To Bristol, the bankruptcy of European Near East diplomacy was exposed in March 1920 by the great British naval demonstration and the subsequent Allied (mostly British) occupation of Constantinople. Bristol dismissed as "simply a farce" the punitive treaty of Sèvres that the European Allies forced upon the impotent sultanate in 1920.[55] With obvious satisfaction, Bristol observed to James Barton that the treaty had brought no peace, as Turkish nationalists continued their warfare against the Armenians in the East, the Greeks in western Anatolia, and the French in Cilicia.[56] He must have been tickled by the complaint of a British admiral when confronted by the limits of sea power: "Oh yes . . . we have a lot of dreadnoughts. The trouble is the damn dreadnoughts haven't got wheels."[57]

Throughout his eight years at Constantinople, Bristol was an earnest "Open Door diplomat" who devoted considerable energy to promoting American business and philanthropic enterprises in the Near East in opposition to the monopolistic Europeans. He quite clearly believed that American businessmen and missionaries were sources of betterment to the Turks.[58] Aiming to encourage a cluster of mutually supportive American enterprises that would assure the United States an important presence in the Near East, the admiral was especially upset when the Guaranty Trust Company of New York, his efforts notwithstanding, sold its Constantinople branch to the Ionian Bank, an Anglo–Greek concern. The whole idea was "one of the rottenest of things," the disappointed admiral fulminated.[59]

Bristol enthusiastically assisted American philanthropy in the Near East, provided it was nonproselytizing and without prejudice as to race or religion. He corresponded with philanthropic and missionary bodies such as the YMCA, the YWCA, the Rockefeller Foundation, the Red Cross, and Near East Relief that he believed could contribute best in education and in medicine. Caleb F. Gates, president of Robert College, shared his views on "race" and religion; Mary Patrick, head of Constantinople College for Women, helped him found the American Hospital at Constantinople, after 1945 known as the Bristol Hospital.[60] The dedicated Near East Relief worker Annie T. Allen and Halib Edib, heroine of the Turkish revolution, kept him in touch with Turkish nationalists.[61] Sometimes, however, Bristol was hard-pressed to keep American philanthropists and businessmen together in support of his policies of square-dealing toward all peoples and religions—as he observed in some despair to his friend L. I. Thomas, a director at SOCONY:

> As you know, I have always worked out here to try to get all of our Americans together for protection of American interests. Thus I have tried to get our businessmen to reconcile the differences with the benevolent institutions rather than criticize them and in the same way have pointed out to the missionaries, educators, and philanthropists that their interests depend largely upon American business interests. I have met with a good deal of success. . . .[62]

For Bristol the final vindication of his warnings and pleas for a square deal for all "races" came in September 1922 when the Turks recaptured Smyrna from the Greeks after a three-year war of national resistance. Fleeing before the Turkish onslaught were thousands of Greeks, whom the Turks in their fury were determined to expel from Anatolia. Bristol quickly responded to appeals from Smyrna by dispatching his chief of staff, Captain Arthur J. Hepburn, and three destroyers to the troubled area. But it soon became evident that Bristol could not just offer protection to American lives and property, as perhaps 250,000 homeless Greeks lined the shores of burning Smyrna with nowhere to go but into the sea. Under the pressure of the moment, Bristol organized a Smyrna Relief Committee at Constantinople, which moved food and other supplies to the stricken. Americans being more acceptable to the Turks than either Greeks or other Europeans, Hepburn was able to persuade the Turks to let Greek ships (flying no flags) with American destroyers attending embark on one of the most dramatic population lifts in history. An estimated 262,578 persons were evacuated from Smyrna and its vicinity.

Attention quickly shifted to Constantinople where a still more disastrous outbreak threatened the multi-ethnic population, as Turkish nationalist forces approached the straits. Responding to Bristol's appeals, the Navy Department eventually provided the admiral with some twenty nimble destroyers for emergency service at Constantinople or elsewhere. Fortunately, the crisis subsided as the European Allies finally concluded a truce with the Turks at Mudros on 11 October 1922, preparatory to fresh peace negotiations at Lausanne.[63]

The State Department directed Bristol to attend the Lausanne Conference as one of three American observers in association with Richard Washburn Child, the ambassador at Rome, and the minister to Switzerland, Joseph C. Grew. The Americans were at Lausanne to facilitate a settlement, not to negotiate a peace treaty; so their public actions were largely confined to statements on such matters as the Open Door, minorities, and capitulations. Bristol was evidently not entirely comfortable, as Ambassador Child, not he, would be the chief American spokesman. Grew liked Bristol for having "the best qualities of the sailorman—square, bluff, and straightforward." Bristol's "pro-Turk" attitude also gave him weight with Ismet (Inonu) Pasha, the leader of the Turkish delegation.[64] He was pleased by the evident determination of the Turks to form "a new and independent Government with modern improvements and reforms," and he watched the British very carefully.[65] The first phase of the conference broke down in early 1923, however, when Turkish pride and Western bluff failed to reach an accommodation.[66] The British later allowed to the State Department that they were displeased by Bristol's "pro-Turkish" attitude at the conference.[67]

The Lausanne Conference resumed later in the spring without Bristol and Child, to conclude a peace treaty that gave the Turks everything they had fought for. Grew then signed a separate Lausanne Treaty with the Turks for the restoration of relations between the United States and Turkey as equals. Bristol himself contributed to the normalization of Turkish–American relations by entering an arrangement at Constantinople later in 1923 that provided machinery for deciding claims by Americans and Turks for damages suffered during the break in relations.[68] In response to Turkish pressures once peace was restored, Bristol's ships were removed from Turkish waters, and the U.S. Navy's Turkish Detachment was dissolved in 1924.[69]

Bristol continued to work for a "square deal" as American high commissioner in Turkey for four years after the Lausanne Conference, partly because the navy offered him a no more interesting job and partly because restoration of relations between the United States and Turkey was held up by the Senate's delay in acting on the American Lausanne Treaty. Bristol's achievements in the Near East were clearly more significant to him and to the State Department than to the navy. When he was devoting his energies to a host of Near East problems in mid-1920, he was stunned to learn that the navy's selection board of senior admirals had passed him over for promotion from temporary to permanent rear admiral.[70] Confident that he was as actively at sea as any flag officer afloat, Bristol decided to stay where he was, to mobilize his friends, and to carry on. The "temporary" was finally removed from his rear admiral's rank about eighteen months later. In 1922, he aspired to add the title of Commander U.S. Naval Forces Europe to that of High Commissioner, but the State Department apparently feared the new assignment would diminish his effectiveness as high commissioner.[71] When three years later he sounded out the Navy Department for an interesting sea job, perhaps command of the Asiatic Fleet, he was told that his Turkish billet did not put him in line for a fleet command.[72] By 1925, the State Department was seriously embarrassed on the Lausanne Treaty from church groups and the Armenians, and President Coolidge indicated beyond doubt that he wanted Bristol to remain where he was.[73]

The Lausanne Treaty failed of ratification by six votes in the Senate in early 1927, whereupon Bristol was called upon to persuade the Turks in Ankara to accept restoration of relations without a treaty.[74] That delicate task accomplished, Bristol radioed the Navy Department that he wanted the Asiatic Fleet, a request the navy then could hardly deny a second time.[75] For Bristol's eight years as an ambassador charged with "duties of unusual difficulty and delicacy," during which he had achieved success "notable in the annals of American diplomacy," the president expressed thanks for himself and for the American government.[76]

When Bristol raised his full admiral's four-star flag as commander in chief on the armored cruiser *Pittsburgh* at Shanghai on 9 September 1927, he confronted conditions that closely resembled those in Turkey from 1919 to 1927. The Kuomintang (Nationalist) campaign to unite China had temporarily halted after Nationalist armies had swept north from their South China base at Canton to occupy the principal Yangtze River ports from Hankow to Shanghai. In China as in Turkey, the Nationalist program called for a national revival and full equality with foreign powers. Bristol found himself sympathetic with these Chinese aspirations even as he strove to work with often discordant American business, missionary, and diplomatic constituencies. Even more than in Turkey, the Open Door and independence of China were major American policy objectives, hallowed by time and by the diplomacy of a line of distinguished secretaries of state. Unlike in the Near East, however, Bristol wore just one official hat in East Asia, that of commander in chief of the U.S. Asiatic Fleet. Although he protested that his job was strictly naval, he sometimes still thought and behaved rather like a high commissioner.

The Asiatic Fleet was a fleet in name only, similar to though more impressive than the Turkish Detachment. Apart from the flagship, the fleet's showpiece, its fighting strength included about eighteen destroyers, a squadron of submarines, and a few tender-based planes. Nine or ten gunboats of as many sizes, ages, and fighting capacities were suited only for patrols on China's rivers. Responding to appeals from frightened Americans before Bristol's arrival, the Navy Department had temporarily reinforced the Asiatic Fleet with a division of three light cruisers, landed the Fourth Marine Regiment at Shanghai, and dispatched 3,000 additional marines to reinforce the 1,000 men of the Army's Fifteenth Infantry at Tientsin. The marines were organized as the Third Marine Brigade under the colorful Brigadier General Smedley D. Butler, whose immediate superior was Admiral Bristol. To the Chinese, if not to the Americans, the American naval and marine units in their country were part of a still larger foreign naval presence that included British, Japanese, French, and some others. The United States thus was intricately involved in China at a time when the American public wanted only to keep the boys at home. During conferences in Washington with the president and at the State and Navy Departments, Bristol was impressed with the importance of avoiding any conflict with the Chinese comparable to the Boxer Uprising.[77]

Bristol was far more accommodating to Chinese nationalism than were most foreigners in China. Upon assuming command, the admiral hastened to Peking to confer with American officials in North China, to meet members of the government of the Old Marshal from Manchuria, Chang Tso-lin, and to look over the situation. To General Butler and to Ferdinand Mayer, the chargé d'affaires at the American legation, Bristol expressed deep misgivings that the large American forces in the Peking–Tientsin area might provoke the very confrontation with the Chinese that they were designed to prevent, especially should the area fall to the Nationalist armies moving up from the South. It would be far better to reduce the forces as a beau geste than to confront an embarrassing Chinese demand for their

Inspecting a landing force in China, circa 1928. Bristol (at left) inspects landing force personnel at the Shanghai race course with Colonel Henry Davis, commander of the Fourth Marine Regiment, and Rear Admiral Yates Stirling, Jr., commander of the Yangtze Patrol. *Courtesy of the National Archives.*

withdrawal, Bristol argued. Only vigorous opposition from Mayer and Butler induced the admiral to maintain the marines at their existing levels for the time being.[78]

Bristol then turned southward to cruise the Yangtze from Hankow to Shanghai, meeting Chinese, Americans, and other foreigners at every port along the way. During a strictly unofficial call at Nanking, Dr. C. C. Wu, foreign minister of the still unrecognized Nationalist regime, welcomed Bristol as a friend of Turkish nationalists who would surely extend a helping hand to China. Wu questioned the admiral as to why the United States had sent such large forces to China and when they would leave, and he embarrassed Bristol by observing that the Americans in Shanghai seemed to "out British the British" in their lordly attitudes toward China's aspirations. Bristol left the interview convinced that the time had come to negotiate a settlement with the new Nanking government, a view not shared by the American legation in Peking. Nevertheless, the admiral was at pains that fall to cultivate such Kuomintang luminaries as Finance Minister T. V. Soong, Soong's three charming sisters, and the rising young general Chiang Kai-shek.[79] By friendly persuasion Bristol also induced the Chinese government's Kiangnan Shipyard at Shanghai to continue work on six gunboats that the United States had ordered for the Yangtze Patrol, notwithstanding the popular Chinese demand that all foreign gunboats leave.[80] And he vigorously objected when Ferdinand Mayer at Peking, without consulting him, suggested to the State Department that his (Bristol's) ships join with other foreign units in operations against pirates in South China waters. Apart from the fact that a diplomat had intruded in his bailiwick, Bristol opposed participation by American forces in any joint action that might link the United States in Chinese minds to the suspected designs of other foreign powers. Nor did he think that American shippers would be threatened by pirates, provided they adopted appropriate precautions.[81]

Bristol concluded before departing for the Philippines in early 1928 that, although normalcy was returning to China, it would be a long time before the Chinese could set their house in order. The Nationalists were squabbling among themselves even as they planned a further march to the North. The British and the Japanese had become more conciliatory toward the Chinese but not, Bristol was sure, because they had experienced any sincere change of heart. Predictably, the admiral held that, because the Chinese trusted Americans, the United States should promote its own policy toward China without becoming involved with others. Here as in Turkey, he found local Americans divided, the businessmen calling for a hard line toward the Chinese, and the missionaries, just the reverse.[82]

Clearly not to be undercut by the British or the Japanese and without consulting the legation in Peking, Bristol radioed the Navy Department from the Philippines that he had been convinced "for some time" that the marines in China should be reduced as they were "out of proportion to our interests as compared with other nations." Moreover, the British had cast the United States in an "unfavorable light" by "decidedly" reducing their landing forces. The admiral agreed to withhold a recommendation for sweeping withdrawals until the fate of North China had been decided, but he still proposed that no replacements be sent to fill vacancies as they appeared in the marine expeditionary force. This plan for reduction by attrition was approved by Admiral Charles F. Hughes, the chief of naval operations.[83]

Bristol's plan immediately provoked outcries from Ferdinand Mayer in Peking and from Minister John V. A. MacMurray, then in Central China. Both diplomats agreed that any reductions might destabilize the situation by encouraging provocations by the Chinese. MacMurray expressed "complete surprise" that Bristol had recommended the reduction without consulting him, the more so since the admiral had usurped "the function of the diplomatic representative" by commenting on Chinese politics.[84] The collision between Bristol and the diplomats having become a matter of turf, Stanley K. Hornbeck, chief of the State Department's Division of Far Eastern Affairs, declared that Bristol had "encroached" on MacMurray's prerogatives and that the admiral's encroachments would "continue and expand" unless halted.[85] Secretary of State Frank B. Kellogg advised the Navy Department that, "since the very crisis for which our forces in China were augmented seems to be approaching, a reduction of strength at this time seemed inappropriate."[86] Without conceding any intrusion on his part, the unflappable Bristol blithely reaffirmed his purpose "to stick to the clearly defined duties of the Commander-in-Chief" and to cooperate "in the closest way possible . . . for the furtherance of American interests, ashore and afloat."[87]

Bristol withdrew from Chinese waters during the early months of 1928 to inspect the navy's outpost at Guam and then to attend the inauguration of Governor General Henry L. Stimson at Manila. His northward return in April and May was marked by lavish British entertainments at Hong Kong, more "unofficial" calls on the Chinese at Canton, and the first official visit by a commander in chief of the Asiatic Fleet to Japan since the great earthquake of 1923. The Japanese regaled the visiting Americans at a series of parties in the flowering spring even as Chinese Nationalists and Japanese clashed at the Shantung provincial capital of Tsinan. Like other admirals, Bristol insisted he wanted a minimum of pomp and entertaining, but like them he probably enjoyed the pageantry of naval visits. At the same time the round of parties did not influence his judgment. Bristol believed the Japanese would adopt all means necessary to gain a special position in China. The Americans could only blame themselves if Japan gained rights prejudicial to the United States, the admiral averred.[88]

The Tokyo pleasantries completed, Bristol made a sixty-nine-hour dash by train and ship for Peking. The admiral was anxious to work things out with MacMurray and to indoctrinate the unpredictable General Butler before the Peking–Tientsin area was engulfed by civil war. Secretary Kellogg, perhaps inadvertently, came to Bristol's support by warning MacMurray that the admiral, being responsible for defense measures, would determine to what extent American forces should cooperate with the forces of other powers.[89] Bristol found the Americans in Peking confident that Chang Tso-lin's trained soldiers could surely resist the Nationalist tide. As it turned out, however, the Kuomintang and its allies swept to victory, and only with some difficulty did Bristol get back to the flagship *Pittsburgh* on 2 June 1928, just ahead of Chang Tso-lin and his fleeing Manchurian army. The marines had been involved in no incidents with the Chinese. Indeed, the admiral concluded that their presence might have restrained the Japanese from attacking the Chinese. He also confirmed to his own satisfaction that the "very charming, agreeable, and intelligent" Minister MacMurray assumed himself to be responsible for directing the U.S. Navy, Bristol included, in the protection of Americans.[90]

Bristol ended his first year in China aware of a new spirit among the Chinese that foreigners could ignore only at their own risk. Unwilling to call this spirit nationalism, communism, or radicalism, the admiral preferred to label it "self assertiveness," believing it arose from a feeling among the Chinese that they were the victims of foreign high-handedness. Foreigners having demonstrated little concern for China in the past, Bristol expected the Chinese to be even less considerate toward foreigners in the future. The Chinese would press for justice as soon as they had the power to do so:

That the spirit of revolution against the old order of things in China is well lodged in the minds of the people there can be no doubt. It is healthy and growing and it may develop rapidly. . . . They will suffer least who recognize soonest this existing situation and prepare to meet it by the cultivation of good relations, square dealing, and fairness.

The admiral doubted that foreign warships or foreign merchantmen would be allowed to operate much longer in China's internal waters. The Chinese like the Turks would be masters in their own house.[91]

Bristol, Butler, and the Navy Department pressed successfully during the last six months of 1928 to secure withdrawal of the bulk of the marines from China. MacMurray repeated in vain the received wisdom from earlier generations of foreigners in China that "the greater more impressive force tends strongly to minimize the danger of ill considered action by Chinese."[92] The final clash between Bristol and MacMurray came when the commander in chief proposed to withdraw all but a 500-man legation guard from North China and to bring the Fourth Marines to full strength at Shanghai, a central point where American interests were far more important than in the North. MacMurray argued for the larger force to be stationed in North China, and Assistant Secretary of State Nelson T. Johnson held that, because Minister MacMurray had primary responsibility for protecting Americans in North China, his view should prevail.[93] Bristol ultimately won, and the admiral radioed the Navy Department on 15 January 1929 that the Third Marine Brigade had ceased to exist with the departure of General Butler, marines, and dependents from Tientsin.[94] The State Department successfully opposed a move to recall the Fourth Marines from Shanghai in May 1929, and the famed unit remained in China until it was finally shifted to the Philippines in late 1941, shortly before the outbreak of World War II.[95]

Meanwhile, Bristol looked to the Americans to guide China's reconstruction. He was pleased when the United States reached a settlement with the Nanking government ahead of other powers and when the Nationalists invited the Kemmerer Commission of American economic experts to advise China on financial reform. He also warmly supported a request from the Chinese naval authorities that Chinese be accepted at the Naval Academy, writing Secretary of the Navy Curtis D. Wilbur:

I have become convinced not only from my own past experiences in the Far East but more particularly since I have been here this time that American influence in China during the present evolution of a new China is most important for the Chinese people, for the nations of the Far East, and for the interests of the world. I believe the Chinese would accept guidance from us when they would hesitate to accept the same from any other country.[96]

The Chinese were turned down, apparently because the navy's Bureau of Navigation did not want to be bothered with training Chinese midshipmen. Bristol must have been disappointed when later in the year the Nanking government contracted to employ British naval officers as instructors in the Chinese navy.[97]

At the conclusion of his cruise in command of the Asiatic Fleet, Bristol summarized his mission and that of the U.S. Navy in East Asia in Asiatic Fleet Order No. 1-29 and in a long letter to Secretary of the Navy Charles Francis Adams. Bristol insisted to Adams that the navy was not just for parade:

> The Navy is not primarily for threatening or active operations against people like the Chinese to enforce our rights at the muzzle of a gun. The Navy as an agent of the Government has a positive mission to assist in the maintenance of peace which is just as important as its warlike mission in defending the country.

Bristol had had "quite a bit of difficulty" with the indoctrination of his officers, who were too much taken by the slogan among certain foreigners "that the Chinese only recognize force and if you took 'a firm stand' and told the Chinese 'where to get off' they would respect you and you lose all prestige if you adopt any other method of dealing with them." There should be no "blustering or threats" but also no hesitation to use force when force was called for. Conceding an inclination among the Chinese to scrap among themselves, he also recognized in them a capacity "to unite as a whole when races or nations from outside interfere with their internal affairs."[98]

In his fleet order, Bristol admonished his command:

> Good will and natural respect of all nations and peoples are not attained by swagger and swashing, or by showing a superiority in dealing with other races having different standards and ideals. Nor are they attained by continually rattling the sword in the scabbard, by parading armed forces and men of war as a display of power, or making fluffs, when the ultimate use of coercion is not contemplated. On the other hand, good will and mutual respect will be established by dignified association with foreign peoples, by treating them with consideration which urges them to give some consideration in return, by recognizing that there are two sides to every story, and by being very fair and square in all dealings.

After repeating the American policies toward China to promote the Open Door, to discourage outside interference in Chinese domestic affairs, and to support the territorial integrity of China, Bristol warned that the Asiatic Fleet bore a "heavy responsibility to prevent incidents which will necessitate the employment of force to protect American interests." Specifically, Bristol directed his men:

1. To avoid bluffing on the assumption that the Chinese would not stand up against force, remembering that a dignified evacuation was far better than defeat.
2. To avoid any collision with Chinese government forces unless American ships were fired upon without provocation.
3. To protect American lives against mobs, by evacuation if necessary.
4. To protect American property but not to the point of killing.
5. To avoid provoking an outbreak comparable to the Boxer Uprising.
6. To assist with the defense of no foreign concession except the International Settlement at Shanghai. Nor to engage in any joint action with other forces under a unified command.
7. To avoid any operations outside the Shanghai International Settlement except in conformity with the Fleet Order.
8. The Legation Guard to remain quartered within the American legation compound unless otherwise directed by the Commander-in-Chief.[99]

The admiral's letter to Secretary Adams and his order to the fleet were vintage Bristol, a clear expression of his philosophy on dealing fairly and squarely with the peoples of the non-Western world. His views accepted the changed conditions of the twentieth century under which older methods of gunboat diplomacy could no longer succeed. They were clearly in advance of many State Department officials in China, the local business community, and probably even the personnel of his own command.

When Bristol hauled down his flag as commander in chief in September 1929, he lost two stars and reverted to the rank of rear admiral, the highest permanent rank in the U.S. Navy at that time. For his last duty, he secured orders to the General Board at the Navy Department, the distinguished group of elder naval statesman who advised the secretary on naval building programs, naval arms limitation, and such other policy matters as the secretary might refer to them. In the spring of 1930, upon the retirement from the board of his friend and classmate Rear Admiral Andrew T. Long, Bristol became the board's senior member and chairman of its executive committee, a position close to the top of the Washington naval establishment, in status if not in power. The Bristols returned to their Washington home in easy stages, taking the trans-Siberian railway to Europe, stopping in Paris, and arriving in Washington in November.[100]

Anglo–American naval relations were frigid when Bristol reported to the General Board. The War Plans Division of Operations held in 1929 that first priority should be given to plans for war against Japan, Britain, or an Anglo–Japanese coalition, a sentiment that quite evidently also extended to the General Board. The immediate point at issue was whether the United States, Britain, and Japan could agree on limitations covering the lesser classes in their navies, especially cruisers, without upsetting the famous 5–5–3 ratio in capital ships and aircraft carriers that the three great naval powers had accepted in the five-power Washington Naval Treaty of 1922. Since 1922 it had been axiomatic in the General Board that the U.S. Navy must preserve parity with the British navy (represented by 5–5), and that the United States should build cruisers only of the most powerful type allowed by the Washington treaty, the so-called treaty cruiser of 10,000 tons mounting 8-inch guns. The subsequent three-power Geneva Naval Conference of 1927 had broken down, however, over the divergent claims of the British for a large number (seventy) of smaller, less heavily gunned (6-inch guns or less) cruisers and of the Americans for a much smaller number of the largest cruisers allowed. The General Board wanted 8-inch-gun cruisers to offset the cruiser preponderance that the British might gain by arming with guns of smaller caliber their numerous merchant ships suitable for conversion. The heavier cruisers also had broader cruising ranges that would permit the Americans to operate against the British and the Japanese where the United States lacked naval bases. The breakdown at Geneva provoked the Congress, prompted by the General Board, to approve a cruiser bill in 1929 that brought to twenty-three the American authorized strength in the large "treaty" cruisers, only two of which actually had been completed by 1930.

The new American administration of Herbert Hoover and the new British Labour cabinet of James Ramsay MacDonald sought to avoid a disastrous Anglo–American naval race by devising a "yardstick" that would provide theoretical "parity" between the world's two greatest navies even as it met their needs for different types of cruisers. Two categories of cruisers would be provided, the heavy 8-inch-gun "treaty" cruiser and a lesser cruiser mounting guns no larger than 6-inch caliber. By applying a complicated yardstick of variables, theoretical parity between the two navies would be assured, allowing the United States a somewhat larger number of the 8-inch-gun cruisers, while Britain would compensate for a smaller number of heavies by maintaining a larger number of 6-inch-gun cruisers. In early September 1929, Britain proposed a scheme whereby the United States could complete only eighteen of the twenty-three 8-inch-gun cruisers authorized by Congress, as compared with fifteen allowed the British. The British scheme, however, would permit the United States to complete 70,000 tons of 6-inch-gun cruisers that the General Board (and Bristol) did not want. Only under pressure from the White House did the General Board concede a reduction of the American heavies to twenty-one but no more. There the matter rested when Britain issued invitations to a five-power naval conference to convene at London in late January 1930.[101]

Bristol, of course, subscribed fully to the General Board's position that the naval needs of the United States should not be sacrificed to British convenience.[102] More accommodating to British wishes and to the Hoover administration's diplomatic priorities, however, was Admiral William V. Pratt, then commander in chief of the United States Fleet, who had been one of the architects of the 1922 Washington Naval Treaty. Whereas Bristol like many others of his generation in the U.S. Navy did not dismiss the possibility of war against Britain, Pratt conceived of a world order resting on Anglo–American understanding that would permit the British the naval types they wanted.[103] Pratt's designation as naval advisor to the American delegation at the forthcoming conference did not augur well for the General Board's position. Bristol could gain some comfort, however, in the fact that Rear Admiral Hilary P. Jones—the navy's leading authority on naval arms limitation, who had clashed with the British in 1927 and whom Bristol had idolized since their Naval Academy days—was also going to London as naval advisor.[104]

From Bristol's point of view, the negotiations leading to the 1930 London Naval Treaty were disastrous. His friend Hilary Jones withdrew from the conference on grounds of ill health, but probably also, as Bristol suspected, because the American delegation ignored his advice for that of Pratt. The American delegation, working with Pratt, agreed to a treaty that essentially incorporated the British proposal on cruisers and raised the ratio of cruisers and destroyers allowed Japan by about ten percent above the Washington Naval Treaty ratio (5–3). Japan's ratio in cruisers and destroyers was increased from 10–6 to 10–7, and Japan received parity in submarines. The London treaty also delayed replacements in the American battleship line by five years.[105]

The ranks of the naval critics were further depleted when Admiral Charles F. Hughes, the chief of naval operations and ex officio chairman of the General Board, suffered a debilitating stroke. Rear Admiral William H. Standley, the assistant chief of naval operations, thus alerted Bristol that he, Bristol, should put together the General Board's case against the treaty.[106] Bristol's immediate reaction to early reports of the London treaty was that the United States had sacrificed the ratios of 1922 at a time when the naval building approved by Congress and the deplorable financial situation of Britain and Japan placed the United States in a commanding bargaining situation. "War between Great Britain and the United States will be banished when mutual respect is established," the admiral grumbled to Assistant Secretary of the Navy Ernest L. Jahncke. "The ugly children of competition in naval armaments" could only be banished by an agreement that would "wipe out the justified feeling of lack of square dealing, fair play, and fifty–fifty compromise."[107]

Before the Senate Committees on Foreign Affairs and Naval Affairs, Bristol read a lengthy prepared statement in which he reviewed the General Board's policy since 1922 of building only cruisers of 10,000 tons mounting 8-inch guns, and he claimed the savings ascribed to the London treaty were negligible. In addition to reducing the U.S. Navy to but eighteen 8-inch gun cruisers, ten fewer than the General Board had sought after the breakdown of the 1927 Geneva Conference, the treaty granted the United States 70,000 additional tons of 6-inch-gun cruisers that, to Bristol, were unsuited to American requirements. The delay in battleship replacement, in Bristol's opinion, would only cause a disorderly rush in big ship construction five years later. Bristol wound up his statement by suggesting that the senators ask themselves a series of questions: "Is the Treaty a square deal?" Did it promote international good will? Was it necessary to abandon the principle of naval parity with Britain that the United States had followed since 1922? And more.

Bristol intended the answer to all these questions to be a resounding "No," as became abundantly clear when the senators pressed him with queries. Given the fact that the United States had but eleven cruisers to Britain's fifty-four at the outset of the conference, it would have been far better in Bristol's view had the United States continued building under its approved program until Britain and Japan were willing to accept a "fair" treaty.[108] Backing up Bristol in his opposition to the treaty were all members of the General Board, Admirals Hughes and Jones, and a good part of the naval establishment. Those supporting the treaty were the state and naval secretaries, Admiral Pratt, and three other able officers. The political clout of the Hoover administration and its peace-loving constituencies moved the Senate to approve the treaty, by a vote of 58 to 9.[109]

Bristol's success as senior member of the General Board would depend on his ability to accommodate to his immediate superior, the chief of naval operations. In September 1930, Admiral Hughes was succeeded as CNO and as ex officio chairman of the General Board by Admiral Pratt, with whom Bristol had differed over the London Naval Treaty. Pratt had graduated two years after Bristol from the Naval Academy; they had been shipmates on the Asiatic Station in the early 1890s; and Bristol had admired Pratt's important but inadequately recognized contributions in the Office of Naval Operations during World War I. Perhaps to avoid unnecessary tangling with his old shipmate, Pratt graciously left to Bristol the conduct of the General Board's business.[110] Pratt attended General Board hearings, but Bristol, unlike his predecessors, signed the board's reports as its senior member. Pratt probably lost far less than he gained by according a dignified, separate status to Bristol, as he retained the freedom to differ with the board in his recommendations to the secretary. As senior officer on the General Board, Bristol was senior among a distinguished group of individuals, many of whom had come from or would be going to important commands. Bristol's task, it seems, was to coordinate and to promote consensus. Although the admiral's views can be sensed in the board's recommendations, Bristol was not in a position to exert the highly visible leadership that he demonstrated over naval air, in Turkey, or in command of the Asiatic Fleet.

Bristol moved in consultation with Pratt, Secretary Adams, and other board members to alter significantly the character of the board by removing its ex officio members: the CNO, the president of the Naval War College, the director of Naval Intelligence, and the commandant of the Marine Corps. It was Bristol's position that the board should be composed of senior officers without administrative or command responsibilities, who could provide the secretary with impartial advice. This was not the case, Bristol argued, when members had their special interests to defend:

You have only to come here to these conferences a few times to notice that the individual is human and he is working for his own special office, and you don't want to put him in that position of trying to do two things, looking out for his own interests and at the same time be perfectly open minded in his recommendations for the service at large.[111]

On 1 March 1932, the Navy Regulations were altered to meet Bristol's wishes that neither the board nor its members should have any executive or administrative duties. Its membership would include five line officers, a majority of them of flag rank, and a general of the Marine Crops if deemed advisable.[112] Only two months before his retirement, Bristol began signing the board's papers as its chairman, not as its senior officer present. For a person of Bristol's strong character, the new system obviously provided the board and its chairman with dignity and independence that they had not enjoyed when they were sitting in the shadow of the CNO. The secretary could look to both the board and the CNO for advice, but he was more likely to heed the CNO should the latter differ with the board. The removal of the board's ex officio members may have separated the board somewhat from the action in the Navy Department, however, and contributed to its gradual demise over the years.

Undoubtedly, the most important objective for Bristol, as for other General Board members, was to build the navy to treaty limits so that there would be no further erosion of naval ratios at the naval conference scheduled for 1935. Apart from the unfinished 8-inch-gun cruisers, the most important new ships allowed under the treaties were 55,200 tons of aircraft carriers and 73,500 tons of the 6-inch-gun "London treaty" cruisers. The London treaty also allowed the United States to build twenty-five percent of its cruisers as "landing deck" cruisers, but Bristol did not share the enthusiasm of such airmen as Rear Admirals William A. Moffett and Harry E. Yarnell for that option. Bristol and the General Board proposed building up the navy during fiscal year 1932 by laying down one 13,800-ton carrier, two 6-inch cruisers, eleven destroyers, and four submarines, a program approved by the administration save for the substitution of a landing deck cruiser for one of the 6-inch-gun cruisers.[113] Bristol supported the 6-inch-gun cruiser on the ground that he must obey the treaty, but he was most skeptical of the landing deck cruiser. He regarded the House Naval Affairs Committee's approval of the landing deck cruiser as evidence of "the tail wagging the dog" where "aircraft is the tail."[114] Unfortunately for the Navy, the bill passed the House but failed to reach the Senate floor before its adjournment on 3 March 1931.

The Great Depression, budget cuts arising therefrom, and President Hoover's predilection for arms limitation destroyed prospects for much more than a slow continuation of the navy's 8-inch-gun cruiser program. Nevertheless, the General Board went through the process of preparing a naval policy to conform with the new treaty situation, at least two building programs for fiscal year 1933, and schedules for building to treaty limits in either ten or fifteen years. The board's first program for 1933 was rejected by the Budget Bureau; Bristol did not know what happened to the second.

The admiral had far more friendly support in the congressional naval committees than in the administration. Carl Vinson, chairman of the House Naval Affairs Committee after the Democrats won the House in 1930, prepared a bill without administration approval that provided for the construction of 120 vessels at a cost of $616,000,000, a bill suspiciously close to the General Board's own ten-year program. Republican Senator Frederick Hale proposed a bill to authorize building the navy to treaty limits at an estimated cost of $988,705,906. Bristol declared himself in favor of either bill or, better still, a combination of the two! Vinson affirmed it the responsibility of Congress to establish naval policy.[115] He would wait two years for a new administration before he could secure congressional authorization to build the navy to treaty limits.

Bristol remained true to the battleship to the end of his career. In the spring of 1931, he and Pratt both joined the fleet at Panama to witness Fleet Problem XII. Perhaps to counter the effects of Fleet Problem IX two years earlier, when carrier-based air evaded defending forces to attack the Panama Canal, the superior Black battleship fleet in the new exercise would attack the Panama and Nicaraguan canals against Blue's superior air power. Bristol concluded that the superior Black battle fleet had won control of the sea by the end of the exercise, and Pratt agreed that the battleship had been demonstrated still to be the backbone of the fleet.[116]

While Bristol was at Panama, the specter was raised that the European powers—Britain, France, and Italy—might use the forthcoming General Disarmament Conference sponsored by the League of Nations as an occasion to strike down the giant battleships, perhaps reducing their upper weight limit from 35,000 to 25,000 tons, and the caliber of their main battery guns from 16 inches to 12 inches. Here was a challenge to the American battle line as serious to Bristol as the British assault on the American cruiser program. At hearings before the General Board, Pratt observed that the issue was not whether the United States wanted 35,000-ton battleships but whether it would be forced to accept less.[117] Indeed, by May 1931, Pratt, with Secretary Adams's concurrence, assured Secretary of State Stimson that, notwithstanding opposition from practically the entire General Board, he would be willing to reduce the battleship upper limit to 27,500 tons, and the big gun calibers to 12 inches, provided all other nations adopted the same standard.[118]

Here again Pratt was accepting compromise, as he had at Washington in 1922 and London in 1930; but Bristol was in no mood to compromise, as he informed the General Board during its discussion of policies that would be followed at the forthcoming conference:

> The Board can't go—and I suggest it should not go—on the principle that we have got to accept anything but what is right. As regards the President or as regards the people we must say what we believe should be the right thing for the Navy of the United States. If that is not acceptable to the civilian body of the United States why then we should be called upon to modify it to suit their instructions and their ideas and then come to a compromise if we have to. . . . We should say what we believe is right.[119]

The General Board, Bristol signing, remained unbending in its support of the existing battle fleet limits without any reduction in numbers, tonnages, or gun calibers:

> Under no consideration should we permit our national security to be threatened by whittling away our battleship strength unless and until it becomes evident that the battleship has ceased to be the backbone of the fleet—a contingency which appears less probable today than ten years ago.

To concede any reduction in the battleship fleet would only diminish the naval strength of the United States as compared with other nations (Britain) that possessed numerous well-placed naval bases and an abundance of ships in other classes. The board urged, therefore, that the United States permit no opening of the battleship question at least until the Washington and London naval treaties came up for reconsideration in 1935. Pratt agreed that the battleship question should be postponed until 1935, but he distanced himself from the General Board's adamant opposition to any reduction in existing limitations. Secretary Adams approved the CNO's position, and Bristol could do no more than note the "action" of the secretary.[120] Bristol's resistance to any erosion of the battle fleet and his warm support of building to treaty limits were both evidence of the horror with which he regarded agitation by "pacifistic societies," which in his view were far more dangerous to the navy and the nation than "communistic agitators" because "pacifistic ideas," unlike the "red influence," were likely to persuade the American people.[121] The statesmen at the 1932 Geneva Disarmament Conference met, debated, and reached no agreement.

The Far East also attracted Bristol's attention after the Japanese invasion of Manchuria in September 1931 and the subsequent spread of Sino–Japanese hostilities to Shanghai. Secretary of State Stimson declared himself "rejoiced" by Bristol's suggestion in October that the two restore their relations to the "old basis" they had enjoyed when Bristol commanded the Asiatic Fleet and Stimson was governor general of the Philippines.[122] The secretary, however, apparently left Bristol watching unhappily from the sidelines without pressing for the admiral's advice. Bristol wanted the United States to uphold impartially and "without bluff" as "an honorable contract" the Nine Power Pact of 1922 in support of China's independence.[123] But his was an isolationist stance that the United States should "put its own house in order without worrying abut other nations unless we can help ourselves by doing so."[124] Obviously disapproving the high profile of Stimson's nonrecognition diplomacy, Bristol feared that the United States by going too far had earned the ill will of both the Chinese and Japanese when the Chinese "would have settled it themselves, though it would have taken them a long time." "We are sitting on a volcano," he complained in the spring of 1932.[125] Bristol clearly agreed with conservatives in the navy who wanted to remain clear of the Sino–Japanese fracas.[126]

Some months before his retirement on 2 May 1932, Bristol allowed that he would welcome a position in business that would enable him to serve the American people and supplement his retirement pay.[127] No tempting offer came, however, to lure the Bristols from Washington. The admiral was clearly delighted by the nomination of his former associate, Franklin D. Roosevelt, as Democratic Party presidential candidate in July 1932. His offer of support was authentic Bristol:

> I am strongly urged that I still have a mission to continue service to the country even after retiring from active service of forty-nine years. The country has a right to expect service from us all, especially under present conditions. You are undertaking to give the greatest service.

I can help you. I want to do anything I can to assist our people to regain their confidence and their belief that the principles of honesty, truthfulness, and square dealing upon which Washington, and our forefathers established our great republic do still and always shall prevail in both our national life and in our international affairs.[128]

Again, apparently, no call came, and Bristol continued to busy himself with various activities open to distinguished retired elders who chose to remain as decorations on the Washington scene—serving on the District of Columbia's Democratic Party Committee, supporting projects on behalf of White Russian refugees or the American Hospital at Istanbul, dabbling in business, and maintaining memberships in a half-dozen clubs in Washington, New York, and Connecticut. Death came to the admiral on 13 May 1939.

Mark Bristol's formative years were the early years of an expanding imperial America when Theodore Roosevelt called the nation to lead by setting an example of fair and square dealing. Like T.R., Bristol was a man of tremendous energy, deeply convinced of his own ability to recognize right and to act on it. Also like T.R., Bristol never doubted his ability to judge impartially. He liked to think of himself as above factionalism and therefore qualified to serve as arbiter between Greeks and Turks, businessmen and missionaries, Asians and Europeans. If he misled anyone, it was himself insofar as he clung to his belief in his own impartiality in human affairs. He differed vigorously with others, but he commonly regarded these differences as a challenge to convert the others to his way of thinking.

Bristol was a sincere patriot when patriotism for most Americans was fairly uncomplicated faith. For him the United States, moved by altruistic and democratic ideals, had a mission to enlighten the world. This patriotism was basic to all his endeavors as a naval diplomat. Surely Bristol will be longest remembered for his sympathy for and successful approach to non-Western peoples. But his championing of Turks and Chinese, of course, was inextricably linked with his ambition to win for the United States a major place in the Near East and East Asia. His suspicions of Great Britain, not uncommon among American naval men of his day, reflected his anxiety that the longtime mistress of the seas was not yet ready to accept the United States and the U.S. Navy as equal. For individual Englishmen, such as Lieutenant General Sir Charles Harrington, the British commander at Constantinople, he had the highest admiration. In his 1917 War College thesis on "Policy," he pointed to Britain as a nation whose policy was based on righteousness and justice as the British people pressed their will on the privileged classes.[129]

Above all, however, Bristol was the epitome of the able, energetic line officer of his day, convinced of his ability to succeed in any mission that might come his way. This conviction was linked from his early years to his enthusiasm for gunnery and battleships. He performed his service with naval air without ever doubting that the airplane was simply another type of naval vessel to be commanded by line officers and fitted into a doctrine of battleship supremacy. Undoubtedly, he would have opted for a command in the battle fleet at the close of World War I; but the accident of his selection for duty in Turkey opened for him a career of far more lasting distinction than he would have received had he mounted a low rung on the ladder of command in the main fleet. Finally, as senior officer on the General Board, he pressed for an institutional reform that would promote his ideals as a line officer, when he sought to enhance that body of distinguished elder statesmen by freeing them from the partisan tugs that even senior line officers were exposed to when serving in active commands and administrative jobs.

FURTHER READING

Mark Bristol is a superb subject for a first-rate biography that has yet to be written, not just because of his achievements as a naval officer but also because of the light that his biography would shed on many naval, diplomatic, and other interests of his day. Moreover, the materials for such a biography survive in abundance. Most notable are the Bristol papers at the Library of Congress, numbering more than 40,000 pieces in over a hundred containers. Much of this Bristol material, including extensive diaries, relates to the admiral in Turkey, but there is a good deal more that Mark and Helen Bristol obviously saved with historians in mind. Bristol's personal letters are especially significant for what they reveal of his personality and his diverse contacts inside and outside the navy. In addition to diplomats' papers that contain occasional Bristol items, Bristol also appears in the papers of such naval men as William S. Sims and Henry C. Mustin at the Library of Congress as well as Lyman Cotten at the University of North Carolina, Chapel Hill. Bristol's official correspondence, apart from copies in his private papers, is located in the State Department and naval records at the National Archives. In addition to the central files of the Navy Department, the naval records include the valuable but unpredictable Naval Records and Library Collection, the General Board records, and extensive but little used bureau records.

The single most important study of Bristol is Peter M. Buzanski's fine dissertation on "Admiral Mark L. Bristol and Turkish American Relations, 1919–1922," which unfortunately deals with only the first four of Bristol's eight years at Constantinople. Bristol's naval work in Turkey may also be glimpsed in Henry P. Beers's brief *U.S. Naval Detachment in Turkish Waters, 1919–1924,* Thomas A. Bryson's *Tars, Turks, and Tankers: The Role of the United States Navy in the Middle East, 1800–1979,* and an article by Admiral Bern Anderson entitled "The High Commissioner to Turkey." For Bristol's nonnaval involvement in the Near East, reference should be made especially to Joseph L. Grabill's *Protestant Diplomacy in the Near East: The Missionary Influence on American Foreign Policy,* John De Novo's *American Interests and Policies in the Middle East, 1900–1939,* and a rewarding article by Thomas Bryson on "Admiral Mark L. Bristol: An Open-Door Diplomat in Turkey." Bristol's role in naval aviation is assessed in Clifford L. Lord's official administrative history, "History of Naval Aviation," which was based on extensive research in the Bureau of Aeronautics and other official records. The published version by Lord and Archibald D. Turnbull, *History of United States Naval Aviation,* is less dependable, partly because Lord's valuable footnotes were omitted. There is a copy of the complete manuscript at the Naval Historical Center. Also helpful is Admiral George van Deurs, *Wings for the Fleet: A Narrative of Naval Aviation's Early Development, 1910–1916.* Especially valuable for understanding the Asiatic Fleet during Bristol's command is Bernard D. Cole's well-balanced *Gunboats and Marines: The United Navy in China, 1925–1928.* An adequate institutional history of the General Board has yet to be written. Bristol's service with the board is mentioned only in passing in other naval historical studies.

NOTES

1. Bristol to Ralph Victor Solitt, 12 March 1909, Mark Lambert Bristol Papers, Box 29, Library of Congress.

2. Charles J. Weeks, "The Life and Career of Admiral Newton A. McCully," 12.

3. Brief summaries of Bristol's early years may be found in Peter M. Buzanski, "Admiral Mark L. Bristol and Turkish American Relations, 1919–1922," 14–16; *Dictionary of American Biography,* XI, Supplement 2, 65–66; *The National Cyclopaedia of American Biography,* Current Volume A, 63–64; Bristol Folder, Biographical Reference Files, Operational Records, Naval Historical Center.

4. Bristol to Taylor, 16 April 1900, Bristol to Secretary of the Navy, 22 September 1906, Bristol Papers, Box 29.

5. Robley, D. Evans, *An Admiral's Log,* 324.

6. Mark L. Bristol Jacket, 1903–1913, Record Group 24: Bureau of Navigation Records, No. 3153, National Archives (henceforth R.G. 24: BuNav Records).

7. Julean Arnold to Bristol, 11 July 1930, Bristol Papers, Box 56.

8. W. J. Coggeshall and J. E. McCarthy, *The United States Naval Torpedo Station, Newport, Rhode Island, 1858–1920*, 25–26.

9. Beekman Winthrop to Bristol, 2 August 1911, R.G. 24: BuNav Records, Nos. 3153–93.

10. Memorandum for American Austin M. Knight, MLB 1-16, Bristol Papers, Box 70.

11. Philip Andrews to Bristol, 15 July 1912, with papers relating to *Albany* grounding, Bristol Papers, Box 29.

12. Charles B. McVay, Jr., to Bristol, 21 June and 17 July 1912, ibid.

13. Bradley A. Fiske, *From Midshipman to Rear Admiral*, 538–39; Annual report by Bristol on naval aviation, 19 January 1916, Bristol Papers, Box 30. Although titled an annual report, this paper is actually Bristol's summary of naval aviation under his charge.

14. Dewey to Secretary of the Navy Daniels, 30 August 1913, Chambers Board to Daniels, 25 November 1913, Bristol Papers, Box 30.

15. Clifford Lord, "History of Naval Aviation," 108; Bristol annual report, 19 January 1916, Bristol Papers, Box 30.

16. Lord, "History of Naval Aviation," 112–30; Bristol–Mustin correspondence, 1914, Bristol Papers, Box 29; George Van Deurs, *Wings of the Fleet*, 103–23.

17. Lord, "History of Naval Aviation," 126–37.

18. Bristol to Fiske, 25 September 1914, Dewey to Secretary of the Navy, 17 November 1914, Bristol Papers, Box 29.

19. Testimony by Bristol, 5 December 1914, *Hearings before the Committee on Naval Affairs of the House of Representatives on Estimates Submitted by the Secretary of the Navy, 1915*, 63rd Cong., 3rd Sess., 275–303; Bristol to Secretary of the Navy, 3 February 1915, Bristol Papers, Box 29.

20. Naval Appropriations Act, 3 March 1915, *United States Statutes at Large*, XXXVIII, Part 1, 1930–39; Lord, "History of Naval Aviation," 137–42.

21. Bristol to Mustin, 11 March 1915, Bristol Papers, Box 29.

22. Bristol annual report, 19 January 1916, Bristol Papers, Box 30; Lord, "History of Naval Aviation," 150–66.

23. Bristol to Secretary of the Navy, 16 August 1915, Bristol to Chief of Naval Operations, 19 January 1916, Bristol Papers, Box 29.

24. Memorandum by Daniels, 12 October 1915, with press statement, R.G. 80: General Board Records, File 449, National Archives.

25. Statement by Bristol, 21 February 1916, *Estimates Submitted by the Secretary of the Navy, 1916*, Hearings before Committee of Naval Affairs, House of Representatives, 64th Cong., 1st Sess., 1815–16.

26. Naval Appropriations Act, 29 August 1916, *United States Statutes at Large*, XXXIX:559, 582.

27. Bristol to Secretary of the Navy, 17 February 1916, Bristol Papers, Box 30.

28. Lord, "History of Naval Aviation," 245.

29. Ibid., 187, 190.

30. Daniels to Chief of Naval Operations, 26 May 1916, Benson to Bristol, 1 June 1916, Bristol Papers, Box 63.

31. Benson to Bristol, 25 July 1916, ibid.; Lord, "History of Naval Aviation," 197–98.

32. Bristol to Gleaves, 17 November 1916, Gleaves to Bristol, 21 November 1916, Bristol to Lieutenant B. L. Smith, 14 December 1917, Lee Palmer to Bristol, 14 December 1917, Bristol Papers, Box 30.

33. Thesis: Policy—Its Relation to War and Its Bearing Upon Preparations for War, Submitted by Captain Mark L. Bristol, 30 March 1917, Bristol Papers, Box 70; Bristol to Benson, 4 February 1917, Bristol to Lee Palmer, 5 February 1917, Bristol Papers, Box 30.

34. USS *North Carolina* History during World War I, R.G. 45: Naval Records Collection of the Office of Naval Records and Library, 1911–1927, OS File, Naval Archives.

35. Papers of USS *Oklahoma*, ibid.

36. Bristol to Force Commander (Sims), 8 December 1918, Bristol Papers, Box 30.

37. Sims to Bristol, 17 December 1918, telegram, ibid.; Benson to Simsadus, 5 January 1919, telegram, R.G. 45: Naval Records Collection, Area M File.

38. Sims to Bristol, 6 January 1919, Bristol Papers, Box 63; OpNav to AmNavPar (Benson), 21 January 1919, R.G. 45: Naval Records Collection, Area M File.

39. Bristol to Sims, 2 February 1919, R.G. 45: Naval Records Collection, Area M File.

40. Buzanski, "Admiral Mark L. Bristol," 31–44.

41. Henry P. Beers, *U.S. Naval Detachment in Turkish Waters, 1919–1924.*

42. Bristol to Force Commander (Sims), 10 April 1919, R.G. 45: Naval Records Collection, Area M File.

43. StaNav (Bristol) to AmMission Paris, 10 November 1919, ibid.; Weeks, "Nathan A. McCully," 207.

44. Bristol to SecState, 13 May 1920, telegram, R.G. 45: Naval Records Collection, Area M File; also see Bristol Papers, Boxes 31–32, for extensive correspondence between Bristol and McCully on the Russian situation.

45. Weeks, "Nathan A. McCully," 249–59.

46. For example, see Bristol to Mrs. Fred W. Upham, 24 August 1922, Bristol Papers, Box 34.

47. Bristol to Sims, 18 May 1919, Bristol Papers, Box 31; Buzanski, "Admiral Mark L. Bristol," 49–52; Beers, *Naval Detachment,* 15–16.

48. Smyrna Commission Conclusion and Recommendations, 13 October 1919, with other documents, *Papers Relating to the Foreign Relations of the United States, 1919: Paris Peace Conference,* IX:36–44; Buzanski, "Admiral Mark L. Bristol," 54–75.

49. For Bristol's view, see especially Bristol to Frank Polk, 10 October 1919, Bristol to Dr. Charles F. Gates, 13 December 1919, Bristol Papers, Box 31; Buzanski, "Admiral Mark L. Bristol," 82–121.

50. Harbord Report, 16 October 1919, *Papers Relating to the Foreign Relations of the United States, 1919,* II:841–74; King–Crane Commission Report, 28 August 1919, ibid., XII:823–45.

51. Bristol to Colonel William H. Haskell, 17 January 1920, Bristol Papers, Box 31.

52. Bristol to Walter George Smith, 27 December 1920, Bristol to James Barton, 28 March 1921, Bristol Papers, Box 32.

53. Buzanski, "Admiral Mark L. Bristol," 182–83.

54. Bristol to SecState, 29 January 1920, 7 March 1920, telegrams, R.G. 45: Naval Records Collection, Area M File.

55. Bristol to SecState, 16 March 1920, 20 March 1920, telegram, ibid.; Bristol to Dr. Caleb F. Gates, 30 March 1920, Bristol Papers, Box 31.

56. Bristol to Vice Admiral Harry P. Huse, 14 September 1920, Bristol to Barton, 19 October 1920, Bristol Papers, Box 32.

57. Memorandum for Bristol by Flag Lieutenant A. E. Willis, 17 June 1920, Bristol Papers, Box 32.

58. Bristol to Elliot G. Mears, 23 January 1922, Bristol Papers, Box 36; Thomas A. Bryson, "Admiral Mark L. Bristol: An Open-Door Diplomat in Turkey," 450–67; Buzanski, "Admiral Mark L. Bristol," 211–46.

59. Bristol to Allen W. Dulles, 14 September 1922, Bristol Papers, Box 37.

60. Plan for Foundation of American Hospital Constantinople, 15 May 1920, Bristol Papers, Box 32.

61. Buzanski, "Admiral Mark L. Bristol," 146–50, 152; Bristol to Miss Etta D. Marden, 17 February 1922, Bristol Papers, Box 36.

62. Bristol to L. I. Thomas, 2 July 1932, Bristol Papers, Box 37.

63. *United States Foreign Relations, 1922,* II:414–92; Beers, *Turkish Detachment,* 21–24; Bern Anderson, "The High Commissioner to Turkey," 21–22; Bristol to William D. Leahy, 28 May 1923, Bristol Papers, Box 37.

64. Joseph C. Grew, *Turbulent Era: A Diplomatic Record of Forty Years, 1904–1945,* I, 503–5, 509; Waldo H. Heinrichs, *American Ambassador: Joseph C. Grew and the Development of the United States Diplomatic Tradition,* 73–78.

65. Bristol to Dulles, 11 December 1922, 19 January 1923, Bristol Papers, Box 38.

66. Bristol to McCully, 20 February 1923, Bristol Papers, Box 38; Grew, *Turbulent Era,* II:552–53.

67. Complaint by Robert Craigie, R.G. 84: Records of the Foreign Service Posts of the Department of State, File No. 133B773, National Archives.

68. *Papers Relating to the Foreign Relations of the United States, 1923,* II:1172–90.

69. Beers, *Turkish Detachment,* 27–28.

70. Bristol to Chief of Naval Operations (Coontz), 17 June 1920, with enclosures, 30 June 1920, Bristol to House, 14 September 1920, Bristol Papers, Box 32.

71. Dulles to Secretary of State, 6 July 1922, R.G. 84: Foreign Service Posts, File No. 123B773/46,95.

72. William R. Shoemaker to Bristol, 9 March 1925, ibid., File No. 123B773/100.

73. Frank B. Kellogg to Secretary of the Navy (Curtis B. Wilbur), 4 May 1925, ibid., File No. 123B773/97.

74. Exchange of notes, 17 February 1927, *Papers Relating to the Relations of the United States, 1927,* III:796–97.

75. StaNav (Bristol) to BuNav, 27 March 1927, telegram, R.G. 45: Naval Records Collection, WT File.

76. Coolidge to Bristol, 1927, quoted in Bristol biographical sketch, Biographical References Files, Operational Records, Naval Historical Center.

77. Bernard D. Cole, *Gunboats and Marines: The United States Navy in China, 1925–1928,* 28–40, 103–5, 136–37; Annual Reports of Commander in Chief Asiatic Fleet, 17 July 1928, 10 April 1929, National Archives Microfilm Publication M971, Reel 12. Bristol refers to conferences in Washington in Bristol to Admiral Charles F. Hughes, 12 January 1928, Bristol Papers, Box 83.

78. Bristol to Hughes, 12 January 1928, Bristol to Butler, 24 December 1927, Bristol Papers, Box 83; CinC Asiatic to OpNav, 10 March 1928, telegram, R.G. 80: General Records of the Department of the Navy, SecNav's Secret Correspondence, 1927–39, EF16/KK.

79. National Interview between Bristol and Wu, 17 October 1927, Bristol to Wilbur, 3 November 1927, R.G. 80: SecNav's Confidential Correspondence, 1927–39, FF6.

80. Bristol to Wilbur, 21 January 1928, ibid.

81. Bristol to Nelson T. Johnson, 20 January 1928, Bristol Papers, Box 83; Mayer to Secretary of State, Kellogg to MacMurray, 6 December 1927, telegrams, *Papers Relating to the Foreign Relations of the United States, 1927,* II:331–41.

82. Bristol to Asa K. Jennings, 11 January 1928, Bristol to Christian Merriman, 15 December 1928, Bristol Papers, Box 83.

83. Bristol to OpNav, 29 February 1928, telegram, R.G. 80: SecNav's Confidential Correspondence, 1927–39, EF16/KK; Hughes to CinC Asiatic, 2 March 1928, telegram, R.G. 80: SecNav's Secret Correspondence, 1927–39, A16-3.

84. Mayer to SecState, 2 March 1929, MacMurray to SecState, 5 March 1928, telegrams, R.G. 59: General Records of the Department of State, State Department Decimal File, 893.00/9784, 9789.

85. Hornbeck endorsement, 5 March 1928, ibid., 893.00/9803.
86. Kellogg to SecNav, 10 March 1928, ibid., 893.0146/29.
87. Bristol to SecNav, 10 March 1928, telegram, ibid., 893.00/9803.
88. Bristol to Wilbur, 4 May 1928, R.G. 80: SecNav's Confidential Correspondence, 1927–39, EF16/PG9-2.
89. Kellogg to Legation Peking, 17 May 1928, 18 May 1928, telegrams, *United States Foreign Relations, 1928,* II:226.
90. Bristol to Wilbur, 23 June 1928, Bristol Papers, Box 84.
91. Bristol Annual Report, 17 July 1928, National Archives Microfilm M971, Reel 12.
92. MacMurray to SecState, 13 July 1928, telegram, R.G. 59: State Department Decimal File, 893.00/0146/67.
93. MacMurray to SecState, 1 November 1928, 5 November 1928, telegrams, ibid., 893.0146/88; Memorandum by NTJ for the Cabinet, 8 November 1928, ibid., 893.00/89.
94. CinC Asiatic to OpNav, 15 January 1929, telegram, R.G. 80; SecNav's Unclassified Correspondence, 1926–40, EF16/P9-2.
95. MacMurray to SecState, 28 April 1929, telegram, R.G. 59: State Department Decimal File, 893.0146/118; Henry L. Stimson to Secretary of the Navy, 30 April 1929, R.G. 80: SecNav's Unclassified Correspondence, 1926–40, FF16.
96. Bristol to Wilbur, 1 December 1928, Bristol Papers, Box 67.
97. William R. Braisted, *The United States Navy in the Pacific, 1909–1922,* 664–65.
98. Bristol to Adams, 26 August 1928, Bristol Papers, Box 56.
99. Asiatic Fleet, General Order No. 1-29, 10 August 1929, ibid.
100. Bristol to Charles B. McVay, 11 January 1930, Information on Trans-Siberian Railway Travel, Bristol Papers, Box 56.
101. Raymond G. O'Connor, *Perilous Equilibrium: The United States and the London Naval Conference of 1930,* 11–46.
102. Memorandum, 12 December 1929, Bristol Papers, Box 105; Memorandum by MLB, 7 January 1930, R.G. 80: General Board Papers, File 438–1.
103. Gerald E. Wheeler, *Admiral William Veazie Pratt, U.S. Navy: A Sailor's Life,* 295–96.
104. Bristol to Jones, 11 January 1930, Bristol to Jules James, 28 February 1930, Bristol to James H. Finley, *New York Times,* 8 March 1930, Bristol Papers, Box 56.
105. London Naval Treaty, 22 April 1930, *Papers Relating to the Relations of the United States, 1930,* I:107–25.
106. Standley to Bristol, 18 April 1930, R.G. 80: General Board Papers, File 438-1.
107. Bristol to Jahncke, 21 April 1930, Bristol Papers, Box 65.
108. *London Naval Treaty of 1930,* Hearings before the Committee on Naval Affairs, United States Senate, 71st Cong., 2nd Sess., 238–68; *Treaty on the Limitation of Armaments,* Hearings before the Committee on Foreign

Relations, United States Senate, 71st Cong., 2nd Sess., 101–21, 137–58, 226–34.

109. Wheeler, *Pratt,* 307–8.

110. Ibid., 323. As chief of naval operations, Pratt was chairman of the General Board, but in his absence Bristol, the senior officer present, signed the board's papers.

111. Hearing on Change of U.S. Navy Regulations, 30 June 1931, General Board Hearings, 1931, R.G. 80: General Board Papers, microfilm edition, I:369.

112. Change No. 15, U.S. Navy Regulations, 1 March 1932, R.G. 80: General Board Papers, G.B. 401; Bristol to Andrew T. Long, 1 April 1932, Bristol Papers, Box 37.

113. Bristol to SecNav, 16 October 1930, R.G. 80: General Board Papers, G.B. 420–2.

114. Armin Rappaport, *The Navy League of the United States,* 36.

115. Hearings before Senate Committee on Naval Affairs on S 51, 72nd Cong., 1st Sess., 21–91; Hearings before the House Naval Affairs Committee, 13 January 1932, 72nd Cong., 1st Sess., microfiche edition, 609–71.

116. Fleet Problem No. XII, February 1931, National Archives Microfilm M964, Reel 13; Bristol Diary on Fleet Maneuvers, February 1931, Bristol Papers, Box 8.

117. Hearing on Displacement of Battleships, 30 June 1931, General Board Hearings, 1931, I:369.

118. Henry L. Stimson Diary, 25 May 1931, XVI: 101.

119. Hearings on Draft Disarmament Convention, 30 September 1931, General Board Hearings, 1931, I:998–99.

120. Bristol to SecNav, 7 January 1932, with endorsements, G.B. 438-1 (1521-G), R.G. 80: SecNav's Confidential Correspondence, 1927–39, A19 File.

121. Bristol to Long, 30 December 1931, Bristol Papers, Box 57.

122. Stimson Diary, 15 October 1931, XVIII:137.

123. Bristol to Arnold, 23 December 1931, Bristol Papers, Box 57.

124. Bristol to R. E. Gregoran, 2 March 1932, ibid.

125. Bristol to F. B. Stern, 6 April 1932, ibid.

126. Bristol to Ellis, 21 July 1932, ibid.

127. Bristol to Myron Taylor, 4 February 1932, 23 February 1932, ibid.

128. Bristol to Franklin D. Roosevelt, 12 July 1932, ibid.

129. Bristol Naval War College Thesis, 30 March 1917, Bristol Papers, Box 30.

WILLIAM A. MOFFETT: STEWARD OF THE AIR REVOLUTION

CLARK G. REYNOLDS

In the generation of American officers produced by the sail–steam, coast defense navy, none played a more far-reaching leadership role during the transition to an air-centered fleet with a global reach than William Adger Moffett. For twelve years, from 1921 to 1933, in spite of strong opposition by the ruling battleship men, Admiral Moffett wielded immense authority in forging the fledgling air arm of the U.S. Navy. His consummate managerial skill enabled him to lay the foundations of American naval striking power during World War II and for the ensuing half-century. His epitaph, the "Father of Naval Aviation," is entirely appropriate.

In terms of national policy and naval strategy, Moffett consistently endorsed the philosophy of worldwide American maritime expansion advocated by Alfred Thayer Mahan and Theodore Roosevelt. Indeed, as a young lieutenant (j.g.), Moffett served under Captain Mahan's command in the protected cruiser *Chicago* in 1893–95, and he attended the Naval War College in the summer of 1896, during Mahan's last tour there. By the time he became an admiral, in the 1920s, Moffett followed Mahan in the belief that the United States needed a revitalized merchant marine and additional colonial possessions as naval bases.

"All virile nations are naturally annexationists," Moffett argued, in favor of American empire. Furthermore, he declared in 1930, "The United States should not have a navy inferior to any other. . . . I am also in favor of a merchant marine inferior to none." American warships, merchantmen, and overseas bases were essential to fill the vacuum being created by the demise of the British Empire.

William A. Moffett. This photograph of Moffett as chief of the Bureau of Aeronautics was taken a few days before his death in 1933. *Courtesy of the Naval Historical Center.*

I can not but feel that Great Britain has reached her pinnacle; that they have a glorious history and traditions but are living on traditions too much. . . . They have traditions and what is generally called aristocracy, but while we are comparatively short on both, we have virility and are a young nation stepping out with vision and confidence, and nothing will stop our being the greatest nation in the world except what we do within ourselves.[1]

Typical of naval officers of his generation, Moffett had the manner of a cool professional devoted to his service. He developed his administrative talents as a line officer in the usual shipboard and shore-side assignments and was not dazzled by innovations in technology. For example, observing the bitter resistance of the line to absorbing engineers, Moffett learned to accept change by understanding and applying technological progress. He took the same attitude with aircraft. "My former service on and experience with steam and the attitude of the Navy toward it," he observed in 1933, "has been of great assistance to me being patient when endeavoring to do all that I could to assist in indoctrinating the Navy as a whole in regard to aviation and its importance."[2]

Moffett's sound intellect and controlled manner stemmed from the circumstances of his youth. Born of Scotch–Irish parents in the genteel and Civil War–devastated port city of Charleston, South Carolina, on 31 October 1869, Moffett grew up in the dual environment of maritime commerce and Southern Reconstruction society. His father, a merchant of the city and former Confederate officer, passed on to him a deep respect for and emulation of the mighty Robert E. Lee. And though the father died in the boy's fifth year, Moffett drew similar strength from his mother. His solid upbringing in a family of nine children (he was number seven) enabled him to become a family man himself with six children of his own. Moffett's calm, Southern demeanor stood him in good stead in the public schools and at the Naval Academy, where he often had to defend the honor of the South against Yankee critics. A fairly mediocre student, he graduated rather far down in the Class of 1890.[3]

Moffett's early career reflected the technological changes transforming the U.S. Navy at the turn of the century: service in sailing and steam sloops, a gunboat once and a monitor twice, cruisers, and predreadnought as well as dreadnought battleships. On board a protected cruiser named after his home town, the *Charleston,* Moffett participated in the capture of Guam and Manila during the War with Spain. His skills were sufficient to lead the Ottoman navy to offer him a senior commission in 1900, though he was but a new lieutenant in the battleship *Kentucky* en route to the Far East. He declined that honor, but received increasingly responsible posts during the expansion of the Roosevelt navy.[4]

Moffett's long seagoing service led him to command of the scout cruiser *Chester* late in 1913. As such, he personally delivered Admiral Henry T. Mayo's ultimatum to the Mexicans at Tampico in April 1914, an action culminating in the Vera Cruz intervention, in which his ship engaged Mexican shore batteries. That August he was given command of the Great Lakes Naval Training Station near Chicago, with additional duty supervising the three naval districts in the region. Here his organizational and innovative genius shone brightly as he upgraded the training program, leading to his promotion to captain in 1916 and his retention in the post throughout America's participation in World War I. From a capacity of 1,600 trainees, Moffett increased the recruit accommodations to some 50,000, making Great Lakes the largest recruit training depot in the navy; it produced nearly 100,000 sailors for wartime service. He even brought in the renowned bandmaster John Philip Sousa to provide music for the station. Moffett's reward, in December 1918, was command of the battleship *Mississippi* for two years.[5]

Like many of his peers, Moffett had been catapulted into the forefront of the managerial revolution sweeping American industry in peacetime as in war. At Great Lakes he not only streamlined the internal organization but learned the art of working effectively through local political and business leaders. He developed an especially close relationship with the chewing gum magnate, William K. Wrigley, Jr. Moffett's fine diplomatic tact even enabled him, at the head of a landing party from the *Mississippi,* to prevent a radical labor demonstration during President Woodrow Wilson's visit to Seattle in September 1919.[6]

Moffett's first real exposure to the new technology of naval aviation occurred early in 1913 when, as executive officer of the new dreadnought *Arkansas,* he went duck hunting at Guantanamo Bay, Cuba, with the young flyers of the U.S. Navy's first seaplane unit. But he took no interest in the crude flying machines. Reflecting the general attitude of his fellow officers, during one hunting foray he remarked to the airmen's commander, Lieutenant John H. Towers: "Towers, you're such a nice chap, why don't you give up this aviation fad? You'll surely get yourself killed. Any man who sticks to it is either crazy or else a plain damned fool!"[7]

The use of military aircraft in the European war and the pressing need to train aviation mechanics at Great Lakes changed his attitude. Working closely with Wrigley, he established an aviation unit of more than 250 planes at the sprawling depot. By the time he got the *Mississippi,* Moffett had begun to appreciate the revolutionary promise of fleet aviation, particularly because Japan had suddenly reemerged as the major enemy across the vast Pacific.[8]

Following experiments on board the *Texas,* Moffett had a ramp installed over a turret on the "Missy" in order to launch scout planes to spot the fall of her shells. (The planes landed ashore.) During gunnery exercises in May and June 1920, these Sopwiths, Jennys, and F5L flying boats under Captain Henry C. Mustin and Commander Towers transmitted the proper ranges by wireless to Moffett's gunnery officer, Commander William L. Calhoun. On one day alone, Moffett signaled the aviators: "Your aeroplanes were our salvation. We thank you." In fact, the planes enabled the *Mississippi* to attain scores so high that they almost equaled those of all the other battleships combined! Among three aerial spotters whom Moffett singled out for high praise was Lieutenant Commander Marc A. Mitscher, an officer who would earn his growing admiration over time and who, as Admiral Mitscher, would lead the famous Fast Carrier Task Force in the war against Japan.[9]

The senior admirals realized that naval aviation was maturing so rapidly that it needed its own bureau organization, their thinking stimulated in no small part by the growing crusade of Brigadier General William "Billy" Mitchell of the U.S. Army's Air Service. Mitchell publicly proclaimed that the navy's air arm should be united with the army's in a new separate and independent air force, geared to land-based strategic bombing. So uncompromising and outspoken was Mitchell that the director of naval aviation, the normally affable Captain Thomas T. Craven, finally refused even to speak to him. As intraservice efforts to create the navy's own bureau of aeronautics accelerated over 1920–21, a tactful but knowledgeable bureau chief was needed, and Moffett was the logical choice. At the urging of Henry Mustin, Moffett approached Bill Wrigley to ask Wrigley's support for his candidacy. A prominent industrialist, Wrigley had become a major power in the Republican Party, and he was pleased to lend his support in recommending Moffett to lead naval aviation. President Warren G. Harding agreed, whereupon Moffett relieved Craven as director in March 1921, then fleeted up to become chief of the new Bureau of Aeronautics (BuAer) upon its creation in July. The post carried the rank of rear admiral.[10]

Moffett's style and philosophy of leadership in naval aviation were immediately obvious and did not change in the twelve years that he held the office. A man of only medium build, the white-haired Moffett was a commanding presence with an erect bearing and quiet, confident manner. Energetic, neat, and well-ordered, he drove about in the latest model LaSalle automobile. Though no flag-waving "prophet" like Mitchell, he was an impressive individual who had to be reckoned with. Indeed, Admiral William V. Pratt, his friend and CNO, remarked to Moffett in front of Secretary of the Navy Charles

Francis Adams in 1930 that, as Moffett recalled it: "I was the most insistent person he had ever known. I told him that when I felt I was right, I would insist to the end." And yet, to the aviation community, in the words of Towers, Bill Moffett was "beloved by all who had the privilege of really knowing him." [11]

The insistence Pratt observed was Moffett's determination to gain for aviation the importance he firmly believed it deserved within the navy. The rigid conservatism of the so-called Gun Club of battleship admirals stood in his way at nearly every turn. Moffett often noted that the problem of selling naval aviation was "lack of knowledge and lack of understanding," both of which he labored energetically to correct. His task was made more difficult by the outspokenness of younger pilots who proclaimed the obsolescence of the battleship, thus further arousing senior admirals already resentful of BuAer's budgetary and manpower needs in an era of stringent economy measures. Moffett's struggles were fought largely within the navy, with colleagues—"the old timers in the Navy who don't appreciate Aviation," he called them. These adversaries held such key positions as CNO, commander in chief United States Fleet (CinCUS), and chief of the Bureau of Navigation (BuNav). The BuNav chief controlled personnel assignments, a subject of major interest in Moffett's attempt to gain control of the assignment of its aviators for BuAer, a goal achieved in the latter years of his tenure as bureau chief. Moffett set out to make BuAer into a superbureau, just as the office of naval aviation had been during the war—that is, an agency reaching into the previously sacrosanct bureaus that had controlled personnel, engineering, weapons, and even medicine. [12]

Moffett thus worked within the system to "sell" naval aviation. Of him, Jack Towers wrote, "I cannot recall any man who more loved a fight and who could think of more ways to win one." Moffett grew so adept at it that he came to be feared by the conservative battleship-weaned admirals. The infighting never let up during his dozen years at the helm of BuAer. Even when he won victories for aviation that became department policy, the criticism and antagonism toward him intensified, so that he felt compelled to counterattack it with pointed letters. For example, in the spring of 1932, he chastised Admiral Frank M. Schofield for being "disloyal" to the navy by criticizing its adoption of Moffett's much-resented dirigible program. Not only was Admiral Schofield the reigning CinCUS, but he also had been an Academy classmate of Moffett's. Moffett then expressed his chagrin to Towers: "Battles are in progress, not daily but hourly. . . . I must say that when we find we are double-crossed here in the Department in regard to flight pay and other Aviation matters, it makes one wonder whether we should continue the fight." [13]

But continue he did. Instead of depending upon his uniformed colleagues in the hope of gaining concessions, he quietly courted presidents and members of Congress for appropriations. His careful testimony in congressional hearings was especially effective, as expert advisers sat behind him to coach him with data. He made speeches to appropriate patriotic and interest groups and utilized the press whenever he believed it necessary, often corresponding with publishers, editors, and reporters he had befriended. (In 1925 he began a letter to Pulitzer Prize winner Herbert Bayard Swope with "Herbert, old man.") He entered naval planes and pilots in air shows to win public recognition. The best of these flyers were his special "pets," notably polar explorer Richard E. Byrd, altitude record holder C. C. Champion, and speed champion Alford J. Williams. He appointed the famous pioneer Naval Aviator Number One, Commander T. G. "Spuds" Ellyson, to head his plans division more for Ellyson's considerable public image than his ability. Moffett shepherded along the struggling aircraft manufacturers to provide ever better planes for the navy, especially with the adoption of the more efficient air-cooled engine over the water-cooled design. He not only established aviation training at the Naval Academy but succeeded in having regular training planes assigned there. [14]

Moffett concentrated on policy and politics, allowing his officer advisers to attend to details. In so doing, he became a master at promoting the cause of aviation within the U.S. Navy. In contrast to Mitchell the crusader, Moffett acted as the steward of the fleet's growing air arm, quietly and effectively overseeing a revolution in naval warfare from the administrative end. He became an organization man in the new age of machine weaponry. In fully appreciating the realities of warfare in the modern world, he placed himself squarely in the future.

To guarantee his own future and reappointment to successive four-year terms as chief of BuAer, Moffett again solicited the support of his good friend Bill Wrigley of Chicago. In 1925 and again in 1929, Wrigley prevailed upon the president (Coolidge and then Hoover) to reappoint Moffett, a brand of politicking thoroughly resented by Moffett's peers and superiors. In both instances, Moffett rebuffed attempts by his superiors to send him to sea or shunt him off to the General Board. Though he would have enjoyed a seagoing flag command, he realized that the position of naval aviation was too tenuous to be left to others with less political finesse and clout. In other words, Moffett made himself indispensable as head of naval aviation and won a resounding battle against Secretary of the Navy Curtis D. Wilbur, CNO Admiral Charles F. Hughes, CinCUS Admiral S. S. Robison, and BuNav Chief R. H. Leigh, who tried to have him reassigned in 1929. Such a triumph, however, led Moffett to take care thereafter, "for as the Good Book says 'Pride goeth before destruction and a haughty spirit before a fall.' "[15]

The closest point of contact between Moffett and the administrations he served was the secretary of the navy, to whom all bureau chiefs reported directly. Edwin Denby gave no particular personal attention to aviation during the formative years of Moffett's rule, but the accession of Wilbur in 1924 brought direct secretarial involvement. A graduate of the Academy two years ahead of Moffett, Wilbur sided with his own classmate Admiral Hughes, CNO from 1927 to 1930, in trying to have Moffett transferred from command of BuAer.

Although the assistant secretary of the navy figured somewhat in these relationships, the creation in 1926 of the new post of assistant secretary of the navy for aeronautics granted naval aviation a unique position within the civilian hierarchy of the navy. It also strengthened Moffett in his battle with the CNO and BuNav because both men who filled the post were strong Moffett supporters. The first appointee held impeccable credentials: Edward P. Warner was a respected aeronautical engineer and educator who quickly became a forceful spokesman alongside Moffett in budgetary hearings. His successor, in 1929, was even more prominent—David S. Ingalls, who had been the navy's only fighter ace in World War I and who as a practicing pilot now personally tested all new naval aircraft. His aeronautical knowledge and pleasing personality never failed to win over congressional inquirers. When Ingalls resigned in 1932 to run for elective office, the post fell vacant as an economy measure, but Moffett had the continued general support of Secretary Adams and Assistant Secretary Ernest L. Jahncke.[16]

In molding BuAer internally, Admiral Moffett surrounded himself with the best available talent from the flying cadre. But too few senior officers were qualified in aviation to fill the senior billets; so he instituted the naval aviation observers course at NAS Pensacola, wherein captains and commanders could learn the rudiments of flight, doing everything—spotting, navigating, operating the radio—except actually flying the plane. Moffett himself had flown down to Pensacola when time permitted him to participate in the course during his first year in office. In June 1922, after accumulating some 150 hours of flight time, he was rated as a naval observer. He kept the program in existence for another ten years, until qualified pilots attained sufficient seniority to fill the increasing number of aviation command slots. [17]

Though only a stopgap solution, the observer program typified Moffett's wise managerial ability to compromise where necessary. Ideally, however, he preferred to have actual pilots advising him, in order to tap their undisputed expertise. Consequently, he selected as his first assistant chief of bureau the innovative pioneer Captain Henry Mustin. After Mustin's premature death in 1923, observer Captain Albert W. Johnson stepped in for a year, to be followed by two pioneer aviators, Commanders Kenneth Whiting and John Rodgers. The latter's fatal plane crash in 1926 led to the appointment of observer Captain Emory S. Land. Though highly talented, Land lacked close contact with the line officer community as a member of the Construction Corps. The three subsequent assistants, however, were aviators: Jack Towers (1929–31), as Naval Aviator Number Three the most experienced and able; Ernest J. King (1928–29); and Arthur B. Cook (1931–33)—the latter two latecomers to the aviation community as qualified pilots. All were superior men who held or attained the rank of captain while in the job.

During his first term, 1921–25, Moffett and his advisers agreed that aviation's primary role was reconnaissance as the "eyes of the fleet," just as it had been in World War I. Naval aircraft should not only spot for the gun ships but fly antisubmarine patrols, conduct long-range scouting against enemy fleet units, and, like scouting ships, provide additional firepower in the form of light bombs and aerial torpedoes. The platforms for these functions were flying boats, shore-based dirigibles, and the experimental aircraft carrier *Langley,* commissioned in 1922.

Though this reconnaissance mission satisfied the conservative admirals, Moffett and his cohorts also believed that the carrier, flying boat, and airship would gain enhanced striking power as wartime technology was replaced by a new advanced generation of delivery systems. Thus they planned to develop the air arm into an offensive force. Under their leadership, the 1920s became a period of transition for aviation, from employment in the traditional scouting role for battleships to use as a primary attack element, which would ultimately—in the 1940s—replace the battleship altogether. The more apparent the future course became, the more antagonistic the Gun Club grew. Moffett proceeded cautiously in the face of such opposition; until the technology matured to develop its offensive role, he carefully insisted that the air arm must only support the battle line.

Between 1921 and 1925 the aircraft carrier moved to the forefront of Moffett's plans. During the Washington naval arms limitation conference of 1921–22, Moffett welcomed a decision allowing the United States to convert two uncompleted battle cruiser hulls into large 33,000-ton carriers. These vessels, the *Lexington* and the *Saratoga*, took most of the decade to design, build, outfit, and provide with special aircraft and squadrons of trained pilots. Experiments with the tiny 11,500-ton *Langley* quickly showed just how powerful the two *Lexington*s would be. As war reparations from Germany, the navy received the rigid dirigible *Los Angeles*, and then it constructed its own *Shenandoah*. Plans called for testing both airships as platforms foreshadowing fleet "flying aircraft carriers," capable of long-range reconnaissance not only alone but operating with a few scout planes launched from a special trapeze mechanism.

The four years of Moffett's first term at BuAer were the most chaotic because of the uncertain promise of carriers and airships, the resentment of aviation within the navy, and Billy Mitchell's continuing assaults. Mitchell vociferously proclaimed that land-based strategic bombers had made armies and navies obsolete, an attitude that did not endear him to the conservative generals in the army, much less to Moffett and the navy. He also insisted on a separate independent air force with control over all military aviation.

Moffett firmly believed that the navy's air arm should remain an integral part of the fleet and not be left to the mercy of land-based zealots, as had occurred under the Royal Air Force in Britain. He thus remained a steadfast opponent of such a unified air force and battled Mitchell continuously in public and in private. When the American Legion endorsed the idea of a separate air force, Moffett wrote to the Legion: "I think that the establishment of a separate, independent air force would almost ruin the national defense." Furthermore, though the majority of the navy's pilots advocated their own naval air corps within the navy, Moffett opposed it because airplanes and ships must work in concert under one fleet command. He preferred to educate the fleet commanders on the proper use of aircraft alongside all ships.[18]

Part of the interservice problem was that no centralized authority existed to establish defense policy, and the army had reverted to its traditional prewar role of defending the continental United States. Its airmen furthermore insisted that the aerial defense of the coasts was their province rather than the navy's. Moffett, by contrast, espoused the navy's position, which was global:

> For the same reason that we need a Navy second to none to defend against attack from overseas, we need an adequate Navy to secure for us the freedom of the seas for trade and commerce. . . . The air defense of the country must be maintained a thousand or more miles at sea which will serve the double purpose of guarding us against attack and protecting our lines of commerce and communication with other nations.

Because the army's bombers could reach out only 250 miles, the immense task had to remain with the navy.[19]

Not only did the navy's newer and better flying boats and carrier-borne planes promise to equal army bombers in their ability to defend the coast, but Moffett firmly believed that the dirigible could greatly extend the navy's range. Ever since 1919, British and German rigids had been crossing the Atlantic; such nonstop staying power offered the fleet a unique observation platform. "The rigid airship today fills a gap in transportation need [sic] that can be filled up by no other means," Moffett declared in 1925, and he thus steadfastly insisted that experimentation continue to improve the rigids.[20]

Events in September 1925 marked a watershed in Moffett's tenure. The rigid Shenandoah crashed in a storm over Ohio, killing many of the crew, and a PN-9 flying boat was lost at sea attempting to fly nonstop between San Francisco and Hawaii (actually, the crew sailed it into the islands in a remarkable ten-day voyage). Mitchell condemned the government, and by implication the navy, for allowing these tragedies to happen, whereupon Moffett threw his energies into destroying Mitchell's credibility—a reaction shared by many of Mitchell's own superiors in the army, who silenced him with a court-martial. President Coolidge appointed the Morrow Board of distinguished aeronautical and engineering experts to establish a national aeronautic policy. Moffett and his advisers, most importantly Jack Towers, presented careful evidence that so impressed the legislators that Congress instituted a five-year plan for naval, army, and commercial aviation, including the creation of assistant secretary of aeronautics posts in both services.[21]

Moffett dusted off a long-range development scheme, devised by the late Henry Mustin, that became the basis for naval aviation's growth between 1926 and 1931. Under it, the navy contracted for the purchase of 1,000 new aircraft, a commensurate increase in pilot training, at least one new carrier, and two fleet dirigibles. With the support of his able assistants and department heads—who found that Moffett usually just signed anything they put in front of him without reading it—the airplane production goal was met one year ahead of schedule. This proved providential, because the onset of the Great Depression delayed construction of the fleet airships *Akron* and *Macon* and the carrier *Ranger* and also slowed other essential aviation programs. As to the coast defense mission, in 1931 CNO Pratt agreed to let the army have primary responsibility for it, a decision that angered Moffett and most of his fellow admirals, who continued to oppose and circumvent it all the way down to World War II.[22]

While Moffett fought the political wars in Washington, he depended upon the theoreticians at Newport and the airmen in the fleet to give him hard data showing exactly what aircraft could do at sea. Moffett corresponded with Admiral William S. Sims, who as president of the Naval War College tested the role of aircraft in war games, and through Sims, in 1922, he had the first pilot assigned to the course and staff there: famed Commander Albert C. Read, who had commanded the NC-4 flying boat on the first transatlantic airplane flight three years before. Moffett wrote to and occasionally visited with successive U.S. Fleet commanding air admirals, who maneuvered their planes with the battleships in weekly exercises and the annual fleet problems. The most progressive of these men was Rear Admiral Joseph Mason Reeves, whose dramatic use of the *Saratoga* to attack the Panama Canal in Fleet Problem IX in 1929 demonstrated the offensive power of the carriers. Moffett and Reeves disagreed over many issues—for example, the location of an airship base in California—but they shared a mutual respect. Moffett was completely honest when he wrote Reeves in 1928 that "in this tactical work . . . I believe that you . . . can make more progress and accomplish more than anyone else." Reeves's successor, Rear Admiral Harry E. Yarnell, however, was a kindred soul to Moffett in every respect, and his expert chief of staff was Moffett's own protegé, Towers.[23]

For both his knowledge of aeronautics and his diplomatic skills, Moffett served as a member of the London naval arms conference in

1930, but he was chagrined to encounter complete apathy toward carriers on the part of all his colleagues except Yarnell. Not only did they not want to build up to the treaty limit for more carriers— perhaps four more—but Moffett had to fend off British attempts to reduce overall carrier tonnage. He finally succeeded in enlightening his colleagues, though only three other senior admirals favored the treaty as a viable solution to avert an arms race. Moffett feared the consequences if the United States did not build up to the limits allowed by the treaty; in his view, the General Board "and the reactionaries . . . are sinking the Navy and doing much more harm than the Japanese ever have or ever will do." He believed the United

In the control car of the USS *Akron*. Moffett is facing the camera and talking with Lieutenant Commander Charles E. Rosendahl. Rosendahl had survived the crash of the *Shenandoah* in 1925 and outfitted the *Akron* when it was brought into service. Moffett died when the *Akron* crashed off Barnegat Light, New Jersey, on 4 April 1933. He was the fifth U.S. Navy flag rank officer to die in the line of duty. *Courtesy of the Naval Historical Center.*

States should keep all its battleships as long as Britain and Japan kept theirs, but he hoped that at the next conference he might scrap them all in favor of carriers and some cruisers. Moffett also came up with a compromise ship type, the "flying deck cruiser"—to him "the ship of the future"—to increase U.S. air strength at sea. The final treaty permitted it, but the U.S. Navy never adopted the idea.[24]

Unfortunately, the aftermath of the London conference left Moffett thoroughly disgusted with the Hoover administration. Because of the deepening depression, Hoover refused to build the navy up to treaty limits—not only in carriers but in other ship types too. Moffett thus welcomed the election of Franklin D. Roosevelt late in 1932: "I believe that the stagnation that we have been going through in [the] Increase of the Navy will end soon after Mr. Roosevelt comes in. So much time has been lost by Mr. Hoover in trying to get Europe to disarm that we find ourselves in a position with nothing to trade." And in February 1933 he elaborated on this theme by delivering an address to Naval Academy alumni entitled "The Decadence of the Navy."[25]

Still in all, now nearing the end of his third term as chief of BuAer, Moffett could take solace in the fact that he had achieved most of his goals, particularly in the knowledge that U.S. naval aviation was far ahead of Japan's. He had produced a strong cadre of trained pilots and had fought, with decreasing success, to retain their flight pay. The carriers had proved their worth and were equipped with new, powerful airplanes. The patrol–bombing flying boat had evolved to the Consolidated P2Y, the last step before the sturdy PBY a year later. All battleships and cruisers carried catapult-launched seaplanes as gunfire spotters for the battle line.

The dirigible, however, remained an unknown quantity, though Moffett hoped it would prove its utility in operations with the fleet. In the face of almost universal opposition to the rigid airships in the navy, Moffett once wrote that "Putting over Lighter-Than-Air has been the toughest job I ever undertook." Moffett loved to go for quiet soaring rides in the dirigible *Akron* out of NAS Lakehurst. During one such flight, on 4 April 1933, the big airship, unable to outmaneuver a violent storm, crashed into a cold night sea, killing most of its crew—and Admiral Moffett. The rigid airship program died with him.[26]

"Life is timing," Moffett had often remarked; he believed that one should leave a job "when the flags were flying and the bands were playing." And so he had done. He never experienced the dreary retirement for age he expected on 1 November of that year. The new president, Franklin Roosevelt, had been disposed to reappoint him later in April, although FDR did not like the idea of such a short-term appointment for anyone. Moffett had wanted to stay on, especially to ensure the appointment of heir-apparent Towers as his successor. "I think all Aviation wants to see Towers here," Moffett had written to Congressman Carl Vinson in 1932. But that would have taken some doing, for Ernest J. King, already selected for rear admiral, had the support of Moffett's opponents, whereas Towers was still a very junior captain.[27]

With Moffett's death, King won out as his successor—and he went on not only to direct the entire World War II fleet but personally to conduct the antisubmarine air war against Germany in the Atlantic. Towers, however, brought naval aviation into that war as chief of BuAer during 1939–42 and then shaped the Pacific Fleet's air doctrine for Chester W. Nimitz in the war against Japan.

William A. Moffett was indeed the father of modern naval aviation. Rooted in the golden age of the steel battleship but foreseeing the age of the Air Navy, he was a key transitional figure in bridging the two eras. As a peerless naval politician and manager, he had battled the service conservatism typical of naval hierarchies but had worked as much as possible within the system, where naval aviation belonged. His quiet, deliberate personality had impressed members of Congress repelled by Billy Mitchell's harangues; and the achievements of his racing and long-distance flyers had won over the public. By deeds rather than words, Moffett used his stewardship over the naval air revolution to lay the foundations of a navy that would dominate the seas during succeeding generations.

FURTHER READING

In spite of the vast collection of documents in the Moffett Collection at the U.S. Naval Academy, the only Moffett biography is Edward Arpee, *From Frigates to Flat-Tops*. An excellent treatment, it was, however, published privately and is difficult to locate. Arranged both chronologically and topically, the work covers Moffett's life in detail, and quotes liberally from his correspondence and published statements. Arpee's analysis of Moffett as both man and leader of naval aviation is done well. The only weakness of the book is its lack of research into other primary documents and official in-house naval histories on specific matters.

One of these internal studies was a massive manuscript history of U.S. naval aviation covering the years to 1939, condensed and published by

Archibald D. Turnbull and Clifford L. Lord as *History of United States Naval Aviation.* The contraction of the original study is so great that this source, the only one on the entire period, suffers from omissions and inaccuracies. Thus it fails to provide full coverage of Moffett, although it remains an indispensable overview for the beginning student.

Two autobiographies add important insights into the admiral in the late 1920s: Eugene E. Wilson, *Slipstream,* and Admiral J. J. Clark, *Carrier Admiral.* Both men were naval aviators who served closely with Moffett in Washington, the former in engine design, the latter as personal pilot. The most analytical examination is in Clark G. Reynolds, "Towers: The Air Admiral," as John H. Towers served as Moffett's alter ego between 1928 and 1933, even when Towers was no longer at BuAer.

In order to understand Moffett's leadership role in the context of the interwar period, three sources are essential. Stephen Roskill's two-volume work *Naval Policy between the Wars,* which divides at 1930, covers U.S. and British naval developments equally well, and the interrelationships between the two navies. Several chapters are devoted to naval aviation. Fred Greene, "The Military View of American National Policy, 1904–1940," succinctly treats the navy's strategic differences with the army. John F. Shiner, "The Air Corps, the Navy, and Coast Defense, 1919–1941," gives a balanced analysis of a very important aspect of this interservice rivalry.

NOTES

1. Moffett to H. Ralph Burton of the National Patriotic League, 3 June 1930; Moffett to inventor and Aeronautical Society member Hudson Maxim, 6 February 1923; Moffett to Congressman Burton L. French, 5 March 1930; Moffett to Captain John H. Towers, 17 February 1930. These documents, and all others not cited herein as belonging to other collections, are from the William A. Moffett Collection, Nimitz Library, U.S. Naval Academy. The author is indebted to Professors William Reynolds Braisted and Paolo E. Coletta for their assistance in obtaining source material.

2. Moffett to Commander C. H. McMorris, Department of English and History, U.S. Naval Academy, in March 1933, quoted in William A. Moffett, Jr., "For the Good of the Ship," 20; Moffett to Captain Joseph Mason Reeves, 28 March 1926.

3. Moffett, "For the Good of the Ship," 19; Edward Arpee, *From Frigates to Flat-Tops,* 3–31. Moffett's father, George Hall Moffett, purchased arms for the Confederacy before enlisting and becoming aide-de-camp to Brigadier General Johnson Hagood in Lee's army. His mother was Elizabeth H. Simonton Moffett. Moffett stood thirty-first in a class of thirty-four, though forty-seven had failed to complete the course. His classmates included future senior admirals Frank H. Schofield, Jehu V. Chase, Montgomery Meigs Taylor, Charles B. McVay, Jr., John H. Dayton, L. A.

Bostwick, and J. L. Latimer. He married Jeannette Beverly Whitton in 1902; all three of his sons graduated from Annapolis and became naval aviators. Livingston Davis, special assistant to Assistant Secretary of the Navy Franklin D. Roosevelt, noted in his diary, 8 May 1918, after dining with the Moffetts at Great Lakes Naval Training Station, that Mrs. Moffett "is perfectly charming" and the captain "as fine a man as I ever met," impressions shared throughout the navy. Davis Diary, Franklin D. Roosevelt Library, Hyde Park, New York.

4. Moffett, "For the Good of the Ship," 19; Arpee, *Frigates*, 32–44. Moffett's early ranks were passed midshipman 1890, ensign 1892, lieutenant (jg) and lieutenant 1899, lieutenant commander 1905, and commander 1914. Early tours of duty: screw steamer *Pensacola*, 1890–91; cruiser *Baltimore*, 1891–92; sloop *Portsmouth*, 1892–93; monitor *Amphitrite*, 1895–96, 1904; Naval War College 1896, 1907–8; sloop *Constellation*, 1896; schoolship *Enterprise*, 1896–98; steam sloop *Mohican*, 1898; *Charleston*, 1898; practice ship *Monongahela*, 1900; *Kentucky*, 1900–1901; gunboat *Marietta*, 1901; sloop *St. Mary's*, 1901–2; cruiser *Minneapolis*, 1902; steam sloop *Lancaster*, 1903; battleship *Maine*, 1903–4; commanding officer, Guantanamo Bay, Cuba, 1904–6; Bureau of Equipment, 1906–7; armored cruiser *Maryland*, 1908–10; lighthouse inspector, San Francisco, 1910–12; and battleship *Arkansas*, 1912–13. Clark G. Reynolds, *Famous American Admirals*, 221–22.

5. Moffett, "For the Good of the Ship," 19; Arpee, *Frigates*, 45–51, 55–70. Though he received the Medal of Honor for his part in the Vera Cruz affair, Congress extravagantly awarded the medal to large numbers of participants hardly deserving of it, Moffett among them.

6. Moffett even came to know the underworld figures of the crime-infested city of Chicago so well that he joked he could have had anyone "eliminated," had he so desired. Mrs. John H. Towers to the author, 9 December 1978.

7. Moffett quoted in Towers's unpublished reminiscences, John H. Towers Collection, Naval Historical Foundation, Library of Congress.

8. Arpee, *Frigates*, 66.

9. Moffett to William K. Wrigley, Jr., 29 July 1921; Arpee, *Frigates*, 51–52; Henry C. Mustin Diary, April–June 1920, Mustin Collection, Naval Historical Foundation, Library of Congress; Theodore Taylor, *The Magnificent Mitscher*, 68–69; Elretta Sudsbury, *Jackrabbits to Jets*, 63. Moffett to Lieutenant Commander M. A. Mitscher, 2 April 1929: "I have always felt greatly indebted to you not only for what you did yourself but for the advice and counsel you gave me" while serving at the Bureau of Aeronautics.

10. Admiral J. J. Clark, *Carrier Admiral*, 36; Arpee, *Frigates*, 83–96. Moffett relieved Craven 7 March 1921, was designated chief of BuAer by Harding 25 July 1921, and assumed the post officially 10 August 1921. Moffett to Captain Powers Symington, USN (Ret.), 16 February 1925: "When I relieved Craven, Craven wouldn't speak to him [Mitchell]." Also, Moffett to Wrigley, 11 June 1921.

11. Inglis M. Uppercu, President, Uppercu Cadillac Corp., New York City, to Moffett, 31 May 1929; Moffett to Towers, 17 February 1930; Towers book review, 1139. See Clark, *Carrier Admiral*, 35–36, and William L. Calhoun quotation in Arpee, *Frigates*, 254, on Moffett's leadership. To his friends Moffett was known as both "Bill" and "Billy."

12. Moffett to Reeves, 22 March 1926; Moffett to Wrigley, 7 May and 13 October 1928.

13. Towers book review, 1139; Moffett to Lieutenant Commander D. C. Ramsey, 19 November 1928; Moffett to Admiral Frank M. Schofield, 29 March 1932; Moffett to Towers, 31 March, 29 April 1932.

14. George van Deurs, *Anchors in the Sky*, 212; Clark, *Carrier Admiral*, 236–37; Eugene E. Wilson, *Slipstream*, 63–64; Moffett to Congressman Carl Vinson, 13 March 1932; Moffett to Herbert Bayard Swope, 16 September 1925.

15. Wrigley to Moffett, 5 November 1924; Moffett to Wrigley, 7 May and 13 October 1928, 29 January and 26 November 1929; Moffett to Ramsey, 13 November, 7 and 11 December 1928; Moffett to Lieutenant Commander Claude Bailey, USN (Ret.), his Academy roommate, 3 April 1929; Arpee, *Frigates*, 114–19, 153–54. Moffett was reappointed chief of BuAer 13 March 1925 and 13 March 1929. He also battled over personnel with Leigh's predececessor Rear Admiral William R. Shoemaker and again with Leigh's successor, Rear Admiral F. Brooks Upham.

16. Moffett to Towers, 10 February 1930.

17. Moffett to Ramsey, 13 November 1928; Moffett to Rear Admiral H. E. Yarnell, 22 January 1932. Moffett was designated naval observer 17 June 1921 and ordered to duty involving flying 1 July 1922.

18. Arpee, *Frigates*, 88–100 and passim; Moffett to SecNav, "Naval Aeronautical Policy," 10 August 1922; Moffett to Charles W. Schick, 3 October 1931; Moffett to French, 5 March 1930; Moffett to Symington, 16 February 1925.

19. Arpee, *Frigates*, 110–12; Moffett to Porter Adams of the National Aeronautic Association, 5 January 1925; Moffett to CNO, 8 April 1928; Moffett to Captain E. S. Land, 1 July and 11 August 1930; Moffett to Towers, 22 August 1931; Fred Greene, "The Military View of American National Policy, 1904–1940," 369–76; John F. Shiner, "The Air Corps, the Navy, and Coast Defense, 1919–1941," 114–18; Shiner, *Foulois and the U.S. Army Air Corps*, 52–54.

20. Arpee, *Frigates*, 200, 214–15.

21. Clark, *Carrier Admiral*, 16–17; Arpee, *Frigates*, 102–4.

22. Wilson, *Slipstream*, 67–68; Moffett to Captain Adolphus Andrews, 24 February 1926; Moffett to Dwight Morrow, 2 March 1926; Shiner, "Coast Defense," 116–17; Shiner, *Foulois*, 54 ff.

23. Moffett to Rear Admiral William S. Sims, 28 February 1922; Moffett to Reeves, 23 February 1928. Reeves to Moffett, 12 March 1926: "You have the hardest job in the Navy." Moffett had tried to have Rear Admiral John Halligan appointed to command the carriers in 1930, but Standley and Leigh reappointed Reeves for a second tour. Moffett to Rear

Admiral J. L. Latimer, 3 May 1930. Reeves opposed Moffett, but in vain, on locating the new West Coast dirigible base at Sunnyvale rather than Camp Kearney near San Diego. Moffett to Captain J. H. Gunnell, 3 June 1930.

24. Statement by Moffett before the Senate Naval Affairs Committee, 22 May 1930; Raymond G. O'Connor, *Perilous Equilibrium,* 76–77; Arpee, *Frigates,* 169 ff.; Moffett to Frank A. Tichenor of *Aero Digest,* 14 January 1931; Moffett to Towers, 3 and 17 February, 31 March, 2 April 1930. The only other admirals to favor the treaty were Pratt, Yarnell, and Arthur J. Hepburn. Moffett to Lieutenant Commander George D. Murray, 4 June 1930; Moffett to David S. Ingalls, 24 February 1930, 30 September 1931; Moffett to Lieutenant A. R. Mead, his aide, 27 February 1930.

25. Moffett to Vice Admiral William H. Standley, 19 December 1932; Moffett speech at annual dinner of the Naval Academy Graduates Association, New York, 17 February 1933; also Arpee, *Frigates,* 164–65.

26. Moffett to Ingalls, 30 September 1931; Arpee, *Frigates,* 232ff., 238ff.

27. Clark, *Carrier Admiral,* 50; Moffett to Towers, 9 and 25 July 1932, 20 March 1933; Moffett to Ingalls, 26 July 1932; Moffett to Yarnell, 19 July 1932, Yarnell Collection, Naval Historical Foundation, Library of Congress; Moffett to Vinson, 22 November 1932. Though Moffett preferred Towers, he held King in high regard, as in Moffett to King, 8 August 1930, 18 November 1932. The date for Moffett's reappointment would have been 22 April 1933, the fourth anniversary of his last confirmation by the Senate.

BIBLIOGRAPHY

DOCUMENTARY SOURCES

Manuscripts

Houghton Library, Harvard University, Cambridge, Massachusetts
  Walter Hines Page Papers
Henry E. Huntington Library, San Marino, California
  James McHenry Papers
Library of Congress, Washington, D.C.
  William S. Benson Papers
  Mark L. Bristol Papers
  William C. Church Papers
  Grover Cleveland Papers
  Josephus Daniels Diaries and Papers
  George Dewey Papers
  Robley D. Evans Papers
  Bradley A. Fiske Diaries
  Stephen B. Luce Papers
  Henry T. Mayo Papers
  Henry C. Mustin Papers
  Mary C. Powell Collection
  William S. Sims Papers
  Henry Clay Taylor Papers
  Charles M. Thomas Papers
  John H. Towers Collection
  Woodrow Wilson Papers
  Henry E. Yarnell Collection
Massachusetts Historical Society, Boston, Massachusetts
  John D. Long Papers
Military Personnel Records Center, St. Louis, Missouri
  Henry Thomas Mayo's Service Record

National Archives, Washington, D.C.
  Annual Reports of Fleets and Task Forces of the U.S. Navy, 1920–41
    (Microfilm M971)
  Bureau of Navigation Records (Record Group 24)
  Fitness Reports and Naval Examining Board Records (Record Group 125)
  General Records of the Department of the Navy (Record Group 80)
  General Records of the Department of State (Record Group 59)
  Naval Records Collection of the Office of Naval Records and Library
    (Record Group 45)
  Records of Foreign Service Posts of the Department of State (Record
    Group 84)
  Records of Naval Operating Forces (Record Group 313)
  Records of the U.S. Naval Academy (Record Group 405)
  Records Relating to U.S. Fleet Problems I to XXII, 1923–1941 (Micro-
    film M964)
Naval Historical Center, Washington, D.C.
  Biographical Files
  General Board Papers
  George Goodwin Dewey Papers
  McCarty Little Papers
  Stephen B. Luce Papers
  Manuscript Item Collection
  Naval War College Archives
  William V. Pratt Papers
Naval War College, Newport, Rhode Island
  Mahan Collection
  Kay Russell Papers
  Charles H. Stockton Papers
  Storer Papers
  Writings of Stephen B. Luce
  "Notes on Comments of Rear Admiral Mahan," ca. 25 February–1 March
    1911
Nimitz Library, U.S. Naval Academy, Annapolis, Maryland
  Board of Visitors Records
  Bradley A. Fiske Diary
  William A. Moffett Collection
  William T. Sampson Collection
  W. S. Schley Collection
Palmyra King's Daughters Free Library, Palmyra, New York
  William T. Sampson File
Public Record Office, London, England
  Admiralty Papers
  Records of the War Cabinet
Franklin D. Roosevelt Library, Hyde Park, New York
  Livingston Davis Diary
  Winfield Scott Schley Memoir

University of North Carolina, Chapel Hill, North Carolina
Lyman Cotton Papers
Vermont Historical Society, Montpelier, Vermont
George Dewey Papers
Yale University Archives, Yale University, New Haven, Connecticut
Edward M. House Diary and Papers
Henry L. Stimson Diary and Papers

Printed Source Materials

"The Adventurous Career of 'Fighting Bob' Evans." *Current Literature* 42 (January 1907): 33–35.

Allen, Gardner W., ed. *Papers of John Davis Long.* Boston: Massachusetts Historical Society, 1939.

Baker, Ray Stannard and William E. Dodd, eds., *The Public Papers of Woodrow Wilson: The New Democracy (1913–1917).* New York: Harper, 1926.

Barker, Albert. *Everyday Life in the Navy.* Boston: Gorham, 1928.

Barnes, James. "Robley D. Evans, Rear-Admiral." *Outlook* 87 (23 November 1907): 674–86.

"Captain Evans' Diplomacy." *Literary Digest* 44 (20 January 1912): 132–33.

Chadwick, French E. "Aids to Navigation." U.S. Naval Institute *Proceedings* 7 (1881): 255–96.

———. "The Great Need of the United States Navy." *Munsey's Magazine* 33 (September 1905): 643–45.

———. "Naval Department Organization." U.S. Naval Institute *Proceedings* 20 (1894): 493–526.

———. "The Navy in the War." *Scribner's* 24 (November 1898): 529–39.

———. "The 'New York' at Santiago." *Century* 58 (May 1899): 111–14.

———. "The Russian and Japanese Naval Situation." *Collier's Weekly* 33 (16 January 1904): 14–15.

Clark, Charles E. *My Fifty Years in the Navy.* Boston: Little, Brown, 1917.

Clark, J. J. and Clark G. Reynolds. *Carrier Admiral.* New York: David McKay Co., 1967.

Cook, Francis, "The 'Brooklyn' at Santiago." *Century* 58 (May 1899): 95–102.

Coolidge, L. A. "Stories of the Fighting Leaders." *McClure's* 11 (June 1898): 181.

"Concerning Admiral Evans." *Bookman* 34 (January 1912): 582–85.

Cronon, E. David, ed. *The Cabinet Diaries of Josephus Daniels, 1913–1921.* Lincoln: University of Nebraska Press, 1963.

Daniels, Josephus. *The Wilson Era: Years of Peace, 1910–1917.* Chapel Hill: University of North Carolina Press, 1946.

———. *The Wilson Era: Years of War and After, 1917–1923.* Chapel Hill: University of North Carolina Press, 1946.

Davis, Charles B., ed. *Adventures and Letters of Richard Harding Davis.* New York: Scribner's, 1917.

Dewey, Adelbert Milton. *The Life and Letters of Admiral Dewey from Montpelier to Manila.* New York: Woolfall, 1899.

Dewey, George. *Autobiography of George Dewey: Admiral of the Navy.* New York: Scribner's, 1913.

Evans, Robley D. *A Sailor's Log: Recollections of Forty Years of Naval Life.* New York: Appleton, 1901.

————. *An Admiral's Log: Being Continued Recollections of Naval Life.* New York: Appleton, 1910.

————. "The Engineer in Naval Warfare." *North American Review* 163 (December 1896): 654–60.

————. "The 'Iowa' at Santiago." *Century* 58 (May 1899): 50–62.

————. "Prince Henry's American Impressions." *McClure's* 19 (May 1902): 27–37.

————. "Reserve Our Anthracite for Our Navy." *North American Review* 174 (January 1907): 246–53.

Fiske, Bradley A. "Admiral Dewey: An Appreciation." U.S. Naval Institute *Proceedings* 43 (March 1917): 433–36.

————. "Air Power, 1914–1943." U.S. Naval Institute *Proceedings* 68 (May 1942): 686–94.

————. "American Naval Policy," U.S. Naval Institute *Proceedings* 31 (January 1905): 1–80.

————. "The Civil and Military Authority." U.S. Naval Institute *Proceedings* 32 (March 1906): 127–30.

————. "The Civilian Electrician in a Modern War." *Science* 16 (24 October 1890): 225–27.

————. "Courage and Prudence." U.S. Naval Institute *Proceedings* 34 (March 1908): 277–308.

————. "The Defense of the Philippines." *North American Review* 213 (June 1921): 721–24.

————. "Delusions of Pacifists." *Forum* 81 (February 1929): 75–77.

————. "The Diplomatic Responsibility of the United States Navy." U.S. Naval Institute *Proceedings* 40 (May–June 1914): 799–802.

————. "The Electric Railway." *Popular Science Monthly* 24 (April 1884): 742–51.

————. "Electricity in Naval Life." U.S. Naval Institute *Proceedings* 22 (September 1896): 323–428.

————. *Electricity in Theory and Practice; or Elements of Electrical Engineering.* New York: D. Van Nostrand, 1887.

————. "A Fair Basis for Competition in Battle Practice." U.S. Naval Institute *Proceedings* 34 (December 1908): 1189–98.

————. *From Midshipman to Rear Admiral.* New York: Century, 1919.

————. "How We Shall Lose the Next War, and When." *The World's Work* 53 (April 1927): 626–35.

————. "The Invention and Development of the Naval Telescope Sight." U.S. Naval Institute *Proceedings* 35 (June 1909): 405–7.

————. "The Naval Battle of the Future." *Forum* 9 (May 1890): 323–32.

————. "Naval Defense." *North American Review* 203 (February 1916): 216–26.

————. "Naval Policy." *North American Review* 203 (January 1916): 63–73.

————. "Naval Power." U.S. Naval Institute *Proceedings* 37 (June 1911): 683–736.

————. "Naval Preparedness." *North American Review* 202 (December 1915): 847–57.

————. "Naval Principles." *North American Review* 202 (November 1915): 693–701.

————. "The Naval Profession." U.S. Naval Institute *Proceedings* 33 (June 1907): 475–78.

————. *The Navy as a Fighting Machine.* New York: Charles Scribner's Sons, 1916.

————. "The Next Five Years of the Navy: What We Shall Get for the Billion Dollars We Shall Spend." *The World's Work* 33 (January 1917): 256–75.

————. "Pacifists and Militarists." *Woman Citizen* n.s. 12 (October 1927): 14–15 and (December 1927): 38–39.

————. "The Paramount Duty of the Army and Navy." U.S. Naval Institute *Proceedings* 41 (July–August 1914): 1073–74.

————. "Possibilities for Disarmament." *Annals of the American Academy of Political and Social Science* 120 (July 1925): 77–80.

————. "Range Finders." U.S. Naval Institute *Proceedings* 27 (June 1901): 432–34.

————. "Stephen B. Luce: An Appreciation." U.S. Naval Institute *Proceedings* 43 (September 1917): 1935–40.

————. "Torpedo Plane and Bomber." U.S. Naval Institute *Proceedings* 48 (September 1922): 1474–78.

————. "War and Peace." *Forum* 81, sup. 46 (March 1929): 75–77.

————. "The Warfare of the Future." U.S. Naval Institute *Proceedings* 47 (February 1921): 157–67.

————. *Wartime in Manila.* Boston: Gorham, 1913.

Goode, W. A. M. "The Destruction of Cervera's Fleet." *McClure's* 11 (September 1898): 423–32.

————. *With Sampson through the War.* New York: Doubleday, 1899.

Goodrich, Caspar F. *Rope Yarns from the Old Navy.* New York: Naval History Society, 1931.

Graham, George Edward. "The Destruction of Cervera's Fleet." *McClure's* 11 (September 1898): 403–21.

————. *Schley and Santiago.* Chicago: Conkey, 1902.

Grew, Joseph C. *Turbulent Era: A Diplomatic Record of Forty Years, 1904–1945,* 2 vols. Boston: Houghton Mifflin, 1952.

Grinnell, Charles E. "A Legal View of the Inquiry Granted to Rear Admiral Schley and of Other Inquiries by Military Courts." *Green Bag* 14 (1902): 99–148.

Gulliver, Louis J. "Sampson and Shafter at Santiago." U.S. Naval Institute *Proceedings* 65 (June 1939): 799–806.

Hayes, John D. and John B. Hattendorf, eds. *The Writings of Stephen B. Luce.* Newport: Naval War College, 1975.

"Honor to a Naval Warrior [Robley D. Evans]." *Outlook* 89 (29 August 1908): 972.

House, Edward Mandell and Charles Seymour, eds. *What Really Happened at Paris: The Story of the Peace Conference, 1918–1919 by American Delegates.* New York: Charles Scribner's Sons, 1921.

King, Ernest J. and Walter Muir Whitehill. *Fleet Admiral King: A Naval Record.* New York: W. W. Norton, 1952.

Link, Arthur S., ed. *The Papers of Woodrow Wilson,* 57 vols. to date. Princeton: Princeton University Press, 1966–87.

Lodge, Henry Cabot. *Selections from the Correspondence of Theodore Roosevelt and Henry Cabot Lodge,* 2 vols. New York: Scribner's, 1925.

———. *The Senate and the League of Nations.* New York: Charles Scribner's Sons, 1925.

Long, John D. *America of Yesterday as Reflected in the Journal of John Davis Long,* ed. Lawrence S. Mayo. Boston: Atlantic Monthly, 1923.

———. *The New American Navy,* 2 vols. New York: Outlook, 1903.

Long, Margaret D., ed. *The Journal of John D. Long.* Ringe, N.H.: Smith, 1956.

Luce, Stephen B. "The Fleet." *North American Review* 188 (October 1908): 564–76.

———. "The Naval War College:" U.S. Naval Institute *Proceedings* 36 (March 1910): 685.

———. "The Spanish–American War." *North American Review* 194 (October 1911): 616–21.

Maguire, Doris D., ed. *French Ensor Chadwick: Selected Letters and Papers.* Washington, D.C.: University Press of America, 1981.

Mahan, Alfred Thayer. "America's Duties to Her New Dependencies." *Engineering Magazine* 16 (January 1899): 521 ff. Reprinted under the title "The Relation of the United States to Their New Dependents" in *Lessons of the War With Spain,* 241–53.

———. "The Apparent Decadence of the Church's Influence." *Churchman* 87 (25 April 1903): 537–38.

———. "Appreciation of Conditions in the Russo–Japanese Conflict." *Collier's Weekly* XXXII (20 February 1904): 7–8 and XXXIII (30 April 1904): 10–13.

———. *Armaments and Arbitration, or the Place of Force in International Relations of States.* New York: Harper, 1912.

———. "The Battle of the Sea of Japan." *Collier's Weekly* XXXV (17 June 1905): 12–13.

———. "The Battleship of All Big Guns." *World's Work* 21 (January 1911): 13888–902.

———. "Capt. Mahan on Expansion." *New York Times,* 1 December 1898.

————. "Christian Progress." *New York Times,* 16 August 1914.

————. "Commerce and War." *New York Times,* 17 and 23 November 1898.

————. "The Effect of Asiatic Conditions upon World Policies." *North American Review* 176 (November 1900): 609–26.

————. "Freedom in the Use of the Prayer Book." *The Churchman* CVIII (November 1913): 623–24.

————. *From Sail to Steam: Recollections of Naval Life.* New York: Harper and Brothers, 1907.

————. "Germany's Naval Ambition." *Collier's Weekly* 43 (24 April 1911): 12–13.

————. "The Hague Conference; the Question of Immunity of Belligerent Merchant Shipping." *National Review* 49 (June 1907): 521–37.

————. "The Hague Conference and the Practical Aspect of War." *National Review* 49 (July 1907): 688–704.

————. *The Harvest Within: Thoughts on the Life of a Christian.* Boston: Little, Brown, 1909.

————. *The Influence of Sea Power upon the French Revolution and Empire,* 2 vols. Boston: Little, Brown, 1892.

————. *The Influence of Sea Power upon History, 1660–1783.* Boston: Little, Brown, 1890; 14th ed., 1898.

————. *The Interest of America in Sea Power, Present and Future.* Boston: Little, Brown, 1897.

————. *Lessons of the War with Spain and Other Articles.* Boston: Little, Brown, 1899.

————. *Naval Administration and Warfare, Some Great Principles With Other Essays.* Boston: Little, Brown, 1908.

————. *Naval Strategy, Compared and Constrasted with the Principles of Military Operations on Land.* Boston: Little, Brown, 1911.

————. "The Panama Canal and Sea Power in the Pacific." *Century* 82 (June 1911): 240–48.

————. "The Panama Canal and the Distribution of the Fleet." *North American Review* 200 (September 1914): 549–68.

————. "Panama Unguarded Might Be Seized." *New York Times,* 27 October 1912.

————. "The Peace Conference and the Moral Aspect of War." *North American Review* 169 (October 1899): 433–47.

————. "Prayer Book Revision." *The Churchman* CX (October 1914): 465–66, 497–98.

————. "The Problem of Asia." *Harper's Monthly* 100 (March, April, May 1900): 536–47, 747–59, 929–41, reprinted in *The Problem of Asia.*

————. *The Problem of Asia and Its Effects upon International Policies.* Boston: Little, Brown, 1900.

————. "The Problems That Rojestvensky and Togo Must Solve." *Collier's Magazine* XXXV (13 May 1905): 12–14.

————. "Reflections, Historic and Others, Suggested by the Battle of the

Sea of Japan." U.S. Naval Institute *Proceedings* 32 (June 1906): 447–71.

————. *Retrospect and Prospect: Studies in International Relations, Naval and Political.* Boston: Little, Brown, 1903.

————. "Retrospect upon the War between Japan and Russia." *National Review* 47 (May 1906): 383–405.

————. "Sampson's Naval Career." *McClure's* 19 (July 1902): 217–21. Published also as "Rear Admiral Wm. R. Sampson" in *Fortnightly Review* 72 (August 1902): 227–39; and in Mahan, *Retrospect and Prospect,* 287–309.

————. *Some Neglected Aspects of War.* Boston: Little, Brown, 1907.

————. "The Submarine and Its Enemies." *Collier's Weekly* 39 (6 April 1907): 17–21.

————. "Subordination in Historical Treatment." Renamed "Writing of History," *Atlantic Monthly* 91 (March 1903): 289–98.

————. *Sea Power in Its Relations to the War of 1812,* 2 vols. Boston: Little, Brown, 1912.

————. "Torpedo Craft vs. Battleships." *Collier's Weekly* XXXIII (21 May 1904): 16–17.

————. "Twentieth Century Christianity." *North American Review* 199 (April 1914): 589–98.

————. "War from the Christian Standpoint." A paper read before the Church Congress, Providence, Rhode Island, 15 November 1900. Printed in *Some Neglected Aspects of War.*

————. "Was Panama 'A Chapter of National Dishonor'?" *North American Review* 196 (October 1912): 549–68.

————. "Writing of History." *Atlantic Monthly* 91 (March 1903): 289–98.

"Mayo at Tampico." *Literary Digest* 48 (2 May 1914): 1056–60.

Mayo, Henry Thomas. "The Atlantic Fleet in the Great War." In *What Really Happened at Paris: The Story of the Peace Conference, 1918–1919,* ed. Edward Mandell House and Charles Seymour, 348–69, 490–94. New York: Scribner's, 1921.

Mayo, Lawrence Shaw, ed. *America of Yesterday as Reflected in the Journal of John Davis Long.* Boston: Atlantic Monthly, 1923.

Morison, Elting E. and John M. Blum, eds. *Letters of Theodore Roosevelt,* 8 vols. Cambridge, Mass.: Harvard University Press, 1951–54.

Nordhoff, Charles. *Man of War Life: A Boy's Experience in the United States Navy, during a Voyage around the World in a Ship of the Line.* With an Introduction and notes by John B. Hattendorf. Annapolis: Naval Institute Press, 1985.

Palmer, Frederick. *With My Own Eyes.* Indianapolis: Bobbs-Merrill, 1932.

Pershing, John J. *My Experiences in the World War,* 2 vols. New York: Stokes, 1931.

Philip, John. "The 'Texas' at Santiago." *Century* 58 (May 1899): 87–94.

Reuterdahl, Henry. "Needs of Our Navy." *McClure's Magazine* XXX (January–February 1908): 251–63, 517–20.

Roosevelt, Theodore. "Admiral Evans." *The Outlook* 100 (13 January 1912): 55–74.
———. *An Autobiography*. New York: Scribner's, 1913 and 1920.
———. *The Works of Theodore Roosevelt*, 20 vols. New York: Scribner's, 1926.
Sampson, William T. "The Atlantic Fleet in the Spanish War." *Century* 57 (April 1899): 886–913.
———. "Face Hardened Armor." U.S. Naval Institute *Proceedings* 20 (1894): 818–21.
———. [Order Establishing Dept. of Discipline, 25 January 1890]. U.S. Naval Institute *Proceedings* 16 (1890): 173–74.
———. "Outline of a Scheme for the Naval Defense of the Coast." U.S. Naval Institute *Proceedings* 15 (March 1889): 169–232.
Sargent, Nathan, comp. *Admiral Dewey and the Manila Campaign*. Washington, D.C.: Naval Historical Foundation, 1947.
Schley, Winfield Scott. "Admiral Schley's Own Story." *Cosmopolitan* 52 (December 1911–May 1912): 4–14, 187–99, 368–78, 523–32, 605–23, 751–60.
———. *Forty-five Years under the Flag*. New York: Appleton, 1904.
———. [Report on the *Baltimore*]. U.S. Naval Institute *Proceedings* 18 (1892): 235–49.
Schley, Winfield Scott and J. R. Soley. *The Rescue of Greely*. New York: Scribner's, 1885.
Schroeder, Seaton. *A Half Century of Naval Science*. New York: Appleton, 1922.
Seager, Robert, II and Doris D. Maguire, eds. *Letters and Papers of Alfred Thayer Mahan*, 3 vols. Annapolis: Naval Institute Press, 1975.
Sims, William S. *The Victory at Sea,* ed. David F. Trask. Annapolis: Naval Institute Press, 1984; original edition, New York: Doubleday, Page, 1920.
Soley, James R. *Historical Sketch of the U.S. Naval Academy*. Washington, D.C.: GPO, 1876.
The Statistical History of the United States from Colonial Times to the Present. Stamford, Conn.: Fairfield, 1965.
Stickney, Joseph L. "With Dewey at Manila." *Harper's New Monthly* 98 (February 1899): 476–84.
Taylor, Henry C. "The 'Indiana' at Santiago." *Century* 58 (May 1899): 62–75.
U.S. Congress. "Floating Batteries." In *House Executive Document No. 49*. 49th Cong., 1st Sess. Washington, D.C.: GPO, 1886.
———. [Inquiry at Mare Island]. *House Executive Document No. 9*. 52nd Cong., 1st Sess. Washington, D.C.: GPO, 1892.
———. *Senate Executive Document No. 56*. 53rd Cong., 3rd Sess. Washington, D.C.: GPO, 1895.
———. *Papers Relating to the Foreign Relations of the United States* [1914]. 63rd Cong., 3rd Sess. Washington, D.C.: GPO, 1922.

————. *Record of Proceedings of a Court of Inquiry in the Case of Rear Admiral Winfield Scott Schley, U.S. Navy*, 2 vols. 57th Cong., 1st Sess. Washington, D.C.: GPO, 1902.

————. *Naval Investigation: Hearings before the Subcommittee of the Committee on Naval Affairs, United States Senate*, 2 vols. 66th Cong. 2nd Sess. Washington, D.C.: GPO, 1920.

————. House of Representatives. Committee on Naval Affairs. *Navy Reorganization: Hearings on the Bill to Combine the Line and Engineer Corps of the Navy.* 55th Cong., 2nd Sess. Washington, D.C.: GPO, 1898.

————. House of Representatives. Committee on Naval Affairs. *Hearings . . . on Estimates Submitted by the Secretary of the Navy, 1915.* 63rd Cong., 3rd Sess. Washington, D.C.: GPO, 1915.

————. House of Representatives. Committee on Naval Affairs. *Hearings . . . on Estimates Submitted by the Secretary of the Navy, 1916.* 64th Cong., 3rd Sess. Washington, D.C.: GPO, 1916.

————. House of Representatives. Committee on Naval Affairs. *Naval Investigation: Hearings before the Subcommittee of the Committee on Naval Affairs, United States Senate*, 2 vols. 66th Cong., 2nd Sess. Washington, D.C.: GPO, 1920.

————. House of Representatives. Committee on Naval Affairs. *Hearings . . . on Estimates Submitted by the Secretary of the Navy, 1930.* 72nd Cong., 1st Sess. Washington, D.C.: GPO, 1932.

————. Senate [Chadwyck, French Ensor]. *Report on the Training System for the Navy and Mercantile Marine of England and on the Naval Training System of France, Made to the Bureau of Equipment and Recruiting, U.S.N. Department, Sept. 1879, Senate Executive Document, No. 52.* 46th Cong., 2nd Sess. Washington, D.C.: GPO, 1880.

————. Senate. *Senate Executive Documents No. 68.* 48th Cong., 2nd Sess. Washington, D.C.: GPO, 1885.

————. Senate. Committee on Foreign Affairs. *Treaty on the Limitation of Armaments, Hearings.* 71st Cong., 2nd Sess. Washington, D.C.: GPO, 1930.

————. Senate. Committee on Naval Affairs. *Naval Investigation: Hearings before the Subcommittee on the Committee on Naval Affairs.* 66th Cong., 2nd Sess. Washington, D.C.: GPO, 1920.

————. Senate. Committee on Naval Affairs. *London Naval Treaty of 1930. Hearings.* 71st Cong., 2nd Sess. Washington, D.C.: GPO, 1930.

————. Senate. Committee on Naval Affairs. *Hearings on S. 51.* 72nd Cong., 1st Sess. Washington, D.C.: GPO, 1932.

U.S. Department of the Navy. *Annual Reports of the Secretary of the Navy.* Washington, D.C.: GPO, 1821–1948.

————. *Official Records of the Union and Confederate Navies in the War of the Rebellion*, ed. Richard Rush et al., 31 vols. and index. Washington, D.C.: GPO, 1894–1922.

————. *Operations of the War with Spain: Appendix to Report of the Chief of Bureau of Navigation.* Washington, D.C.: GPO, 1899.

————. *Report of the Board of Visitors to the United States Naval Academy, Annapolis, Maryland, May 1, 1929.* Washington, D.C.: GPO, 1929.

————. *Report of the Board of Visitors to the United States Naval Academy, Annapolis, Maryland, May 1, 1930.* Washington, D.C.: GPO, 1930.

————. *Revised Organization Orders of the Office of Naval Operations (1 August 1919).* Washington, D.C.: GPO, 1919.

U.S. Department of State. *Foreign Relations of the United States, 1891.* Washington, D.C.: GPO, 1892.

————. *Papers Relating to the Foreign Relations of the United States, 1918–1930,* 32 vols. Washington, D.C.: GPO, 1930–45.

————. *Papers Relating to the Foreign Relations of the United States, 1919: The Paris Peace Conference,* 13 vols. Washington, D.C.: GPO, 1942–47.

U.S. Department of War, Adjutant-General's Office. *Correspondence Relating to the War with Spain and Conditions Growing Out of the Same . . . April 15, 1898, to July 30, 1902,* 2 vols. Washington, D.C.: GPO, 1902.

U.S. *Statutes at Large,* vols. 38–39. Washington, D.C.: GPO, 1915–17.

Wainwright, Richard. "William Thomas Sampson," U.S. Naval Institute *Proceedings* 28 (June 1902): 456.

Washington Post. *Pictorial History of the Schley Court of Inquiry.* Washington, D.C.: Washington Post, 1901.

"When 'Fighting Bob' Was 'Little Breeches.' " *Literary Digest* 44 (24 February 1912): 390–91.

Wilson, Eugene E. *Slipstream: The Autobiography of an Air Craftsman,* 2nd ed. New York: Science Press, 1965.

Wilson, H. W. "The Schley Court of Inquiry." *National Review* [London] 38 (February 1902): 788–800.

SECONDARY SOURCES

Books and Dissertations

Abbazia, Patrick. *Mr. Roosevelt's Navy.* Annapolis: Naval Institute Press, 1975.

Albion, Robert G. *Makers of Naval Policy, 1798–1947,* ed. Rowena Reed. Annapolis: Naval Institute Press, 1979.

Alden, Carroll S. and Ralph Earle. *Makers of the Naval Tradition.* New York: Ginn, 1926.

Alden, John D. *American Steel Navy: A Photographic History of the U.S. Navy from the Introduction of the Steel Hull in 1883 to the Cruise of the Great White Fleet, 1907–1909.* Annapolis: Naval Institute Press and New York: American Heritage Press, 1972.

Arpee, Edward. *From Frigates to Flat-Tops: The Story of the Life and Achievements of Rear Admiral William Adger Moffett, U.S.N.* Lake Forest, Ill.: Privately printed, 1953.

Arthur, Reginald Wright. *Contact: Careers of U.S. Naval Aviators Assigned Numbers 1–2000.* Washington, D.C.: Naval Aviators Register, 1967.

Beach, Edward L. *The United States Navy: Two Hundred Years.* New York: Holt, 1986.

Beers, Henry P. *U.S. Naval Detachment in Turkish Waters, 1919–1924.* Washington, D.C.: Navy Department, 1943.

Benjamin, Park. *The United States Naval Academy.* New York: Putnam's, 1900.

Bennett, Frank M. *The Steam Navy of the United States.* Pittsburgh: W. T. Nicholson, 1896.

Bradford, James C., ed. *Captains of the Old Steam Navy: Makers of the American Naval Tradition, 1840–1880.* Annapolis: Naval Institute Press, 1986.

Braisted, William R. *The United States Navy in the Pacific, 1897–1909.* Austin: University of Texas Press, 1958.

————. *The United States Navy in the Pacific, 1909–1922.* Austin: University of Texas Press, 1971.

Brodie, Bernard. *Seapower in the Machine Age.* Princeton: Princeton University Press, 1941.

Browning, Robert S., III. *Two if by Sea: The Development of American Coastal Defense Policy.* Westport, Conn.: Greenwood, 1984.

Bryson, Thomas A. *Tars, Turks, and Tankers: The Role of the United States Navy in the Middle East, 1800–1979.* Metuchen, N.J.: Scarecrow, 1980.

Busch, Briton C. *The War against the Seals: A History of the North American Seal Fishery.* Kingston, Ont.: McGill-Queen's, 1985.

Bush, Lewis, W. *Seventy-seven Samarai: Japanese Embassy to America.* Tokyo: Kodansha, 1968.

Buzanski, Peter M. "Admiral Mark L. Bristol and Turkish American Relations, 1919–1922." Ph.D. dissertation, University of California, Berkeley, 1960.

Callahan, Edward W. *List of Officers of the Navy of the United States and of the Marine Corps from 1775 to 1900.* New York: L. R. Hamersley & Co., 1901.

Calvert, James. *The Naval Profession.* New York: McGraw Hill, 1965.

Calvert, Monte A. *The Mechanical Engineer in America, 1830–1910: Professional Cultures in Conflict.* Baltimore: Johns Hopkins University Press, 1967.

Chadwick, French E. *The Relations of the United States and Spain: Diplomacy.* New York: Scribner's, 1909.

————. *The Relations of the United States and Spain: The Spanish–American War,* 2 vols. New York: Scribner's, 1911.

Challener, Richard. *Admirals, Generals, and American Foreign Policy, 1898–1914.* Princeton: Princeton University Press, 1973.

Cherpak, Evelyn, comp. *Register of the Stephen B. Luce Papers.* Newport: Naval War College, 1987.

Coggeshall, W. J. and J. E. McCarthy. *The United States Naval Torpedo Station, Newport, Rhode Island, 1858–1920.* Newport: Training Station, 1920.

Cole, Bernard D. *Gunboats and Marines: The United States Navy in China,*

1925–1928. Newark: University of Delaware, 1983.

Coletta, Paolo E. *Admiral Bradley A. Fiske and the American Navy.* Lawrence: Regents Press of Kansas, 1979.

———. *Bowman Hendry McCalla: A Fighting Sailor.* Washington, D.C.: University Press of America, 1979.

———. *French Ensor Chadwick: Scholarly Warrior.* Lanham, Md.: University Press of America, 1980.

———. *William Jennings Bryan: Progressive Politician and Moral Statesman, 1909–1915.* Lincoln: University of Nebraska Press, 1969.

Coletta, Paolo E., K. Jack Bauer, and Robert G. Albion, eds. *American Secretaries of the Navy,* 2 vols. Annapolis: Naval Institute Press, 1980.

Cooling, Benjamin Franklin. *Benjamin Franklin Tracy: Father of the Modern American Fighting Navy.* Hamden, Conn.: Shoe String, 1973.

———. *Gray Steel and Blue Water Navy: The Formative Years of America's Military–Industrial Complex, 1881–1917.* Hamden, Conn.: Archon, 1979.

Cooper, James Fenimore. *The History of the Navy of the United States of America,* 2 vols. Philadelphia: Lea & Blanchard, 1839.

Cosmas, Graham A. *An Army for Empire: The United States Army in the Spanish–American War.* Columbia: University of Missouri Press, 1971.

Costello, Daniel J. "Planning for War: A History of the General Board of the Navy, 1900–1914." Ph.D. dissertation, Fletcher School of Law and Diplomacy, Tufts University, 1968.

Davenport, Charles Benedict. *Naval Officers: Their Heredity and Development.* Washington, D.C.: Carnegie Institution of Washington, 1919.

Davis, George T. *A Navy Second to None: The Development of Modern American Naval Policy.* New York: Harcourt, Brace, 1940.

De Novo, John A. *American Interests and Policies in the Middle East, 1900–1939.* Minneapolis: University of Minnesota Press, 1963.

Dowart, Jeffrey M. *Conflict of Duty: The U.S. Navy's Intelligence Dilemma, 1919–1945.* Annapolis: Naval Institute Press, 1983.

Eccles, Henry E. *Military Concepts and Philosophy.* New Brunswick, N.J.: Rutgers University Press, 1965.

Falk, Edwin A. *Fighting Bob Evans.* New York: Cornwall Press, 1931.

The First Japanese Embassy to the United States of America. Tokyo: American Japan Society, 1920.

Friedel, Frank B. *Franklin D. Roosevelt: The Apprenticeship.* Boston: Little, Brown, 1952.

Frothingham, Tomas G. *The Naval History of the World War,* 3 vols. Cambridge, Mass.: Harvard University Press, 1924–26.

Grabill, Joseph L. *Protestant Diplomacy and the Near East: Missionary Influence in American Policy, 1810–1927.* Minneapolis: University of Minnesota Press, 1971.

Gleaves, Albert. *Life and Letters of Stephen B. Luce.* New York: Putnam's, 1925.

———. *The Life of an American Sailor: Rear Admiral William Hemsley Emory, USN.* New York: Doran, 1923.

Goldberg, Joyce S. *The Baltimore Affair*. Lincoln: University of Nebraska Press, 1986.

Gorshkov, S. G. *Red Star Rising at Sea*. Annapolis: Naval Institute Press, 1974.

———. *The Sea Power of the State*. Annapolis: Naval Institute Press, 1979.

Gould, Lewis L. *The Spanish–American War and President McKinley*. Lawrence: University Press of Kansas, 1982.

Grant, Robert M. *U-Boats Destroyed: The Effect of Anti-submarine Warfare, 1914–1918*. London: Putnam, 1964.

———. *U-Boat Intelligence, 1914–1918*. London: Putnam, 1969.

Hagan, Kenneth J. *American Gunboat Diplomacy and the Old Navy, 1877–1889*. Westport, Conn.: Greenwood, 1973.

Hagan, Kenneth J., ed. *In Peace and War: Interpretations of American Naval History, 1775–1984*, 2nd ed. Westport, Conn.: Greenwood, 1984.

Halpern, Paul G. *The Naval War in the Mediterranean, 1914–1918*. Annapolis: Naval Institute Press, 1987.

Halstead, Murat. *Life and Achievements of Admiral Dewey: From Montpelier to Manila*. Chicago: Dominion, 1899.

Hamersly, Lewis Randolph, comp. *The Records of Living Officers of the U.S. Navy and Marine Corps*. Philadelphia: L. R. Hamersly & Co., [5th ed.] 1894, [7th ed.] 1902.

Hammond, Paul Y. *Organizing for Defense: The American Military Establishment in the Twentieth Century*. Princeton: Princeton University Press, 1961.

Hart, Robert A. *The Great White Fleet: Its Voyage around the World, 1907–1909*. Boston: Little, Brown, 1965.

Hattendorf, John, comp. *Register of the Alfred Thayer Mahan Papers*. Newport: Naval War College, 1987.

Hattendorf, John B. and Lynn C. Hattendorf, comps. *A Bibliography of the Works of Alfred Thayer Mahan*. Newport: Naval War College, 1986.

Hattendorf, John B., B. Mitchell Simpson III, and John R. Wadleigh. *Sailors and Scholars: The Centennial History of the U.S. Naval War College*. Newport: Naval War College, 1984.

Healy, Laurin Hall and Luis Kutner. *The Admiral [Dewey]*. Chicago: Ziff-Davis, 1944.

Heinl, Robert D. *Dictionary of Military and Naval Quotations*. Annapolis: Naval Institute Press, 1966.

Heinrichs, Waldo H. *American Ambassador: Joseph C. Grew and the Development of the United States Diplomatic Tradition*. Boston: Little, Brown, 1966.

Herrick, Walter R., Jr. *The American Naval Revolution*. Baton Rouge: Louisiana State University Press, 1966.

Hewes, James E., Jr. *From Root to McNamara: Army Organization and Administration, 1900–1963*. Washington, D.C.: GPO, 1963.

Horsfield, John. *The Art of Leadership in War: The Royal Navy from the Age of Nelson to the End of World War II*. Westport, Conn.: Greenwood Press, 1980.

Howarth, L. S. *History of Communications—Electronics in the United States Navy.* Washington, D.C.: GPO, 1963.

Howe, M. A. De Wolfe. *George von Lengerke Meyer.* New York: Dodd, Mead, 1920.

Huntington, Samuel P. *The Soldier and the State: The Theory and Politics of Civil—Military Relations.* Cambridge, Mass.: Harvard University Press, 1957.

Johnson, Allan, Dumas Malone, et al., eds. *Dictionary of American Biography,* 20 vols. and 7 supplements. New York: Scribner's, 1927–81.

Johnson, Robert Erwin. *Far China Station: The U.S. Navy in Asian Waters, 1800–1898.* Annapolis: Naval Institute Press, 1979.

———. *Rear Admiral John Rodgers, 1812–1882.* Annapolis: Naval Institute Press, 1967.

———. *Thence Around Cape Horn: The Story of United States Naval Forces on Pacific Stations, 1818–1923.* Annapolis: Naval Institute Press, 1963.

Johnson, Virginia W. *The Unregimented General: A Biography of Nelson A. Miles.* Boston: Houghton Mifflin, 1962.

Jomini, Antoine-Henri. *The Art of War,* trans. G. H. Mendell and W. P. Craighill, 1862. Philadelphia: Lippincott, 1892.

Karsten, Peter. *The Naval Aristocracy: The Golden Age of Annapolis and the Emergency of Modern American Navalism.* New York: Free Press, 1972.

Kipling, Rudyard. *The Cat That Walked by Himself.* New York: Hawthorn, 1970.

Kilpatrick, Carroll, ed. *Roosevelt and Daniels: A Friendship in Politics.* Chapel Hill: University of North Carolina Press, 1952.

Kittredge, Tracy B. *Naval Lessons of the Great War: A Review of the Senate Naval Investigations of the Criticisms of Admiral Sims of the Policies and Methods of Josephus Daniels.* Garden City, N.Y.: Doubleday, Page, 1921.

Klachko, Mary. "Anglo—American Naval Competition, 1918–1922." Ph.D. dissertation, Columbia University, 1962.

Klachko, Mary with David F. Trask. *Admiral William Shepherd Benson: First Chief of Naval Operations.* Annapolis: Naval Institute Press, 1987.

Kranzberg, Melvin and Carroll W. Pursell, Jr., eds. *Technology and Western Civilization,* 2 vols. New York: Oxford University Press, 1967.

Langley, Lester D. *The Banana Wars: An Inner History of American Empire, 1900–1934.* Lexington: University Press of Kentucky, 1983.

Leech, Margaret. *In the Days of McKinley.* New York: Harper & Brothers, 1959.

Library of Congress, Manuscript Department Reference Division. *Naval Historical Foundations Collections: Part 7, David Foot Sellers and Stephen B. Luce.* Washington, D.C.: Library of Congress, 1968.

Linderman, Gerald F. *The Mirror of War: American Society and the Spanish—American War.* Ann Arbor: University of Michigan Press, 1974.

Link, Arthur S. *Woodrow Wilson and the Progressive Era, 1910–1917.* New York: Harper and Row, 1954.

Livezey, William E. *Mahan on Sea Power.* Norman: University of Oklahoma Press, 1947.

Livingston, Dorothy M. *Master of Light: Albert A. Michelson.* Chicago: University of Chicago Press, 1973.

Lord, Clifford L. and Archibald D. Turnbull. *History of United States Naval Aviation.* New Haven: Yale University Press, 1949.

Love, Robert William, Jr., ed. *The Chiefs of Naval Operations.* Annapolis: Naval Institute Press, 1980.

Maclay, Edgar Stanton. *History of the Navy,* 3 vols. New York: Appleton, 1901.

Mahan, Alfred T. *Types of Naval Officers.* London: Sampson Low, Marston & Co., 1904.

Marder, Arthur J. *From Dreadnoughts to Scapa Flow: The Royal Navy in the Fisher Era, 1904–1919,* 5 vols. New York: Oxford University Press, 1961–70.

Millett, Allan R. and Peter Maslowski. *For the Common Defense: A Military History of the United States of America.* New York: Free Press, 1984.

Millis, Walter. *The Martial Spirit.* Cambridge, Mass.: Riverside, 1931.

Morison, Elting E. *Admiral Sims and the Modern American Navy.* Boston: Houghton Mifflin, 1942.

———. *Men, Machines, and Modern Times.* Cambridge, Mass.: MIT Press, 1966.

Morrison, Joseph L. *Josephus Daniels: The Small-d Democrat.* Chapel Hill: University of North Carolina Press, 1966.

Musicant, Ivan. *U.S. Armored Cruisers: A Design and Operational History.* Annapolis: Naval Institute Press, 1985.

National Cyclopedia of American Biography, 63 vols. and vols. A to M. New York: White, 1872–1959.

Nicholson, Philip Y. "George Dewey and the Transformation of American Foreign Policy." Ph.D. dissertation, University of New Mexico, 1971.

Notter, Harley. *The Origins of the Foreign Policy of Woodrow Wilson.* Baltimore: Johns Hopkins University Press, 1937.

O'Connor, Raymond G. *Perilous Equilibrium: The United States Navy and the London Naval Conference of 1930.* Lawrence: University Press of Kansas, 1962.

Padfield, Peter. *Guns at Sea.* New York: St. Martin's, 1974.

Paterson, Thomas G. *American Foreign Policy: A History to 1914,* 2nd ed. Lexington, Mass.: D. C. Heath, 1983.

Paullin, Oscar. *Paullin's History of Naval Administration, 1775–1911.* Annapolis: Naval Institute Press, 1968.

Pike, Frederick B. *Chile and the United States, 1880–1962: The Emergence of Chile's Social Crisis and the Challenge to United States Diplomacy.* South Bend, Ind.: University of Notre Dame Press, 1963.

Potter, E. B., ed. *Sea Power: A Naval History,* 2nd ed. Annapolis: Naval Institute Press, 1981.

Potter, E. B. and J. Roger Fredland, eds. *The United States and World Sea Power.* Englewood Cliffs, N.J.: Prentice-Hall, 1955.

Pratt, Julius W. *Expansionists of 1898: The Acquisition of Hawaii and the Spanish Islands.* Baltimore: Johns Hopkins University Press, 1936.

Puleston, W. D. *Annapolis: Gangway to the Quarterdeck.* New York: Appleton, 1942.

————. *Mahan: The Life and Work of Captain Alfred Thayer Mahan, U.S.N.* New Haven: Yale University Press, 1939.

Quick, Robert E. *An Affair of Honor: Woodrow Wilson and the Occupation of Vera Cruz.* New York: W. W. Norton, 1962.

Ranft, Bryan and Geoffrey Till. *The Sea in Soviet Strategy.* Annapolis: Naval Institute Press, 1983.

Rappaport, Armin. *The Navy League of the United States.* Detroit: Wayne State University Press, 1962.

Reed, Rowena. *Combined Operations in the Civil War.* Annapolis: Naval Institute Press, 1978.

Reynolds, Clark G. *Famous American Admirals.* New York: Van Nostrand Reinhold Co., 1978.

————. "Towers: The Air Admiral." Annapolis: Naval Institute Press, forthcoming.

Rickover, Hyman G. *How the Battleship "Maine" Was Destroyed.* Washington, D.C.: Naval Historical Center, 1976.

Roskill, Stephen. *Naval Policy between the Wars.* Vol. 1, *The Period of Anglo-American Antagonism, 1919–1929.* London: Collins, St. James, 1968.

Rudin, Harry R. *Armistice, 1918.* New Haven: Yale University Press, 1944.

Seager, Robert, II. *Alfred Thayer Mahan: The Man and His Letters.* Annapolis: Naval Institute Press, 1977.

Shiner, John F. *Foulois and the U.S. Army Corps, 1931–1935.* Washington, D.C.: Office of Air Force History, 1983.

Spector, Ronald. *Admiral of the New Empire: The Life and Career of George Dewey.* Baton Rouge: Louisiana State University Press, 1974.

————. *Professors of War: The Naval War College and the Development of the Naval Profession.* Newport: Naval War College, 1977.

Spiller, Roger J., Joseph G. Dawson, and T. Harry Williams, eds. *Dictionary of American Military Biography,* 3 vols. Westport, Conn.: Greenwood, 1984.

Sprout, Harold and Margaret Sprout. *The Rise of American Naval Power, 1776–1918.* Princeton: Princeton University Press, 1939. Reprinted with new introduction, 1966.

————. *Toward a New Order of Sea Power: American Naval Policy and the World Scene, 1918–1922.* Princeton: Princeton University Press, 1943.

Still, William N. *American Sea Power in the Old World: The United States Navy in European and Near Eastern Waters, 1865–1917.* Westport, Conn.: Greenwood, 1980.

Stillson, Albert Charles. "The Development and Maintenance of the American Naval Establishment, 1901–1909." Ph.D. dissertation, Columbia University, 1959.

Sudsbury, Elretta. *Jackrabbits to Jets: The History of North Island, San Diego, California*. San Diego: Neyenesch, 1967.

Sweetman, Jack. *The Landing at Vera Cruz: 1914*. Annapolis: Naval Institute Press, 1968.

———. *The U.S. Naval Academy: An Illustrated History*. Annapolis: Naval Institute Press, 1979.

Taylor, Theodore. *The Magnificent Mitscher*. New York: W. W. Norton, 1957.

Taylor, Charles C. *The Life of Admiral Mahan*. London: John Murray, 1920.

Todorich, Charles. *The Spirited Years: A History of the Antebellum Naval Academy*. Annapolis: Naval Institute Press, 1984.

Trask, David F. *Captains and Cabinets: Anglo–American Naval Relations, 1917–1918*. Columbia: University of Missouri Press, 1972.

———. *The United States in the Supreme War Council: American War Aims and Inter-Allied Strategy, 1917–1918*. Middletown, Conn.: Wesleyan University Press, 1961.

———. *The War with Spain in 1898*. New York: Macmillan, 1981.

Turk, Richard W. *The Ambiguous Relationship: Theodore Roosevelt and Alfred Thayer Mahan*. Westport, Conn.: Greenwood, 1988.

Turnbull, Archibald D. and Clifford L. Lord. *History of United States Naval Aviation*. New Haven: Yale University Press, 1949.

U.S. Navy Department. *Dictionary of American Naval Fighting Ships*, 8 vols. Washington, D.C.: GPO, 1959–81.

Van der Vat, Dan. *The Atlantic Campaign: World War II's Great Struggle at Sea*. New York: Harper & Row, 1988.

Van Deurs, George. *Anchors in the Sky: Spuds Ellyson, the First Naval Aviator*. San Rafael, Calif.: Presidio Press, 1978.

———. *Wings for the Fleet: A Narrative of Naval Aviation's Early Development, 1910–1916*. Annapolis: Naval Institute Press, 1966.

Von Doenhoff, Richard A., ed. *Versatile Guardian: Research in Naval History*. Washington, D.C.: Howard University Press, 1979.

Varg, Paul. *The Making of a Myth: The United States and China, 1897–1912*. East Lansing: Michigan State University Press, 1968.

Warner, Oliver. *Command at Sea: Great Fighting Admirals from Hawke to Nimitz*. New York: St. Martin's Press, 1976.

Weber, Gustavus A. *The Naval Observatory: Its History, Activities, and Organization*. Baltimore: Johns Hopkins University Press, 1926.

Webster's American Military Biographies. Springfield, Mass.: Merriam, 1978.

Weeks, Charles T. "The Life and Career of Admiral Newton A. McCully." Ph.D. dissertation, Georgia State University, 1975.

West, Richard S., Jr. *Admirals of the American Empire*. Indianapolis: Bobbs-Merrill, 1948.

Wheeler, Gerald. *Admiral William Veazie Pratt, U.S. Navy: A Sailor's Life*. Washington, D.C.: Naval History Division, 1974.

Williams, William Appleman. *Empire as a Way of Life*. New York: Oxford University Press, 1980.

————. *The Great Evasion: An Essay on the Contemporary Relevance of Karl Marx and on the Wisdom of Admitting the Heretic into the Dialogue about America's Future*. Chicago: Quadrangle Books, 1964.

Williams, William Appleman, ed. *From Colony to Empire: Essays in the History of American Foreign Relations*. New York: John Wiley & Sons, 1972.

Williams, Vernon L. "The U.S. Navy in the Philippines Insurrection and Subsequent Native Unrest, 1898–1906." Ph.D. dissertation, Texas A&M University, 1985.

Articles and Essays

Allard, Dean C., Jr. "Admiral William S. Sims and the United States Naval Policy in World War I." *American Neptune* 35 (April 1975): 97–110.

————. "Anglo-American Naval Differences during World War I." *Military Affairs* 44 (April 1980): 75–81.

Allin, Lawrence C. "The Naval Institute, Mahan, and the Naval Profession." *Naval War College Review* 31 (Summer 1978): 29–48.

Anderson, Bern. "The High Commissioner to Turkey." U.S. Naval Institute *Proceedings* 83 (1957): 21–22.

Bailey, Thomas A. "Dewey and the Germans at Manila Bay." *American Historical Review* 45 (October 1939): 59–81.

Bauer, K. Jack. "The Korean Expedition of 1871." U.S. Naval Institute *Proceedings* 64 (February 1948): 197–203.

Bowling, R. A. "The Negative Influence of Mahan on Anti-submarine Warfare." *Journal of the Royal United Services Institute for Defense Studies* (December 1977): 52–59.

Braisted, William R. "The Philippine Naval Base Problem, 1898–1909." *Mississippi Valley Historical Review* 41 (June 1954): 21–40.

Brent, Robert. "Mahan—Mariner or Misfit?" U.S. Naval Institute *Proceedings* 92 (April 1966): 92–103.

Brodie, Bernard. "New Tactics in Naval Warfare." *Foreign Affairs* 26 (January 1946): 210–23.

Bryson, Thomas A. "Admiral Mark L. Bristol: An Open-Door Diplomat in Turkey." *International Journal of Middle East Studies* 5 (1974): 450–67.

"Captain Benson Is Appointed Chief of Naval Operations." *Philadelphia Inquirer,* 29 April 1915.

Clements, Kendrick. "Woodrow Wilson's Mexican Policy, 1913–15." *Diplomatic History* 4 (Spring 1980): 113–36.

Coletta, Paolo E. "Bradley A. Fiske: Naval Inventor." In *Versatile Guardian,* ed. Richard A. Von Doenhoff, 87–101. Washington, D.C.: Howard University Press, 1979.

————. "The 'Nerves' of the New Navy." *American Neptune* 38 (April 1978): 122–30.

————. "The Perils of Invention: Bradley A. Fiske and the Torpedo Plane." *American Neptune* 37 (April 1977): 111–27.

Crowl, Philip A. "Alfred Thayer Mahan: The Naval Historian." In *Makers of Modern Strategy from Machiavelli to the Nuclear Age,* ed. Peter Paret, 444–77. Princeton: Princeton University Press, 1986.

Dennett, Tyler. "Mahan's 'The Problem of Asia.' " *Foreign Affairs* 13 (January 1935): 464–72.

Dorwart, Jeffrey M. "William Sowden Sims." In *Dictionary of American Military Biography,* ed. Roger J. Spiller et al., III: 1003–6.

Duncan, Francis. "Mahan—Historian with a Purpose." U.S. Naval Institute *Proceedings* 83 (May 1957): 498–503.

Etzold, Thomas. "Is Mahan Still Valid?" U.S. Naval Institute *Proceedings* 106 (August 1980): 38–43.

Eyre, James K. "Japan and the American Annexation of the Philippines." *Pacific Historical Review* 11 (March 1942): 55–71.

Field, James A. "Alfred Thayer Mahan Speaks for Himself." *Naval War College Review* 29 (Fall 1976): 47–60.

————. "American Imperialism: The Worst Chapter in Almost Any Book." *American Historical Review* 83 (June 1978): 644–68.

Foner, Philip S. "Why the United States Went to War with Spain in 1898." *Science and Society* 32 (Winter 1968): 39–65.

Godfrey, Jack E. "Mahan": The Man, His Writings and Philosophy." *Naval War College Review* 21 (March 1969): 59–68.

Gosnell, H. A. "The Navy in Korea, 1871." *The American Neptune* 7 (April 1947): 107–14.

Greene, Fred. "The Military View of American National Policy, 1904–1940." *American Historical Review* 66 (January 1961): 354–77.

Hacker, Louis M. "The Holy War of 1898." *American Mercury* 22 (November 1930): 316–26.

————. "The Incendiary Mahan: A Biography." *Scribner's* 95 (April 1934): 263–68, 311–12.

Hagan, Kenneth J. "Alfred Thayer Mahan." In *Makers of American Diplomacy,* 2 vols., ed. Frank J. Merli and Theodore A. Wilson, 279–304. New York: Scribner's, 1974.

Hattendorf, John B. "Luce's Idea of the Naval War College." *Naval War College Review* 37 (September–October 1984): 35–43.

Heffron, Paul T. "Secretary Moody and Naval Administrative Reform." *American Neptune* 29 (January 1969): 30–53.

Herrick, Walter R. "William C. Whitney." In *American Secretaries of the Navy,* ed. Paolo E. Colletta, I: 405–12.

Herwig, Holger H. and David F. Trask. "The Failure of Imperial Germany's Offensive against World Shipping, February 1917–October 1918." *Historian* 33 (August 1971): 611–36.

Johnson, A. B. "The Light House Establishment." In *The Naval Encyclopedia,* 430–31. Philadelphia: Hamersly, 1881.

Karsten, Peter. "The Nature of 'Influence': Roosevelt, Mahan and the Concept of Sea Power." *American Quarterly* 23 (October 1971): 585–600.

Kellogg, E. S. "Enemies: Hitherto Unpublished Footnote to History." Naval Institute *Proceedings* 63 (September 1937): 1239–40.

Knapp, H. S. "The Naval Officer in Diplomacy." Naval Institute *Proceedings* 53 (1927): 309–17.

Knudson, David L. T. "A Note on Walter LaFeber, Captain Mahan, and the Use of Historical Sources." *Pacific Historical Review* 40 (November 1971): 519–22.

Livermore, Seward W. "Theodore Roosevelt, the American Navy, and the Venezuelan Crisis of 1902–1903." *American Historical Review* 51 (April 1946): 425–71.

Mead, Lucia Ames. "Some Fallacies of Captain Mahan." *Arena* 40 (September 1908): 163–70.

Moll, Kenneth L. "Mahan: American Historian." *Military Affairs* 27 (Fall 1963): 131–37.

Moffett, William A., Jr. "For the Good of the Ship." *Shipmate* 48 (January–February 1985): 19–20.

Neumann, William L. "Franklin Delano Roosevelt: A Disciple of Admiral Mahan." U.S. Naval Institute *Proceedings* 78 (July 1952): 712–29.

Pandolfe, Frank C. "Soviet Seapower in the Light of Mahan's Principles." U.S. Naval Institute *Proceedings* 106 (August 1980): 44–46.

Paullin, Charles O. "Half Century of Naval Administration." Part 10. U.S. Naval Institute *Proceedings* 40 (January–February 1914): 111–28.

Pratt, Julius W. "Alfred Thayer Mahan." In *The Marcus W. Jernegan Essays in American Historiography,* ed. William T. Hutchinson, 207–26. Chicago: University of Chicago Press, 1937.

———. "The 'Large Policy' of 1898." *Mississippi Valley Historical Review* 19 (September 1932): 219–43.

"Prepare for War to Assure Peace: Advice of Admiral Benson." *North American Review,* 6 June 1915.

Reitzel, William. "Mahan on the Use of the Sea." *Naval War College Review* 25 (May–June 1973): 73–82.

Rice, Wallace. "Some Current Fallacies of Captain Mahan." *Dial* 28 (16 March 1900): 198–200.

Romance, Francis J. "A Chinese Commentary of Mahan's Theory of Seapower." U.S. Naval Institute *Proceedings* 105 (April 1979): 110–12.

Rohwer, Jurgen. "Admiral Gorshkov and the Influence of History upon Sea Power," trans. Christine Ulrich. U.S. Naval Institute *Proceedings* 107 (May 1981): 150–73.

St. John, Ronald B. "European Naval Expansion and Mahan, 1889–1906." *Naval War College Review* 23 (March 1971): 74–83.

Scammell, J. M. "Thucydides and Sea Power." U.S. Naval Institute *Proceedings* 47 (May 1921): 701–14.

Seager, Robert, II. "Alfred Thayer Mahan." *In Dictionary of American Military Biography,* ed. Roger J. Spiller et al., II: 711–14.

———. "Alfred Thayer Mahan." In *Dictionary of Literary Biography: Amer-*

ican Historians, 1866–1912, ed. Clyde N. Wilson, 162–73. Detroit: Gale Research, 1986.

———. "A Biography of a Biographer: Alfred Thayer Mahan." In *Changing Interpretations and New Sources in Naval History,* ed. Robert W. Love, Jr., 278–92. New York: Garland, 1980.

———. "Ten Years Before Mahan: The Unofficial Case for the New Navy, 1880–1890." *Mississippi Valley Historical Review* 40 (December 1953): 491–512.

Shiner, John F. "The Air Corps, the Navy, and Coast Defense, 1919–1941." *Military Affairs* 45 (October 1981): 113–20.

Shippee, Lester B. "Germany and the Spanish–American War." *American Historical Review* 30 (July 1925): 754–77.

Smith, Richard W. "Mahan's Historical Method." U.S. Naval Institute *Proceedings* 90 (January 1964): 50–51.

Sprout, Margaret Tuttle. "Mahan: Evangelist of Sea Power." In *Makers of Modern Strategy: Military Thought from Machiavelli to Hitler,* ed. Edward Mead Earle, 415–45. Princeton: Princeton University Press, 1943.

Stevens, William Oliver. "Scrapping Mahan." *Yale Review* 12 (1923): 528–42.

Thompson, J. A. "William Appleman Williams and the American Empire." *Journal of American Studies* 7 (April 1973): 91–104.

Trask, David F. "The American Navy in a World at War, 1914–1919." In *Peace and War,* ed. Kenneth J. Hagan, 205–20.

———. "William Shepherd Benson." In *The Chiefs of Naval Operations,* ed. Robert Love, Jr., 3–22. Annapolis: Naval Institute Press, 1980.

West, Richard S., Jr. "The Superintendents of the Naval Academy." U.S. Naval Institute *Proceedings* 71 (July 1945): 801–11.

Williams, William Appleton. "Confessions of an Intransigent Revisionist." *Socialist Revolution* 3 (September–October 1973): 87–98.

Zevin, Robert. "An Interpretation of American Imperialism." *Journal of Economic History* 32 (March 1972): 316–60.

NOTES ON CONTRIBUTORS

John B. Hattendorf is Ernest J. King Professor of Maritime History at the Naval War College, Newport, Rhode Island. Educated first at Kenyon College, he spent nearly eight years as an active-duty naval officer, including duty on board destroyers in both the Atlantic and Pacific fleets, at the Naval Historical Center in Washington, D.C., and at the Naval War College. He received his doctorate from Oxford University, and then returned to the civilian faculty of the Naval War College. In 1981–83 he was visiting professor of military and naval history at the National University of Singapore. His publications include *On His Majesty's Service: Observations in the British Home Fleet from the Diary, Reports, and Letters of Joseph H. Wellings; The Writings of Stephen B. Luce;* and *Sailors and Scholars: A Centennial History of the Naval War College.*

Robert Seager II served as a deck officer in the U.S. Merchant Marine in all war theaters in 1943–46. He later took B.A. and M.A. degrees at Rutgers and Columbia universities and a Ph.D. at the Ohio State University. He has taught U.S. naval and diplomatic history at Denison University, the U.S. Naval Academy, the University of Maine, and the University of Kentucky, and was senior editor of the Papers of Henry Clay at the University of Kentucky before his recent retirement. His publications include *And Tyler Too,* a biography of the tenth president; *America's Major Wars: Critics, Crusaders and Scholars,* 2 vols.; *The Letters and Papers of Alfred Thayer Mahan,* 3 vols.; and *Alfred Thayer Mahan,* a biography of the philosopher of sea power. He is currently working on a biography of Henry Clay.

Richard W. Turk is professor of history at Allegheny College. He received a Ph.D. from the Fletcher School of Law and Diplomacy and is the author of *The Ambiguous Relationship: Theodore Roosevelt and Alfred Mayer Mahan,* as well as numerous articles and essays dealing with various facets of pre–World War I naval history.

Malcolm Muir, Jr., professor of history at Austin Peay State University, Clarksville, Tennessee, holds a B.A. from Emory University, an M.A. from Florida State University, and a Ph.D. from the Ohio State University. He has published articles on naval matters in a variety of journals and a book on *Iowa*-class battleships. He has taught at the Ohio State University and the U.S. Military Academy at West Point. In 1987 he became the first recipient of the SecNav Research Chair in Naval History at the Naval Historical Center in Washington, D.C.

Benjamin Franklin Cooling serves as chief, special histories branch, and senior historian for contract programs, Office of Air Force History, Washington, D.C. He has previously been associated with the U.S. Army Center of Military History, the U.S. Army Military History Institute, and the National Park Service. A graduate of Rutgers University, he received M.A. and Ph.D. degrees from the University of Pennsylvania. His publications on military and naval history include *Benjamin Franklin Tracy: Father of the Modern American Navy; Symbol, Sword, and Shield: Defending Washington during the Civil War; War, Business, and American Society* (editor); *New American State Papers, Military Series,* 20 vols. (editor); *Gray Steel and Blue Water Navy: Formative Years of America's Military–Industrial Complex; Combined Operations in Peace and War* (coauthor); *Forts Donelson and Henry: Key to the Confederate Heart;* and *Mr. Lincoln's Fort: A Guide to the Civil War Defenses of Washington* (coauthor).

Joseph G. Dawson III is associate professor of history and director of the Military Studies Institute at Texas A&M University. He received B.A., M.A., and Ph.D. degrees from Louisiana State University. He was the associate editor of the three-volume reference work, *Dictionary of American Military Biography.*

Harold D. Langley is curator of naval history, National Museum of American History, Smithsonian Institution, and adjunct professor of history at the Catholic University of America in Washington, D.C. His undergraduate education was completed at the Catholic University, and he received M.A. and Ph.D. degrees from the University of Pennsylvania. He is the author of *Social Reform in the U.S. Navy, 1798–1862,* the coeditor of *Roosevelt and Churchill: Their Secret Wartime Correspondence,* and the editor of *So Proudly We Hail: The History of the United States Flag* and *To Utah With the Dragoons.* His numerous articles and essays on naval and diplomatic leaders include "Robert F. Stockton: A Naval Officer and a Reformer" in *Command Under Sail,* the first volume in the *Makers of the American Naval Tradition* series. His current research focuses on the history of medicine in the U.S. Navy.

Vernon L. Williams, a member of the Department of History at Abilene Christian University in Abilene, Texas, received a B.A. from Abilene Christian, an M.A. from Southwest Texas State University, and a Ph.D.

from Texas A&M University in 1985. He is the author of *Lieutenant Patton and the American Army on the Punitive Expedition, 1915–1916* and has recently completed two manuscripts, "Company C Goes to War: Austin County and Waller's 13th Texas Cavalry in the Trans-Mississippi West, 1861–1865" and "Crucible of the New Navy: The U.S. Navy in the Philippines, 1898–1906."

James C. Bradford, associate professor of history at Texas A&M University, was educated at Michigan State University where he received B.A. and M.A. degrees, and the University of Virginia where he received a Ph.D. His work on John Paul Jones includes a comprehensive microfilm edition of *The Papers of John Paul Jones,* a select letterpress edition of *The Correspondence of John Paul Jones,* currently in press, and an essay on Jones in *Command Under Sail,* the first volume in the *Makers of the American Naval Tradition* series, which he edits.

David F. Trask, a free-lance historian, received a B.A. from Wesleyan University and M.A. and Ph.D. degrees from Harvard University. He taught at Boston University, Wesleyan University, the University of Nebraska at Lincoln, and the State University of New York at Stony Brook before becoming director of the Office of the Historian, U.S. Department of State, and later the chief historian of the U.S. Army Center of Military History. He has served as president of the Society for History in the Federal Government and as a member of the National Historical Publications and Records Commission. His nine volumes include five on World War I, among them *The United States in the Supreme War Council: American War Aims and Inter-Allied Strategy, 1917–1918; World War I at Home;* and his most recent work, *Admiral William Shepherd Benson: First Chief of Naval Operations,* which he wrote with Mary Klachko. He is now at work on a book treating the role of the United States in World War I.

Mary Klachko, free-lance researcher, writer, and lecturer, is a native of Ukraine, where she completed her undergraduate studies at the St. Josaphat Teachers Seminary in Lviv. She earned M.A. and Ph.D. degrees in political science from Columbia University. Her works on the early twentieth century include her dissertation, "Anglo–American Naval Competition, 1918–1922," and *Admiral William Shepherd Benson: First Chief of Naval Operations,* recently published with David F. Trask. She is currently compiling a collection of documents on the involvement of the United States in the Polish–Ukrainian conflict between 1914 and 1923, and writing "Archbishop Count Andrei Sheptyts'kyi: Special Mission to Western Europe and the Americas, 1920–1923," with coauthor Eva Piddubcheshen.

William Reynolds Braisted is professor of history at the University of Texas at Austin. He received a B.A. from Stanford in 1939 and a Ph.D. from the University of Chicago in 1950. The author of *The United States Navy in the Pacific, 1897–1909; The United States Navy in the Pacific, 1909–1922;* and *Meiroku Zasshi: Journal of the Japanese Enlightenment,* he is, as the Secretary of the Navy's Research Professor of Naval History for 1988–89, engaged in extending his study of the U.S. Navy in the Pacific to 1941.

Clark G. Reynolds received a B.A. from the University of California, Santa Barbara, in 1961 and an M.A. and a Ph.D. in history from Duke University in 1964 and has taught at the U.S. Naval Academy, University of Maine, and U.S. Merchant Marine Academy. He chairs the history department of the College of Charleston and is the author of several naval history works, including *The Fast Carriers: The Forging of an Air Navy; Command of the Sea: The History and Strategy of Maritime Empires; Famous American Admirals; The Fighting Lady;* and *Towers: The Air Admiral.*

INDEX

419

ADMIRALS OF THE NEW STEEL NAVY

Composed by Vail-Ballou
in Garamond no. 3

Printed by The Maple Press Company on
60-lb. Glatco Matte Smooth white
and bound in Holliston Roxite B with
Mohawk Ticonderoga endsheets